Mastering Java 11
Second Edition

Develop modular and secure Java applications using
concurrency and advanced JDK libraries

Dr. Edward Lavieri

BIRMINGHAM - MUMBAI

Mastering Java 11
Second Edition

Commissioning Editor: Aaron Lazar
Acquisition Editor: Denim Pinto
Content Development Editor: Akshada Iyer
Technical Editor: Gaurav Gala
Copy Editor: Safis Editing
Project Coordinator: Prajakta Naik
Proofreader: Safis Editing
Indexer: Rekha Nair
Graphics: Jisha Chirayil
Production Coordinator: Nilesh Mohite

First published: October 2017
Second edition: September 2018

Production reference: 1260918

Published by Packt Publishing Ltd.
Livery Place
35 Livery Street
Birmingham
B3 2PB, UK.

ISBN 978-1-78913-761-3

www.packtpub.com

To IBB, my love, partner, and best friend.

– Ed Lavieri

`mapt.io`

Mapt is an online digital library that gives you full access to over 5,000 books and videos, as well as industry leading tools to help you plan your personal development and advance your career. For more information, please visit our website.

Why subscribe?

- Spend less time learning and more time coding with practical eBooks and videos from over 4,000 industry professionals

- Improve your learning with Skill Plans built especially for you

- Get a free eBook or video every month

- Mapt is fully searchable

- Copy and paste, print, and bookmark content

Packt.com

Did you know that Packt offers eBook versions of every book published, with PDF and ePub files available? You can upgrade to the eBook version at `www.packt.com` and as a print book customer, you are entitled to a discount on the eBook copy. Get in touch with us at `customercare@packtpub.com` for more details.

At `www.packt.com`, you can also read a collection of free technical articles, sign up for a range of free newsletters, and receive exclusive discounts and offers on Packt books and eBooks.

Contributors

About the author

Dr. Edward Lavieri is a veteran developer with a strong academic background. He has earned a doctorate in computer science from Colorado Technical University, an MS in management information systems (Bowie State University), an MS in education (Capella University), and an MS in operations management (University of Arkansas).

He has been creating and teaching computer science courses since 2002. Edward retired from the US Navy as a Command Master Chief after 25 years of active service. As the founder and creative director of *three19*, a software design and development studio. Edward is constantly designing and developing software.

This is Edward's 10th book.

About the reviewer

Mandar Jog is an expert IT trainer with over 15 years of training experience. He is an expert with technologies such as Java, Spring, Hibernate, and Android. He also possesses SCJP and SCWCD certifications. He is an occasional blogger; he makes the readers to feel "I can" with complex concepts in Java and J2EE. He is a regular speaker at many engineering colleges in technical seminars and workshops. He worked as a technical reviewer on *Modular Programming in Java 9* and *Mastering Java 9* by Packt Publishing.

> *Thank you Tejaswini (my wife) for your constant and inspirational support. I am equally grateful to my son, Ojas; his lovely smiles always make me push myself further.*

Packt is searching for authors like you

If you're interested in becoming an author for Packt, please visit `authors.packtpub.com` and apply today. We have worked with thousands of developers and tech professionals, just like you, to help them share their insight with the global tech community. You can make a general application, apply for a specific hot topic that we are recruiting an author for, or submit your own idea.

Table of Contents

Preface   1

Chapter 1: The Java 11 Landscape   7
  Technical requirements   7
  Understanding the Java platform's new versioning model   8
    Feature-driven releases   8
    Time-based releases   8
  Understanding the significance of Java 9   9
    Breaking the monolith   10
    Using the Java Shell   11
    Taking control of external processes   11
    Boosting performance with G1   12
    Measuring performance with JMH   12
    Getting ready for HTTP 2.0   13
    Encompassing reactive programming   13
  Benefiting from changes introduced with Java 10   13
    Local variable type inference   14
    Consolidation of the JDK forest into a single repository   14
    Garbage collection interface   14
    Parallel full garbage collector for G1   15
    Application class-data sharing   15
    Thread-local handshakes   15
    Removal of the native-header generation tool (javah)   15
    Additional Unicode language-tag extensions   15
    Heap allocation on alternative memory devices   15
    Experimental Java-based JIT compiler   16
    Root certificates   16
  Benefiting from changes introduced with Java 11   16
    Dynamic class-file constants   16
    Epsilon – an arbitrarily low-overhead garbage collector   17
    Removal of the Java EE and CORBA modules   17
    Local variable syntax for Lambda parameters   17
  Summary   17
  Questions   18
  Further reading   18

Chapter 2: Discovering Java 11   19
  Technical requirements   20
  Improved contended locking   21
    Improvement goals   22

Segmented code cache   22
Memory allocation   23
Smart Java compilation   23
Resolving lint and doclint warnings   24
Tiered attribution for Javac   25
Annotations pipeline 2.0   26
New version-string scheme   27
Generating runtime compiler tests automatically   28
Testing class-file attributes generated by Javac   29
Storing interned strings in class-data sharing archives   30
The problem   31
The Java 9 solution   31
The Java 10 improvement   31
Class determination   32
AppCDS archive creation   32
Using the AppCDS archive   32
Preparing JavaFX UI controls and Cascading Style Sheet APIs for modularization   33
JavaFX overview   33
Implications for Java 9, 10, and 11   34
Compact strings   36
Merging selected Xerces 2.11.0 updates into JAXP   36
Updating JavaFX/Media to the newer version of GStreamer   37
HarfBuzz font-layout engine   38
HiDPI graphics on Windows and Linux   38
Marlin graphics renderer   39
Unicode 8.0.0   40
New in Unicode 8.0.0   40
Updated classes in Java 9   40
Reserved stack areas for critical sections   41
The pre-Java 9 situation   41
New in Java 9   42
Dynamic linking of language-defined object models   43
Proof of concept   43
Additional tests for humongous objects in G1   43
Improving test-failure troubleshooting   45
Environmental information   45
Java process information   45
Optimizing string concatenation   46
HotSpot C++ unit-test framework   46
Enabling GTK3 on Linux   47
New HotSpot build system   48
Consolidating the JDF forest into a single repository   49

Summary   49
Questions   50
Further reading   50

Chapter 3: Java 11 Fundamentals   51
  Technical requirements   52
  Working with variable handlers   52
    Working with the AtoMiC ToolKit   54
    Using the sun.misc.Unsafe class   55
  Import statement depreciation warnings   56
  Milling Project Coin   57
    Using the @SafeVarargs annotation   57
    The try-with-resource statement   58
    Using the diamond operator   59
    Discontinuing use of the underscore   60
    Making use of private interface methods   61
  Import statement processing   63
  Inferring local variables   64
    Inferring declarations with the var identifier   65
    Local variable syntax for Lambda parameters   65
  Thread-local handshakes   66
  Heap allocation on alternative memory devices   66
  Root certificates   66
  Dynamic class-file constants   67
  Removal of the Java EE and CORBA modules   68
  Summary   68
  Questions   69
  Further reading   69

Chapter 4: Building Modular Applications with Java 11   71
  Technical requirements   72
  A modular primer   72
  The modular JDK   74
    Modular source code   77
    JDK source code organization before modularization   78
      Development tools   79
        Deployment   79
        Internationalization   79
        Monitoring   80
        RMI   80
        Security   80
        Troubleshooting   80
        Web services   81
      JavaFX tools   81
      Java runtime environment   81
      Source code   81

Libraries   82
C header files   83
Database   84
JDK source code reorganization   84
Modular runtime images   84
Adopting a runtime format   85
Runtime image restructure   85
Supporting common operations   87
Deprivileging JDK classes   87
Preserving existing behaviors   87
Module system   87
Module paths   88
Access-control boundary violations   89
Runtime   89
Modular Java application packaging   91
An advanced look at the Java Linker   92
Java Packager options   92
The Java Linker   96
Encapsulating most internal APIs   98
Summary   98
Questions   99
Further reading   99

Chapter 5: Migrating Applications to Java 11   101
Technical requirements   102
A quick review of Project Jigsaw   102
Classpath   103
The monolithic nature of the JDK   103
How modules fit into the Java landscape   104
Base module   105
Reliable configuration   107
Strong encapsulation   108
Migration planning   109
Testing a simple Java application   109
Potential migration issues   112
The JRE   112
Accessing internal APIs   113
Accessing internal JARs   114
JAR URL depreciation   114
Extension mechanism   115
The JDK's modularization   116
Advice from Oracle   117
Preparatory steps   118
Getting the JDK early access build   118
Running your program before recompiling   118
Updating third-party libraries and tools   119

Compiling your application   119
    Pre-Java 9 -source and -target options   121
    Java 10 and 11 -source and -target options   122
Running jdeps on your code   122
Breaking encapsulation   126
    The --add-opens option   126
    The --add-exports option   126
    The --permit-illegal-access option   127
Runtime image changes   127
Java version schema   127
JDK and JRE's layout   128
What has been removed?   131
Updated garbage collection   132
Deploying your applications   133
Selecting your JRE version   133
Serialized applets   133
JNLP update   134
    Nested resources   134
    FX XML extension   134
    JNLP file syntax   136
    Numeric version comparison   137
Useful tools   137
Java Environment -jEnv   137
Maven   139
Obtaining the M2Eclipse IDE   140
Summary   143
Questions   143
Further reading   143
Chapter 6: Experimenting with the Java Shell   145
Technical requirements   145
Understanding JShell   146
Getting started with JShell   147
Practical uses of JShell   153
Feedback modes   154
    Creating a custom feedback mode   158
Listing your assets   160
Editing in JShell   161
    Modifying text   161
    Basic navigation   162
    Historical navigation   162
    Advanced editing commands   162
Working with scripts   162
Startup scripts   163
Loading scripts   163
Saving scripts   164

Advanced scripting with JShell   164
Summary   166
Questions   166
Further reading   167
Chapter 7: Leveraging the Default G1 Garbage Collector   169
Technical requirements   170
Overview of garbage collection   170
    Object life cycle   170
        Object creation   171
        Object mid-life   171
        Object destruction   172
    Garbage collection algorithms   172
        Mark and sweep   172
        Concurrent Mark Sweep (CMS) garbage collection   173
        Serial garbage collection   173
        Parallel garbage collection   174
        G1 garbage collection   174
    Garbage collection options   174
    Java methods relevant to garbage collection   178
        The System.gc() method   178
        The finalize() method   179
The pre-Java 9 garbage collection schema   181
    Visualizing garbage collection   182
    Garbage collection upgrades in Java 8   183
    Case study – games written with Java   183
Collecting garbage with the new Java platform   184
    Default garbage collection   185
    Depreciated garbage collection combinations   186
    Unified garbage collection logging   188
    Unified JVM logging   188
        Tags   188
        Levels   189
        Decorations   189
        Output   190
        Command-line options   190
    Unified GC logging   190
        Garbage collection logging options   191
        The gc tag   192
        Macros   192
        Additional considerations   193
    Garbage collection interface   193
    Parallel full garbage collection for G1   194
    Epsilon – an arbitrarily low-overhead GC   194
Persistent issues   194
    Making objects eligible for garbage collection   195
Summary   197

Questions	198
Further reading	198
Chapter 8: Microbenchmarking Applications with JMH	199
Technical requirements	199
Microbenchmarking overview	200
Approach to using JMH	201
Installing Java and Eclipse	201
Hands-on experiment	202
Microbenchmarking with Maven	204
Benchmarking options	211
Modes	212
Time units	212
Techniques for avoiding microbenchmarking pitfalls	213
Power management	213
OS schedulers	213
Timesharing	214
Eliminating dead-code and constant folding	214
Run-to-run variance	215
Cache capacity	215
Summary	216
Questions	216
Further reading	216
Chapter 9: Making Use of the Process API	217
Technical requirements	218
Introducing processes	218
Working with the ProcessHandle interface	219
Getting the PID of the current process	220
Getting information about processes	220
Listing processes	222
Listing children	223
Listing descendants	223
Listing all processes	225
Waiting for processes	226
Terminating processes	226
Reviewing a sample process controller app	229
Main class	229
Parameters class	230
ParamsAndHandle	231
ControlDaemon	232
Summary	235
Questions	235
Further reading	236
Chapter 10: Fine-Grained Stack Tracing	237

Technical requirements   238
Overview of the Java Stack   238
The importance of stack information   239
    Example – restricting callers   240
    Example – getting loggers for callers   243
Working with StackWalker   244
    Getting an instance of StackWalker   244
    Enum options   245
        RETAIN_CLASS_REFERNCE 245
        SHOW_REFLECT_FRAMES   245
        SHOW_HIDDEN_FRAMES   245
        Final thoughts on enum constants 249
    Accessing classes   249
    Walking methods   249
StackFrame   251
Performance   252
Summary   253
Questions   253
Chapter 11: New Tools and Tool Enhancements   255
Technical requirements   256
Working with the HTTP client   256
    The pre-Java 9 HTTP client   256
    The Java 11 HTTP client   258
    Limitations of the HTTP client API   259
Understanding Javadoc and the Doclet API   261
    The pre-Java 9 Doclet API   261
        API enums   263
        API classes   263
        API interfaces   263
    Problems with the pre-existing Doclet API   264
    Java 9's Doclet API   264
        Compiler tree API   264
        Language model API   267
            The AnnotatedConstruct interface 268
            The SourceVersion enum 268
            The UnknownEntityException exception 270
    Using the HTML5 Javadoc   271
    Javadoc search   276
        Introducing Camel Case search 277
Changes to the Multiple JRE feature   277
JavaScript Parser   278
    Nashorn   278
        Using Nashorn as a command-line tool 279
        Using Nashorn as an embedded interpreter 282
    ECMAScript   283
    Parser API   284

Multiple-release JAR files   286
  Identifying multi-release JAR files   287
  Related JDK changes   288
Java-level JVM Compiler Interface   289
  BeanInfo annotations   290
    JavaBean   290
    BeanProperty   291
  SwingContainer   291
  BeanInfo classes   292
TIFF support   292
Platform logging   295
  The java.util.logging package   295
  Logging in the modern Java platform   297
XML Catalogs   298
  The OASIS XML Catalog standard   299
  JAXP processors   299
  Earlier XML Catalogs   299
  Current XML Catalogs   300
Collections   300
  Using collections prior to the modern Java platform   301
  Using new collection literals   303
Platform-specific desktop features   304
Enhanced method handling   305
  The reason for the enhancement   305
  Lookup functions   306
  Argument handling   306
  Additional combinations   307
Enhanced depreciation   308
  What the @Deprecated annotation really means   309
The native header generation tool (javah)   309
Summary   309
Questions   310
Further reading   310

Chapter 12: Concurrency Enhancements   311
  Technical requirements   311
  Reactive programming   312
    Reactive programming standardization   313
  The Flow API   315
    The Flow.Publisher interface   315
    The Flow.Subscriber interface   315
    The Flow.Subscription interface   316
    The Flow.Processor interface   316
    Sample implementation   317
  Additional concurrency updates   318

Java concurrency   318
  Concurrency explained   318
  System configurations   319
  Java threads   320
Concurrency improvements   323
CompletableFuture API enhancements   324
  Class details   325
  Enhancements   329
Spin-wait hints   330
Summary   331
Questions   331
Further reading   331

Chapter 13: Security Enhancements   333
Technical requirements   333
Datagram Transport Layer Security   334
  DTLS protocol version 1.0   335
  DTLS protocol version 1.2   336
  DTLS support in Java   339
Creating PKCS12 keystores   340
  Keystore primer   340
  Java Keystore (JKS)   341
    Understanding the KeyStore.Builder   342
    The CallbackHandlerProtection class   342
    The PasswordProtection class   343
    The PrivateKeyEntry class   343
    The SecretKeyEntry class   343
    The TrustedCertificateEntry class   344
  PKCS12 default in Java 9, 10, and 11   345
Improving security application performance   345
  Security policy enforcement   346
  Permission evaluation   347
  The java.Security.CodeSource package   347
  Package checking algorithm   348
The TLS application-layer protocol negotiation extension   349
  TLS ALPN extension   349
  The javax.net.ssl package   350
  The java.net.ssl package extension   351
Leveraging CPU instructions for GHASH and RSA   353
  Hashing   353
OCSP stapling for TLS   355
  OCSP stapling primer   356
  Recent changes to the Java platform   357
DRBG-based SecureRandom implementations   358
Summary   359
Questions   360

Further reading   360

Chapter 14: Command-Line Flags   361
  Technical requirements   361
  Unified JVM logging   362
    Command-line options   363
    Decorations   365
    Levels   366
    Working with Xlog output   366
    Tags   367
  Compiler control   367
    Compilation modes   367
      The C1 compilation mode   368
      The C2 compilation mode   368
      Tiered compilation   368
    Compiler control in Java 11   369
  Diagnostic commands   371
  The heap profiling agent   372
  Removing your JHAT   372
  Command-line flag argument validation   373
  Compiling for older platform versions   375
  The experimental Java-based JIT compiler   377
  Summary   377
  Questions   377
  Further reading   378

Chapter 15: Additional Enhancements to the Java Platform   379
  Technical requirements   379
  Support for UTF-8   380
    The ResourceBundle class   380
      The nested class   381
      Fields and constructors   385
      Methods   386
    Changes in the modern Java platform   392
  Unicode support   392
    The java.lang package   393
    The java.text package   393
    Additional significance   394
  Linux/AArch64 port   395
  Multiresolution images   396
  Common Locale Data Repository   397
  Summary   398
  Questions   398

Chapter 16: Future Directions   399
  Technical requirements   399

An overview of the JDK Enhancement Proposal 400
JEP Candidates 401
    JEP 326: Raw String Literals 401
    JEP 334: JVM Constants API 401
    JEP 337: RDMA Network Sockets 402
    JEP 338: Vector API 402
    JEP 339: Edwards-Curve Digital Signature Algorithm 402
JEP Submitted 402
JEP Drafted 403
Ongoing special projects 404
    Annotations Pipeline 2.0 405
    Audio Synthesis Engine 405
    Caciocavallo 405
    Common VM Interface 406
    Compiler Grammar 406
    Device I/O 406
    Graal 406
    HarfBuzz integration 406
    Kona 407
    OpenJFX 407
    Panama 407
    Shenandoah 407
Summary 408
Questions 408

Chapter 17: Contributing to the Java Platform 409
Technical requirements 410
The Java Community 410
Participating in a Java User Group 411
Java Community Process 411
Oracle Technology Network 412
Writing technical articles 412
Summary 413
Questions 413

Appendix A: Assessment 415
Chapter 1 415
Chapter 2 415
Chapter 3 416
Chapter 4 416
Chapter 5 417
Chapter 6 418
Chapter 7 419
Chapter 8 420

Chapter 9   421

Chapter 10   421

Chapter 11   422

Chapter 12   423

Chapter 13   424

Chapter 14   425

Chapter 15   425

Chapter 16   426

Chapter 17   427

Other Books You May Enjoy   429

Index   433

Preface

Java 11 and its new features add to the richness of the language—one of the most commonly-used programming languages for building robust software applications. Java 11 expands the capabilities of the Java platform. This book is your one-stop guide to mastering the changes made to the Java platform since Java 9.

This book gives an overview and explanation of the new features introduced in Java 11 and their importance. You will be provided with practical guidance in applying your newly acquired knowledge of Java 11 as well as information on future developments to the the Java platform. This book aims to improve your productivity by making your applications faster. By learning the best practices in Java, you will become the go-to person in your organization for Java.

By the end of this book, you will not only learn the important concepts of Java 11 but you will also gain a nuanced understanding of the important aspects of programming with this great language.

Who this book is for

This book is for enterprise developers and existing Java developers. Basic knowledge of Java is necessary.

What this book covers

Chapter 1, *The Java 11 Landscape*, explores the newly implemented time-based versioning system for the Java platform. We survey the current Java landscape with a specific focus on changes introduced with Java 9, 10 (18.3), and 11 (18.9). Our exploration includes an overview of Java 9's modularity, Java Shell, external process control, garbage collection, JHM, and more. For Java 10, we will highlight key changes to include local variable type inference, JDK consolidation, garbage collection, application class-data sharing, and root certificates, to name a few. Finally, we will explore changes introduced in Java 11, including dynamic class-file constants, garbage collection, and local variable type inference for lambdas.

Chapter 2, *Discovering Java 11*, looks at several internal changes introduced in the Java platform, including changes from Java 9, 10, and 11. Java 9 represented a major release to the Java platform; Java 10 and 11 were timed releases. Collectively, these releases consisted of a large number of internal changes, representing a tremendous set of new possibilities for Java developers, some stemming from developer requests, others from Oracle-inspired enhancements.

Chapter 3, *Java 11 Fundamentals*, covers changes to the Java platform that impact variable handlers, import statements, improvements to Project Coin, local variable type inference, root certificates, dynamic class-file constants, and more. These represent changes to the Java language itself.

Chapter 4, *Building Modular Applications with Java 11*, examines the structure of a Java module as specified by Project Jigsaw. We take a deep dive into how Project Jigsaw is implemented as part of the Java platform. We also review key internal changes to the Java platform as they relate to the modular system.

Chapter 5, *Migrating Applications to Java 11*, explores how to migrate our existing applications to the current Java platform. We look at both manual and semi-automated migration processes. This chapter aims to provide you with insights and processes to get your non-modular Java code working with the current Java platform.

Chapter 6, *Experimenting with the Java Shell*, takes a look at the new command line, the **Read-Eval-Print-Loop** (also referred to as **REPL**) tool in Java, and the **Java Shell** (**JShell**). We start with introductory information regarding the tool, the REPL concept, and move into the commands and command-line options for use with JShell. We take a practitioner's approach to our review of JShell and include examples you can try on your own.

Chapter 7, *Leveraging the Default G1 Garbage Collector*, takes an in-depth look at garbage collection and how it is handled in Java. We start with an overview of garbage collection and then look at specifics in the pre-Java 9 realm. Armed with that foundational information, we look at specific garbage collection changes in the Java 9 platform. Lastly, we look at some garbage collection issues that persist, even after Java 11.

Chapter 8, *Microbenchmarking Applications with JMH*, looks at how to write performance tests using the **Java Microbenchmark Harness** (**JMH**), a Java harness library for writing benchmarks for the **Java Virtual Machine** (**JVM**). We use Maven along with JMH to help illustrate the power of microbenchmarking with the new Java platform.

Chapter 9, *Making Use of the Process API*, focuses on the updates to the Process class and the java.lang.ProcessHandle API. In earlier versions of Java, prior to Java 9, managing processes in Java was difficult. The API was insufficient with some features lacking and some tasks needed to be solved in a system-specific manner. For example, in Java 8, giving a process access to its own **process identifier** (PID) was an unnecessarily difficult task.

Chapter 10, *Fine-Grained Stack Tracing*, focuses on Java's StackWalker API. The API supports special functionality that is rarely needed by ordinary programs. The API can be useful for some very special cases, such as with functionality that is delivered by a framework. So, if you want an efficient means of stack walking that gives you filterable access to stack trace information, you will enjoy using the StackWalker API. The API provides fast and optimized access to the call stack, implementing lazy access to the individual frames.

Chapter 11, *New Tools and Tool Enhancements*, covers over a dozen tools and tool enhancements relevant to the modern Java platform. The featured changes will cover a wide range of tools and updates to APIs that are aimed at making developing with Java easier and enhance the ability to create optimized Java applications.

Chapter 12, *Concurrency Enhancements*, covers concurrency enhancements to the Java platform. Our primary focus is the support for reactive programming, a concurrency enhancement that is provided by the Flow class API. Reactive programming was first released in Java 9 and remains an important feature of Java 10 and 11. We also explore additional concurrency enhancements.

Chapter 13, *Security Enhancements*, looks at several recent changes made to the JDK that involve security. The size of these changes does not reflect their significance. The security enhancements to the modern Java platform provide developers with a greater ability to write and maintain applications that are more secure than previously possible.

Chapter 14, *Command-Line Flags*, explores several changes to the modern Java platform with the common theme of command-line flags. These include the following concepts: unified JVM logging, compiler control, diagnostic commands, the heap profiling agent, removing your JHAT, command-line flag argument validation, compiling for older platform versions, and the experimental Java-based JIT compiler.

Chapter 15, *Additional Enhancements to the Java Platform*, focuses on best practices with additional utilities provided with the Java platform. Specifically, this chapter covers support for UTF-8, Unicode support, Linux/AArch64 port, multi-resolution images, and the Common Locale Data Repository.

`Chapter 16`, *Future Directions*, provides an overview of the future development of the Java platform beyond Java 11. We look at what is planned for Java 19.3 and 19.9 and what further changes we are likely to see in the future. We start with a brief overview of the **JDK Enhancement Program (JEP)**.

`Chapter 17`, *Contributing to the Java Platform*, discusses the Java community and ways developers can contribute to the Java platform. Specifically, the chapter covers the following Java community-related topics, such as the Java community, participating in a Java user group, the Java community process, **Oracle Technology Network (OTN)**, and writing technical articles.

To get the most out of this book

You are encouraged to download the Java 11 JDK in order to follow the examples provided in this book.

Download the example code files

You can download the example code files for this book from your account at `www.packt.com`. If you purchased this book elsewhere, you can visit `www.packt.com/support` and register to have the files emailed directly to you.

You can download the code files by following these steps:

1. Log in or register at `www.packt.com`.
2. Select the **SUPPORT** tab.
3. Click on **Code Downloads & Errata**.
4. Enter the name of the book in the **Search** box and follow the onscreen instructions.

Once the file is downloaded, please make sure that you unzip or extract the folder using the latest version of:

- WinRAR/7-Zip for Windows
- Zipeg/iZip/UnRarX for Mac
- 7-Zip/PeaZip for Linux

The code bundle for the book is also hosted on GitHub at `https://github.com/PacktPublishing/Mastering-Java-11-Second-Edition`. In case there's an update to the code, it will be updated on the existing GitHub repository.

We also have other code bundles from our rich catalog of books and videos available at `https://github.com/PacktPublishing/`. Check them out!

Download the color images

We also provide a PDF file that has color images of the screenshots/diagrams used in this book. You can download it here: `https://www.packtpub.com/sites/default/files/downloads/9781789137613_ColorImages.pdf`.

Conventions used

There are a number of text conventions used throughout this book.

`CodeInText`: Indicates code words in text, database table names, folder names, filenames, file extensions, pathnames, dummy URLs, user input, and Twitter handles. Here is an example: "Mount the downloaded `WebStorm-10*.dmg` disk image file as another disk in your system."

A block of code is set as follows:

```
try ( Scanner xmlScanner = new Scanner(new File(xmlFile)); {
    while (xmlScanner.hasNext()) {
        // read the xml document and perform needed operations
```

When we wish to draw your attention to a particular part of a code block, the relevant lines or items are set in bold:

```
public default void fastWalk() {
    Scanner scanner = new Scanner(System.in);
    System.out.println("Enter desired pacing: ");
```

Any command-line input or output is written as follows:

```
$ java --version
```

Bold: Indicates a new term, an important word, or words that you see onscreen. For example, words in menus or dialog boxes appear in the text like this. Here is an example: "Select **System info** from the **Administration** panel."

Warnings or important notes appear like this.

 Tips and tricks appear like this.

Get in touch

Feedback from our readers is always welcome.

General feedback: If you have questions about any aspect of this book, mention the book title in the subject of your message and email us at customercare@packtpub.com.

Errata: Although we have taken every care to ensure the accuracy of our content, mistakes do happen. If you have found a mistake in this book, we would be grateful if you would report this to us. Please visit www.packt.com/submit-errata, selecting your book, clicking on the Errata Submission Form link, and entering the details.

Piracy: If you come across any illegal copies of our works in any form on the Internet, we would be grateful if you would provide us with the location address or website name. Please contact us at copyright@packt.com with a link to the material.

If you are interested in becoming an author: If there is a topic that you have expertise in and you are interested in either writing or contributing to a book, please visit authors.packtpub.com.

Reviews

Please leave a review. Once you have read and used this book, why not leave a review on the site that you purchased it from? Potential readers can then see and use your unbiased opinion to make purchase decisions, we at Packt can understand what you think about our products, and our authors can see your feedback on their book. Thank you!

For more information about Packt, please visit packt.com.

The Java 11 Landscape

In this chapter, we will explore the newly implemented, time-based versioning system for the Java platform. We will survey the current Java landscape with a specific focus on changes introduced with Java 9, 10 (18.3), and 11 (18.9). Our exploration will include an overview of Java 9's modularity, Java Shell, external process control, garbage collection, **Java Microbenchmark Harness** (**JMH**), and more. For Java 10, we will highlight key changes to include local variable type inference, **Java Development Kit** (**JDK**) consolidation, garbage collection, application **class-data sharing** (**CDS**), root certificates, and more. Finally, we will explore changes introduced in Java 11, including dynamic class-file constants, garbage collection, local variable type inference for Lambdas, and more.

Things we will learn by the end of this chapter include:

- Understanding the Java platform's new versioning model
- Understanding the significance of Java 9
- Benefiting from changes introduced with Java 10
- Benefiting from changes introduced with Java 11

Technical requirements

This chapter and subsequent chapters feature Java 11. The **Standard Edition** (**SE**) of the Java platform can be downloaded from Oracle's official download site (`http://www.oracle.com/technetwork/java/javase/downloads/index.html`).

An **integrated development environment** (**IDE**) software package is sufficient. IntelliJ IDEA, from JetBrains, was used for all coding associated with this chapter and subsequent chapters. The Community version of IntelliJ IDEA can be downloaded from the site (`https://www.jetbrains.com/idea/features/`).

Understanding the Java platform's new versioning model

The first version of Java was released as Java 1 in 1996. Since then, there have been several incremental releases, each of which followed a feature-driven release model. Starting with Java 10, Oracle has implemented a new, time-based release model. In this section, we will look at the original model to provide a foundation to show how the Java platform evolved, and look at the new versioning model and why it matters.

Feature-driven releases

Following the 1996 launch of Java 1, subsequent releases had the nomenclature of 1.1, 1.2, 1.3, and 1.4. With the release of 1.5, the Java platform was referred to as Java 5. Frequent updates were released for Java 5 until Java 6 was released followed by Java 7, Java 8, and Java 9.

The following table provides a condensed view of the Java release history until Java 9:

Release Name	Version	Year Released	Code Name
Java 1	1.0	1996	Oak
Java 1.1	1.1	1997	(Abigail, Brutus, Chelsea)
Java 2	1.2	1998	Playground
Java 3	1.3	2000	Kestrel
Java 4	1.4	2002	Merlin
Java 5	1.5	2004	Tiger
Java 6	1.6	2006	Mustang
Java 7	1.7	2011	Dolphin
Java 8	1.8	2014	Spider
Java 9	9	2017	*Code names no longer used

The release of Java 9 was a significant change to the Java platform and how each of the versions was numbered. With the post-Java 9 releases, Oracle decided to abandon their feature-based model, opting for a time-released model instead.

Time-based releases

Java 9 was released in 2017 and two releases were scheduled for 2018. Those releases were Java 10 and Java 11. The version numbers for these post-Java 9 releases followed the *YY.M* format. So, with Java 10 released in March 2018, the version number was 18.3. Java 11, released in September 2018, has a version number of 18.9.

The general premise behind the new time-based release model is to have releases scheduled predictably and frequently. Here are the details:

- **Feature releases**: Issued every six months (each March and September)
- **Update releases**: Issued every quarter
- **Long-term support release**: Issued every three years

There are great gains to be had, from a developer's perspective, with this model. Developers no longer need to wait long for releases to the Java platform. More significant is the fact that no release will represent a major change to the platform of the kind that Java 9 was.

Understanding the significance of Java 9

Unarguably, the modularization of the Java platform, developed as part of Project Jigsaw, was the greatest change introduced to the Java platform with Java 9. Initially planned for Java 8, but postponed, Project Jigsaw was one of the main reasons why the final release of Java 9 was itself postponed. Jigsaw also introduced a few notable changes to the Java platform and was one of the reasons Java 9 was considered a major release. We will explore these features in detail in subsequent chapters.

Apart from the Jigsaw-related Java enhancement proposals, there is a long list of other enhancements that made it in Java 9. This section explores the most significant features introduced in Java 9, specifically:

- Breaking the monolith
- Using the Java Shell
- Taking control of external processes
- Boosting performance with G1
- Measuring performance with **Java Microbenchmark Harness (JMH)**
- Getting ready for HTTP 2.0
- Encompassing reactive programming

Breaking the monolith

Over the years, the utilities of the Java platform have continued to evolve and increase, making it into one big monolith. In order to make the platform more suitable for embedded and mobile devices, the publication of stripped-down editions, such as Java **Connected Device Configuration** (**CDC**) and Java **Micro Edition** (**ME**), was necessary. These, however, did not prove to be flexible enough for modern applications with varying requirements in terms of the functionality provided by the JDK. In that regard, the need for a modular system came in as a vital requirement, not only to address the modularization of the Java utilities (overall, there are more than 5,000 Java classes and 1,500 C++ source files with more than 250,000 lines of code for the HotSpot runtime), but also to provide a mechanism for developers to create and manage modular applications using the same module system as that used in the JDK. Java 8 provided an intermediate mechanism to enable applications to use only a subset of the APIs provided by the entire JDK, and that mechanism was named **compact profiles**. In fact, compact profiles also provided the basis for further work that had to be done in order to break dependencies between the various distinct components of the JDK. This breaking of dependencies was required to enable the implementation of a module system in Java.

The module system itself was developed under the name of Project Jigsaw, on the basis of which several Java enhancement proposals and a target **Java Specification Request** (**JSR 376**) were formed. A complete restructuring of the JDK code base was made, along with a complete reorganization of the JDK distributable images.

There was considerable controversy in the community as to whether an existing and mature Java module system, such as OSGi, should be adopted as part of the JDK, instead of providing a completely new module system. However, OSGi targets runtime behavior, such as the resolution of module dependencies, installation, uninstallation, starting and stopping of modules (also named bundles in terms of OSGi), custom module classloaders, and so on.

 OSGi refers to the **OSGi Alliance**, formally known as the **Open Services Gateway Initiative**. OSGi is an open standard for a Java platform modular system.

Project Jigsaw, however, targets a compile-time module system where the resolution of dependencies happens when the application is compiled. Moreover, installing and uninstalling a module as part of the JDK eliminates the need to include it explicitly as a dependency during compilation. Furthermore, the loading of module classes is made possible through the existing hierarchy of classloaders (the bootstrap, and the extension and system classloaders).

Additional benefits from the Java module system include enhanced security and performance. By modularizing the JDK and applications into Jigsaw modules, developers are able to create well-defined boundaries between components and their corresponding domains. This separation of concerns aligns with the security architecture of the platform and is an enabler of better resource utilization.

Using the Java Shell

For a long time, there has been no standard shell shipped with the Java programming language to experiment with new language features or libraries, or for rapid prototyping. If you wanted to do this, you could write a test application with a `main()` method, compile it with `javac`, and run it. This could be done either in the command line or using a Java IDE; however, in both cases, this is not as convenient as having an interactive shell for the purpose.

Starting an interactive shell in JDK 9 is as simple as running the following command (assuming the `bin` directory of your JDK 9 installation is in the current path):

```
jshell
```

You may find it somewhat puzzling that an interactive shell has not been introduced earlier in the Java platform, as many programming languages, such as Python, Ruby, and a number of others, already come with an interactive shell in their earliest versions. However, this didn't make it on the priority features list until Java 9. The Java Shell makes use of a JShell API that provides capabilities to enable autocompletion or evaluation of expressions and code snippets, among other features. Chapter 6, *Experimenting with the Java Shell*, is dedicated to discussing the details of the Java Shell so that developers can make the best use of it.

Taking control of external processes

Up to JDK 9, if you wanted to create a Java process and handle process input/output, you had to use one of the following approaches:

- The `Runtime.getRuntime.exec()` method, which allows us to execute a command in a separate OS process. Using this approach would require you to get a `java.lang.Process` instance over which to provide certain operations in order to manage the external process.

- The new `java.lang.ProcessBuilder` class, which has some more enhancements with regard to interacting with the external process. You would also need to create a `java.lang.Process` instance to represent the external process.

Both approaches were inflexible and also nonportable, as the set of commands executed by the external processes were highly dependent on the operating system. An additional effort had to be exerted in order to make the particular process operations portable across multiple operating systems. Chapter 9, *Making Use of the Process API*, is dedicated to the new process API, providing developers with the knowledge to create and manage external processes in a much easier way.

Boosting performance with G1

The G1 garbage collector was already introduced in JDK 7 and is now enabled by default in JDK 9. It is targeted for systems with multiple processing cores and a lot of available memory. What are the benefits of the G1 compared to previous types of garbage collectors? How does it achieve these improvements? Is there a need to tune it manually, and in what scenarios? These and several more questions regarding G1 will be discussed in Chapter 7, *Leveraging the Default G1 Garbage Collector*.

Measuring performance with JMH

On many occasions, Java applications may suffer from performance degradation. Exacerbating the issue is a lack of performance tests that can provide at least a minimal set of guarantees that performance requirements are met and, moreover, the performance of certain features will not degrade over time. Measuring the performance of Java applications is not trivial, especially due to the fact that there are a number of compiler and runtime optimizations that may affect performance statistics. For that reason, additional measures, such as warm-up phases and other tricks, must be used in order to provide more accurate performance measurements. The JMH is a framework that incorporates a number of techniques, along with a convenient API that can be used for this purpose. It is not a new tool but was included with the distribution of Java 9. If you have not added JMH to your toolbox yet, read Chapter 8, *Microbenchmarking Applications with JMH*, to learn about the use of JMH in the context of Java application development.

Getting ready for HTTP 2.0

HTTP 2.0 is the successor to the HTTP 1.1 protocol, and this new version of the protocol addresses some limitations and drawbacks of the previous one. HTTP 2.0 improves performance in several ways and provides capabilities such as request/response multiplexing in a single TCP connection, sending of responses in a server push, flow control, and request prioritization, among others. Java provides the `java.net.HttpURLConnection` utility that can be used to establish a nonsecure HTTP 1.1 connection. However, the API was considered difficult to maintain, an issue which was further complicated by the need to support HTTP 2.0 and, so, an entirely new client API was introduced in order to establish a connection via the HTTP 2.0 or the web socket protocols. The HTTP 2.0 client, along with the capabilities it provides, will be covered in `Chapter 11`, *New Tools and Tool Enhancements*.

Encompassing reactive programming

Reactive programming is a paradigm used to describe a certain pattern for the propagation of changes in a system. Reactiveness is not built in Java itself, but reactive data flows can be established using third-party libraries, such as RxJava or Project Reactor (part of the Spring Framework). JDK 9 also addressed the need for an API that aids the development of highly responsive applications built around the idea of reactive streams by providing the `java.util.concurrent.Flow` class for the purpose. The `Flow` class, along with other related changes introduced in JDK 9, will be covered in `Chapter 12`, *Concurrency Enhancements*.

Benefiting from changes introduced with Java 10

Java 10 was released in March 2018 and had the 11 features listed here, in addition to the previously covered time-based versioning:

- Local variable type inference
- Consolidation of the JDK forest into a single repository
- Garbage collection interface
- Parallel full garbage collector for G1
- Application class-data sharing
- Thread-local handshakes

- Removal of the native-header generation tool (javah)
- Additional Unicode language-tag extensions
- Heap allocation on alternative memory devices
- Experimental Java-based JIT compiler
- Root certificates

A brief overview of these features is covered in this chapter, with more detailed coverage in subsequent chapters.

Local variable type inference

Starting with Java 10, declaring local variables has been simplified. Developers no longer have to include manifest declarations of local variable types. This is accomplished using the new `var` identifier, as shown in this example:

```
var myList = new ArrayList<String>();
```

Using the preceding code, `ArrayList<String>` is inferred, so we no longer need to use `ArrayList<String> myList = new ArrayList<String>();`.

Local variable type inference is covered in `Chapter 3`, *Java 11 Fundamentals*.

Consolidation of the JDK forest into a single repository

Prior to Java 10, there were eight repositories for the JDK (CORBA, HotSpot, JDK, JAXP, JAX-WS, langtools, Nashorn, and ROOT). With Java 10, these repositories have been consolidated into a single code base. Notably, Java FX was not part of this consolidation. This topic will be explained further in `Chapter 2`, *Discovering Java 11*.

Garbage collection interface

Java 10 ushered in enhancements to the garbage collection process. A new garbage collector interface results in improvements that will be detailed in `Chapter 7`, *Leveraging the Default G1 Garbage Collector*.

Parallel full garbage collector for G1

In Java 10, the G1 full garbage collector was made parallel. Starting with Java 9, G1 was made the default garbage collector, so this change was of special significance. This change will be detailed in Chapter 7, *Leveraging the Default G1 Garbage Collector*.

Application class-data sharing

Class-data sharing (**CDS**) has been extended to support faster application startup and smaller footprints. Using CDS, developers can have specific class files pre-parsed and stored in a shareable archive. We will explore this change to the Java platform in Chapter 2, *Discovering Java 11*.

Thread-local handshakes

With Java 10 and beyond, it is possible to stop individual threads without having to perform a global virtual machine safepoint. We will fully explore this change in Chapter 3, *Java 11 Fundamentals*.

Removal of the native-header generation tool (javah)

A concerted effort was undertaken to remove the javah tool from the JDK. This change was warranted because of the functionality available in javac. We will detail this change in Chapter 11, *New Tools and Tool Enhancements*.

Additional Unicode language-tag extensions

The Java platform has supported language tags since Java 7. In Java 10, changes were made to java.util.Local and related APIs to incorporate additional Unicode language tags. Details will be covered in Chapter 2, *Discovering Java 11*.

Heap allocation on alternative memory devices

The HotSpot virtual machine, as of Java 10, supports non-DRAM memory devices. This will be explained in Chapter 3, *Java 11 Fundamentals*.

Experimental Java-based JIT compiler

Java 9 introduced us to a Java-based **just-in-time** (**JIT**) compiler. This JIT compiler has been enabled for Linux/x64 platforms. This experimental compiler will be further explored in Chapter 14, *Command-Line Flags*.

Root certificates

Starting with the release of Java 10, there has been a default set of **Certification Authority** (**CA**) certificates as part of the JDK. This change and its benefits will be covered in Chapter 3, *Java 11 Fundamentals*.

Benefiting from changes introduced with Java 11

Java 11, was released in September 2018 and had four features, as listed here:

- Dynamic class-file constants
- Epsilon—an arbitrarily low-overhead garbage collector
- Removal of the Java EE and CORBA modules
- Local variable syntax for Lambda parameters

A brief overview of these features is covered in this chapter, with more detailed coverage in subsequent chapters.

Dynamic class-file constants

In Java 11, the file format for Java class files was extended to support CONSTANT_Dynamic, which delegates creation to a bootstrap method. This change will be fully explored in Chapter 3, *Java 11 Fundamentals*.

Epsilon – an arbitrarily low-overhead garbage collector

Garbage collection enhancements are seemingly part of every Java platform release. Java 11, includes a passive garbage collector that does not reclaim memory. We will explore this in `Chapter 7`, *Leveraging the Default G1 Garbage Collector*.

Removal of the Java EE and CORBA modules

The **Java Enterprise Edition (Java EE)** and **Common Object Request Broker Architecture (CORBA)** modules were depreciated in Java 9 and have been removed from the Java platform as of Java 11. Details are provided in `Chapter 3`, *Java 11 Fundamentals*.

Local variable syntax for Lambda parameters

As discussed earlier in this chapter, the `var` identifier was introduced in Java 10. With the latest version, Java 11, `var` can be used in implicitly typed Lambda expressions. This use of the `var` identifier is covered in `Chapter 3`, *Java 11 Fundamentals*.

Summary

In this chapter, we explored the newly implemented, time-based versioning system for the Java platform. We also learned, at a high level, the changes introduced in Java 9, 10, and 11 (referred to as versions 9, 18.3, and 18.9 respectively). Java 9's most significant change was modularity based on Project Jigsaw and included additional changes focusing on the Java shell, controlling external process, garbage collection, JHM, and more. Key features of Java 10 were covered, including local variable type inference, JDK consolidation, garbage collection, application CDS, root certificates, and more. Changes introduced in Java 11 included dynamic class-file constants, garbage collection, local variable type inference for Lambdas, and more.

In the next chapter, we will look at several internal changes introduced in the Java platform, including changes from Java 9, 10, and 11.

Questions

1. What will the first Java version be in 2019?
2. What is a key benefit of the new Java time-based release model?
3. What was the most significant change to the Java platform with JDK 9?
4. What was removed with Java 11: CORBA, Lambda, or G1?
5. Does CDS support faster startup or more efficient garbage collection?
6. What is Epsilon?
7. Is `var` a datatype, identifier, reserved word, or keyword?
8. Which Java release introduced root certificates to the Java platform?
9. Which release included enhancements to garbage collection?
10. What is the default garbage collector in Java?

Further reading

This survey chapter took a broad-brush approach to recent changes to the Java platform. If any of the concepts were unfamiliar to you, consider brushing up on your Java knowledge with one or more of the following resources:

- *Java: Object-Oriented Programming Concepts [Integrated Course]*, available at `https://www.packtpub.com/application-development/java-object-oriented-programming-concepts-integrated-course`.

- *Java 9 High Performance*, available at `https://www.packtpub.com/application-development/java-9-high-performance`.

Discovering Java 11 2

In the previous chapter, we explored the newly-implemented time-based versioning system for the Java platform. We also learned, at a high-level, the changes introduced in Java 9, 10, and 11, also referred to as versions 9, 18.3, and 18.9 respectively. Java 9's most significant change was the introduction of modularity based on Project Jigsaw and included additional changes focusing on the Java Shell, controlling external process, garbage collection, JHM, and more. Key features of Java 10 were covered, including local variable type inference, JDK consolidation, garbage collection, application **class-data sharing** (**CDS**), root certificates, and more. Changes introduced in Java 11 included dynamic class-file constants, garbage collection, local variable type inference for Lambdas and more.

In this chapter, we will look at several internal changes introduced to the Java platform, including changes from Java 9, 10, and 11. Java 9 represented a major release to the Java platform; Java 10 and 11 were timed-releases. Collectively, these releases consisted of a large number of internal changes, representing a tremendous set of new possibilities for Java developers, some stemming from developer requests, others from Oracle-inspired enhancements.

In this chapter, we will review 29 of the most important changes. Each change is related to a **JDK Enhancement Proposal** (**JEP**). JEPs are indexed and housed at `openjdk.java.net/jeps/0`. You can visit this link for additional information on each JEP.

 The JEP program is part of Oracle's support for open source, open innovation, and open standards. While other open source Java projects can be found, OpenJDK is the only one supported by Oracle.

In this chapter, we will cover the following:

- Improved contended locking [JEP 143]
- Segmented code cache [JEP 197]
- Smart Java compilation, phase two [JEP 199]
- Resolving lint and doclint warnings [JEP 212]

- Tiered attribution for Javac [JEP 215]
- Annotations pipeline 2.0 [JEP 217]
- New version-string scheme [JEP 223]
- Generating runtime compiler tests automatically [JEP 233]
- Testing class-file attributes generated by Javac [JEP 235]
- Storing interned strings in CDS archives [JEP 250]
- Preparing JavaFX UI controls and CSS APIs for modularization [JEP 253]
- Compact strings [JEP 254]
- Merging selected Xerces 2.11.0 updates into JAXP [JEP 255]
- Updating JavaFX/Media to the newer version of GStreamer [JEP 257]
- HarfBuzz font-layout engine [JEP 258]
- HiDPI graphics on Windows and Linux [JEP 263]
- Marlin graphics renderer [JEP 265]
- Unicode 8.0.0 [JEP 267 and JEP 314]
- Reserved stack areas for critical sections [JEP 270]
- Dynamic linking of language-defined object models [JEP 276]
- Additional tests for humongous objects in G1 [JEP 278]
- Improving test-failure troubleshooting [JEP 279]
- Optimizing string concatenation [JEP 280]
- HotSpot C++ unit-test framework [JEP 281]
- Enabling GTK3 on Linux [JEP 283]
- New HotSpot build system [JEP 284]
- Consolidating the JDF Forest into a single repository [JEP 296]

Technical requirements

This chapter and subsequent chapters feature Java 11. The **Standard Edition** (**SE**) of the Java platform can be downloaded from Oracle's official download site at the link (`http://www.oracle.com/technetwork/java/javase/downloads/index.html`).

An **Integrated Development Environment** (IDE) software package is sufficient. IntelliJ IDEA, from JetBrains, was used for all coding associated with this chapter and subsequent chapters. The Community version of IntelliJ IDEA can be downloaded from the website (https://www.jetbrains.com/idea/features/).

This chapter's source code is available at GitHub at the URL (https://github.com/ PacktPublishing/Mastering-Java-11-Second-Edition).

Improved contended locking

The JVM uses heap space for classes and objects. The JVM allocates memory on the heap whenever we create an object. This helps facilitate Java's garbage collection, which releases memory previously used to hold objects that no longer have a memory reference. Java stack memory is a bit different and is usually much smaller than heap memory.

The JVM does a good job of managing data areas that are shared by multiple threads. It associates a monitor with every object and class; these monitors have locks that are controlled by a single thread at any one time. These locks, controlled by the JVM, are, in essence, giving the controlling thread the object's monitor. So, what contends locking? When a thread is in a queue for a currently locked object, it is said to be in contention for that lock. The following diagram shows a high-level view of this contention:

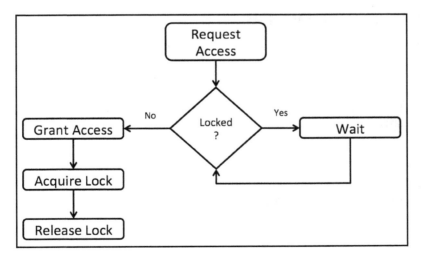

As you can see in the preceding diagram, any threads in waiting cannot use a locked object until it is released.

Improvement goals

The general goal of JEP 143 was to increase the overall performance of how the JVM manages contention over locked Java object monitors. The improvements to contended locking were all internal to the JVM and do not require any developer actions to benefit from them. The overall improvement goals were related to faster operations. These include:

- Faster monitor enter
- Faster monitor exit
- Faster notifications

The notifications are the `notify()` and `notifyAll()` operations that are called when the locked status of an object is changed. Testing this improvement is not something you can easily accomplish. Greater efficiency at any level is welcome, so this improvement is one we can be thankful for.

Segmented code cache

Java's segmented code cache upgrade was completed and results in faster, more efficient execution time. At the core of this change was the segmentation of the code cache into three distinct segments—non-method, profiled, and non-profiled code.

 A code cache is the area of memory where the JVM stores generated native code.

Each of the aforementioned code cache segments will hold a specific type of compiled code. As you can see in the following diagram, the code heap areas are segmented by type of compiled code:

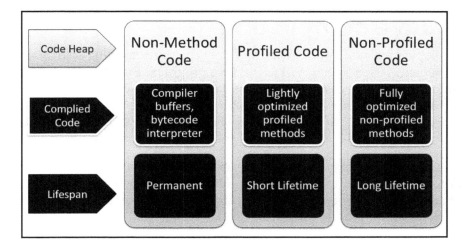

Memory allocation

The code heap containing non-method code is used for JVM internal code and consists of a 3 MB fixed memory block. The rest of the code cache memory is equally allocated for the profiled code and non-profiled code segments. You have control of this via command line commands.

The following command can be used to define the code heap size for the non-method compiled code:

```
-XX:NonMethodCodeHeapSize
```

The following command can be used to define the code heap size for the profiled compiled methods:

```
-XX:ProfiledCodeHeapSize
```

The following command can be used to define the code heap size for the non-profiled compiled methods:

```
-XX:NonProfiledCodeHeapSize
```

This feature certainly stands to improve Java application efficiency. It also impacts other processes that employ the code cache.

Smart Java compilation

All Java developers will be familiar with the `javac` tool for compiling source code to bytecode, which is used by the JVM to run Java programs. Smart Java compilation, also referred to as Smart Javac and `sjavac`, adds a smart wrapper around the `javac` process. Perhaps the core improvement added by `sjavac` is that only the necessary code is recompiled. Necessary code, in this context, is code that has changed since the last compile cycle.

This enhancement might not get developers excited if they only work on small projects. Consider, however, the tremendous gains in efficiency when you continuously have to recompile your code for medium and large projects. The time developers stand to save is reason enough to embrace JEP 199.

How will this change the manner in which you compile your code? It probably won't, at least not yet. Javac will remain the default compiler. While `sjavac` offers efficiencies regarding incremental builds, Oracle has deemed it to not have sufficient stability to become part of the standard compilation workflow.

Resolving lint and doclint warnings

Lint and doclint are sources that report warnings to `javac`. Let's take a look at each one:

- Lint analyzes bytecode and source code for `javac`. The goal of lint is to identify security vulnerabilities in the code being analyzed. Lint can also provide insights into scalability and thread locking concerns. There is more to lint and the overall purpose is to save developers time.

 You can read more about lint here:
http://openjdk.java.net/jeps/212

- Doclint is similar to lint and is specific to `javadoc`. Both lint and doclint report errors and warnings during the compile process. Resolution of these warnings was the focus of JEP 212. When using core libraries, there should not be any warnings. This mindset led to JEP 212, which has been resolved and implemented in Java 9.

A comprehensive list of the lint and doclint warnings can be reviewed in the **JDK Bug System (JBS)**, available at `https://bugs.openjdk.java.net`.

Tiered attribution for Javac

Javac's type-checking has been streamlined. Let's first review how type-checking works in Java 8; then we will explore the changes in the modern Java platform.

In Java 8, type-checking of poly expressions is handled by a speculative attribution tool.

Speculative attribution is a method of type-checking as part of `javac`'s compilation process. It has a significant processing overhead.

Using the speculative attribution approach to type-checking is accurate, but lacks efficiency. These checks include argument position and are exponentially slower when testing in the midst of recursion, polymorphism, nested loops, and Lambda expressions. So, the update was intended to change the type-checking schema to create faster results. The results themselves were not inaccurate with speculative attribution; they were just not generated rapidly.

The new approach, available in Java 9-11, uses a tiered attribution tool. This tool implements a tiered approach for type-checking argument expressions for all method calls. Permissions are also made for method overriding. In order for this new schema to work, new structural types are created for each of the following listed types of method arguments:

- Lambda expressions
- Poly expressions
- Regular method calls
- Method references
- Diamond instance creation expressions

The changes to `javac` are more complex than what has been highlighted in this section. There is no immediate impact to developers, other than a more efficient `javac` and time saved.

Annotations pipeline 2.0

Java annotations refer to a special kind of metadata that resides inside your Java source code files. They are not stripped by `javac` so that they can remain available to the JVM at runtime.

Annotations look similar to JavaDocs references because they start with the @ symbol. There are three types of annotations. Let's examine each of these as follows:

- The most basic form of annotation is a marker annotation. These are standalone annotations, with the only component being the name of the animation. Here is an example:

  ```
  @thisIsAMarkerAnnotation
  public double computeSometing(double x, double y) {
      // do something and return a double
  }
  ```

- The second type of annotation is one that contains a single value, or piece of data. As you can see in the following code, the annotation, which starts with the @ symbol, is followed by parentheses containing data:

  ```
  @thisIsAMarkerAnnotation (data="compute x and y coordinates")
  public double computeSometing(double x, double y) {
      // do something and return a double
  }
  ```

  An alternative way of coding the single value annotation type is to omit the `data=` component, as illustrated in the following code:

  ```
  @thisIsAMarkerAnnotation ("compute x and y coordinates")
  public double computeSometing(double x, double y) {
      // do something and return a double
  }
  ```

- The third type of annotation is when there is more than one data component. With this type of annotation, the `data=` component cannot be omitted. Here is an example:

  ```
  @thisIsAMarkerAnnotation (data="compute x and y coordinates",
  purpose="determine intersecting point")
  public double computeSometing(double x, double y) {
      // do something and return a double
  }
  ```

So, what has changed in Java 9, 10, and 11? To answer this question, we need to recall a couple of changes introduced with Java 8 that impacted Java annotations:

- Lambda expressions
- Repeated annotations
- Java type annotations

These Java 8-related changes impacted Java annotations but did not usher in a change to how `javac` processed them. There were some hardcoded solutions that allowed `javac` to handle the new annotations, but they were not efficient. Moreover, this type of coding (hardcoding workarounds) is difficult to maintain.

So, JEP 217 focused on refactoring the `javac` annotation pipeline. This refactoring was all internal to `javac`, so it should not be evident to developers.

New version-string scheme

Prior to Java 9, the release numbers did not follow industry standard versioning—semantic versioning. For example, the last four JDK 8 releases were as follows:

- Java SE 8 Update 144
- Java SE 8 Update 151
- Java SE 8 Update 152
- Java SE 8 Update 161
- Java SE 8 Update 162

Semantic versioning uses a major, minor, patch (0.0.0) schema as follows:

- **Major** equates to new API changes that are not backward compatible
- **Minor** is when functionality is added that is backward compatible
- **Patch** refers to bug fixes or minor changes that are backward compatible

Oracle has embraced semantic versioning starting with Java 9 and beyond. For Java, a major-minor-security schema will be used for the first three elements of Java version numbers:

- **Major**: A major release consisting of a significant new set of features
- **Minor**: Revisions and bug fixes that are backward compatible
- **Security**: Fixes deemed critical to improve security

There were three releases of Java 9; the initial release and two updates. The versions listed as follows demonstrate the major-minor-security schema:

- Java SE 9
- Java SE 9.0.1
- Java SE 9.0.4

As detailed in `Chapter 1`, *The Java 11 Landscape*, versioning past Java 9 will follow the time-release schema of *YY.MM*. Using that schema, the four releases following Java 9 are and will be as follows:

- Java SE 18.3 (March 2018)
- Java SE 18.9 (September 2018)
- Java SE 19.3 (March 2019)
- Java SE 19.9 (September 2019)

Generating runtime compiler tests automatically

Java is arguably the most commonly used programming language and resides on an increasingly diverse number of platforms. This exacerbates the problem of running targeted compiler tests in an efficient manner. The new Java platform includes a tool that automates the runtime compiler tests.

This new tool starts by generating a random set of Java source code and/or bytecode. The generated code will have three key characteristics:

- It will be syntactically correct
- It will be semantically correct
- It will use a random seed that permits reusing the same randomly generated code

The source code that is randomly generated will be saved in the following directory:

```
hotspot/test/testlibrary/jit-tester
```

These test cases will be stored for later reuse. They can be run from the `j-treg` directory or from the tool's makefile. One of the benefits of rerunning saved tests is to test the stability of your system.

Testing class-file attributes generated by Javac

The lack of, or insufficient, capability to create tests for class-file attributes was the impetus behind the effort to ensure `javac` creates a class-file's attributes completely and correctly. This suggests that even if some attributes are not used by the class-file, all class-files should be generated with a complete set of attributes. There also needs to be a way of testing that the class-files were created correctly, in regards to the file's attributes.

Prior to Java 9, there was no method of testing a class-file's attributes. Running a class and testing the code for anticipated or expected results were the most commonly used method of testing `javac` generated class-files. This technique falls short of testing to validate the file's attributes.

There are three categories of class-file attributes—attributes used by the JVM, optional attributes, and attributes not used by the JVM.

Attributes used by the JVM include the following:

- `BootstrapMethods`
- `Code`
- `ConstantValue`
- `Exceptions`
- `StackMapTable`

Optional attributes include the following:

- `Deprecated`
- `LineNumberTable`
- `LocalVariableTable`
- `LocalVariableTypeTable`
- `SourceDebugExtension`
- `SourceFile`

Attributes not used by the JVM include the following:

- `AnnotationDefault`
- `EnclosingMethod`
- `InnerClasses`

- MethodParameters
- RuntimeInvisibleAnnotations
- RuntimeInvisibleParameterAnnotations
- RuntimeInvisibleTypeAnnotations
- RuntimeVisibleAnnotations
- RuntimeVisibleParameterAnnotations
- RuntimeVisibleTypeAnnotations
- Signature
- Synthetic

Storing interned strings in class-data sharing archives

In Java 5 through Java 8, the method in which strings were stored and accessed to and from CDS archives was inefficient, excessively time-consuming, and wasted memory.
The following diagram illustrates the method by which Java stored interned strings in a CDS archive prior to Java 9:

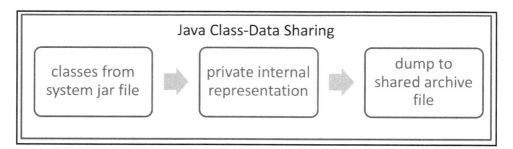

The inefficiency stemmed from the storage schema. This was especially evident when the CDS tool dumped the classes into the shared archive file. The constant pools containing CONSTANT_String items have a UTF-8 string representation.

 UTF-8 is an 8-bit variable-length character encoding standard.

The problem

With the use of UTF-8 prior to Java 9, the strings had to be converted to string objects, that is, instances of the `java.lang.String` class. This conversion took place on-demand, which usually resulted in slower systems and unnecessary memory usage. The processing time was extremely short, but the memory usage was excessive. Every character in an interned string required at least three bytes of memory and potentially more.

A related problem is that the stored strings were not accessible to all JVM processes.

The Java 9 solution

CDS archives, starting with Java 9, allocate specific space on the heap for strings. This process is illustrated in the following diagram:

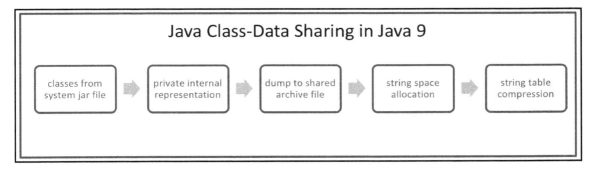

The string space is mapped using a shared-string table, hash tables, and deduplication.

 Deduplication is a data compression technique that eliminates duplicative information in an archive.

The Java 10 improvement

Java 9 introduced more efficient CDS and Java 10 further improved upon the feature, specifically to support the addition of application classes to the shared archive. The intention of JEP 310, application CDS, was not to bloat the archives, slow startup times, or consume more memory than needed. Those outcomes are nonetheless possible without a purposeful approach to CDS.

We use a three-step process with CDS archives: determine what classes to include, create the archive, and use the archive:

1. Class determination
2. AppCDS archive creation
3. Using the AppCDS archive

Let's examine the details of each step.

Class determination

The best practice for using CDS is to only archive the classes that are used. This will help keep the archive from bloating unnecessarily. We can use the following command line and flags to determine which classes are loaded:

```
java -Xshare:off -XX:+UseAppCDS -XX:DumpLoadedClassList=ch2.lst - cp
cp2.jar Chapter2
```

AppCDS archive creation

Once we know which classes are loaded, we can create our AppCDS archive. Here are the command line and flag options to use:

```
java  -Xshare:dump -XX:+UseApsCDS \
    -XX:SharedClassListFile=ch2.lst \
    -XX:SharedArchiveFile=ch2.jsa -cp ch2.jar
```

Using the AppCDS archive

To use the AppCDS archive, we issue the -Xshare:on command line option, as shown here:

```
java -Xshare:on -XX:+UseAppCDS -XX:SharedArchiveFile=ch2.jsa -cp ch2.jar
Chapter2
```

Preparing JavaFX UI controls and Cascading Style Sheet APIs for modularization

JavaFX is a set of packages that permit the design and development of media-rich graphical user interfaces. JavaFX applications provide developers with a great API for creating a consistent interface for applications. **Cascading Style Sheets (CSS)** can be used to customize the interfaces. One of the great things about JavaFX is that the tasks of programming and interface design can easily be separated.

JavaFX overview

JavaFX contains a wonderful visual scripting tool called Scene Builder, which allows you to create graphical user interfaces by using drag-and-drop and property settings. Scene Builder generates the necessary FXML files that are used by your IDE, such as NetBeans.

Here is a sample UI created with Scene Builder:

And here is the FXML file created by Scene Builder:

```
<?xml version="1.0" encoding="UTF-8"?>
<?import java.lang.*?>
<?import java.util.*?>
<?import javafx.scene.control.*?>
<?import javafx.scene.layout.*?>
<?import javafx.scene.paint.*?>
<?import javafx.scene.text.*?>
```

```
<AnchorPane id="AnchorPane" maxHeight="-Infinity"
  maxWidth="-Infinity" minHeight="-Infinity"
  minWidth="-Infinity" prefHeight="400.0" prefWidth="600.0"
  xmlns:fx="http://javafx.com/fxml/1"
  xmlns="http://javafx.com/javafx/2.2">
  <children>
    <TitledPane animated="false" collapsible="false"
      layoutX="108.0" layoutY="49.0" text="Sample">
    <content>
      <AnchorPane id="Content" minHeight="0.0" minWidth="0.0"
        prefHeight="180.0" prefWidth="200.0">
      <children>
        <CheckBox layoutX="26.0" layoutY="33.0"
          mnemonicParsing="false" prefWidth="94.0"
          text="CheckBox" />
        <ColorPicker layoutX="26.0" layoutY="65.0" />
        <Hyperlink layoutX="26.0" layoutY="103.0"
          text="Hyperlink" />
        <Label alignment="CENTER" layoutX="14.0" layoutY="5.0"
          prefWidth="172.0" text="This is a Label"
          textAlignment="CENTER">
          <font>
            <Font size="14.0" />
          </font>
        </Label>
        <Button layoutX="81.0" layoutY="146.0"
          mnemonicParsing="false" text="Button" />
      </children>
      </AnchorPane>
    </content>
    </TitledPane>
  </children>
</AnchorPane>
```

Implications for Java 9, 10, and 11

Prior to Java 9, JavaFX controls and CSS functionality were only available to developers by interfacing with internal APIs. Java 9's modularization has made the internal APIs inaccessible. Therefore, JEP 253 was created to define public, instead of internal, APIs.

This was a larger undertaking than it might seem. Here are a few actions that were taken as part of this JEP:

- Moving JavaFX control skins from the internal to public API (`javafx.scene.skin`)

- Ensuring API consistencies
- Generation of a thorough `javadoc`

The following classes were moved from internal packages to a public `javafx.scene.control.skin` package:

AccordionSkin	ButtonBarSkin	ButtonSkin	CellSkinBase
CheckBoxSkin	ChoiceBoxSkin	ColorPickerSkin	ComboBoxBaseSkin
ComboBoxListViewSkin	ComboBoxPopupControl	ContextMenuSkin	DateCellSkin
DatePickerSkin	HpyerLinkSkin	LabelSkin	LabeledSkinBase
ListCellSkin	ListViewSkin	MenuBarSkin	MenuButtonSkin
MenuButtonSkinBase	NestedTableColumnHeader	PaginationSkin	ProgressBarSkin
ProgressIndicatorSkin	RadioButtonSkin	ScrollBarSkin	ScrollPanelSkin
SeparatorSkin	SliderSkin	SpinnerSkin	SplitMenuButtonSkin
SplitPaneSkin	TabPaneSkin	TableCellSkin	TableCellSkinBase
TableColumnHeader	TableHeaderRow	TableHeaderSkin	TabelRowSkinBase
TableViewSkin	TableViewSkinBase	TextAreaSkin	TextFieldSkin
TextInputControlSkin	TitledPaneSkin	ToggleButtonSkin	ToolBarSkin
TooltipSkin	TreeCellSkin	TreeTableCellSkin	TreeTableRowSkin
TreeTableViewSkin	TreeViewSkin	VirtualContainerBase	VirtualFlow

The public `javafx.css` package now has the following additional classes:

- `CascadingStyle.java:public class CascadingStyle implements Comparable<CascadingStyle>`
- `CompoundSelector.java:final public class CompoundSelector extends Selector`
- `CssError.java:public class CssError`
- `Declaration.java:final public class Declaration`
- `Rule.java:final public class Rule`
- `Selector.java:abstract public class Selector`
- `SimpleSelector.java:final public class SimpleSelector extends Selector`
- `Size.java:final public class Size`
- `Style.java:final public class Style`
- `Stylesheet.java:public class Stylesheet`
- `CssParser.java:final public class CssParser`

Compact strings

The string data type is an important part of nearly every Java app. Prior to Java 9, string data was stored as an array of `chars`. This required 16 bits for each `char`. It was determined that the majority of string objects could be stored with only 8 bits, or 1 byte of storage. This is due to the fact that most strings consist of Latin-1 characters.

 The **Latin-1 characters** refers to the Latin-1 character set established by the International Organization for Standardization. The character set consists of a single byte set of character's encodings.

Starting with Java 9, strings are now internally represented using a `byte` array, along with a flag field for encoding references.

Merging selected Xerces 2.11.0 updates into JAXP

Xerces is a library used for parsing XML in Java. It was updated to 2.11.0 in late 2010, and JAXP was updated to incorporate changes in Xerces 2.11.0.

 JAXP is Java's API for XML processing.

Prior to Java 9, the JDK's latest update regarding XML processing was based on Xerces 2.7.1. There were some additional changes to JDK 7 based on Xerces, 2.10.0. Java now has a further refinement of the JAXP based on Xerces 2.11.0.

Xerces 2.11.0 supports the following standards:

- XML 1.0, Fourth Edition
- Namespaces in XML 1.0, Second Edition
- XML 1.1, Second Edition
- Namespaces in XML 1.1, Second Edition
- XML Inclusions 1.0, Second Edition

- **Document Object Model (DOM):**
  - Level 3:
    - Core
    - Load and save
  - Level 2:
    - Core
    - Events

- Traversal and Range
- Element Traversal, First Edition
- Simple API for XML 2.0.2
- Java APIs for XML Processing (JAXP) 1.4
- Streaming API for XML 1.0
- XML Schema 1.0
- XML Schema 1.1
- XML Schema Definition Language

The JDK was updated to include the following Xerces 2.11.0 categories:

- Catalog resolver
- Datatypes
- Document Object Model Level 3
- XML Schema Validation
- XPointer

The public API for JAXP was not changed in Java 9, 10, or 11.

Updating JavaFX/Media to the newer version of GStreamer

JavaFX is used for creating desktop and web applications. JavaFX was created to replace Swing as Java's standard GUI library. The `Media` class, `javafx.scene.media.Media`, is used to instantiate an object representing a media resource. JavaFX/`Media` refers to the following class:

```
public final class Media extends java.lang.Object
```

This class provides referential data to a media resource. The `javafx.scene.media` package provides developers with the ability to incorporate media into their JavaFX applications. JavaFX/`Media` utilizes a GStreamer pipeline.

 GStreamer is a multimedia processing framework that can be used to build systems that take in media from several different formats and, after processing, export them in selected formats.

The update to the modern Java platform ensures JavaFX/Media was updated to include the latest release of GStreamer for stability, performance, and security assurances.

HarfBuzz font-layout engine

Prior to Java 9, the layout engine was used to handle font complexities, specifically fonts that have rendering behaviors beyond what the common Latin fonts have. Java used the uniform client interface, also referred to as ICU, as the de facto text rendering tool. The ICU layout engine has been depreciated and, in Java 9, has been replaced with the HarfBuzz font layout engine.

HarfBuzz is an OpenType text rendering engine. This type of layout engine has the characteristic of providing script-aware code to help ensure text is laid out as desired.

 OpenType is an HTML formatted font format specification.

The impetus for the change from the ICU layout engine to the HarfBuzz font layout engine was IBM's decision to cease supporting the ICU layout engine. Therefore, the JDK was updated to contain the HarfBuzz font layout engine.

HiDPI graphics on Windows and Linux

A concerted effort was made to ensure the crispness of on-screen components relative to the pixel density of the display. The following terms are relevant to this effort and are provided along with the accompanying listed descriptive information:

- **DPI-aware application**: An application that is able to detect and scale images for the display's specific pixel density.

- **DPI-unaware application**: An application that makes no attempt to detect and scale images for the display's specific pixel density.
- **HiDPI graphics**: High dots-per-inch graphics.
- **Retina display**: This term was created by Apple to refer to displays with a pixel density of at least 300 pixels per inch. Displaying graphics, both images, and graphical user interface components, to the user is typically of paramount performance. Displaying this imagery in high quality can be somewhat problematic. There is large variability in computer monitor DPIs. There are three basic approaches to developing for displays:
  - Develop apps without regard for the potential different display dimensions. In other words, create a DPI-unaware application.
  - Develop a DPI-aware application that selectively uses pre-rendered image sizes for a given display.
  - Develop a DPI-aware application that properly scales images up/down to account for the specific display on which the application is run.

Clearly, the first two approaches are problematic and for different reasons. With the first approach, the user experience is not considered. Of course, if the application was being developed for a very specific display with no expected pixel density variability, then this approach could be viable.

The second approach requires a lot of work on the design and development end to ensure images for each expected display density are created and implemented programmatically. In addition to the tremendous amount of work, the app size will unnecessarily increase, and new and different pixel densities will not have been accounted for.

The third approach is to create a DPI-aware application with efficient and effective scaling capabilities. This approach works well and has been proven with the Mac retina displays.

Prior to Java 9, automatic scaling and sizing was already implemented in Java for the macOS X. This capability was added in Java 9 for Windows and Linux operating systems.

Marlin graphics renderer

The Pisces graphics rasterizer has been replaced with the Marlin graphics renderer in the Java 2D API. This API is used to draw 2D graphics and animations.

The goal was to replace Pisces with a rasterizer/renderer that was much more efficient and without any quality loss. This goal was realized in Java 9. An intended collateral benefit was to include a developer-accessible API. Previously, the means of interfacing with the AWT and Java 2D was internal.

Unicode 8.0.0

Unicode 8.0.0 was released on June 17, 2015. Java's relevant APIs were updated to support Unicode 8.0.0.

New in Unicode 8.0.0

Unicode 8.0.0 added nearly 8,000 characters. Here are the highlights of the release:

- Ahom script for the Tai Ahom language (India)
- Arwi, Tamil language (Arabic)
- Cherokee symbols
- CJK unified ideographs
- Emoji symbols along with flesh-tone symbol modifiers
- Georgian Lari currency symbol
- Ik language (Uganda)
- Kulango language (Cote d'Ivoire)

Updated classes in Java 9

In order to fully comply with the new Unicode standard, several Java classes were updated. The following listed classes were updated for Java 9 to comply with the new Unicode standard:

- `java.awt.font.NumericShaper`
- `java.lang.Character`
- `java.lang.String`
- `java.text.Bidi`
- `java.text.BreakIterator`
- `java.text.Normalizer`

Reserved stack areas for critical sections

Problems stemming from stack overflows during the execution of critical sections have been mitigated. This mitigation takes the form of reserving additional thread stack space.

The pre-Java 9 situation

The JVM throws StackOverflowError when it is asked to perform data computation in a thread that has insufficient stack space and does not have permission to allocate additional space. This is an asynchronous exception. The JVM can also throw the StackOverflowError exception synchronously when a method is invoked.

When a method is invoked, an internal process is used to report the stack overflow. While the current schema works sufficiently for reporting the error, there is no room for the calling application to easily recover from the error. This can result in being more than a nuisance for developers and users. If the StackOverflowError was thrown during a critical computational operation, the data might be corrupted, causing additional problems.

While not the sole cause of these problems, the effected status of locks from the ReentrantLock class were a common cause of undesirable outcomes. This issue was evident in Java 7 because the ConcurrentHashMap code implemented the ReentrantLock class. The ConcurrentHashMap code was modified for Java 8, but problems still persisted for any implementation of the ReentrantLock class. Similar problems existed beyond just ReentrantLock class usage.

The following diagram provides a broad overview of the StackOverflowError problem:

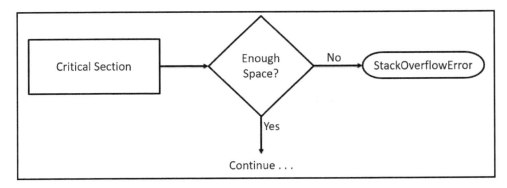

In the next section, we will look at how this issue was resolved for Java 9.

New in Java 9

With the changes to the modern Java platform, a critical section will automatically be given additional space so that it can complete its execution and not suffer from `StackOverflowError`. This is predicated on the additional space allocation needs being small. The necessary changes have been made to the JVM to permit this functionality.

The JVM actually delays `StackOverflowError`, or at least attempts to, while critical sections are executing. In order to capitalize on this new schema, methods must be annotated with the following:

```
jdk.internal.vm.annotation.ReservedStackAccess
```

When a method has this annotation and a `StackOverflowError` condition exists, temporary access to the reserved memory space is granted. The new process is, at a high-level of abstraction, presented as follows:

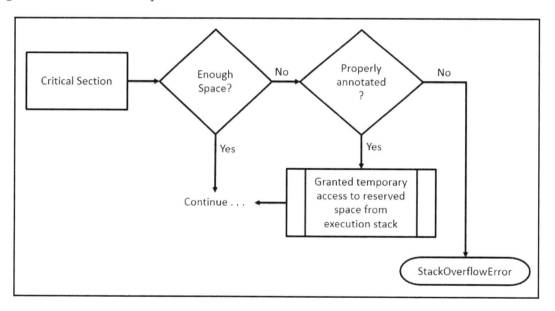

Dynamic linking of language-defined object models

Java interoperability has been enhanced. The necessary JDK changes were made to permit runtime linkers from multiple languages to coexist in a single JVM instance. This change applies to high-level operations, as you would expect. An example of a relevant high-level operation is the reading or writing of a property with elements such as accessors and mutators.

The high-level operations apply to objects of unknown types. They can be invoked with INVOKEDYNAMIC instructions. Here is an example of calling an object's property when the object's type is unknown at compile time:

```
INVOKEDYNAMIC "dyn:getProp:age"
```

Proof of concept

Nashorn is a lightweight, high-performance, JavaScript runtime that permits embedding JavaScript in Java applications. This was created for Java 8 and replaced the previous JavaScript scripting engine that was based on Mozilla Rhino. Nashorn already has this functionality. It provides linkage between high-level operations on any object of unknown types, such as obj.something, where it produces the following:

```
INVOKEDYNAMIC "dyn.getProp.something"
```

The dynamic linker springs into action and provides, when possible, the appropriate implementation.

Additional tests for humongous objects in G1

One of the long-favored features of the Java platform is the behind-the-scenes garbage collection. An improvement goal was to create additional WhiteBox tests for humongous objects as a feature of the G1 garbage collector.

 WhiteBox testing is an API used to query JVM internals. The WhiteBox testing API was introduced in Java 7 and upgraded in Java 8 and Java 9.

The G1 garbage collector worked extremely well, but there was room for some improved efficiency. The way the G1 garbage collector worked was based on first dividing the heap into regions of equal size, illustrated as follows:

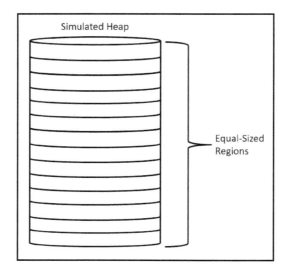

The problem with the G1 garbage collector was how humongous objects were handled.

 A humongous object, in the context of garbage collection, is any object that takes up more than one region on the heap.

The problem with humongous objects was that if they took up any part of a region on the heap, the remaining space was not able to be allocated for other objects. In Java 9, the WhiteBox API was extended with four types of new methods:

- Methods with the purpose of blocking full garbage collection and initiating concurrent marking.
- Methods that can access individual G1 garbage collection heap regions. Access to these regions consist of attribute reading, such as with the current state of the region.
- Methods with direct access to the G1 garbage collection internal variables.
- Methods that can determine if humongous objects reside on the heap and, if so, in what regions.

Improving test-failure troubleshooting

Additional functionality has been added in Java to automatically collect information to support troubleshooting test failures as well as timeouts. Collecting readily available diagnostic information during tests stands to provide developers and engineers with greater fidelity in their logs and other output.

There are two basic types of information in the context of testing:

- Environmental
- Process

Each type of information is described in the following section.

Environmental information

When running tests, the testing environment information can be important for troubleshooting efforts. This information includes the following:

- CPU loads
- Disk space
- I/O loads
- Memory space
- Open files
- Open sockets
- Processes running
- System events
- System messages

Java process information

There is also information available during the testing process directly related to Java processes. These include the following:

- C stacks
- Core dumps
- Mini dumps

- Heap statistics
- Java stacks

For additional information on this concept, read about the JDK's regression test harness (`jtreg`).

Optimizing string concatenation

Prior to Java 9, string concatenation was translated by `javac` into `StringBuilder : :` `append` chains. This was a suboptimal translation methodology, often requiring `StringBuilder` presizing.

The enhancement changed the string concatenation bytecode sequence, generated by `javac`, so that it uses `INVOKEDYNAMIC` calls. The purpose of the enhancement was to increase optimization and to support future optimizations without the need to reformat the `javac`'s bytecode.

See JEP 276 for more information on `INVOKEDYNAMIC`.

The use of `INVOKEDYAMIC` calls to `java.lang.invoke.StringConcatFactory` allows us to use a methodology similar to Lambda expressions, instead of using `StringBuilder`'s stepwise process. This results in more efficient processing of string concatenation.

HotSpot C++ unit-test framework

HotSpot is the name of the JVM. This Java enhancement was intended to support the development of C++ unit tests for the JVM. Here is a partial, non-prioritized, list of goals for this enhancement:

- Command line testing
- Creating appropriate documentation
- Debugging compile targets
- Framework elasticity
- IDE support

- Individual and isolated unit testing
- Individualized test results
- Integrating with existing infrastructure
- Internal test support
- Positive and negative testing
- Short execution time testing
- Supporting all JDK 9 build platforms
- Test compile targets
- Test exclusion
- Test grouping
- Testing that requires the JVM to be initialized
- Tests co-located with source code
- Tests for platform-dependent code
- Writing and executing unit testing (for classes and methods)

This enhancement is evidence of the increasing extensibility.

Enabling GTK3 on Linux

GTK+, formally known as the GIMP toolbox, is a cross-platform tool used for creating graphical user interfaces. The tool consists of widgets accessible through its API. Java's enhancement ensures GTK 2 and GTK 3 are supported on Linux when developing Java applications with graphical components. The implementation supports Java apps that employ JavaFX, AWT, and Swing.

We can create Java graphical applications with JavaFX, AWT, and Swing. Here is a table summarizing those three approaches as they relate to GTK, prior to Java 9:

Approach	Remarks
JavaFX	• Uses a dynamic GTK function lookup • Interacts with AWT and Swing via JFXPanel • Uses AWT printing functionality
AWT	• Uses a dynamic GTK function lookup
Swing	• Uses a dynamic GTK function lookup

So, what changes were necessary to implement this enhancement? For JavaFX, three specific things were changed:

- Automated testing was added for both GTK 2 and GTK 3
- Functionality was added to dynamically load GTK 2
- Support was added for GTK 3

For AWT and Swing, the following changes were implemented:

- Automated testing was added for both GTK 2 and GTK 3
- `AwtRobot` was migrated to GTK 3
- `FileChooserDilaog` was updated for GTK 3
- Functionality was added to dynamically load GTK 3
- The Swing GTK LnF was modified to support GTK 3

 Swing GTK LnF is short for Swing GTK look and feel.

New HotSpot build system

The Java platform used, prior to Java 9-11, was a build system riddled with duplicate code, redundancies, and other inefficiencies. The build system has been reworked for the modern Java platform based on the build-infra framework. In this context, infra is short for infrastructure. The overarching goal of this enhancement was to upgrade the build system to one that was simplified.

Specific goals included:

- Leveraging the existing build system
- Creating maintainable code
- Minimizing duplicate code
- Simplification
- Supporting future enhancements

 You can learn more about Oracle's infrastructure framework at the following link `http://www.oracle.com/technetwork/oem/frmwrk-infra-496656.html`.

Consolidating the JDF forest into a single repository

The Java 9 platform consisted of eight distinct repositories, as depicted in the following diagram. In Java 10, all of these repositories were combined into a single repository:

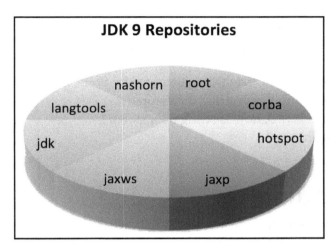

Repository consolidation helps streamline development. Moreover, it increases the ease of maintaining and updating the Java platform.

Summary

In this chapter, we covered some impressive new features of the Java platform introduced with Java 9, 10, and 11. We focused on `javac`, JDK libraries, and various test suites. Memory management improvements, including heap space efficiencies, memory allocation, and improved garbage collection represent a powerful new set of Java platform enhancements. Changes regarding the compilation process that result in greater efficiencies were part of our chapter. We also covered important improvements, such as with the compilation process, type testing, annotations, and automated runtime compiler tests.

In the next chapter, we will look at several minor language enhancements introduced in Java 9, 10, and 11.

Questions

1. What is contented locking?
2. What is a code cache?
3. What is the command-line code used to define the code heap size for the profiled compiled methods?
4. What are lint and doclint in the context of warnings?
5. What is the directory used when auto-generating run-time compiler tests?
6. What flag is used with the `-Xshare` command-line option for CDS class determination?
7. What is the file name extension generated by Scene Builder?
8. Prior to Java 9, how was string data stored?
9. Starting with Java 9, how is string data stored?
10. What is OpenType?

Further reading

The books listed here, also available as eBooks, will help you to dive deeper into Java 9 and JavaFX:

- *Java 9 High Performance*, available at `https://www.packtpub.com/application-development/java-9-high-perfor mance`.
- *JavaFX Essentials*, available at `https://www.packtpub.com/web-development/ javafx-essentials`.

Java 11 Fundamentals 3

In the last chapter, we covered some impressive new features of the Java platform introduced with Java 9, 10, and 11. We focused on javac, JDK libraries, and various test suites. Memory management improvements, including heap space efficiencies, memory allocation, and improved garbage collection represent a powerful new set of Java platform enhancements. Changes regarding the compilation process resulting in greater efficiencies were part of our chapter. We also covered important improvements, such as those regarding the compilation process, type testing, annotations, and automated runtime compiler tests.

This chapter covers some changes to the Java platform that impact variable handlers, import statements, improvements to Project Coin, local variable type inference, root certificates, dynamic class-file constants, and more. These represent changes to the Java language itself.

The specific topics we will cover in this chapter are as follows:

- Variable handlers
- Import statement depreciation warnings
- Project Coin
- Import statement processing
- Inferring local variables
- Thread-local handshakes
- Heap allocation on alternative memory devices
- Root certificates
- Dynamic class-file constants
- Removal of the Java EE and CORBA modules

Technical requirements

This chapter and subsequent chapters feature Java 11. The **Standard Edition** (**SE**) of the Java platform can be downloaded from Oracle's official download site (http://www.oracle.com/technetwork/java/javase/downloads/index.html).

An IDE software package is sufficient. IntelliJ IDEA, from JetBrains, was used for all coding associated with this chapter and subsequent chapters. The Community version of IntelliJ IDEA can be downloaded from the website (https://www.jetbrains.com/idea/features/).

This chapter's source code is available on GitHub at the URL (https://github.com/PacktPublishing/Mastering-Java-11-Second-Edition).

Working with variable handlers

Variable handlers are typed references to variables and are governed by the java.lang.invoke.VarHandle abstract class. The VarHandle method's signature is polymorphic. This provides for great variability in both method signatures and return types. Here is a code sample demonstrating how VarHandle might be used:

```
. . .
class Example {
  int myInt;
  . . .
}
. . .
class Sample {
  static final VarHandle VH_MYINT;

  static {
    try {
      VH_MYINT =
        MethodHandles.lookup().in(Example.class)
        .findVarHandle(Example.class, "myInt", int.class);
    }
    catch (Exception e) {
      throw new Error(e);
    }
  }
}
. . .
```

As you can see in the preceding code snippet, `VarHandle.lookup()` performs the same operation as those that are performed by a `MethodHandle.lookup()` method.

The aim of this change to the Java platform was to standardize the way in which methods of the following classes are invoked:

- `java.util.concurrent.atomic`
- `sun.misc.Unsafe`

Specifically, methods that did the following:

- Accessed/mutated object fields
- Accessed/mutated elements of an array

In addition, this change resulted in two fence operations for memory ordering and object reachability. In the spirit of due diligence, special attention was given to ensure the safety of the JVM. It was important to ensure that memory errors did not result from these changes. Data integrity, usability, and, of course, performance were key components of the aforementioned due diligence and are explained as follows:

- **Safety**: Corrupt memory states must not be possible.
- **Data integrity**: It must be ensured that access to an object's field uses identical rules:
  - `getfield` bytecode
  - `putfield` bytecode

- **Usability**: The benchmark for usability was the `sun.misc.Unsafe` API. The goal was to make the new API easier to use than the benchmark.
- **Performance**: There could be no degradation of performance compared to the use of the `sun.misc.Unsafe` API. The goal was to outperform that API.

 In Java, a fence operation is what javac does to force a constraint on memory in the form of a barrier instruction. These operations occur before and after the barrier instruction, essentially fencing them in.

Working with the AtoMiC ToolKit

The `java.util.concurrent.atomic` package is a collection of 12 subclasses that support operations on single variables that are thread-safe and lock-free. In this context, thread-safe refers to code that accesses or mutates a shared single variable without impeding on other threads executing on the variable at the same time. This superclass was introduced in Java 7.

Here is a list of the 12 subclasses in the AtoMiC ToolKit. The class names, as you would expect, are self-descriptive:

- `java.util.concurrent.atomic.AtomicBoolean`
- `java.util.concurrent.atomic.AtomicInteger`
- `java.util.concurrent.atomic.AtomicIntegerArray`
- `java.util.concurrent.atomic.AtomicIntegerFieldUpdater<T>`
- `java.util.concurrent.atomic.AtomicLong`
- `java.util.concurrent.atomic.AtomicLongArray`
- `java.util.concurrent.atomic.AtomicLongFieldUpdater<T>`
- `java.util.concurrent.atomic.AtomicMarkableReference<V>`
- `java.util.concurrent.atomic.AtomicReference<V>`
- `java.util.concurrent.atomic.AtomicReferenceArray<E>`
- `java.util.concurrent.atomic.AtomicReferenceFieldUpdater<T,V>`
- `java.util.concurrent.atomic.AtomicStampedReference<V>`

The key to using the AtoMIC ToolKit is having an understanding of volatile variables. Volatile variables, fields, and array elements can be asynchronously modified by concurrent threads.

 In Java, the `volatile` keyword is used to inform the javac utility to read the value, field, or array element from the main memory and not to cache them.

Here is a code snippet that demonstrates the use of the `volatile` keyword for an instance variable:

```
public class Sample {
  private static volatile Sample myVolatileVariable; // a volatile
  //
instance
  //variable
```

```
  // getter method
  public static Sample getVariable() {
    if (myVolatileVariable != null) {
      return myVolatileVariable;
    }

    // this section executes if myVolatileVariable == null
    synchronized(Sample.class) {
      if (myVolatileVariable == null) {
        myVolatileVariable = new Sample();
      }
    }
    return null;
  }
}
```

Using the sun.misc.Unsafe class

The sun.misc.Unsafe class, like other sun classes, is not officially documented or supported. It has been used to circumvent some of Java's built-in memory management safety features. While this can be viewed as a window to greater control and flexibility in our code, it is a terrible programming practice.

The class had a single private constructor, so an instance of the class could not easily be instantiated. So, if we tried to instantiate an instance with myUnsafe = new Unsafe(), SecurityException would be thrown in most circumstances. This somewhat unreachable class has over 100 methods that permitted operations on arrays, classes, and objects. Here is a brief sampling of those methods:

Arrays	Classes	Objects
arrayBaseOffset	defineAnonymousClass	allocateInstance
arrayIndexScale	defineClass	objectFieldOffset
	ensureClassInitialized	
	staticFieldOffset	

Here is a secondary grouping of the `sun.misc.Unsafe` class method for information, memory, and synchronization:

Information	Memory	Synchronization
addressSize	allocateMemory	compareAndSwapInt
pageSize	copyMemory	monitorEnter
	freeMemory	monitorExit
	getAddress	putOrderedEdit
	getInt	tryMonitorEnter
	putInt	

The `sun.misc.Unsafe` class was earmarked for removal in Java 9. There was actually some opposition to this decision in the programming industry. To put their concerns to rest, the class has been depreciated, but will not be completely removed.

Import statement depreciation warnings

Quite often, when we compile our programs, we receive many warnings and errors. The compiler errors must be fixed, as they are typically syntactical in nature. The warnings, on the other hand, should be reviewed and appropriately addressed. Some of the warning messages are ignored by developers.

Java 9 provided a slight reduction in the number of warnings we received. Specifically, depreciation warnings caused by import statements were no longer generated. Prior to Java 9, we could suppress deprecated warning messages with the following annotation:

```
@SupressWarnings
```

Now the compiler will suppress depreciated warnings if one or more of the following cases is true:

- If the `@Deprecated` annotation is used
- If the `@SuppressWarnings` annotation is used
- If the use of the warning-generating code and the declaration are within the ancestor class
- If the use of the warning-generating code is within an `import` statement

Milling Project Coin

Project Coin was a feature set of minor changes introduced in Java 7. These changes are listed as follows:

- Strings in `switch` statements
- Binary integral literals
- Using underscores in numeric literals
- Implementing multi-catch
- Allowing for more precise rethrowing of exceptions
- Generic instance creation improvements
- Addition of the `try`-with-resource statement
- Improvements to invoking `varargs` methods

Detailed information can be found in the following Oracle presentation (`http://www.oracle.com/us/technologies/java/project-coin-428201.pdf`).

For the Java 9 release, there were five improvements to Project Coin. These enhancements are detailed in the sections that follow.

Using the @SafeVarargs annotation

Starting with Java 9, we could use the `@SafeVarargs` annotation with private instance methods. When we use this annotation, we are asserting that the method does not contain any harmful operations on the `varargs` passed as parameters to the method.

The syntax for use is as follows:

```
@SafeVarargs // this is the annotation
static void methodName(...) {

/*
  The contents of the method or constructor must not
  perform any unsafe or potentially unsafe operations
  on the varargs parameter or parameters.
*/
}
```

Use of the `@SafeVarargs` annotation is restricted to the following:

- Static methods
- Final instance methods
- Private instance methods

The try-with-resource statement

The `try`-with-resource statement previously required a new variable to be declared for each resource in the statement when a `final` variable was used. Here is the syntax for the `try`-with-resource statement prior to Java 9 (in Java 7 or 8):

```
try ( // open resources ) {
  // use resources
} catch (// error) {
  // handle exceptions
}
// automatically close resources
```

Here is a code snippet using the preceding syntax:

```
try ( Scanner xmlScanner = new Scanner(new File(xmlFile)); {
  while (xmlScanner.hasNext()) {
    // read the xml document and perform needed operations
  }
  xmlScanner.close();
  } catch (FileNotFoundException fnfe) {
  System.out.println("Your XML file was not found.");
}
```

Since Java 9, the `try`-with-resource statement can manage `final` variables without requiring a new variable declaration. So, we can now rewrite the earlier code in Java 9, 10, or 11, as shown here:

```
Scanner xmlScanner = new Scanner(newFile(xmlFile));
try ( while (xmlScanner.hasNext()) {
  {
    // read the xml document and perform needed operations
  }
  xmlScanner.close();
} catch (FileNotFoundException fnfe) {
    System.out.println("Your XML file was not found.");
  }
```

As you can see, the `xmlScanner` object reference is contained inside the `try`-with-resource statement block, which provides for automatic resource management. The resource will automatically be closed as soon as the `try`-with-resource statement block is exited.

> You can also use a `finally` block as part of the `try`-with-resource statement.

Using the diamond operator

Introduced in Java 9, the diamond operator can be used with anonymous classes if the inferred data type is denotable. When a data type is inferred, it suggests that the Java compiler can determine the data types in a method's invocation. This includes the declaration and any arguments contained within.

> The diamond operator is the less than and greater than symbol pair (<>). It is not new to Java 9; rather, the specific use with anonymous classes is.

The diamond operator was introduced in Java 7 and made instantiating generic classes simpler. Here is a pre-Java 7 example:

```
ArrayList<Student> roster = new ArrayList<Student>();
```

Then, in Java 7, we could rewrite it:

```
ArrayList<Student> roster = new ArrayList<>();
```

The problem was that this method could not be used for anonymous classes. Here is an example in Java 8 that works fine:

```
public interface Example<T> {
  void aMethod() {
    // interface code goes here
  }
}

Example example = new Example<Integer>()
{
```

```
  @Override
  public void aMethod() {
    // code
  }
};
```

While the preceding code works fine, when we change it to use the diamond operator, as shown here, a compiler error will occur:

```
public interface Example<T> {
  void aMethod() {
    // interface code goes here
  }
}

Example example = new Example<>()
{
  @Override
  public void aMethod() {
    // code
  }
};
```

The error results from using the diamond operator with anonymous inner classes. Java 9 to the rescue! While the preceding code results in a compile-time error in Java 8, it works fine in Java 9, 10, and 11.

Discontinuing use of the underscore

The underscore character (_) can no longer be used as a legal identifier name.
Earlier attempts to remove the underscore in an identifier name were incomplete. The use of the underscore would generate a combination of errors and warnings. Since Java 9, the warnings are now errors. Consider the following sample code:

```
public class UnderscoreTest {
  public static void main(String[] args) {
    int _ = 319;
    if ( _ > 300 ) {
      System.out.println("Your value us greater than 300.");
    }
    else {
      System.out.println("Your value is not greater than 300.");
    }
  }
}
```

The preceding code, in Java 8, will result in compiler warnings for the int _ = 319; and if (_ > 300) statements. The warning is: As of Java 9, '_' is a keyword, and may not be used as an identifier. So, in Java 9, 10 or 11, you are not able to use the underscore by itself as a legal identifier.

> It is considered bad programming practice to use identifier names that are not self-descriptive. So, the use of the underscore character by itself as an identifier name should not be a problematic change.

Making use of private interface methods

Lambda expressions were a big part of the Java 8 release. As a follow-up to that improvement, private methods in interfaces are now feasible. Previously, we could not share data between nonabstract methods of an interface. With Java 9, 10, and 11, this data sharing is possible. Interface methods can now be private. Let's look at some sample code.

This first code snippet is how we might code an interface in Java 8:

```
. . .
public interface characterTravel {
  public default void walk() {
    Scanner scanner = new Scanner(System.in);
    System.out.println("Enter desired pacing: ");
    int p = scanner.nextInt();
    p = p +1;
  }
  public default void run() {
    Scanner scanner = new Scanner(System.in);
    System.out.println("Enter desired pacing: ");
    int p = scanner.nextInt();
    p = p +4;
  }
  public default void fastWalk() {
    Scanner scanner = new Scanner(System.in);
    System.out.println("Enter desired pacing: ");
    int p = scanner.nextInt();
    p = p +2;
  }
  public default void retreat() {
    Scanner scanner = new Scanner(System.in);
    System.out.println("Enter desired pacing: ");
    int p = scanner.nextInt();
```

```
      p = p - 1;
    }
    public default void fastRetreat() {
      Scanner scanner = new Scanner(System.in);
      System.out.println("Enter desired pacing: ");
      int p = scanner.nextInt();
      p = p - 4;
    }
  }
```

Starting in Java 9, we can rewrite this code. As you can see in the following snippet, the redundant code has been moved into a single private method called characterTravel:

```
  . . .
  public interface characterTravel {
    public default void walk() {
      characterTravel("walk");
    }
    public default void run() {
      characterTravel("run");
    }
    public default void fastWalk() {
      characterTravel("fastWalk");
    }
    public default void retreat() {
      characterTravel("retreat");
    }
    public default void fastRetreat() {
      characterTravel("fastRetreat");
    }
    private default void characterTravel(String pace) {
      Scanner scanner = new Scanner(System.in);
      System.out.println("Enter desired pacing: ");
      int p = scanner.nextInt();
      if (pace.equals("walk")) {
        p = p +1;
      }
      else if (pace.equals("run")) {
        p = p + 4;
      }
      else if (pace.equals("fastWalk")) {
        p = p + 2;
      }
      else if (pace.equals("retreat")) {
        p = p - 1;
      }
      else if (pace.equals("fastRetreat"))
```

```
    {
       p = p - 4;
    }
    else
    {
       //
    }
  }
}
```

Import statement processing

JDK Enhancement Proposal (JEP) 216 was issued as a fix to javac in regard to how import statements are processed. Prior to Java 9, there were instances where the order of import statements would impact if the source code was accepted or not.

When we develop applications in Java, we typically add import statements as we need them, resulting in an unordered list of import statements. IDEs do a great job of color-coding import statements that are not used, as well as informing us of import statements we need, but that has not been included. It should not matter what order the import statements are in; there is no applicable hierarchy.

javac compiles classes in two primary steps. Specific to handling import statements, these steps are as follows:

- **Type resolution**: The type resolution consists of a review of the abstract syntax tree to identify declarations of classes and interfaces
- **Member resolution**: The member resolution includes determining the class hierarchy and individual class variables and members

Starting with Java 9, the order in which we list import statements in our classes and files will no longer impact the compilation process. Let's look at an example:

```
package samplePackage;

import static SamplePackage.OuterPackage.Nested.*;
import SamplePackage.Thing.*;

public class OuterPackage {
  public static class Nested implements Inner {
    // code
  }
}
```

```
package SamplePackage.Thing;

public interface Inner {
  // code
}
```

In the preceding example, type resolution occurs and results in the following realizations:

- `SamplePackage.OuterPackage` exists
- `SamplePackage.OuterPackage.Nested` exists
- `SamplePackage.Thing.Innner` exists

The next step is member resolution, and this is where the problem existed prior to Java 9. Here is an overview of the sequential steps javac would use to conduct the member resolution for our sample code:

1. Resolution of `SamplePackage.OuterPackage` begins.
2. The `SamplePackage.OuterPackage.Nested` import is processed.
3. Resolution of the `SamplePackage.Outer.Nested` class begins.
4. The inner interface is type checked, although, because it is not in scope at this point, the inner interface cannot be resolved.
5. Resolution of `SamplePackage.Thing` begins. This step includes importing all member types of `SamplePackage.Thing` into scope.

So, the error occurs, in our example, because `Inner` is out of scope when resolution is attempted. If steps 4 and 5 were swapped, it would not have been a problem.

The solution to the problem, implemented in Java 9, was to break the member resolution steps into additional substeps. Here are those steps:

1. Analyze the import statements
2. Create the hierarchy (class and interfaces)
3. Analyze class headers and type parameters

Inferring local variables

Starting with Java 10, declaring local variables has been simplified. Developers no longer have to include manifest declarations of local variable types; rather, declarations can be inferred through use of the new `var` identifier.

Inferring declarations with the var identifier

We can use the new `var` identifier, as with the following example, to infer our data type. So, instead of explicitly declaring data types, we can infer them:

```
var myList = new ArrayList<String>();
```

The preceding code infers `ArrayList<String>`, so we no longer need to use the verbose `ArrayList<String> myList = new ArrayList<String>();` syntax.

 The introduction of the `var` identifier should not be construed as adding a new keyword to the Java language. The `var` identifier is technically a reserved type name.

There are a few restrictions to using the `new` identifier. For example, they cannot be used when any of the following conditions exist:

- No initializer is used
- Multiple variables are being declared
- Array dimension brackets are used
- A reference to the initialized variable is used

As expected, javac will issue specific error messages if `var` is used incorrectly.

Local variable syntax for Lambda parameters

As discussed earlier in this chapter, the `var` identifier was introduced in Java 10. With the latest version, Java 11, `var` can be used in implicitly typed Lambda expressions. The following is an example of two equivalent Java statements:

- `(object1, object2) -> object1.myMyethod(object2)`
- `(var object1, var object2) -> object1.myMethod(object2)`

In the first statement, the `var` identifier is not used. In the second statement, `var` is used. It is important to note that if `var` is used in an implicitly typed Lambda expression, it must be used for all formal parameters.

Thread-local handshakes

One of the features added to the Java platform in version 10 was the ability to stop threads individually without having to perform a global virtual machine safe point. The benefits of having this capability include biased lock revocation improvement, virtual machine latency reduction, safer stack tracing, and omitting memory barriers.

This change is evident in x64 and **SPARC** (short for **Scalable Processor Architecture**) systems. If we want to select normal safepoints, we would use the following option:

```
XX: ThreadLocalHandshakes
```

Heap allocation on alternative memory devices

The HotSpot virtual machine, as of Java 10, supports non-DRAM memory devices. We can use the following option to allocate the Java object heap in alternative memory devices:

```
XX:AllocateHeapAt=<file system path>
```

Location conflicts and security concerns can be important to address when allocating memory using alternative device filesystems. Specifically, ensure that the proper permissions are used and that the heap is wiped upon application termination.

Root certificates

Starting with the release of Java 10, there is a default set of **Certification Authority** (**CA**) certificates as part of the JDK. The JDK's `cacerts` and `keystore` prior to Java 10, did not contain a set of certificates. Prior to this Java release, developers were required to create and configure a set of root certificates for `cacerts` and `keystore`.

Now, the Java platform includes a set of root certificates in `cacerts` and `keystore`, issued by Oracle. The specific CA is part of the Java SE Root CA program.

As of Java 10, the following CAs, authenticated by Oracle, are included in the root certificates:

- Actalis S.p.A.
- Buypass AS
- Camerfirma
- Certum
- Chunghwa Telecom Co., Ltd.
- Comodo CA Ltd.
- Digicert Inc.
- DocuSign
- D-TRUST GmbH
- IdenTrust
- Let's Encrypt
- LuxTrust
- QuoVadis Ltd.
- Secom Trust Systems
- SwissSign AG
- Tella
- Trustwave

It is likely that additional CAs will be added in each subsequent release of the Java platform.

Dynamic class-file constants

In Java 11, the file format for Java class files was extended to support `CONSTANT_Dynamic`, which delegates creation to a bootstrap method. A new constant form, `CONSTANT_Dynamic`, has been added to the Java platform and has two components:

- `CONSTANT_InvokeDynamic`
- `CONSTANT_NameAndType`

Additional details regarding this feature enhancement can be found by following the link in the *Further reading* section of this chapter.

Removal of the Java EE and CORBA modules

The **Java Enterprise Edition (Java EE)** and **Common Object Request Broker Architecture (CORBA)** modules were depreciated in Java 9 and have been removed from the Java platform as of Java 11.

The following Java SE modules contained Java EE and CORBA modules and have been removed:

- Aggregator module (`java.se.ee`)
- Common Annotations (`java.xml.ws.annotation`)
- CORBA (`java.corba`)
- JAF (`java.activation`)
- JAX-WS (`java.xml.ws`)
- JAX-WS tools (`jdk.xml.ws`)
- JAXB (`java.xml.bind`)
- JAXB tools (`jdk.xml.bind`)
- JTA (`java.transaction`)

Summary

In this chapter, we covered several changes to the Java platform that impact variable handlers, import statements, improvements to Project Coin, local variable type inference, root certificates, dynamic class-file constants, and more. We also covered depreciation warnings and why they are now suppressed under specific circumstances. Finally, we explored the improvements to import statement processing.

In the next chapter, we will examine the structure of a Java module as specified by Project Jigsaw. We will take a deep dive into how Project Jigsaw is implemented as part of the Java platform. Code snippets are used throughout the chapter to demonstrate Java's modular system. Internal changes to the Java platform, in regard to the modular system, will also be discussed.

Questions

1. What is a fence operation?
2. What is Project Coin?
3. What type of methods can `@SafeVarargs` be used with?
4. What was the significance of the change to import statement processing?
5. Where does Java store root certificates?
6. `var` is not a keyword. What is it?
7. What is `var` used for?
8. What change was made to the Java platform in regard to the underscore character (_)?
9. How many subclasses are in the AtoMiC package?
10. Which class governs variable handlers?

Further reading

The following link listed will help you dive deeper into the concepts presented in this chapter:

- *Learning Java Lambdas* (`https://www.packtpub.com/application-development/learning-java-lambdas`)

4
Building Modular Applications with Java 11

In the last chapter, we covered the recent changes to the Java platform with regards to variable handlers and how they related to the AtoMiC ToolKit. We also covered depreciation warnings and why they are suppressed under specific circumstances. Project Coin-related changes were explored as well as import statement processing, inferring local variables, and thread-local handshakes. We further explored changes to the Java language with a look at heap allocation, root certificates, dynamic class-file constants, and removal of the Java EE and CORBA modules.

In this chapter, we will examine the structure of a Java module as specified by Project Jigsaw. We will take a deep dive into how Project Jigsaw is implemented as part of the Java platform. We will also review key internal changes to the Java platform as they relate to the modular system.

We will look at the following topics:

- A modular primer
- The modular JDK
- Modular runtime images
- Module system
- Modular Java application packaging
- The Java Linker
- Encapsulating most internal APIs

Technical requirements

This chapter and subsequent chapters feature Java 11. The **Standard Edition** (**SE**) of the Java platform can be downloaded from Oracle's official download site (`http://www.oracle.com/technetwork/java/javase/downloads/index.html`).

An IDE software package is sufficient. IntelliJ IDEA, from JetBrains, was used for all coding associated with this chapter and subsequent chapters. The Community version of IntelliJ IDEA can be downloaded from the site (`https://www.jetbrains.com/idea/features/`).

A modular primer

We can define the term **modular** as a type of design or construction, in our context, of computer software. This type of software design involves a set of modules that collectively comprise the whole. A house, for example, can be built as a single structure or in a modular fashion where each room is constructed independently and joined to create a home. With this analogy, you could selectively add or not add modules in the creation of your home.

The collection of modules, in our analogy, becomes the design of your home. Your design does not need to use every module, only the ones you want. So, for example, if there are basement and bonus room modules and your design does not include those modular rooms, those modules are not used to build your home. The alternative would be that every home would include every room, not just the ones that are used. This, of course, would be wasteful. Let's see how that correlates to software.

This concept can be applied to computer architecture and software systems. Our systems can be comprised of several components instead of one behemoth system. As you can probably imagine, this provides us with some specific benefits:

- We should be able to scale our Java applications to run on small devices
- Our Java applications will be smaller
- Our modular code can be more targeted
- Increased use of the object-oriented programming model
- There are additional opportunities for encapsulation
- Our code will be more efficient
- Java applications will have increased performance
- The overall system complexity is reduced

- Testing and debugging is easier
- Code maintenance is easier

The shift to a modular system for Java was necessary for several reasons. Here are the primary conditions of the Java platform prior to Java 9 that led to the creation of the modular system in the current Java platform:

- The **Java Development Kit (JDK)** was simply too big. This made it difficult to support small devices. Even with the compact profiles discussed in the next section, supporting some small devices was difficult at best and, in some cases, not possible.
- Due to the oversized JDK, it was difficult to support truly optimized performance with our Java applications. In this case, smaller is better.
- The **Java Runtime Environment (JRE)** was too large to efficiently test and maintain our Java applications. This results in time-consuming, inefficient testing, and maintenance operations.
- The **Java ARchive (JAR)** files were also too large. This made supporting small devices problematic.
- Because the JDK and JRE were all-encompassing, security was of great concern. Internal APIs, for example, that were not used by the Java application, were still available due to the nature of the public access modifier.
- Finally, our Java applications were unnecessarily large.

Modular systems have the following requirements:

- There must be a common interface to permit interoperability among all connected modules
- Isolated and connected testing must be supported
- Compile time operations must be able to identify which modules are in use
- There must be runtime support for modules

The module concept was first introduced in Java 9; it is a named collection of data and code. Specifically, Java modules are a collection of the following:

- Packages
- Classes
- Interfaces
- Code
- Data
- Resources

Key to successful implementation, a module is self-described in its modular declaration. Module names must be unique and typically use the reverse domain name schema. Here is an example declaration:

```
module com.three19.irisScan { }
```

Module declarations are contained in a `module-info.java` file that should be in the module's `root` folder. As one might expect, this file is compiled into a `module-info.class` file and will be placed in the appropriate output directory. These output directories are established in the module source code.

In the next sections, we will look at specific changes to the Java platform in regards to modularity.

The modular JDK

The core aim of JEP-200 was to modularize the JDK using the **Java Platform Module System** (**JPMS**). Prior to Java 9, our familiarity with the JDK includes awareness of its major components:

- The JRE
- The interpreter (Java)
- The compiler (Javac)
- The archiver (JAR)
- The document generator (Javadoc)

The task of modularizing the JDK was to break it into components that could be combined at compile time or runtime. The modular structure is based on the following modular profiles established as compact profiles in Java 8. Each of the three profiles is detailed in the following tables:

- **Compact profile 1**:

java.io	java.lang.annotation	java.lang.invoke
java.lang.ref	java.lang.reflect	java.math
java.net	java.nio	java.nio.channels
java.nio.channels.spi	java.nio.charset	java.nio.charset.spi
java.nio.file	java.nio.file.attribute	java.nio.file.spi
java.security	java.security.cert	java.security.interfaces
java.security.spec	java.text	java.text.spi
java.time	java.time.chrono	java.time.format

java.time.temporal	java.time.zone	java.util
java.util.concurrent	java.util.concurrent.atomic	java.util.concurrent.locks
java.util.function	java.util.jar	java.util.logging
java.util.regex	java.tuil.spi	java.util.stream
java.util.zip	javax.crypto	javax.crypto.interfaces
javax.crypto.spec	javax.net	javax.net.ssl
javax.script	javax.security.auth	javax.security.auth.callback
javax.security.auth.login	javax.security.auth.spi	javax.security.auth.spi
javax.security.auth.x500	javax.security.cert	

- **Compact profile 2**:

java.rmi	java.rmi.activation	java.rmi.drc
java.rmi.registry	java.rmi.server	java.sql
javax.rmi.ssl	javax.sql	javax.transaction
javax.transaction.xa	javax.xml	javax.xml.database
javax.xml.namespace	javax.xml.parsers	javax.xml.stream
javax.xml.stream.events	javax.xml.stream.util	javax.xml.transform
javax.xml.transform.dom	javax.xml.transform.sax	javax.xml.transform.stax
java.xml.transform.stream	javax.xml.validation	javax.xml.xpath
org.w3c.dom	org.w3c.dom.bootstrap	org.w3c.dom.events
org.w3c.dom.ls	org.xml.sax	org.xml.sax.ext
org.xml.sax.helpers		

- **Compact profile 3**:

java.lang.instrument	java.lang.management	java.security.acl
java.util.prefs	javax.annotation.processing	javax.lang.model
javax.lang.model.element	javax.lang.model.type	javax.lang.model.util
javax.management	javax.management.loading	javax.management.modelmbean
javax.management.monitor	javax.management.openmbean	javax.management.relation
javax.management.remote	javax.management.remote.rmi	javax.management.timer
javax.naming	javax.naming.directory	javax.naming.event
javax.naing.ldap	javax.naming.spi	javax.security.auth.kerberos
javax.security.sasl	javax.sql.rowset	javax.sql.rowset.serial
javax.sql.rowset.spi	javax.tools	javax.xml.crypto
javax.xml.crypto.dom	javax.xml.crypto.dsig	javax.xml.crypto.dsig.dom
javax.xml.crypto.dsig.keyinfo	javax.xml.crypto.dsig.spec	org.ieft.jgss

The three compact module profiles represent the basis for the standardized modular system in the current Java platform. The effectiveness of this standardization relies on the following six principles:

- All JCP-governed modules must start with the string `java`. So, if a module on spatial utilities was being developed, it would have a name such as `java.spatial.util`.

 JCP refers to the **Java Community Process**. JCP allows developers to create technical specifications for Java. You can learn more about JCP and become a member at the official JCP website at `https://www.jcp.org/en/home/index`.

- Non-JCP modules are considered part of the JDK and their names must start with the string `jdk`.
- Ensure method invocation chaining works properly. This is best illustrated with the following flowchart:

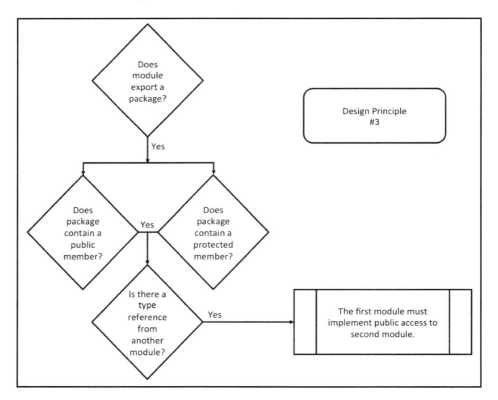

As you can see in the preceding flowchart, it only applies to modules that export a package.

- The fourth principle deals with both standard and nonstandard API packages being used in a standard module. The following flowchart illustrates the implementation of this principle's covenants:

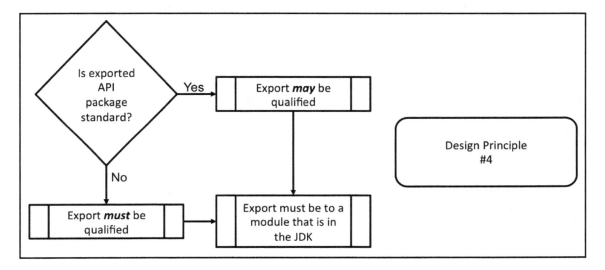

- The fifth design principle is that standard modules can be dependent upon more than one nonstandard module. While this dependency is permitted, implied readability access to nonstandard modules is not.
- The final design principle ensures nonstandard modules do not export standard API packages.

Modular source code

As previously mentioned, Project Jigsaw had the goal of modularization. The envisioned standard modular system would be applied to the Java SE platform and the JDK. In addition to efficiency gains, the modular shift would result in better security and ease maintainability. The enhancement detailed in JEP-201 focused on JDK source code reorganization. Let's take a closer look.

Reorganizing the JDK's source code is a significant task and was accomplished with the following subset of goals:

- Provide JDK developers insights and familiarity with the new Java 9 modular system. So, this goal was aimed at developers of the JDK, not mainstream developers.
- Ensure modular boundaries are established and maintained throughout the JDK build process.
- The third goal was to ensure future enhancements, specifically with Project Jigsaw, could be easily integrated into the new modular system.

The significance of this source code reorganization cannot be overstated. The pre-Java 9 source code organization was 20 years old. This overdue JDK source code reorganization will make the code much easier to maintain. Let's look at the previous organization of the JDK source code and then examine the changes.

JDK source code organization before modularization

The JDK is a compilation of code files, tools, libraries, and more. The following diagram provides an overview of the JDK components:

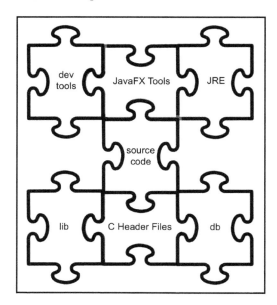

The pre-modular organization of the JDK components in the preceding diagram is detailed in the next seven subsections.

Development tools

The development tools are located in the \bin directory. These tools include seven broad categorizations, each detailed in the subsequent sections.

Deployment

This is a set of tools intended to help deploy Java applications:

- appletviewer: This tool gives you the ability to run and debug Java applets without the need for a web browser.
- extcheck: This tool allows you to find conflicts in JAR files.
- jar: This tool is used for creating and manipulating JAR files. JAR files are Java Archive files.
- java: This is the Java application launcher.
- javac: This is the Java compiler.
- javadoc: This tool generates API documentation.
- javah: This tool allows you to write native methods; it generates C header files.
- javap: This tool disassembles class files.
- javapackager: For signing and packaging Java applications, including JavaFX.
- jdb: This is the Java debugger.
- jdeps: This is an analyzer for Java class dependencies.
- pack200: This is a tool that compresses JAR files into pack200 files. The compression ratio using this tool is impressive.
- unpack200: This tool unpacks pack200 files resulting in JAR files.

Internationalization

If you are interested in creating localizable applications, the following tool might come in handy:

- native2ascii: This tool creates Unicode Latin-1 from normal text

Monitoring

Monitoring tools used for providing JVM performance data include the following:

- `jps`: This is the JVM process status tool (`jps`). It provides a list of HotSpot JVMs on a specific system.
- `jstat`: This is the JVM statistics monitoring tool. It collects log data and performance information from a machine with a HotSpot JVM.
- `jstatd`: This is the `jstat` daemon tool. It runs an RMI server app for monitoring HotSpot JVM operations.

RMI

RMI tools are **Remote Method Invocation** tools. They help developers create applications that operate over a network to include the internet:

- `rmic`: This tool can generate stubs and skeletons for objects over a network
- `rmiregistry`: This is a registry service for remote objects
- `rmid`: This tool is an activation system daemon for RMI
- `serialver`: This tool returns the class `serialVersionUID` value

Security

This set of security tools empowers developers to create security policies that can be enforced on the developer's computer system as well as on remote systems:

- `keytool`: This tool manages security certificates and keystores
- `jarsigner`: This tool generates and verifies JAR signatures for creating/opening JAR files
- `policytool`: This tool has a graphical user interface that helps developers manage their security policy files

Troubleshooting

These experimental troubleshooting tools are useful for very specific troubleshooting. They are experimental and, therefore, not officially supported:

- `jinfo`: This tool provides configuration information for specific processes, files, or servers
- `jhat`: This is a heap dump tool. It instantiates a web server so that a heap can be viewed with a browser

- `jmap`: This displays heap and shared object memory maps from a process, file, or server
- `jsadebugd`: This is Java's Serviceability Agent Debug Daemon. It acts as a debug server for a process or file
- `jstack`: This is a Java Stack Trace tool that provides a thread stack trace for a process, file, or server

Web services

This set of tools provides a utility that can be used with **Java Web Start** and other web services:

- `javaws`: This is a command line tool that launches Java Web Start.
- `schemagen`: This tool generates schemas for Java architecture. These schemas are used for XML binding.
- `wsgen`: This tool is used for generating JAX-WS artifacts that are portable.
- `wsimport`: This tool is used for importing portable JAX-WS artifacts.
- `xjc`: This is the binding compiler that is used for XML binding.

JavaFX tools

The JavaFX tools are located in a few different places including \bin, \man, and \lib directories.

Java runtime environment

The JRE is located in the \jre directory. Key contents include the JVM and class libraries.

Source code

The JDK's source code, pre-Java 9, had the following basic organizational schema:

```
source code / [shared, OS-specific] / [classes / native] / Java API package
name / [.file extension]
```

Let's look at this a bit closer. After the source code, we have two options. If the code is cross-platform, then it is a shared directory; otherwise, it is operating system specific. For example:

```
src/share/...
src/windows/...
```

Next, we have the classes directory or a native language directory. For example:

```
src/share/classes/...
src/share/classes/java/...
```

Next, we have the name of the Java API package followed by the file extension. The file extensions depend on content such as `.java`, `.c`, and more.

Libraries

The `\lib` directory houses class libraries that are needed by one or more of the development tools in the `\bin` directory. Here is a list of files in a typical Java 8 `\lib` directory:

```
Select Command Prompt                                        —    □    ×
C:\Program Files\Java\jdk1.8.0_121>dir
 Volume in drive C is OS
 Volume Serial Number is 608F-FF3F

 Directory of C:\Program Files\Java\jdk1.8.0_121

02/06/2017  09:42 AM    <DIR>          .
02/06/2017  09:42 AM    <DIR>          ..
02/06/2017  09:41 AM    <DIR>          bin
12/12/2016  07:45 PM             3,244 COPYRIGHT
02/06/2017  09:41 AM    <DIR>          db
02/06/2017  09:41 AM    <DIR>          include
02/06/2017  09:41 AM         5,094,117 javafx-src.zip
02/06/2017  09:41 AM    <DIR>          jre
02/06/2017  09:41 AM    <DIR>          lib
02/06/2017  09:41 AM                40 LICENSE
02/06/2017  09:41 AM               159 README.html
02/06/2017  09:41 AM               528 release
02/06/2017  09:41 AM           110,114 THIRDPARTYLICENSEREADME-JAVAFX.txt
02/06/2017  09:41 AM           177,094 THIRDPARTYLICENSEREADME.txt
               7 File(s)      5,385,296 bytes
               7 Dir(s)  844,536,442,880 bytes free

C:\Program Files\Java\jdk1.8.0_121>
```

Reviewing the directory listing does not provide a great level of granular insight. We can list the classes contained in any of the `.jar` files with the following command: `jar tvf fileName.jar`. As an example, here is the class listing generated from executing `jar tvf javafx-mx.jar` at the command line:

```
Command Prompt                                                    —    □    ×

C:\Program Files\Java\jdk1.8.0_121\lib>jar tvf javafx-mx.jar
     0 Mon Dec 12 12:01:10 CST 2016 META-INF/
    25 Mon Dec 12 12:01:10 CST 2016 META-INF/MANIFEST.MF
     0 Mon Dec 12 12:00:54 CST 2016 com/
     0 Mon Dec 12 12:00:54 CST 2016 com/oracle/
     0 Mon Dec 12 12:00:54 CST 2016 com/oracle/javafx/
     0 Mon Dec 12 12:00:56 CST 2016 com/oracle/javafx/jmx/
   963 Mon Dec 12 12:00:54 CST 2016 com/oracle/javafx/jmx/MXExtensionImpl.class
   667 Mon Dec 12 12:00:54 CST 2016 com/oracle/javafx/jmx/SGMXBean.class
   728 Mon Dec 12 12:00:56 CST 2016 com/oracle/javafx/jmx/SGMXBeanImpl$1.class
 12268 Mon Dec 12 12:00:56 CST 2016 com/oracle/javafx/jmx/SGMXBeanImpl.class
     0 Mon Dec 12 12:00:56 CST 2016 com/oracle/javafx/jmx/json/
   744 Mon Dec 12 12:00:56 CST 2016 com/oracle/javafx/jmx/json/ImmutableJSONDocument.class
  1052 Mon Dec 12 12:00:56 CST 2016 com/oracle/javafx/jmx/json/JSONDocument$IteratorWrapper.class
  1068 Mon Dec 12 12:00:56 CST 2016 com/oracle/javafx/jmx/json/JSONDocument$Type.class
 11846 Mon Dec 12 12:00:56 CST 2016 com/oracle/javafx/jmx/json/JSONDocument.class
   893 Mon Dec 12 12:00:56 CST 2016 com/oracle/javafx/jmx/json/JSONException.class
   936 Mon Dec 12 12:00:56 CST 2016 com/oracle/javafx/jmx/json/JSONFactory.class
  1973 Mon Dec 12 12:00:56 CST 2016 com/oracle/javafx/jmx/json/JSONReader$EventType.class
   800 Mon Dec 12 12:00:56 CST 2016 com/oracle/javafx/jmx/json/JSONReader.class
   590 Mon Dec 12 12:00:56 CST 2016 com/oracle/javafx/jmx/json/JSONWriter$Container.class
  1115 Mon Dec 12 12:00:56 CST 2016 com/oracle/javafx/jmx/json/JSONWriter$ContainerType.class
  4781 Mon Dec 12 12:00:56 CST 2016 com/oracle/javafx/jmx/json/JSONWriter.class
     0 Mon Dec 12 12:00:56 CST 2016 com/oracle/javafx/jmx/json/impl/
  1288 Mon Dec 12 12:00:56 CST 2016 com/oracle/javafx/jmx/json/impl/JSONMessages.class
  4966 Mon Dec 12 12:00:56 CST 2016 com/oracle/javafx/jmx/json/impl/JSONScanner.class
  2273 Mon Dec 12 12:00:56 CST 2016 com/oracle/javafx/jmx/json/impl/JSONStreamReaderImpl$1.class
  8241 Mon Dec 12 12:00:56 CST 2016 com/oracle/javafx/jmx/json/impl/JSONStreamReaderImpl.class
  5486 Mon Dec 12 12:00:56 CST 2016 com/oracle/javafx/jmx/json/impl/JSONSymbol.class
   916 Mon Dec 12 12:00:56 CST 2016 com/oracle/javafx/jmx/json/impl/JSONMessagesBundle.properties
  1968 Mon Dec 12 12:00:56 CST 2016 com/oracle/javafx/jmx/json/impl/JSONMessagesBundle_ja.properties
  1284 Mon Dec 12 12:00:56 CST 2016 com/oracle/javafx/jmx/json/impl/JSONMessagesBundle_zh_CN.properties

C:\Program Files\Java\jdk1.8.0_121\lib>
```

C header files

The `/include` directory contains C header files. These files primarily support the following:

- **Java Native Interface (JNI)**: This is used for native-code programming support. The JNI is used to embed Java native methods and the JVM into native apps.
- **JVM tool interface (JVM TI)**: This is used by tools for state inspections and execution control for apps running the JVM.

Database

The Apache Derby relational database is stored in the /db directory. You can learn more about Java DB at the following sites:

- http://docs.oracle.com/javadb/support/overview.html
- http://db.apache.org/derby/manuals/#docs_10.11

JDK source code reorganization

In a previous section, you learned that the pre-Java 9 source code organization schema was as follows:

```
source code / [shared, OS-specific] / [classes / native] / Java API package
name / [.file extension]
```

In the current Java platform, we have a modular schema. That schema follows:

```
source code / module / [shared, OS-specific] / [classes / native /
configuration] / [ package / include / library ] / [.file extension]
```

There are a few differences in the new schema, most notably the module name. After the shared or OS-specific directory, there is either the classes directory, the native directory for C or C++ source files, or a configuration directory. This seemingly rudimentary organization schema changes results in a much more maintainable code base.

Modular runtime images

Java's modular system, introduced in Java 9, required changes to the runtime images for compatibility. The benefits of these changes include enhancements in the following areas:

- Maintainability
- Performance
- Security

Core to these changes was a new URI schema used for resource naming. These resources include modules and classes.

A **Uniform Resource Identifier (URI)** is similar to a **URL (Uniform Resource Locator)** in that it identifies the name and location of something. For a URL, that something is a web page; for a URI, it is a resource.

There were five primary goals for JEP-220, and these are detailed in the following sections.

Adopting a runtime format

A runtime format was created for Java 9, for adoption by stored classes and other resource files. This format is applicable for stored classes and resources under the following circumstances:

- When the new runtime format has greater efficiencies (time and space) than the pre-Java 9 JAR format.

 A **JAR** file is a **Java ARchive** file. This is a compressed file format based on the legacy ZIP format.

- When stored classes and other resources can be individually isolated and loaded.
- When JDK and library classes and resources can be stored. This includes app modules as well.
- When they are devised in such a way as to promote future enhancements. This requires them to be extensible, documented, and flexible.

Runtime image restructure

There are two types of runtime images in Java: JDK and JRE. Beginning with Java 9, both of these image types were restructured to differentiate between files that can be used and modified by users to internal files that can be used but not modified by developers and their apps.

The JDK build system, prior to Java 9, produced both a JRE and a JDK. The JRE is a complete implementation of the Java platform. The JDK includes the JRE as well as other tools and libraries. A notable change in Java 9 is that the JRE subdirectory is no longer part of the JDK image. This change was made, in part, to ensure both image types (JDK and JRE) have identical image structures. With a common and reorganized structure, future changes will be more efficiently integrated.

 If you created custom plugins prior to Java 9 that address a specific structure, your app might not work in Java 9. This is also true if you are explicitly addressing `tools.jar`.

The following diagram provides a high-level view of the contents of each image before Java 9's release:

JRE Image	JDK Image
• bin • lib	• jre • bin • demo • sample • man • include • lib

The Java 9 runtime images are illustrated in the following diagram. As shown, a full JDK image contains the same directories as a modular runtime image as well as `demo`, `sample`, `man`, and includes directories:

Modular RunTime Image	Full JDK Image
• bin • conf • lib	• bin • conf • lib • demo • sample • man • include

There is no longer a difference between a JRE and JDK image. With the current Java platform, a JDK image is a JRE image that contains a full set of dev tools.

Supporting common operations

Developers occasionally must write code that performs operations requiring access to the runtime image. Java 9 includes support for these common operations. This is possible due to the restructuring and standardized JDK and JRE runtime image structures.

Deprivileging JDK classes

The current Java platform allows privilege revocation for individual JDK classes. This change strengthens system security in that it ensures JDK classes only receive the permissions required for system operations.

Preserving existing behaviors

The final goal of the JEP-220 was to ensure currently existing classes are not negatively impacted. This refers to applications that do not have dependencies on internal JDK or JRE runtime images.

Module system

You will recall that the modular system was created to provide reliable configuration and strong encapsulation for Java programs. Key to this implementation was the concept of link time. As illustrated here, link time is an optional phase in between compile time and runtime. This phase allows the assembly of the appropriate modules into an optimized runtime image.

This is possible, in part, due to the JLink linking tool, which you will learn more about later in this chapter:

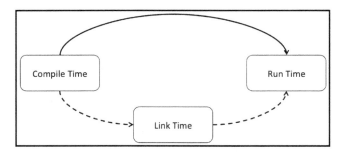

Module paths

It is important to organize modules so that they can be easily located. The module path, a sequence of module components or directories, provides the organizational structure used by searches. These path components are searched for in order, returning the first path component that comprises a module.

Modules and their paths should not be considered to be the same as packages or classpaths. They are indeed different and have a greater level of fidelity. The key difference is that, with classpaths, a singular component is searched for. Module path searches return complete modules. This type of search is possible by searching the following paths, in the presented order, until a module is returned:

- Compilation module path
- Upgrade module path
- System modules
- Application module path

Let's briefly review each of these paths. The compilation module path is only applicable at compile time and contains the module definitions. The upgrade module path has the compiled module definitions. The system modules are built-in and include Java SE and JDK modules. The final path, the application module path, has the compiled module definitions from the application modules as well as the library modules.

Access-control boundary violations

As a professional developer, you always want your code to be secure, portable, and bug-free, which requires strict adherence to Java constructs such as encapsulation. There are occasions, such as with white box testing, that you need to break the encapsulation that the JVM mandates. This mandate permits cross-modular access.

To permit breaking the encapsulation, you can add an `add-exports` option in your module declaration. Here is the syntax you will use:

```
module com.three19.irisScan
{
  - - add-exports <source-module>/<package> = <target-module>
  (, <target-module> )*
}
```

Let's take a closer look at the preceding syntax. The `<source-module>` and `<targetmodule>` are module names, and `<package>` is the name of the package. Using the `add-exports` option permits us to violate access-control boundaries.

There are two rules regarding using the `add-exports` option:

- It can be used multiple times in a module
- Each use must be a unique pairing of `<source-module>` and `<targetmodule>`

It is not recommended that the `add-exports` option is used unless absolutely necessary. Its use permits dangerous access to a library module's internal API. This type of use makes your code dependent on the internal API not changing, which is beyond your control.

Runtime

The HotSpot virtual machine implements `<options>` for the `jmod` and `jlink` command-line tools.

Here is the list of `<options>` for the `jmod` command-line tool:

```
Command Prompt                                                    —    □    ×

C:\Program Files\Java\jdk-9\bin>jmod --help
Usage: jmod (create|extract|list|describe|hash) <OPTIONS> <jmod-file>

Main operation modes:
  create    - Creates a new jmod archive
  extract   - Extracts all the files from the archive
  list      - Prints the names of all the entries
  describe  - Prints the module details
  hash      - Records hashes of tied modules.

Option                                Description
------                                -----------
  --class-path <path>                 Application jar files|dir containing
                                        classes
  --cmds <path>                       Location of native commands
  --config <path>                     Location of user-editable config files
  --dir <path>                        Target directory for extract
  --dry-run                           Dry run of hash mode
  --exclude <pattern-list>            Exclude files matching the supplied
                                        comma separated pattern list, each
                                        element using one the following
                                        forms: <glob-pattern>, glob:<glob-
                                        pattern> or regex:<regex-pattern>
  -h, --help                          Print this usage message
  --hash-modules <regex-pattern>      Compute and record hashes to tie a
                                        packaged module with modules
                                        matching the given <regex-pattern>
                                        and depending upon it directly or
                                        indirectly. The hashes are recorded
                                        in the JMOD file being created, or a
                                        JMOD file or modular JAR on the
                                        module path specified the jmod hash
                                        command.
  --header-files <path>               Location of header files
  --help-extra                        Print help on extra options
  --legal-notices <path>              Location of legal notices
  --libs <path>                       Location of native libraries
  --main-class <class-name>           Main class
  --man-pages <path>                  Location of man pages
  --module-version <module-version>   Module version
  -p, --module-path <path>            Module path
  --target-platform <target-platform> Target platform
  --version                           Version information
  @<filename>                         Read options from the specified file

C:\Program Files\Java\jdk-9\bin>
```

Here is the list of `<options>` for the `jlink` command-line tool:

```
Command Prompt                                          —    □    ×
C:\Program Files\Java\jdk-9\bin>jlink --help
Usage: jlink <options> --module-path <modulepath> --add-modules <module>[,<module>...]
Possible options include:
        --add-modules <mod>[,<mod>...]    Root modules to resolve
        --bind-services                   Link in service provider modules and
                                          their dependences
  -c, --compress=<0|1|2>                  Enable compression of resources:
                                              Level 0: No compression
                                              Level 1: Constant string sharing
                                              Level 2: ZIP
        --disable-plugin <pluginname>     Disable the plugin mentioned
        --endian <little|big>             Byte order of generated jimage
                                          (default:native)
  -h, --help                              Print this help message
        --ignore-signing-information      Suppress a fatal error when signed
                                          modular JARs are linked in the image.
                                          The signature related files of the
                                          signed modular JARs are not copied to
                                          the runtime image.
        --launcher <name>=<module>[/<mainclass>]
                                          Add a launcher command of the given
                                          name for the module and the main class
                                          if specified
        --limit-modules <mod>[,<mod>...]  Limit the universe of observable
                                          modules
        --list-plugins                    List available plugins
  -p, --module-path <path>                Module path
        --no-header-files                 Exclude include header files
        --no-man-pages                    Exclude man pages
        --output <path>                   Location of output path
        --save-opts <filename>            Save jlink options in the given file
  -G, --strip-debug                       Strip debug information
        --suggest-providers [<name>,...]  Suggest providers that implement the
                                          given service types from the module path
  -v, --verbose                           Enable verbose tracing
        --version                         Version information
        @<filename>                       Read options from file
C:\Program Files\Java\jdk-9\bin>
```

Modular Java application packaging

One of the great improvements in Java 9 and persisting with Java 10 and 11 is the size of the runtime binaries generated by the **Java Packager**. This is possible in part due to the **Java Linker**, which is covered in the next section. The Java Packager's workflow has essentially remained the same in current Java 11 as it was in Java 8. There have been, as you will see later in this section, new tools added to the workflow.

The Java Packager solely creates JDK applications. This change to the Java Packager is intended to streamline and make the process of generating runtime images more efficient. So, the Java Packager will only create runtime images for the SDK version that it is associated with.

An advanced look at the Java Linker

Prior to the Java Linker tool, `jlink`, introduced in Java 9, runtime image creation included copying the entire JRE. Then, unused components are removed. Simply put, `jlink` facilitates the creation of runtime images with only the required modules. `jlink` is used by the Java Packager to generate an embedded runtime image.

Java Packager options

The syntax for the Java Packager is as follows:

```
javapackager -command [-options]
```

There are five different commands (`-command`) that can be used. They are described as follows:

Command	Description
-createbss	This command is used for converting files from CSS to binary.
-createjar	This command, used along with additional parameters, creates a JAR archive file.
-deploy	This command is used to generate Java Network Launch Protocol (JNLP) and HTML files.
-makeall	This command combines the -createjar, -deploy, and compilation steps.
-signJar	This command creates and signs a JAR file.

The `[-options]` for the `-createbss` command include the following:

```
-outdir <dir>
        name of the directory to generate output file to.
-srcdir <dir>
        Base dir of the files to pack.
-srcfiles <files>
        List of files in srcdir. If omitted, all files in srcdir (which
        is a mandatory argument in this case) will be used.
```

The `[-options]` for the `-createjar` command include the following:

```
-appclass <application class>
        qualified name of the application class to be executed.
-preloader <preloader class>
        qualified name of the preloader class to be executed.
-paramfile <file>
        properties file with default named application parameters.
-argument arg
        An unnamed argument to be put in <fx:argument> element in the JNLP
        file.
-classpath <files>
        list of dependent jar file names.
-manifestAttrs <manifest attributes>
        List of additional manifest attributes. Syntax: "name1=value1,
        name2=value2,name3=value3.
-noembedlauncher
        If present, the packager will not add the JavaFX launcher classes
        to the jarfile.
-nocss2bin
        The packager won't convert CSS files to binary form before copying
        to jar.
-runtimeversion <version>
        version of the required JavaFX Runtime.
-outdir <dir>
        name of the directory to generate output file to.
-outfile <filename>
        The name (without the extension) of the resulting file.
-srcdir <dir>
        Base dir of the files to pack.
-srcfiles <files>
        List of files in srcdir. If omitted, all files in srcdir (which
        is a mandatory argument in this case) will be packed.
```

The first set of `[-options]` for the `-deploy` command include the following:

```
-native <type>
        generate self-contained application bundles (if possible).
        If type is specified then only bundle of this type is created.
        List of supported types includes: installer, image, exe, msi, dmg, pkg, rpm, deb.
-name <name>
        name of the application.
-appclass <application class>
        qualified name of the application class to be executed.
-outdir <dir>
        name of the directory to generate output file to.
-outfile <filename>
        The name (without the extension) of the resulting file.
-srcdir <dir>
        Base dir of the files to pack.
-srcfiles <files>
        List of files in srcdir. If omitted, all files in srcdir (which
        is a mandatory argument in this case) will be used.
-m <modulename>[/<mainclass>]
--module <modulename>[/<mainclass>]
        the initial module to resolve, and the name of the main class
        to execute if not specified by the module
-p <module path>
--module-path <module path>...
        A : separated list of directories, each directory
        is a directory of modules.
--add-modules <modulename>[,<modulename>...]
        root modules to resolve in addition to the initial module
--limit-modules <modulename>[,<modulename>...]
        limit the universe of observable modules
--strip-native-commands <true/false>
        include or exclude the native commands
-title <title>
        title of the application.
-vendor <vendor>
```

The remaining set of [-options] for the -deploy command include the following:

```
-description <description>
        description of the application.
-embedjnlp
        If present, the jnlp file will be embedded in the html document.
-embedCertificates
        If present, the certificates will be embedded in the jnlp file.
-allpermissions
        If present, the application will require all security permissions
        in the jnlp file.
-updatemode <updatemode>
        sets the update mode for the jnlp file.
-isExtension
        if present, the srcfiles are treated as extensions.
-callbacks
        specifies user callback methods in generated HTML. The format is
        "name1:value1,name2:value2,..."
-templateInFilename
        name of the html template file. Placeholders are in form of
        #XXXX.YYYY(APPID)#
-templateOutFilename
        name of the html file to write the filled-in template to.
-templateId
        Application ID of the application for template processing.
-argument arg
        An unnamed argument to be put in <fx:argument> element in the JNLP
        file.
-preloader <preloader class>
        qualified name of the preloader class to be executed.
-paramfile <file>
        properties file with default named application parameters.
-htmlparamfile <file>
        properties file with parameters for the resulting applet.
-width <width>
        width of the application.
-height <height>
        height of the application.
```

The [-options] for the -makeall command include the following:

```
-appclass <application class>
        qualified name of the application class to be executed.
-preloader <preloader class>
        qualified name of the preloader class to be executed.
-classpath <files>
        list of dependent jar file names.
-name <name>
        name of the application.
-width <width>
        width of the application.
-height <height>
        height of the application.
-v      enable verbose output.
```

The [-options] for the -signJar command include the following:

```
-keyStore <file>
        Keystore filename.
-alias
        Alias for the key.
-storePass
        Password to check integrity of the keystore or unlock the keystore.
-keyPass
        Password for recovering the key.
-storeType
        Keystore type, the default value is "jks".
-outdir <dir>
        name of the directory to generate output file(s) to.
-srcdir <dir>
        Base dir of the files to signed.
-srcfiles <files>
        List of files in srcdir. If omitted, all files in srcdir (which
        is a mandatory argument in this case) will be signed.
```

The Java Packager is divided into two modules:

- jdk.packager
- jdk.packager.services

The Java Linker

The Java Linker, commonly referred to as JLink, is a tool that was created to create custom runtime images. This tool collects the appropriate modules along with their dependencies, then optimizes them to create the image. This represents a big change for Java, with the release of Java 9. Before the Java Linker tool, JLink, was available, runtime image creation included initially copying the entire JRE. In a subsequent step, the unused components were removed. In the current Java platform, jlink creates runtime images with only the required modules. jlink is used by the Java Packager to generate an embedded runtime image.

As illustrated in a previous section, recent changes to the Java platform resulted in link time as an optional phase between compile time and runtime. It is in this phase that the appropriate modules are assembled into an optimized runtime image.

JLink is a command-line linking tool that permits the creation of runtime images containing a smaller subset of the JDK modules. This results in smaller runtime images. The following syntax consists of four components—the jlink command, options, the module path, and the output path:

```
$ jlink <options> ---module-path <modulepath> --output <path>
```

Here is a list of the options that can be used with the `jlink` tool along with brief descriptions of each:

```
Command Prompt                                          —    □    ×

C:\Program Files\Java\jdk-9\bin>jlink --help
Usage: jlink <options> --module-path <modulepath> --add-modules <module>[,<module>...]
Possible options include:
        --add-modules <mod>[,<mod>...]    Root modules to resolve
        --bind-services                   Link in service provider modules and
                                          their dependences
  -c,   --compress=<0|1|2>               Enable compression of resources:
                                              Level 0: No compression
                                              Level 1: Constant string sharing
                                              Level 2: ZIP
        --disable-plugin <pluginname>     Disable the plugin mentioned
        --endian <little|big>             Byte order of generated jimage
                                          (default:native)
  -h,   --help                            Print this help message
        --ignore-signing-information      Suppress a fatal error when signed
                                          modular JARs are linked in the image.
                                          The signature related files of the
                                          signed modular JARs are not copied to
                                          the runtime image.
        --launcher <name>=<module>[/<mainclass>]
                                          Add a launcher command of the given
                                          name for the module and the main class
                                          if specified
        --limit-modules <mod>[,<mod>...]  Limit the universe of observable
                                          modules
        --list-plugins                    List available plugins
  -p,   --module-path <path>              Module path
        --no-header-files                 Exclude include header files
        --no-man-pages                    Exclude man pages
        --output <path>                   Location of output path
        --save-opts <filename>            Save jlink options in the given file
  -G,   --strip-debug                     Strip debug information
        --suggest-providers [<name>,...]  Suggest providers that implement the
                                          given service types from the module path
  -v,   --verbose                         Enable verbose tracing
        --version                         Version information
        @<filename>                       Read options from file

C:\Program Files\Java\jdk-9\bin>
```

The module path tells the linker where to find the modules. The linker will not use exploded modules or JAR/JMOD files.

The output path simply informs the linker where to save the custom runtime image.

Encapsulating most internal APIs

JEP-260 was implemented to make the Java platform more secure. The core of this JEP's goal was to encapsulate the majority of internal APIs. Specifically, most of the JDK's internal APIs are no longer accessible by default. Currently, internal APIs deemed to be critical and widely-used remain accessible. In the future, we are likely to see functionality to replace them, and at that time, those internal APIs will not be accessible by default.

So, why is this change necessary? There are a few widely-used APIs that are unstable and, in some cases, not standardized. Unsupported APIs should not have access to internal details of the JDK. Therefore, JEP-260 resulted in increased security of the Java platform. Generally speaking, you should not use unsupported APIs in your development projects.

The aforementioned critical APIs (internal to the JDK) are as follows:

- `sun.misc`
- `sun.misc.Unsafe`
- `sun.reflect.Reflection`
- `sun.reflect.ReflectionFactory.newConstrutorForSerialization`

The aforementioned critical internal APIs are still accessible in the current Java platform. They will be accessible with the `jdk.unsupported` JDK module. Full JRE and JDK images will contain the `jdk.unsupported` module.

 You can use the Java Dependency Analysis Tool, `jdeps`, to help determine if your Java program has any dependencies on JDK internal APIs.

This is an interesting change to watch. It is likely that the currently accessible internal APIs will not be accessible by default in future Java releases.

Summary

In this chapter, we examined the structure of Java modules as specified by Project Jigsaw and took an in-depth look at how Project Jigsaw was implemented to improve the Java platform. We also reviewed key internal changes to the Java platform as they relate to the modular system. Our review started with a modular primer, where we learned about Java's modular system in terms of benefits and requirements.

We explored the seven primary tool categories that make up the JDK. As we learned, modularity in Java also extends to runtime images resulting in more maintainability, better performance, and increased security. The concept of link time was introduced as an optional phase between compile-time and runtime. We concluded the chapter with a look at the Java Linker and how Java encapsulates internal APIs.

In the next chapter, we will explore how to migrate our existing applications to the current Java platform. We will look at both manual and semi-automated migration processes.

Questions

1. What were the major contributing factors leading up to the Java platform's modularization?
2. What are the four mandatory requirements for modular systems?
3. Java modules are a collection of which six components?
4. What prefix do all JCP-governed modules start with?
5. What are the seven major components of the JDK?
6. What are the benefits of modular runtime images?
7. Which directories are in the modular runtime image?
8. Which directories are in the full JDK image?
9. What is the optional phase between compile time and runtime?
10. What is the reason that binaries created by the Java Packager are smaller than in previous Java versions?

Further reading

The references listed here will help you dive deeper into the concepts presented in this chapter:

- *Learning Java 9 – Modular Programming*, available at `https://www.packtpub.com/application-development/learning-java-9---modular-programming-video`.
- *Learning JShell with Java 9 – Step by Step*, available at `https://www.packtpub.com/application-development/learn-jshell-java-9-step-step-video`.

Migrating Applications to Java 11

5

In the previous chapter, we took a close look at the structure of Java modules as specified by Project Jigsaw and examined how Project Jigsaw was implemented to improve the Java platform. We also reviewed key internal changes to the Java platform with a specific focus on the new modular system. We started with a modular primer, where we learned about Java's modular system in terms of benefits and requirements. Next, we explored how the JDK's modularity including a look at how the source code has been reorganized. We also explored the JDK's seven primary tool categories and learned that Java modularity extends to runtime images, resulting in more maintainability, better performance, and increased security. The concept of **link time** was introduced as an optional phase between compile-time and runtime. We concluded the chapter with a look at the Java Linker and how Java encapsulates internal APIs.

In this chapter, we will explore how to migrate our existing applications to the current Java platform. We will look at both manual and semi-automated migration processes. This chapter aims to provide you with insights and processes to get your non-modular Java code working with the current Java platform.

The topics we will cover in this chapter are the following:

- A quick review of Project Jigsaw
- How modules fit into the Java landscape

- Migration planning
- Advice from Oracle
- Deployment
- Useful tools

Technical requirements

This chapter, and subsequent chapters, features Java 11. The **Standard Edition** (**SE**) of the Java platform can be downloaded from Oracle's official download site (`http://www.oracle.com/technetwork/java/javase/downloads/index.html`).

An **Integrated Development Environment** (**IDE**) software package is sufficient. IntelliJ IDEA, from JetBrains, was used for all coding associated with this chapter and subsequent chapters. The Community version of IntelliJ IDEA can be downloaded from the website (`https://www.jetbrains.com/idea/features/`).

This chapter's source code is available at GitHub at the URL (`https://github.com/PacktPublishing/Mastering-Java-11-Second-Edition`).

A quick review of Project Jigsaw

Project Jigsaw is the Java project that encompasses several change recommendations to the Java platform. As you have read in earlier chapters, the most significant change to the Java platform in Java 9 involves modules and modularity. The initiative to move to modules in Java was driven by Project Jigsaw. The need for modularity stemmed from two major challenges with Java:

- Classpath
- JDK

Next, we will review both of those challenges and see how they were addressed and overcome with the current Java platform.

Classpath

Prior to Java 9, the classpath was problematic and the source of developer anguish. This was evident in the numerous developer forums and, fortunately, Oracle was paying attention. Here are the several instances in which the classpath can be problematic; here are two primary cases:

- The first case involves having two or more versions of a library on your development computer. The way this was previously handled by the Java system was inconsistent. Which library was used during the class loading process was not easily discernible. This resulted in an undesired lack of specificity—not enough details regarding which library was loaded.
- The second case is in exercising the most advanced features of the class loader. Often times, this type of class loader usage resulted in the most errors and bugs. These were not always easy to detect and resulted in a lot of extra work for developers.

Classpaths, before Java 9, were almost always very lengthy. Oracle, in a recent presentation, shared a classpath that contained 110 JAR files. This type of unwieldy classpath makes it difficult to detect conflicts or even determine if anything is missing and if so, what might be missing. The re-envisioning of the Java platform as a modular system made these classpath issues a thing of the past.

 Modules solve the pre-Java 9 classpath problem by providing reliable configuration.

The monolithic nature of the JDK

Java has continually evolved in an impressive fashion since 1995, and with each evolutionary step, the JDK grew larger. As with Java 8, the JDK had become prohibitively large. Prior to Java 9, there were several problematic issues stemming from the monolithic nature of the JDK, including the following ones:

- Because the JDK was so large, it did not fit on very small devices. In some development sectors, this is enough reason to find a non-Java solution for software engineering problems.

- The oversized JDK resulted in waste. It was wasteful in terms of processing and memory when running on devices, networks, and the cloud. This stemmed from the fact that the entire JDK was loaded, even when only a small subset of the JDK was required.
- While the Java platform had great performance when running, the startup performance, in terms of load and launch times, left much to be desired.
- The vast number of internal APIs was also a pain point. Because so many internal APIs existed and were used by developers, the system was difficult to evolve.
- The existence of internal APIs made it difficult to make the JDK secure and scalable. With so many internal dependencies, isolating security and scalability issue was overly problematic.

The answer to the monolithic woes of the JDK is the module. Java 9 introduced the module and its own modular system. One of the great updates to the platform is that only the modules needed are compiled, as opposed to the entire JDK. This modular system is covered throughout this book.

 Modules solve the pre-Java 9 JDK monolithic issue by providing strong encapsulation.

How modules fit into the Java landscape

As you can see from the following diagram, packages are comprised of classes and interfaces, and modules are comprised of packages. Modules are a container of packages. This is the basic premise, at a very high level, of Java's modular system. It is important to view modules as part of the modular system and not simply as a new level of abstraction above packages, as the following diagram suggests:

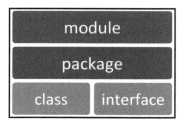

So, modules are new to Java 9 and as you would expect, they require declaration before they can be used. A module's declaration includes names of other modules in which it has a dependency. It also exports packages for other modules that have dependencies to it. Modular declarations are arguably the most important modular issue to address as you start developing with Java. Here is an example:

```
module com.three19.irisScan {
    // modules that com.three19.irisScan depends upon
    requires com.three19.irisCore;
    requires com.three19.irisData;

    // export packages for other modules that are
    // dependent upon com.three19.irisScan
    exports com.three19.irisScan.biometric;
}
```

When programming a Java application, your module declarations will be placed in a `module-info.java` file. Once this file is completed, you simply run Javac, the Java compiler, to generate the `module-info.class` Java class file. You accomplish this task in the same manner that you currently compile your `.java` files into `.class` files.

You can also create modular JAR files that have your `module-info.class` file at its root. This represents a great level of flexibility.

Next, let's review three important concepts regarding Java modules:

- Base module
- Reliable configuration
- Strong encapsulation

Base module

Core to the concept of Java modules is understanding the base module. When programming Java applications or porting existing applications programmed with older versions of Java, the base module (`java.base`) must be used. Every module requires the `java.base` module because it defines the critical, or foundational, Java platform APIs.

Here are the contents of the `java.base` module:

```
module java.base {
    exports java.io;
    exports java.lang;
    exports java.lang.annotation;
    exports java.lang.invoke;
    exports java.lang.module;
    exports java.lang.ref;
    exports java.lang.reflect;
    exports java.math;
    exports java.net;
    exports java.net.spi;
    exports java.nio;
    exports java.nio.channels;
    exports java.nio.channels.spi;
    exports java.nio.charset;
    exports java.nio.charset.spi;
    exports java.nio.file;
    exports java.nio.file.attribute;
    exports java.nio.file.spi;
    exports java.security;
    exports java.security.aci;
    exports java.security.cert;
    exports java.security.interfaces;
    exports java.security.spec;
    exports java.text;
    exports java.text.spi;
    exports java.time;
    exports java.time.chrono;
    exports java.time.format;
    exports java.time.temporal;
    exports java.time.zone;
    exports java.util;
    exports java.util.concurrent;
    exports java.util.concurrent.atomic;
    exports java.util.concurrent.locks;
    exports java.util.function;
    exports java.util.jar;
    exports java.util.regex;
    exports java.util.spi;
    exports java.util.stream;
    exports java.util.zip;
    exports java.crypto;
    exports java.crypto.interfaces;
    exports java.crytpo.spec;
    exports java.net;
    exports java.net,ssi;
```

```
        exports java.security.auth;
        exports java.security.auth.callbak;
        exports java.security.auth.login;
        exports java.security.auth.spi;
        exports java.security.auth.x500;
        exports java.security.cert;
}
```

As you can see, the `java.base` module does not require any modules and it exports numerous packages. It can be useful to have a list of these exports handy so you know what is available to you as you start creating applications using the Java platform.

You will notice that, in the previous section, we did not include the required `java.base`: the line of code in our declaration of our `com.three19.irisScan` module. The updated code is provided as follows and now includes the required `java.base` line of code:

```
module com.three19.irisScan {
    // modules that com.three19.irisScan depends upon
    requires java.base; // optional inclusion
    requires com.three19.irisCore;
    requires com.three19.irisData;

    // export packages for other modules that are
    // dependent upon com.three19.irisScan
    exports com.three19.irisScan.biometric;
}
```

If you do not include the required `java.base;` the line of code in your module declarations, the Java compiler will automatically include it.

Reliable configuration

As suggested earlier in this chapter, modules provide a reliable configuration of our Java applications that solve the classpath problem in earlier versions of the Java platform.

Java reads and interprets modular declarations making the modules readable. These readable modules permit the Java platform to determine whether any modules are missing, whether there are duplicate libraries declared, or whether there are any other conflicts. In Java, versions 9, 10, and 11, very specific error messages will be generated and output by the compiler or at runtime. Here is an example of a compile-time error:

```
src/com.three19.irisScan/module-info.java: error: module not found:
com.three19.irisScan
requires com.three19.irisCore;
```

Here is an example of a runtime error that would occur if the module `com.three19.isrisCore` was not found, but required by the `com.three19.irisScan` app:

```
Error occurred during initialization of VM
java.lang.module.ResolutionException: Module com.three19.irisCore not
found, required by com.three19.irisScan app
```

Strong encapsulation

Earlier in this chapter, you read that Java's strong encapsulation remedied the monolithic JDK issue.

 Encapsulation, a core OOP concept, protects objects from external code. The characterization of **strong** encapsulation refers to a well-programmed implementation of encapsulation.

Encapsulation, in Java, is driven by the information in the `module-info.java` file. The information in this file lets Java know what modules are dependent upon others and what each of them exports. This underscores the importance of ensuring our `moduleinfo-java` files are properly configured. Let's look at an example written with standard Java code, before modularization:

```
com.three19.irisScan

package com.three19.irisScanner.internal;

public class irisScanResult {
  . . .
}
```

```
com.three19.access

package com.three19.access;

import com.three19.irisScanner.internal.irisScanResult;

public class Main {
  private irisScanResult scan1 = new irisScanResult();
  . . .
}
```

In the preceding example, the `com.three19.irisScan` module has an
`irisScanner` package intended for internal use and an `irisScanResult` class. If
the `com.three19.access` application tries to import and use the `irisScanResult` class,
the following error message will be produced by the Java compiler:

```
src/com.three19.access/com/three19/access/Main.java: error: irisScanResult
is not accessible because package com.three19.irisScanner.internal is not
exported private irisSanResult scan1 = new irisScanResult();
```

If the compiler does not catch this error, which would be very unlikely, the following
runtime error would occur:

```
Exception in thread "main" java.lang.IllegalAccessError: class
com.three19.access.Main (in module: com.three19.access) cannot access class
com.three19.irisScanner.internal.irisScanResult (in module:
com.three19.irisScan), com.three19.irisScanner.internal is not exported to
com.three19.access.
```

The detailed error messages will make debugging and troubleshooting much easier.

Migration planning

If you are maintaining Java applications that you built with Java 8 or earlier, you should
consider updating your application to the modern Java platform. Because the post-Java 8
platform is significantly different from earlier versions, a purposeful approach is warranted
in migrating your apps. It is prudent to plan ahead and consider the issues you are most
likely to encounter. Before we look at these issues, let's test a simple Java application in the
next section.

Testing a simple Java application

The following code consists of a single Java class, `GeneratePassword`. This class
prompts the user for the desired password length and then generates a password based on
the user's requested length. If the user asks for a length shorter than eight, the default
length of eight will be used. This code was written with the Java SE 1.7 JRE System Library:

```
/*
 * This is a simple password generation app
 */

import java.util.Scanner;
public class GeneratePassword {
```

```java
public static void main(String[] args) {

    // passwordLength int set up to easily change the schema
    int passwordLength = 8; //default value
    Scanner in = new Scanner(System.in);
    System.out.println("How long would you like your password (min 8)?");

    int desiredLength;
    desiredLength = in.nextInt();

    // Test user input
    if (desiredLength >8) {
        passwordLength = desiredLength;
    }

    // Generate new password
    String newPassword = createNewPassword(passwordLength);

    // Prepare and provide output
    String output = "\nYour new " + passwordLength + "-character password
    is: ";
    System.out.println(output + newPassword);
}

public static String createNewPassword(int lengthOfPassword) {
    // Start with an empty String
    String newPassword = "";
    // Populate password
    for (int i = 0; i < lengthOfPassword; i++) {
        newPassword = newPassword +
            randomizeFromSet("aAbBcCdDeEfFgGhHiIjJkKlLmMnNoOpPqQrR
            sStTuUvVwWxXyYzZ0123456789+-*/?!@#$%");
    }
    return newPassword;
}

public static String randomizeFromSet(String characterSet) {
    int len = characterSet.length();
    int ran = (int)(len * Math.random());
    return characterSet.substring(ran, ran + 1);
}
}
```

In the following screenshot, we test the GeneratePassword app on a Mac running Java 8. As you can see, we start by querying Java to verify the current version. In this test, Java 1.8.0_121 was used. Next, we compile the GeneratePassword Java file using the javac utility. Lastly, we run the app:

```
●  ●  ●                  🏠 edljr — -bash — 80×24
Edwards-iMac:~ edljr$ java -version
java version "1.8.0_121"
Java(TM) SE Runtime Environment (build 1.8.0_121-b13)
Java HotSpot(TM) 64-Bit Server VM (build 25.121-b13, mixed mode)
Edwards-iMac:~ edljr$
Edwards-iMac:~ edljr$
Edwards-iMac:~ edljr$ javac GeneratePassword.java
Edwards-iMac:~ edljr$
Edwards-iMac:~ edljr$
Edwards-iMac:~ edljr$ java GeneratePassword
How long would you like your password (min 8)?
32

Your new 32-character password is: B#CZy0z1Mq0WI@dkFfiuG9BrHw$w9KFg
```

As you can see from the preceding test, GeneratePassword.java was
successfully compiled with the GeneratePassword.class file resulting. The application
was run using the java GeneratePassword command. The user was prompted for the
desired password length and 32 was entered. The application then successfully generated a
32-character random password and provided the appropriate output.

This test demonstrated that the example application works successfully using JDK 1.8.
Next, let's test the same application using JDK 10:

```
●  ●  ●                  🏠 edljr — -bash — 80×16
Edwards-iMac:~ edljr$ java -version
java version "10" 2018-03-20
Java(TM) SE Runtime Environment 18.3 (build 10+46)
Java HotSpot(TM) 64-Bit Server VM 18.3 (build 10+46, mixed mode)
Edwards-iMac:~ edljr$
Edwards-iMac:~ edljr$
Edwards-iMac:~ edljr$ javac GeneratePassword.java
Edwards-iMac:~ edljr$
Edwards-iMac:~ edljr$
Edwards-iMac:~ edljr$ java GeneratePassword
How long would you like your password (min 8)?
32

Your new 32-character password is: INQGRPyX1S+yirmcnBnCLm%qtJ169TSB
Edwards-iMac:~ edljr$ ▯
```

As you can see, we clearly demonstrated that a pre-Java 9 application has the potential to successfully run on Java 10 without having to make any modifications. This is a simple case study and features a very basic Java program. This is, of course, the best case scenario, and cannot be assumed. You will want to test your applications to ensure they run as expected on the current Java platform.

In the next section, we will review some potential issues you might encounter when testing your pre-Java 9 applications using the new Java platform.

Potential migration issues

The potential migration issues featured in this section include direct access to the JRE, access to internal APIs, accessing internal JARs, JAR URL depreciation, the extension mechanism, and the JDK's modularization. Let's look at each of these potential migration issues.

The JRE

Creating Java's modular system resulted in some simplification with respect to the number and location of development and utility tools. One such example is the JDK's consumption of the JRE. In all pre-Java 9 versions, the Java platform included the JDK and JRE as two separate components. Starting with Java 9, these components have been combined. This is a significant change and one that developers should be keenly aware of. If you have an application that specifically points to the JRE directory, you will need to make changes to avoid problems. The JRE contents are shown as follows:

Accessing internal APIs

The current Java platform encapsulates internal APIs to increase the security of the platform and applications written in Java. Applications that you program in Java 9, 10, or 11 will not have default access to the JDK's internal APIs, unlike previous versions of the Java platform. Oracle has identified some internal APIs as critical—those APIs remain accessible via the `jdk.unsupported` JDK module.

The aforementioned critical APIs (internal to the JDK) are as follows:

- `sun.misc`
- `sun.misc.Unsafe`
- `sun.reflect.Reflection`
- `sun.reflect.ReflectionFactory.newConstrutorForSerialization`

If you have pre-Java 9 applications that implement any `sun.*` or `com.sun.*` package, you will likely run into problems migrating your applications to the current Java platform. To address this issue, you should review your class files for use of `sun.*` and `com.sun.*` packages. Alternatively, you can use the Java dependency analysis tool, `jdeps`, to help determine whether your Java program has any dependencies on JDK internal APIs.

 The `jdeps` tool is the Java dependency analysis tool; it can be used to help determine whether your Java program has any dependencies on JDK internal APIs.

Accessing internal JARs

Starting with version 9, Java does not permit access to internal JARs such as `lib/ant-javax.jar`, `lib/dt.jar` and others listed in the `lib` directory shown here:

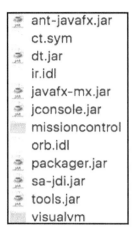

The key thing to note here is that if you have Java applications that are dependent on one of these tools residing in the `lib` folder, you will need to modify your code accordingly.

 It is recommended that you test your IDE once you start using Java 10 and 11 to ensure the IDE is updated and officially supports the latest version of Java. If you use more than one IDE for Java development, test each one to avoid surprises.

JAR URL depreciation

JAR file URLs were, prior to Java 9, used by some APIs to identify specific files in the runtime image. These URLs contain a `jar:file:` prefix with two paths—one to the `jar` and one to the specific resource file within the `jar`. Here is the syntax for the pre-Java 9 JAR URL:

```
jar:file:<path-to-jar>!<path-to-file-in-jar>
```

With the advent of Java's modular system, containers will house resource files instead of individual JARs. The new syntax for accessing resource files is as follows:

```
jrt:/<module-name>/<path-to-file-in-module>
```

A new URL schema, `jrt`, is now in place for naming resources within a runtime image. These resources include classes and modules. The new schema allows for the identification of a resource without introducing a security risk to the runtime image. This increased security ensures that the runtime image's form and structure remain concealed. The following is the new schema:

```
jrt:/[$MODULE[/$PATH]]
```

Interestingly, a `jrt` URL's structure determines its meaning, suggesting that the structure can take one of several forms. Here are three examples of different `jrt` URL structures:

- `jrt:/$MODULE/$PATH`: This structure provides access to the resource file, identified with the `$PATH` parameter, within the module specified with the `$MODULE` parameter
- `jrt:/$MODULE`: This structure provides reference to all resource files within the module specified with the `$MODULE` parameter
- `jrt:/`: This structure provides reference to all resource files in the runtime image

If you have preexisting code that uses URL instances returned by APIs, you should not have any problems. On the other hand, if your code is dependent on the `jar` URL structure, you will have problems.

Extension mechanism

The Java platform previously had an extension mechanism that gave developers the ability to make custom APIs available to all applications. As you can see from the following diagram, extensions are plugins of sorts or add-ons to the Java platform. The APIs and classes in each extension are, by default, automatically available:

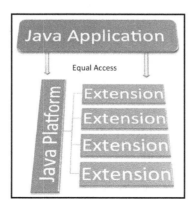

As the diagram suggests, Java applications have access both to the Java platform and extensions without requiring classpaths. This feature was deprecated in Java 8 and no longer exists in the current version of Java.

The JDK's modularization

By now, you have a firm appreciation of Java's modularization. An old adage in Java, and another object-oriented programming language, is *everything is a class*. Now, *everything is a module* is a new adage. There are three types of modules, as explained here:

Module type	Description
Automatic	When a JAR is placed on a new module path, modules are automatically created.
Explicit/Named	These modules are manually defined by editing the `module-info.java` file.
Unnamed	When a JAR is placed on a classpath, unnamed modules are created.

When you migrate your applications from 8 or earlier, your application and its libraries become unnamed modules. So, you will need to ensure all the modules are in the module path.

Another thing to be aware of is that your runtime image will not contain the entire JDK. Instead, it will only contain the modules your application requires. It is worth reviewing how the JDK is modularized in Java. The following table contains the API specification for the current JDK:

`jdk.accessibility`	`jdk.attach`	`jdk.charsets`	`jdk.compiler`
`jdk.crypto.cryptoki`	`jdk.crypto.ec`	`jdk.dynalink`	`jdk.editpad`
`jdk.hotspot.agent`	`jdk.httpserver`	`jdk.incubator.httpclient`	`jdk.jartool`
`jdk.javadoc`	`jdk.jcmd`	`jdk.jconsole`	`jdk.jdeps`
`jdk.jdi`	`jdk.jdwp.agent`	`jdk.jlink`	`jdk.jshell`
`jdk.jsobject`	`jdk.jstatd`	`jdk.localedata`	`jdk.management`
`jdk.management.agent`	`jdk.naming.dns`	`jdk.naming.rmi`	`jdk.net`
`jdk.pack`	`jdk.packager.services`	`jdk.policytool`	`jdk.rmic`
`jdk.scripting.nashorn`	`jdk.sctp`	`jdk.security.auth`	`jdk.security.jgss`
`jdk.snmp`	`jdk.xml.dom`	`jdk.zipfs`	

The following table contains the API specification for Java SE:

java.activation	java.base	java.compiler	java.corba
java.datatransfer	java.desktop	java.instrument	java.logging
java.management	java.management.rmi	java.naming	java.prefs
java.rmi	java.scripting	java.se	java.se.ee
java.security.jgss	java.security.sasl	java.sql	java.sql.rowset
java.transaction	java.xml	java.xml.bind	java.xml.crypto
java.xml.ws	java.xml.ws.annotation		

Remember, all applications will have access to java.base as it is in the module path by default.

The following table contains the API specification for JavaFX in Java:

javafx.base	javafx.controls	javafx.fxml	javafx.graphics
javafx.media	javafx.swing	javafx.web	

There are two additional modules:

- java.jnlp defines the API for **JNLP** (short for **Java Network Launch Protocol**).
- java.smartcardio defines the API for the Java smart card input/output.

For details on any of these modules, visit Oracle's *Java® Platform, Standard Edition Java Development Kit Version 10 API Specification* website: http://docs.oracle.com/javase/10/docs/api/overview-summary.html.

Advice from Oracle

Oracle has done a great job in continually updating the Java platform. Their insights into migrating from older versions to the new JDK is worth reviewing. In this section, we will look at preparatory steps, breaking encapsulation, changes to the runtime image, components such as tools and APIs that have been removed, changes to garbage collection, and deployment.

Preparatory steps

Oracle provides a five-step process to help developers migrate their Java applications from pre-Java 9 versions to a modern version, 9, 10, or 11. These steps are listed as follows and then covered in subsequent sections:

1. Get the JDK early access build
2. Run your program before recompiling
3. Update third-party libraries and tools
4. Compile your application
5. Run `jdeps` on your code

Getting the JDK early access build

If you are reading this book before Java 11 (18.9) is officially released, then you can obtain a JDK 11 early access build from this link: `http://jdk.java.net/11/`.

Early release builds are available for Windows (32 and 64), macOS (64), Linux (32 and 64), and various Linux ARM, Solaris, and Alpine Linux versions.

Taking the time to test your applications for Java 9 and get them migrated before Java 11 is officially released, will help ensure you do not experience any downtime for services that rely on your Java applications.

You can download versions 9 and 10 from the following links:

- `http://jdk.java.net/9/`
- `http://jdk.java.net/10/`

Running your program before recompiling

As indicated earlier in this chapter, there is a chance that your existing Java applications will run without modification on the Java 11 platform. So, before you make any changes, try running your current application on the Java 9 platform. If your application works fine on Java 11, great, but your work is not complete. Review the next three sections on updating third-party libraries and tools, compiling your application, and running `jdeps` on your code.

Updating third-party libraries and tools

Third-party libraries and tools can help extend our applications and shorten development time. For Java compatibility, it is important to ensure that each third-party library and tool you use is compatible with and supports the latest version of the JDK. Running your application on Java 11 will not provide you with the level of insight you need to ensure you do not have compatibility issues down the road. It is recommended that you review the official website for each library and tool to verify compatibility with and support of JDK 18.9.

If a library or tool that you use does have a version that supports JDK 18.9, download and install it. If you find one that does not yet support JDK 18.9, consider finding a replacement for it.

In our context, tools include IDE. NetBeans, Eclipse, and IntelliJ all have IDE versions that support JDK 11. Links to those sites are provided as follows:

- **NetBeans**: http://bits.netbeans.org/download/trunk/nightly/latest/
- **Eclipse**: http://www.eclipse.org/downloads/packages/release/oxygen/m2
- **IntelliJ**: https://www.jetbrains.com/idea/download/#section=windows

Compiling your application

Your next step is to compile your application using the JDK's `javac`. This is important, even if your app works fine with the newest JDK. You might not receive compiler errors but watch for warnings, too. Here are the most common reasons your applications might not compile with the new JDK, assuming they compiled fine prior to Java 9.

First, as indicated earlier in this chapter, most of the JDK's internal APIs are not accessible by default. Your indication will be an `IllegalAccessErrors` error at runtime or compile-time. You will need to update your code so that you are using accessible APIs.

A second reason your pre-Java 9 applications might not compile with JDK 18.9 is if you use the underscore character as a single character identifier. According to Oracle, this practice generates a warning in Java 8 and an error in Java 9, 10, and 11. Let's look at an example. The following Java class instantiates an `Object` named _ and prints a singular message to the console:

```java
public class Underscore {
    public static void main(String[] args) {
        Object _ = new Object();
        System.out.println("This ran successfully.");
```

```
        }
    }
```

When we compile this program with Java 8, we receive a warning that the use of _ as an identifier might not be supported in releases after Java SE 8:

```
● ● ●                    🏠 edljr — -bash — 80×9
Edwards-iMac:~ edljr$ javac Underscore.java
Underscore.java:6: warning: '_' used as an identifier
                Object _ = new Object();
                       ^
  (use of '_' as an identifier might not be supported in releases after Java SE
8)
1 warning
Edwards-iMac:~ edljr$
```

As you can see in the following screenshot, that is just a warning and the application runs fine:

```
● ● ●                🏠 edljr — -bash — 46×5


Edwards-iMac:~ edljr$ java Underscore
This ran successfully.
Edwards-iMac:~ edljr$
```

Now let's try compiling the same class using JDK 9:

```
C:\Command Prompt                                          —    □    ×

C:\Users\elavi\Desktop>javac Underscore.java
Underscore.java:6: warning: '_' used as an identifier
                Object _ = new Object();
                       ^
  (use of '_' as an identifier might not be supported in releases after Java SE 8)
1 warning

C:\Users\elavi\Desktop>Java Underscore
This ran successfully.

C:\Users\elavi\Desktop>
```

As you can see, use of the underscore as a single character identifier still only resulted in a warning and not an error. The application ran successfully. This test was run when JDK 9 was still in early release.

With Java 10 and 11, using _ as an identifier is illegal. The following screenshot shows an attempt to compile the Underscore.java application:

```
Edwards-iMac:~ edljr$ javac Underscore.java
Underscore.java:6: error: as of release 9, '_' is a keyword, and may not be used
 as an identifier
                 Object _ = new Object();
                        ^
1 error
Edwards-iMac:~ edljr$
```

A third potential reason for your pre-Java 9 programmed application not to compile with JDK 9, 10, or 11 is if you are using the -source and -target compiler options. Let's take a look at the -source and -target compiler options pre-Java 9 and with Java 10.

Pre-Java 9 -source and -target options

The -source option specifies the Java SE version and has the following acceptable values:

Value	Description
1.3	javac does not support features introduced after Java SE 1.3.
1.4	javac accepts code with language features introduced in Java SE 1.4.
1.5 or 5	javac accepts code with language features introduced in Java SE 1.5.
1.6 or 6	javac reports encoding errors as errors instead of warnings. Of note, no new language features were introduced with Java SE 1.6.
1.7 or 7	javac accepts code with language features introduced in Java SE 1.7. This is the default value if the -source option is not used.

The `-target` option tells `javac` what version of the JVM to target. The acceptable values for the `-target` option are: 1.1, 1.2, 1.3, 1.4, 1.5 or 5, 1.6 or 6 and 1.7 or 7. If the `-target` option is not used, the default JVM target is dependent on the value used with the `-source` option. Here is a table of `-source` values with their associated `-target`:

`-source` **value**	default `-target`
unspecified	1.7
1.2	1.4
1.3	1.4
1.4	1.4
1.5 or 5	1.7
1.6 or 6	1.7
1.7	1.7

Java 10 and 11 -source and -target options

In Java 9, the supported values are shown as follows:

Supported Values	Remarks
11	This will likely become the default when JDK 11 is released.
10	As of JDK 10, this is the default, should no value be specified.
9	Sets support to 1.9.
8	Sets support to 1.8.
7	Sets support to 1.7.
6	Sets support to 1.6 and generates a warning (not an error) to indicate JDK 6 is depreciated.

Running jdeps on your code

The `jdeps` class dependency analysis tool is not new to Java but perhaps has never been as important to developers than with the advent of Java's modular system. An important step to migrating your applications to Java 9, 10, or 11 is to run the `jdeps` tool to determine the dependencies your applications and its libraries have. The `jdeps` tool does a great job of suggesting replacements if your code has dependencies on any internal APIs.

The following screenshot shows the options available to you when using the `jdeps` analyzer:

```
Edwards-iMac:~ edljr$ jdeps -help
Usage: jdeps <options> <path ...>]
<path> can be a pathname to a .class file, a directory, a JAR file.

Possible options include:
  -dotoutput <dir>
  --dot-output <dir>           Destination directory for DOT file output
  -s        -summary           Print dependency summary only.
  -v        -verbose           Print all class level dependences
                               Equivalent to -verbose:class -filter:none.
  -verbose:package             Print package-level dependences excluding
                               dependences within the same package by default
  -verbose:class               Print class-level dependences excluding
                               dependences within the same package by default
  -apionly
  --api-only                   Restrict analysis to APIs i.e. dependences
                               from the signature of public and protected
                               members of public classes including field
                               type, method parameter types, returned type,
                               checked exception types etc.
  -jdkinternals
  --jdk-internals              Finds class-level dependences on JDK internal
                               APIs. By default, it analyzes all classes
                               on --class-path and input files unless -include
                               option is specified. This option cannot be
                               used with -p, -e and -s options.
                               WARNING: JDK internal APIs are inaccessible.
  -cp <path>
  -classpath <path>
  --class-path <path>          Specify where to find class files
  --module-path <module path>  Specify module path
  --upgrade-module-path <module path>  Specify upgrade module path
  --system <java-home>         Specify an alternate system module path
  --add-modules <module-name>[,<module-name>...]
                               Adds modules to the root set for analysis
  --multi-release <version>    Specifies the version when processing
                               multi-release jar files.  <version> should
                               be integer >= 9 or base.
  -q        -quiet             Suppress warning messages
  -version --version           Version information
```

When you use the jdeps -help command, you will also see module
dependent analysis options, options to filter dependencies and options to
filter classes to be analyzed.

Let's take a look at an example. Here is a simple Java class called DependencyTest:

```
import sun.misc.BASE64Encoder;

public class DependencyTest {
  public static void main(String[] args) throws InstantiationException,
```

```
        IllegalAccessException {
        BASE64Encoder.class.newInstance();
        System.out.println("This Java app ran successfully.");
    }
}
```

Now let's use `javac` to compile this class using Java 8:

```
edljr — -bash — 85×14
Edwards-iMac:~ edljr$ javac DependencyTest.java
DependencyTest.java:1: warning: BASE64Encoder is internal proprietary API and may be
removed in a future release
import sun.misc.BASE64Encoder;
           ^
DependencyTest.java:6: warning: BASE64Encoder is internal proprietary API and may be
removed in a future release
                BASE64Encoder.class.newInstance();
                ^
2 warnings
Edwards-iMac:~ edljr$ java DependencyTest
This Java app ran successfully.
Edwards-iMac:~ edljr$
```

As you can see, Java 8 successfully compiled the class and the application ran. The compiler did give us a `DependencyTest.java:6: warning: BASE64Encoder is internal proprietary API and may be removed in a future release` warning. Now let's see what happens when we try to compile this class using Java 9:

```
Command Prompt                                                      —  □  ×
C:\Users\elavi\Desktop>javac DependencyTest.java
DependencyTest.java:1: warning: BASE64Encoder is internal proprietary API and may be removed in a
 future release
import sun.misc.BASE64Encoder;
           ^
DependencyTest.java:6: warning: BASE64Encoder is internal proprietary API and may be removed in a
 future release
                BASE64Encoder.class.newInstance();
                ^
2 warnings
```

In this case, with Java 9, the compiler gave us two warnings instead of one. The first warning is for the `import sun.misc.BASE64Encoder;` statement and the second for the `BASE64Encoder.class.newInstance();` method call. As you can see, these are just warnings and not errors, so the `DependencyTest.java` class file is successfully compiled.

Next, let's run the application:

```
Command Prompt                                                    —    □    ×

C:\Users\elavi\Desktop>java DependencyTest
Exception in thread "main" java.lang.NoClassDefFoundError: sun/misc/BASE64Encoder
        at DependencyTest.main(DependencyTest.java:6)
Caused by: java.lang.ClassNotFoundException: sun.misc.BASE64Encoder
        at java.base/jdk.internal.loader.BuiltinClassLoader.loadClass(Unknown Source)
        at java.base/jdk.internal.loader.ClassLoaders$AppClassLoader.loadClass(Unknown Source)
        at java.base/java.lang.ClassLoader.loadClass(Unknown Source)
        ... 1 more

C:\Users\elavi\Desktop>
```

Now we can clearly see that Java 9 will not allow us to run the application. Next, let's run a dependency test using the `jdeps` analyzer tool. We will use the following command-line syntax—`jdeps DependencyTest.class`:

```
Command Prompt                                                    —    □    ×

C:\Users\elavi\Desktop>jdeps DependencyTest.class
DependencyTest.class -> C:\Program Files\Java\jdk1.8.0_121\jre\lib\rt.jar
   <unnamed> (DependencyTest.class)
      -> java.io
      -> java.lang
      -> sun.misc                              JDK internal API (rt.jar)

C:\Users\elavi\Desktop>
```

As you can see, we have three dependencies: `java.io`, `java.lang`, and `sun.misc`. Here we are given the suggestion to replace our `sun.misc` dependency with `rt.jar`.

For a final test, we will try to compile `DependencyTest` using Java 10:

```
●  ●  ●              🏠 edljr — -bash — 75×6

Edwards-iMac:~ edljr$ javac DependencyTest.Java
error: Class names, 'DependencyTest.Java', are only accepted if annotation
processing is explicitly requested
1 error
Edwards-iMac:~ edljr$ ▯
```

Here, we see that we simply cannot compile the application. Both JDK 10 and 11 provide the same error.

Breaking encapsulation

The current Java platform is more secure than its predecessor versions due to, in part, the increased encapsulation that resulted from the modular reorganization. That being said, you might have a requirement to break through the modular system's encapsulation. Breaking through these access control boundaries is permitted by Java 9, 10, and 11.

As you read earlier in this chapter, most internal APIs are strongly encapsulated. As previously suggested, you might look for replacement APIs when updating your source code. Of course, that is not always feasible. There are three additional approaches you can take—using the `--add-opens` option at runtime; employing the `--add-exports` option; and `--permit-illegal-access` command-line option. Let's look at each of those options.

The --add-opens option

You can use the `--add-opens` runtime option to allow your code to access non-public members. This can be referred to as **deep reflection**. Libraries that do this deep reflection are able to access all members, private and public. To grant this type of access to your code, you use the `--add-opens` option. Here is the syntax:

```
--add-opens <module>/<package>=<target-module>(,<target-module>)*
```

This allows the given module to open the specified package. The compiler will not produce any errors or warnings when this is used.

The --add-exports option

You can use `--add-exports` to break encapsulation so that you can use an internal API whose default is to be inaccessible. Here is the syntax:

```
--add-exports <source-module>/<package>=<target-module>(,<target-module>)*
```

This command-line option gives code in the `<target-module>` access to types in the `<source-module>` package.

Another method of breaking encapsulation is with a JAR file's manifest. Here is an example:

```
--add-exports:java.management/sun.management
```

 The `--add-exports` command-line option should only be used if deemed absolutely necessary. It is not advisable to use this option except for short-term solutions. The danger of using it routinely is that any updates to referenced internal APIs could result in your code not working properly.

The --permit-illegal-access option

A third option for breaking encapsulation is to use the `--permit-illegal-access` option. Of course, it is prudent to check with third-party library creators to see if they have an updated version. If that is not an option, you use `--permit-illegal-access` to gain illegal access to operations to be implemented on the classpath. Due to the significantly illegal operation here, you will receive warnings each time one of these operations occurs.

Runtime image changes

The current Java is significantly different from Java 8 and earlier with regard to the JDK and the JRE. Much of these changes are related to modularity and have been covered in other chapters. There are still a few more things you should consider.

Java version schema

With Java 9, the way the Java platform's version is displayed has changed. Here is an example of a Java 8 version format:

```
edljr — -bash — 65×8
Last login: Sat Jul 15 15:04:45 on ttys000
Edwards-iMac:~ edljr$ java -version
java version "1.8.0_121"
Java(TM) SE Runtime Environment (build 1.8.0_121-b13)
Java HotSpot(TM) 64-Bit Server VM (build 25.121-b13, mixed mode)
Edwards-iMac:~ edljr$ 
```

Now let's look at how Java 9 reports its version:

As you can see, with Java 9, the version schema is $MAJOR.$MINOR.$SECURITY.$PATCH. This is markedly different from previous versions of Java. This will only impact your applications if you have code that parses the string returned by the `java -version` command and option.

Lastly, let's see how Java 10 (18.3) reports its version:

With Java 10, 11, and for the foreseeable future, the version schema is $YY.$MM. This is a change starting with Java 10. If you have any code that evaluates what is returned by the `java -version` command and option, you will likely need to update your code.

JDK and JRE's layout

How files are organized in the JDK and the JRE has changed in the new version of Java. It is worth your time to familiarize yourself with the new filesystem layout. The following screenshot shows the file structure of the JDK's `/bin` folder:

```
Command Prompt - dir /s/w/p                                    —    □    ×

Volume in drive C is OS
Volume Serial Number is 608F-FF3F

Directory of C:\Program Files\Java\jdk-9\bin

[.]                               [..]
appletviewer.exe                  attach.dll
awt.dll                           bci.dll
dcpr.dll                          decora_sse.dll
deploy.dll                        [dtplugin]
dt_shmem.dll                      dt_socket.dll
eula.dll                          fontmanager.dll
fxplugins.dll                     glass.dll
glib-lite.dll                     gstreamer-lite.dll
idlj.exe                          instrument.dll
j2pcsc.dll                        j2pkcs11.dll
jaas_nt.dll                       jabswitch.exe
jaccessinspector.exe              jaccesswalker.exe
jar.exe                           jarsigner.exe
java.dll                          java.exe
javaaccessbridge.dll              javac.exe
javacpl.exe                       javadoc.exe
javafx_font.dll                   javafx_font_t2k.dll
javafx_iio.dll                    javah.exe
javajpeg.dll                      javap.exe
javapackager.exe                  javaw.exe
javaws.exe                        jawt.dll
jcmd.exe                          jconsole.exe
jdb.exe                           jdeprscan.exe
jdeps.exe                         jdwp.dll
jfxmedia.dll                      jfxwebkit.dll
jhsdb.exe                         jimage.dll
jimage.exe                        jinfo.exe
jjs.exe                           jli.dll
jlink.exe                         jmap.exe
jmod.exe                          jp2iexp.dll
jp2native.dll                     jp2ssv.dll
jps.exe                           jrunscript.exe
jshell.exe                        jsound.dll
jsoundds.dll                      jstack.exe
jstat.exe                         jstatd.exe
jweblauncher.exe                  kcms.dll
keytool.exe                       kinit.exe
klist.exe                         ktab.exe
lcms.dll                          le.dll
management.dll                    management_agent.dll
management_ext.dll                mlib_image.dll
msvcp120.dll                      msvcr120.dll
net.dll                           nio.dll
orbd.exe                          pack200.exe
[plugin2]                         policytool.exe
prefs.dll                         prism_common.dll
prism_d3d.dll                     prism_sw.dll
rmi.dll                           rmic.exe
rmid.exe                          rmiregistry.exe
sawindbg.dll                      schemagen.exe
serialver.exe                     [server]
servertool.exe                    splashscreen.dll
ssvagent.exe                      sunec.dll
sunmscapi.dll                     t2k.dll
tnameserv.exe                     unpack.dll
unpack200.exe                     verify.dll
w2k_lsa_auth.dll                  windowsaccessbridge-64.dll
wsdetect.dll                      wsgen.exe
wsimport.exe                      xjc.exe
zip.dll
            116 File(s)     56,430,864 bytes

Directory of C:\Program Files\Java\jdk-9\bin\dtplugin

[.]              [..]                  deployJava1.dll
npdeployJava1.dll
              2 File(s)      2,209,872 bytes

Directory of C:\Program Files\Java\jdk-9\bin\plugin2

[.]              [..]        msvcp120.dll  msvcr120.dll    npjp2.dll
              3 File(s)      1,841,000 bytes

Directory of C:\Program Files\Java\jdk-9\bin\server

[.]        [..]        jvm.dll
              1 File(s)     10,332,712 bytes

     Total Files Listed:
            122 File(s)     70,814,448 bytes
             11 Dir(s)  890,921,709,568 bytes free

C:\Program Files\Java\jdk-9\bin>
```

Here is the layout of the `\lib` folder:

```
Command Prompt - dir /s/w/p                                           —    □    ×
Volume in drive C is OS
Volume Serial Number is 608F-FF3F

 Directory of C:\Program Files\Java\jdk-9\lib

[.]                              [..]
ant-javafx.jar                   classlist
ct.sym                           [deploy]
deploy.jar                       fontconfig.bfc
fontconfig.properties.src        [fonts]
java.jnlp.jar                    javacpl.cpl
javafx-swt.jar                   javafx.properties
javaws.jar                       jdk.deploy.jar
jdk.javaws.jar                   jdk.plugin.dom.jar
jdk.plugin.jar                   jrt-fs.jar
jvm.cfg                          jvm.lib
modules                          plugin-legacy.jar
plugin.jar                       psfont.properties.ja
psfontj2d.properties             sawindbg.dll.manifest
[security]                       [server]
src.zip                          tzdb.dat
tzmappings
              27 File(s)     249,507,799 bytes

 Directory of C:\Program Files\Java\jdk-9\lib\deploy

[.]                              [..]
messages.properties              messages_de.properties
messages_es.properties           messages_fr.properties
messages_it.properties           messages_ja.properties
messages_ko.properties           messages_pt_BR.properties
messages_sv.properties           messages_zh_CN.properties
messages_zh_HK.properties        messages_zh_TW.properties
splash.gif
              13 File(s)          60,861 bytes

 Directory of C:\Program Files\Java\jdk-9\lib\fonts

[.]                              [..]
LucidaBrightDemiBold.ttf         LucidaBrightDemiItalic.ttf
LucidaBrightItalic.ttf           LucidaBrightRegular.ttf
LucidaSansDemiBold.ttf           LucidaSansRegular.ttf
LucidaTypewriterBold.ttf         LucidaTypewriterRegular.ttf
               8 File(s)       2,068,932 bytes

 Directory of C:\Program Files\Java\jdk-9\lib\security

[.]                      [..]                    blacklist
blacklisted.certs        cacerts                 default.policy
public_suffix_list.dat   trusted.libraries
               6 File(s)        254,000 bytes

 Directory of C:\Program Files\Java\jdk-9\lib\server

[.]          [..]        Xusage.txt
               1 File(s)          1,383 bytes

    Total Files Listed:
              55 File(s)    251,892,975 bytes
              14 Dir(s)  890,920,189,952 bytes free

C:\Program Files\Java\jdk-9\lib>
```

What has been removed?

Another area of change for the new version of the Java platform is that many platform components have been removed. The following sections represent the most significant components.

Notably, the `rt.jar` and `tools.jar` and `dt.jar` have been removed. These JAR files contained class and other resources files and all resided in the `/lib` directory.

The endorsed standards override mechanism has been removed. In Java, both `javac` and `java` will exit if they detect this mechanism. The mechanism was used for application servers to override some JDK components. In Java, you can use upgradeable modules to achieve the same result.

As previously covered in this chapter, the *extension mechanism* has also been removed.

The following listed APIs were previously deprecated and have been removed and are not accessible in the current Java platform. Removal of these APIs is the result of the modularization of the Java platform:

- `apple.applescript`
- `com.apple.concurrent`
- `com.sun.image.codec.jpeg`
- `java.awt.dnd.peer`
- `java.awt.peer`
- `java.rmi.server.disableHttp`
- `java.util.logging.LogManager.addPropertyChangeListener`
- `java.util.logging.LogManager.removePropertyChangeListener`
- `java.util.jar.Pack200.Packer.addPropertyChangeListener`
- `java.util.jar.Pack200.Packer.removePropertyChangeListener`
- `java.util.jar.Pack200.Unpacker.addPropertyChangeListener`
- `java.util.jar.Pack200.Unpacker.removePropertyChangeListener`
- `javax.management.remote.rmi.RMIIIOPServerImpl`
- `sun.misc.BASE64Encoder`
- `sun.misc.BASE64Decoder`
- `sun.rmi.transport.proxy.connectTimeout`

- `sun.rmi.transport.proxy.eagerHttpFallback`
- `sun.rmi.transport.proxy.logLevel`
- `sun.rmi.transport.tcp.proxy`

The following listed tools have been removed. In each case, the tool was previously depreciated or its functionality superseded by better alternatives:

- `hprof`
- `java-rmi.cgi`
- `java-rmi.exe`
- `JavaDB`
- `jhat`
- `native2ascii`

Two additional things that have been removed in Java are the following:

- AppleScript engine. This engine was deemed as unusable and has been dropped without replacement.
- Windows 32-bit client virtual machine. JDK 9 does support a 32-bit server JVM, but not a 32-bit client VM. This change was made to focus on the increased performance of 64-bit systems.

Updated garbage collection

Garbage collection has been one of Java's great claims to fame. In Java 9, the **Garbage-First** (**G1**) garbage collector is now the default garbage collector on both 32-and 64-bit servers. In Java 8, the default garbage collector was the parallel garbage collector. Oracle reports that there are three garbage collection combinations that will prohibit your application from starting in Java 9. Those combinations are as follows:

- DefNew + CMS
- Incremental CMS
- ParNew + SerialOld

We will take an in-depth look at Java 9 garbage collection in `Chapter 7`, *Leveraging the Default G1 Garbage Collector*.

Deploying your applications

There are three issues that you should be aware of, in the context of migrating to the current Java platform from Java 8 or earlier, when you are deploying your applications. These issues are JRE version selection, serialized applets, and the update to the JNLP.

 JNLP is the acronym for **Java Network Launch Protocol** and is covered in a later section of this chapter.

Selecting your JRE version

Prior to Java 9, 10 and 11, developers could request a JRE version other than the version being launched when launching an application. This could be accomplished with a command-line option or with a proper JAR file manifest configuration. This feature has been removed in JDK 9 because of the way we typically deploy applications. Here are the three primary methods:

- Active installers
- **Java Web Start** using JNLP
- Native OS packaging systems

Serialized applets

Java no longer supports the ability to deploy applets as serialized objects. In the past, applets were deployed as serialized objects to compensate for slow compression and JVM performance issues. With the current Java platform, compression techniques are advanced and the JVM has great performance.

If you attempt to deploy your applets as serialized objects, your object attributes and parameter tags will simply be ignored when your applet launches. Starting with Java 9, you can deploy your applets using standard deployment strategies.

JNLP update

The JNLP is used for launching applications on a desktop client using resources located on a web server. JNLP clients include Java Web Start and Java plug-in software because they are able to launch applets that are remotely hosted. This protocol is instrumental in launching RIAs.

RIAs (short for **Rich Internet Applications**), when launched with JNLP, have access to the various JNLP APIs that, with user permission, can access the user's desktop.

The JNLP specification was updated in Java 9. There are four specific updates as detailed in the following sections.

Nested resources

The ability to use component extensions with nest resources in Java or j2se elements was previously supported but not documented in the specification. The specification has now been updated to reflect this support. The previous specification read as follows:

> *No Java elements can be specified as part of the resources.*

The updated specification now reads as follows:

> *A Java element in a component extension will not govern what version of Java is used but may be used containing nested resource elements, and then those resources may be used only when using a Java version that matches the given version as specified in section 4.6.*

This specific change ensures that extension JLP files must have Java or j2se resources and those resources will not dictate what JRE is used. Nested resources are permitted when using the specified version.

FX XML extension

When using the JNLP, you create a JNLP file. Following is an example:

```
<?xml version="1.0" encoding="UTF-8"?>
<jnlp spec="1.0+" codebase="" href="">
  <information>
    <title>Sample/title>
    <vendor>The Sample Vendor</vendor>
    <icon href="sample-icon.jpg"/>
    <offline-allowed/>
```

```
        </information>
        <resources>
          <!-- Application Resources -->
          <j2se version="1.6+"
          href="http://java.sun.com/products/autodl/j2se"/>
          <jar href="Sample-Set.jar" main="true" />
        </resources>
        <application-desc
          name="Sample Application"
          main-class="com.vendor.SampleApplication"
          width="800"
          height="500">
          <argument>Arg1</argument>
          <argument>Arg2</argument>
          <argument>Arg3</argument>
        </application-desc>
        <update check="background"/>
    </jnlp>
```

Two changes have been made to the `<application-desc>` element. First, the optional `type` attribute has been added to the type of application that can be annotated. The default type is `Java`, so if your program is a Java app, you need not include the `type` attribute.

Alternatively, you can specify `Java` as your type, as follows:

```
<application-desc
  name="Another Sample Application"
  type="Java" main-class="com.vendor.SampleApplication2"
  width="800"
  height="500">
  <argument>Arg1</argument>
  <argument>Arg2</argument>
  <argument>Arg3</argument>
</application-desc>
```

We can indicate other application types to include `JavaFX`, as shown here:

```
<application-desc
  name="A Great JavaFX Application"
  type="JavaFX" main-class="com.vendor.GreatJavaFXApplication"
  width="800"
  height="500">
  <argument>Arg1</argument>
  <argument>Arg2</argument>
  <argument>Arg3</argument>
</application-desc>
```

If you indicate an application type that is not supported by the JNLP client, your application launch will fail. For more information about JNLP, you can consult the official documentation: `https://docs.oracle.com/javase/7/docs/technotes/guides/javaws/developersguide/faq.html`.

The second change to the `<application-desc>` element is the addition of the `param` subelement. This allows us to provide the name of parameters along with their value using the `value` attribute. Following is an example of how an `<application-desc` element of a JNLP file looks with the `param` subelement and the `value` attribute included.

This example shows three sets of parameters:

```
<application-desc
  name="My JRuby Application"
  type="JRuby"
  main-class="com.vendor.JRubyApplication"
  width="800"
  height="500">
  <argument>Arg1</argument>
  <argument>Arg2</argument>
  <argument>Arg3</argument>
  <param name="Parameter1" value="Value1"/>
  <param name="Parameter2" value="Value2"/>
  <param name="Parameter3" value="Value3"/>
</application-desc>
```

If the application `type` is Java, then any `param` subelements you use will be ignored.

JNLP file syntax

JNLP file syntax is now in complete compliance with XML specifications. Prior to Java 9, you could use & to create complex comparisons. That is not supported with standard XML. You can still create complex comparisons in JNLP files. Now you will use `&amp;` instead of `&`.

Numeric version comparison

The JNLP specification has been changed to reflect how numeric version elements were compared against non-numeric version elements. Previous to the change, version elements were compared lexicographically by ASCII value. With the current Java platform and this JNLP specification change, elements are still compared lexicographically by ASCII value. The change is evident when the two strings have different lengths. In new comparisons, the shorter string will be padded with leading zeros to match the length of the longer string.

 Lexicographical comparisons use a mathematical model that is based on alphabetical order.

Useful tools

This section highlights three tools that can help facilitate migrating your applications to the current Java platform.

Java Environment -jEnv

If you develop on a computer with Linux or macOS, you might consider using **jEnv**, an open source Java environment management tool. This is a command-line tool, so do not expect a GUI. You can download the tool at this URL:
https://github.com/gcuisinier/jenv.

Here is the installation command for Linux:

```
$ git clone https://github.com/gcuisinier/jenv.git ~/.jenv
```

To download using macOS with Homebrew, use this command:

```
$ brew install jenv
```

You can also install on Linux or macOS using Bash, as follows:

```
$ echo 'export PATH="$HOME/.jenv/bin:$PATH"' >> ~/.bash_profile
$ echo 'eval "$(jenv init -)"' >> ~/.bash_profile
```

Alternatively, you can install on Linux or macOS using **Zsh**, as follows:

```
$ echo 'export PATH="$HOME/.jenv/bin:$PATH"' >> ~/.zshrc
$ echo 'eval "$(jenv init -)"' >> ~/.zshrc
```

After you have **jEnv** installed, you will need to configure it on your system, as shown here. You will need to modify the script to reflect your actual path:

```
$ jenv add /Library/Java/JavaVirtualMachines/jdk17011.jdk/Contents/Home
```

You will want to repeat the `jenv add` command for each version of the JDK on your system. With each `jenv add` command, you will receive confirmation that the specific JDK version was added to jEnv, as follows:

```
$ jenv add /System/Library/Java/JavaVirtualMachines/1.6.0.jdk/Contents/Home
oracle64-1.6.0.39 added
```

```
$ jenv add /Library/Java/JavaVirtualMachines/jdk17011.jdk/Contents/Home
oracle64-1.7.0.11 added
```

You can check to see what JDK versions you have added to your jEnv by using `$ jenv versions` at the Command Prompt. This will result in an output list.

Here are three additional jEnv commands:

- `jenv global <version>`: This sets the global version
- `jenv local <version>`: This sets the local version
- `jenv shell <version>`: This sets the instance version for the shell

Maven

Maven is an open source tool that can be used for building and managing Java-based projects. It is part of the **Apache Maven Project**. If you are not already using Maven and you do a lot of Java development, you might be enticed by the following Maven objectives:

- Making the build process easy
- Providing a uniform build system
- Providing quality project information
- Providing guidelines for best practices development
- Allowing transparent migration to new features

You can read more specifics about each of the Maven objectives at this site: `https://maven.apache.org/what-is-maven.html`. To download Maven, visit this site: `https://maven.apache.org/download.cgi`. Installation instructions for Windows, macOS, Linux, and Solaris are available here: `https://maven.apache.org/install.html`.

Maven can be integrated with Eclipse (M2Eclipse), JetBrains IntelliJ IDEA, and the NetBeans IDE. The M2Eclipse IDE, as an example, provides rich integration with Apache Maven and boasts the following features:

- You can launch Maven builds from within Eclipse
- You can manage your dependencies for the Eclipse build path
- You can easily resolve Maven dependencies (you can do this directly from Eclipse and not have to install a local Maven repository)
- You can automatically download required dependencies (from remote Maven repositories)
- You can use software wizards to create new Maven projects, create `pom.xml` files, and to enable Maven support for your plain Java projects
- Use can perform a rapid dependency search of Maven's remote repositories

Obtaining the M2Eclipse IDE

To obtain the M2Eclipse IDE, you must first have Eclipse installed. Here are the steps:

1. Start by opening your current Eclipse IDE. Next, select **Preferences | Install/Update | Available Software Sites**, as shown in the following screenshot:

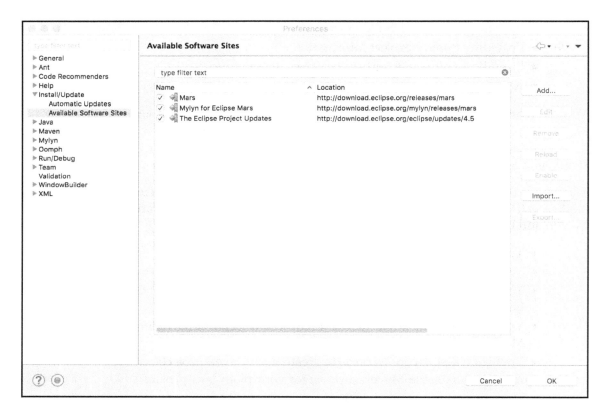

2. The next task is to add the M2Eclipse repository site to your list of **Available Software Sites**. To accomplish this, click the **Add** button and enter values in the **Name** and **Location** text input boxes. For **Name**, enter something to help you remember that M2Eclipse is available at this site. For **Location**, enter the URL: `http://download.eclipse.org/technology/m2e/releases`. Then, click the **OK** button:

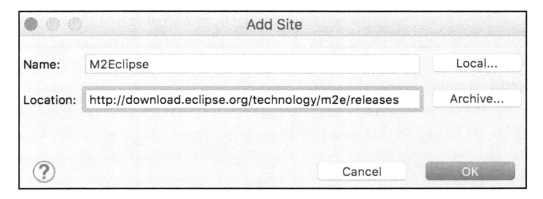

3. You should now see the **M2Eclipse** site listed in your list of **Available Software Sites**, as shown in the following screenshot. Your final step is to click the **OK** button:

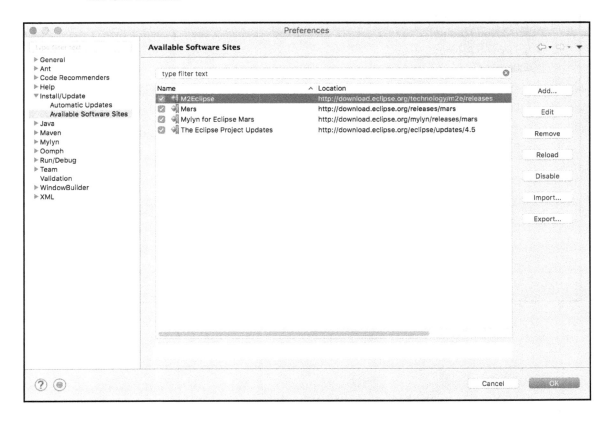

4. Now, when you start a new project, you will see **Maven Project** as an option:

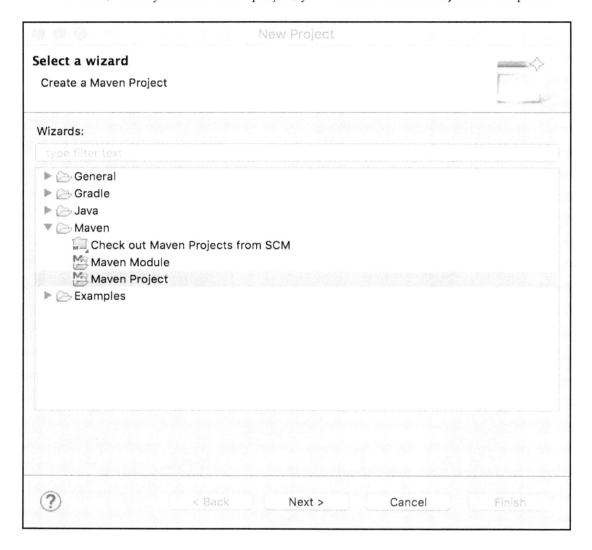

Summary

In this chapter, we explored potential issues involved in migrating our existing applications to the current Java platform. We looked at both manual and semi-automated migration processes. This chapter provided you with insights and processes to get your Java 8 code working with the new Java platform. Specifically, we conducted a quick review of Project Jigsaw, looked at how modules fit into the Java landscape, provided tips for migration planning, shared advice from Oracle regarding migration, and shared tools that you can use to help you as you get started.

In the next chapter, we will take a close look at the Java shell and the JShell API. We will demonstrate the JShell API and the JShell tool's ability to interactively evaluate declarations, statements, and expressions of the Java programming language. We will demonstrate features and the use of this command-line tool.

Questions

1. What was problematic about the classpath that has been resolved with the new modular Java platform?
2. In which version of Java was the modular system introduced?
3. What major problem did the modular system solve?
4. Which module is always required?
5. What drives encapsulation in Java?
6. Which module provides access to critical internal APIs?
7. Which file can be edited to identify explicitly named modules?
8. What is JNLP?
9. What is the significance of the underscore as a single character identifier?
10. What three command-line options can be used to break encapsulation?

Further reading

The reference listed here will help you dive deeper into the concepts presented in this chapter:

- *Maven Crash Course*, available at https://www.packtpub.com/application-development/maven-crash-course-video.

6
Experimenting with the Java Shell

In the previous chapter, we explored how to migrate pre-Java 9 applications to the new Java platform. We examined several issues that might cause your current applications to have problems when running on Java 9. We started with a review of Project Jigsaw and then looked at how modules fit into the new Java platform. We provided you with insights and processes to get your Java 8 code working with Java 9, 10, or 11. Specifically, we provided tips for migration planning, shared advice from Oracle regarding migration, and shared tools that you can use to help you as you get started with Java 18.x.

In this chapter, we will take our first look at the new command line, the **Read-Eval-Print Loop** (also referred to as **REPL**) tool in Java, and the **Java Shell (JShell)**. We will start by going over some introductory information regarding the tool, the REPL concept, and move into the commands and command-line options that you can use with JShell. We will take a practitioner's approach to our review of the JShell and include examples that you can try on your own.

The following topics will be covered in this chapter:

- What is JShell?
- Getting started with JShell
- Practical uses of JShell
- Working with scripts

Technical requirements

This chapter features Java 11. The **Standard Edition (SE)** of the Java platform can be downloaded from Oracle's official download site (`http://www.oracle.com/technetwork/java/javase/downloads/index.html`).

An IDE software package is sufficient. IntelliJ IDEA, from JetBrains, was used for all coding associated with this chapter and subsequent chapters. The Community version of IntelliJ IDEA can be downloaded from the site (`https://www.jetbrains.com/idea/features/`).

This chapter's source code is available on GitHub at the URL (`https://github.com/PacktPublishing/Mastering-Java-11-Second-Edition`).

Understanding JShell

JShell is an important tool that is relatively new to the Java platform. It was introduced with JDK 9. It is an interactive REPL tool that is used to evaluate the following Java programming language components—declarations, statements, and expressions. It has its own API so that it can be used by external applications.

 Read-Eval-Print Loop is often referred to as **REPL**, taking the first letter from each word in the phrase. It is also known as a language shell or interactive top level.

The introduction of JShell was a result of **JDK Enhancement Proposal** (**JEP**) 222. Here are the stated goals of this JEP in regards to the Java Shell command-line tool:

- Facilitates rapid investigation
- Facilitates rapid coding
- Provides an edit history

The rapid investigation and coding listed previously include statements and expressions. Impressively, these statements and expressions do not need to be part of a method. Furthermore, variables and methods are not required to be part of a class, making this tool especially dynamic.

In addition, the following listed features were included to make JShell much easier to use and to make your time using JShell as time-efficient as possible:

- Tab completion
- Autocompletion for end-of-statement semicolons
- Autocompletion for imports
- Autocompletion for definitions

Getting started with JShell

JShell is a command-line tool that is located in the /bin folder. The syntax for this tool is as follows:

```
jshell <options> <load files>
```

As you can see in the following screenshot, there are several options that can be used with this tool:

```
●●●                    ⬆ edljr — -bash — 82×40
Last login: Sat Apr 14 13:08:00 on ttys000
Edwards-iMac:~ edljr$ jshell -h
Usage:   jshell <option>... <load-file>...
where possible options include:
    --class-path <path>    Specify where to find user class files
    --module-path <path>   Specify where to find application modules
    --add-modules <module>(,<module>)*
                           Specify modules to resolve, or all modules on the
                               module path if <module> is ALL-MODULE-PATHs
    --startup <file>       One run replacement for the startup definitions
    --no-startup           Do not run the startup definitions
    --feedback <mode>      Specify the initial feedback mode. The mode may be
                               predefined (silent, concise, normal, or verbose) or
                               previously user-defined
    -q                     Quiet feedback.  Same as: --feedback concise
    -s                     Really quiet feedback.  Same as: --feedback silent
    -v                     Verbose feedback.  Same as: --feedback verbose
    -J<flag>               Pass <flag> directly to the runtime system.
                               Use one -J for each runtime flag or flag argument
    -R<flag>               Pass <flag> to the remote runtime system.
                               Use one -R for each remote flag or flag argument
    -C<flag>               Pass <flag> to the compiler.
                               Use one -C for each compiler flag or flag argument
    --version              Print version information and exit
    --show-version         Print version information and continue
    --help                 Print this synopsis of standard options and exit
    --help-extra, -X       Print help on non-standard options and exit

A file argument may be a file name, or one of the predefined file names: DEFAULT,
PRINTING, or JAVASE.
A load-file may also be "-" to indicate standard input, without interactive I/O.

For more information on the evaluation context options (--class-path,
--module-path, and --add-modules) see:
        /help context

A path lists the directories and archives to search. For Windows, use a
semicolon (;) to separate items in the path. On other platforms, use a
colon (:) to separate items.
Edwards-iMac:~ edljr$ ▯
```

You have already seen the -h option, which we executed with `jshell -h`. This provided the listing of JShell options.

To log into your JShell, you can simply use the `jshell` command. You will see that the prompt in the command window changes accordingly:

```
●  ○  ●                    ⌂ edljr — java ‹ jshell — 70×5
Edwards-iMac:~ edljr$ jshell
|   Welcome to JShell -- Version 10
|   For an introduction type: /help intro

jshell> ▯
```

Exiting the shell is as easy as entering `/exit`. Once inside the JShell, you can enter any of the following commands:

Command	Functionality
/drop	Use this command to delete a source entry that is referenced by name or id. Here is the syntax: `/drop <name or id>`
/edit	With this command, you can edit a source entry using name or id reference. Here is the syntax: `/edit <name or id>`
/env	This powerful command allows you to view or change the evaluation context. Here is the syntax: `/env [-class-path <path>] [-module-path <path>] [-add-modules <modules>]`
/exit	This command is used to exit the JShell. The syntax is simply `/exit` without any options or parameters available.
/history	The history command provides a history of what you have typed. The syntax is simply `/history` without any options or parameters available.
/<id>	This command is used to rerun a previous snippet by referencing the id. Here is the syntax: `/<id>` You can also run a specific snippet by referencing the nth previous snippet with `/-<n>`.
/imports	You can use this command to list the imported items. The syntax is `/imports` and it does not accept any options or parameters.
/list	This command will list the source you typed. Here is the syntax: `/list [<name or id>	-all	-start]`

/methods	This command lists all declared methods as well as their signatures. Here is the syntax: `/methods [<name or id> | -all | -start]`
/open	Using this command, you can open a file as a source input. Here is the syntax: `/open <file>`
/reload	The `reload` command gives you the ability to reset and replay relevant history. Here is the syntax: `/reload [-restore] [-quiet] [-class-path <path>] [-module-path <path>]`
/reset	This command resets the JShell. Here is the syntax: `/reset [-class-path <path>] [-module-path <path>] [-add-modules <modules]`
/save	This command saves the snippet source to a file specified by you. Here is the syntax: `/save [-all | -history | -start] <file>`
/set	This command is used to set the JShell configuration information. Here is the syntax: `/set editor | start | feedback | mode | prompt | truncation | format`
/types	This command simply lists declared types. Here is the syntax: `/types [<name or id> | -all | -start]`
/vars	This command lists all declared variables as well as their values. Here is the syntax: `/vars [<name or id> | -all | -start]`
/!	This command will rerun the last snippet. The syntax is simply `/!`

Several of the previously listed commands use the term **snippet**. In the context of Java and JShell, a snippet is one of the following:

- `ClassDeclaration`
- `Expression`
- `FieldDeclaration`
- `ImportDeclaration`
- `InterfaceDeclaration`
- `MethodDeclaration`

Entering the /help or /? command in the JShell provides a complete list of commands and syntax that can be used in the shell. This list is provided as follows:

```
                           ⬆ edljr — java ‹ jshell — 83×63
jshell> /?
|  Type a Java language expression, statement, or declaration.
|  Or type one of the following commands:
|  /list [<name or id>|-all|-start]
|       list the source you have typed
|  /edit <name or id>
|       edit a source entry
|  /drop <name or id>
|       delete a source entry
|  /save [-all|-history|-start] <file>
|       Save snippet source to a file
|  /open <file>
|       open a file as source input
|  /vars [<name or id>|-all|-start]
|       list the declared variables and their values
|  /methods [<name or id>|-all|-start]
|       list the declared methods and their signatures
|  /types [<name or id>|-all|-start]
|       list the type declarations
|  /imports
|       list the imported items
|  /exit [<integer-expression-snippet>]
|       exit the jshell tool
|  /env [-class-path <path>] [-module-path <path>] [-add-modules <modules>] ...
|       view or change the evaluation context
|  /reset [-class-path <path>] [-module-path <path>] [-add-modules <modules>]...
|       reset the jshell tool
|  /reload [-restore] [-quiet] [-class-path <path>] [-module-path <path>]...
|       reset and replay relevant history -- current or previous (-restore)
|  /history
|       history of what you have typed
|  /help [<command>|<subject>]
|       get information about using the jshell tool
|  /set editor|start|feedback|mode|prompt|truncation|format ...
|       set configuration information
|  /? [<command>|<subject>]
|       get information about using the jshell tool
|  /!
|       rerun last snippet -- see /help rerun
|  /<id>
|       rerun snippets by ID or ID range -- see /help rerun
|  /-<n>
|       rerun n-th previous snippet -- see /help rerun
|
|  For more information type '/help' followed by the name of a
|  command or a subject.
|  For example '/help /list' or '/help intro'.
|
|  Subjects:
|
|  intro
|       an introduction to the jshell tool
|  id
|       a description of snippet IDs and how use them
|  shortcuts
|       a description of keystrokes for snippet and command completion,
|       information access, and automatic code generation
|  context
|       a description of the evaluation context options for /env /reload and /reset
|  rerun
|       a description of ways to re-evaluate previously entered snippets
|
jshell> ▯
```

You are encouraged to experiment with JShell commands. You can use the preceding screenshot to remind yourself of the proper syntax.

The /help command can be especially helpful if you are still new to JShell. As you can see in the following screenshot, we can obtain an introduction to JShell by simply entering the /help intro command:

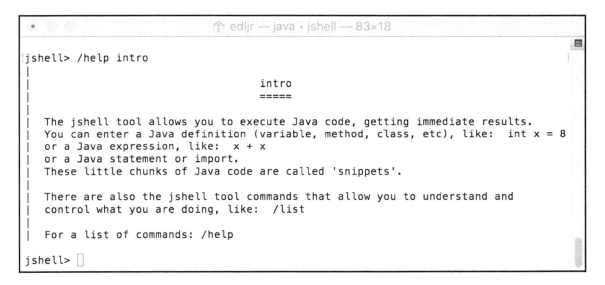

If you find yourself using JShell often, you might benefit from one or more of the following listed shortcuts. These can be listed at any time from within JShell by using the `/help shortcuts` command:

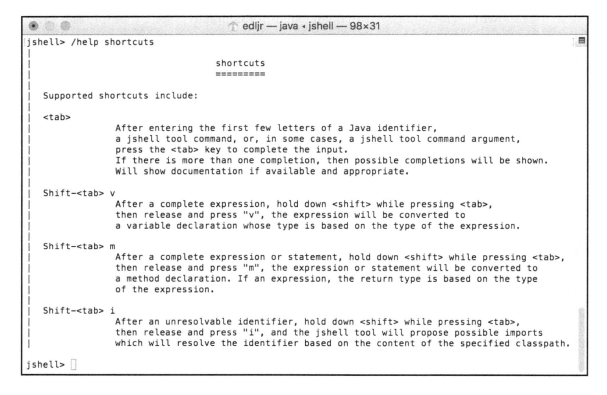

Additional help can be obtained from within the JShell by using the `/help` command followed by the command you want additional help on. For example, entering `/help reload` provides detailed information regarding the `/reload` command. This information is provided as follows:

```
●  ○  ○                      ⌂ edljr — java ‹ jshell — 98×32
jshell> /help reload

                                /reload
                                =======

  Reset the jshell tool code and execution state then replay each valid snippet
  and any /drop commands in the order they were entered.

  /reload
        Reset and replay the valid history since the jshell tool was entered, or
        a /reset or /reload command was executed -- whichever is most
        recent

  /reload -restore
        Reset and replay the valid history between the previous and most
        recent time that the jshell tool was entered, or a /reset, /reload, or /env
        command was executed. This can thus be used to restore a previous
        jshell tool session

  /reload [-restore] -quiet
        With the '-quiet' argument the replay is not shown, however any errors
        will be displayed

  Each of the above accepts evaluation context options, see:

        /help context

  For example:

        /reload -add-modules com.greetings -restore

jshell> []
```

Practical uses of JShell

Whether you are a new or seasoned developer or just new to Java, you are bound to find the JShell very useful. In this section, we will look at some practical uses of JShell. Specifically, we will cover the following:

- Feedback modes
- Listing your assets
- Editing in the JShell

Feedback modes

Command-line tools usually provide relatively sparse feedback in an effort to not overcrowd the screen, otherwise, it may become a nuisance to developers. JShell has several feedback modes in addition to giving developers the ability to create their own custom modes.

As you can see, in the following screenshot, there are four feedback modes: `concise`, `normal`, `silent`, and `verbose`. We can enter the `/set feedback` command without any parameters to list the feedback modes as well as to identify the current feedback mode. The first line of output (see the following screenshot) displays the command-line command and argument set that would be used to set the feedback mode:

```
●  ◉  ●              ⬆ edljr — java ‹ jshell — 54×11

jshell> /set feedback
|    /set feedback normal
|
|    Available feedback modes:
|        concise
|        normal
|        silent
|        verbose

jshell> ▯
```

We can dictate which mode we want to enter when we first enter JShell by including an option when we launch JShell. Here are the command-line options:

Command-line command and option	Feedback mode
jshell -q	concise
jshell -n	normal
jshell -s	silent
jshell -v	verbose

You will notice that we use `-q` for `concise` mode instead of `-c`. The `-c` option has the `-c<flag>` syntax and is used to pass `<flag>` to the compiler. For additional information about these flags, refer to the resources listed in the *Further reading* section of this chapter.

The best way to review the differences between the feedback modes is to use examples. Starting with the `normal` mode, we will execute command-line commands to accomplish the following ordered feedback demonstration:

1. Create a variable.
2. Update the variable's value.
3. Create a method.
4. Update the method.
5. Run the method.

To start our first test, we will execute the `/set feedback normal` command at the `jshell>` prompt, which sets the JShell feedback mode to `normal`. After entering the `normal` feedback mode, we will enter the necessary commands to run our demonstration:

```
● ○ ●                    edljr — java ‹ jshell — 89×20
jshell> /set feedback normal
|  Feedback mode: normal

jshell> int myVar = 3
myVar ==> 3

jshell> int myVar = 10
myVar ==> 10

jshell> void quickMath() {System.out.println("Your result is " + (x*30 + 19));}
|  created method quickMath(), however, it cannot be invoked until variable x is declared

jshell> void quickMath() {System.out.println("Your result is " + (myVar*30 + 19));}
|  modified method quickMath()

jshell> quickMath();
Your result is 319

jshell> []
```

After entering `normal` feedback mode, we entered `int myVar = 3` and received `myVar ==> 3` as feedback. In our next command, we changed the value of the same variable and received the same output with the new value. Our next statement, `void quickMath() {System.out.println("Your result is " + (x*30 + 19));}`, used a variable that was not declared, and you see the resulting two-part feedback—one part indicating that the method was created and the other to inform you that the method cannot be invoked until the undeclared variable is declared. Next, we changed our method to include the `myVar` variable, and the feedback reported that the method was modified. Our last step was to run the method using `quickMath();`, and the results were as we expected.

Let's try this same feedback demonstration in `concise` mode:

```
● ● ●                    ⬆ edljr — java ‹ jshell — 90×10

jshell> /set feedback concise
jshell> int myVar = 3
jshell> int myVar = 10
jshell> void quickMath() {System.out.println("Your result is " + (x*30 + 19));}
|  created method quickMath(), however, it cannot be invoked until variable x is declared
jshell> void quickMath() {System.out.println("Your result is " + (myVar*30 + 19));}
jshell> quickMath();
Your result is 319
jshell> []
```

As you can see from the preceding screenshot, the `concise` feedback mode provides us with much less feedback. We created and modified the variables and received no feedback. When we created the method with an undeclared variable, we received the same feedback that we did in `normal` mode. We updated the method without confirmation or other feedback.

Our next use of the feedback demonstration will be in `silent` mode:

```
●  ⬡  ⬡                   ⬆ edljr — java ‹ jshell — 90×10

jshell> /set feedback silent
-> int myVar = 3
-> int myVar = 10
-> void quickMath() {System.out.println("Your result is " + (x*30 + 19));}
-> quickMath();
-> void quickMath() {System.out.println("Your result is " + (myVar*30 + 19));}
-> quickMath();
Your result is 319
-> []
```

When we entered `silent` feedback mode, as you can see in the preceding screenshot, the JShell prompt changed from `jshell>` to `->`. There was no feedback provided when we created the `myVar` variable, modified the `myVar` variable, or created the `quickMath()` method. We intentionally created the `quickMath()` method to use an undeclared variable. Because we were in `silent` feedback mode, we were not informed that the method had an undeclared variable. Based on this lack of feedback, we ran the method and were not provided with any output or feedback. Next, we updated the method to include the `myVar` declared variable and then ran the method.

The `silent` feedback mode might seem pointless as no feedback is provided, but there is a great utility with this mode. Using `silent` mode might be appropriate for pipelining or simply when you want to minimize the amount of Terminal output. You can include specific, conditional outputs with implicit `System.out.println` commands, as an example.

Our last use of the feedback demonstration is in `verbose` feedback mode. This feedback mode, as you would assume from its name, provides the most amount of feedback. Here are our test results:

```
edljr — java · jshell — 90×24

jshell> /set feedback verbose
|  Feedback mode: verbose

jshell> int myVar = 3
myVar ==> 3
|  created variable myVar : int

jshell> int myVar = 10
myVar ==> 10
|  modified variable myVar : int
|    update overwrote variable myVar : int

jshell> void quickMath() {System.out.println("Your result is " + (x*30 + 19));}
|  created method quickMath(), however, it cannot be invoked until variable x is declared

jshell> void quickMath() {System.out.println("Your result is " + (myVar*30 + 19));}
|  modified method quickMath()
|    update overwrote method quickMath()

jshell> quickMath();
Your result is 319

jshell>
```

In our feedback demonstration, when using `verbose` feedback mode, we receive a bit more feedback as well as a nicer format for the feedback.

Creating a custom feedback mode

While the internal feedback modes (normal, concise, silent, and verbose) cannot be modified, you can create your own custom feedback mode. The first step in this process is to copy an existing mode. The following example demonstrates how to copy the verbose mode to a myCustom mode with the /set mode myCustom verbose – command command string:

```
● ● ●                    🏠 edljr — java ‹ jshell — 79×5

jshell> /set mode myCustom verbose –command
|  Created new feedback mode: myCustom

jshell>
```

We used the –command option to ensure that we would receive the command feedback. You can make various changes to your feedback mode by using the /set command along with one of the options listed in the following screenshot:

```
● ● ●                    🏠 edljr — java ‹ jshell — 74×17

jshell> /set
|   /set editor –default
|   /set start –default
|   /set feedback verbose
|
|   Available feedback modes:
|       concise
|       myCustom
|       normal
|       silent
|       verbose
|
|   To show mode settings use '/set prompt', '/set truncation', ...
|   or use '/set mode' followed by the feedback mode name.

jshell>
```

As an example, let's walk through the truncation setting that mandates how many characters are displayed on each output line. Using the /set truncation command, as illustrated in the following screenshot, shows the current truncation settings:

```
jshell> /set truncation
|    /set truncation myCustom 80
|    /set truncation myCustom 1000 expression,varvalue
|    /set truncation normal 80
|    /set truncation normal 1000 expression,varvalue
|    /set truncation silent 80
|    /set truncation silent 1000 expression,varvalue
|    /set truncation concise 80
|    /set truncation concise 1000 expression,varvalue
|    /set truncation verbose 80
|    /set truncation verbose 1000 expression,varvalue

jshell>
```

As you can see, our `myCustom` feedback mode has a truncation of 80. We will change that to 60 with the `/set truncation myCustom 60` command and then use the `/set truncation` command for verification:

```
jshell> /set truncation myCustom 60

jshell> /set truncation
|    /set truncation myCustom 60
|    /set truncation normal 80
|    /set truncation normal 1000 expression,varvalue
|    /set truncation silent 80
|    /set truncation silent 1000 expression,varvalue
|    /set truncation concise 80
|    /set truncation concise 1000 expression,varvalue
|    /set truncation verbose 80
|    /set truncation verbose 1000 expression,varvalue

jshell>
```

As you can see in the previous screenshot, the truncation for our `myCustom` feedback mode was successfully changed from the 80 inherited from the `verbose` mode to 60, based on our use of the `/set truncation myCustom 60` JShell command.

Listing your assets

There are a few JShell commands that are convenient for listing assets that you have created. Using the feedback demonstration from the previous section, we executed the /vars, /methods, and /list commands to provide a list of variables, methods, and all sources, respectively:

```
                    edljr — java · jshell — 83×14
jshell> /vars
|    int myVar = 10

jshell> /methods
|    void quickMath()

jshell> /list

   2 : int myVar = 10;
   4 : void quickMath() {System.out.println("Your result is " + (myVar*30 + 19));}
   5 : quickMath();

jshell>
```

We can also use the /list -all command and option combination to see what packages JShell imported. As you can see in the following screenshot, JShell imported several packages that make our work within the shell more convenient, saving us time having to import these standard packages in our methods:

```
                    edljr — java · jshell — 83×19
jshell> /list -all

   s1 : import java.io.*;
   s2 : import java.math.*;
   s3 : import java.net.*;
   s4 : import java.nio.file.*;
   s5 : import java.util.*;
   s6 : import java.util.concurrent.*;
   s7 : import java.util.function.*;
   s8 : import java.util.prefs.*;
   s9 : import java.util.regex.*;
  s10 : import java.util.stream.*;
   1 : int myVar = 3;
   2 : int myVar = 10;
   3 : void quickMath() {System.out.println("Your result is " + (x*30 + 19));}
   4 : void quickMath() {System.out.println("Your result is " + (myVar*30 + 19));}
   5 : quickMath();

jshell>
```

If you just want to list the startup imports, you can use the `/list -start` command and option combination. As you can see in the following screenshot, each startup import has an `s` prefix and is numerically ordered:

```
●  ●  ●                    ⌂ edljr — java ‹ jshell — 83×15                        ▣
[jshell> /list -start                                                            ]

    s1 :  import java.io.*;
    s2 :  import java.math.*;
    s3 :  import java.net.*;
    s4 :  import java.nio.file.*;
    s5 :  import java.util.*;
    s6 :  import java.util.concurrent.*;
    s7 :  import java.util.function.*;
    s8 :  import java.util.prefs.*;
    s9 :  import java.util.regex.*;
   s10 :  import java.util.stream.*;

jshell> []
```

Editing in JShell

JShell is not a full-featured text editor, but there are several things you can do within the shell. This section provides you with editing techniques, grouped into modifying text, basic navigation, historical navigation, and advanced editing commands.

Modifying text

The default text edit/entry mode makes it so that the text you type will appear at the current cursor position. You have several options available to you when you want to delete text. Here is a complete list:

Delete action	PC keyboard combination	Mac keyboard combination
Delete the character at the current cursor location	*Delete*	*delete*
Delete the character to the left of the cursor	*Backspace*	*delete*
Delete the text from the cursor location to the end of the line	*Ctrl + K*	*cmd + K*
Delete the text from the cursor location to the end of the current word	*Alt + D*	*alt + D*
Delete from the cursor location to the previous white space	*Ctrl + W*	*cmd + W*

Paste the most recently deleted text at the cursor location	*Ctrl* + *Y*	*cmd* + *Y*
When *Ctrl* + *Y* (or *cmd* + *Y* on Macintosh) is used, you will be able to use the *Alt* +*Y* keyboard combination to cycle through previously deleted text	*Alt* + *Y*	*alt* + *Y*

Basic navigation

While navigational control inside the JShell is similar to most command-line editors, it is helpful to have a list of basic navigational controls:

Key/Key combination	Navigation action
Left arrow	Move backward one character
Right arrow	Move forward one character
Up arrow	Move up one line through history
Down arrow	Move down one line forward through history
Return	Enter (submit) the current line
Ctrl + *A* (*cmd* + *A* on Macintosh)	Jump to the beginning of the current line
Ctrl + *E* (*cmd* +*E* on Macintosh)	Jump to the end of the current line
Alt + *B*	Jump back one word
Alt + *F*	Jump forward one word

Historical navigation

JShell remembers the snippets and commands that you enter. It maintains this history so that you can reuse snippets and commands you have already entered. To cycle through snippets and commands, you can hold down the *Ctrl* key (*cmd* on Macintosh) and then use the up and down arrow keys until you see the snippet or command you want.

Advanced editing commands

There are several more editing options available so that you can include search functionality, macro creation and use, and more. JShell's editor is based on JLine2, a Java library for parsing console input and editing. You can learn more about JLine2 here: `https://github.com/jline/jline2/wiki/JLine-2.x-Wiki`.

Working with scripts

Up to this point, you have entered data directly into JShell from the keyboard. You now have the ability to work with JShell scripts, which are a sequence of JShell commands and snippets. The format is the same as other scripting formats, with one command per line.

In this section, we will look at startup scripts, examine how to load scripts, how to save scripts, and then end with a look at advanced scripting with JShell.

Startup scripts

Each time the JShell is launched, the startup scripts are loaded. This also occurs each time the `/reset`, `/reload`, and `/env` commands are used.

By default, the `DEFAULT` startup script is used by JShell. If you want to use a different startup script, you merely need to use the `/set start <script>` command. Here is an example:

```
/set start MyStartupScript.jsh
```

Alternatively, you can use the JShell `start MyStartupScript.jsh` command at the Command Prompt to launch JShell and load the `MyStartupScript.jsh` JShell startup script.

When you use the `/set start <script>` command with the `-retain` option, you are telling JShell to use the new startup script the next time you launch JShell.

Loading scripts

Loading scripts in the JShell can be accomplished with one of the following methods:

- You can use the `/open` command along with the name of the script as a parameter. For example, if our script name is `MyScript`, we would use `/open MyScript`.
- The second option for loading scripts is to use the `jshell MyScript.jsh` command at the Command Prompt. This will launch JShell and load the `MyScript.jsh` JShell script.

Saving scripts

In addition to creating JShell scripts in external editors, we can create them within the JShell environment as well. When taking this approach, you will need to use the /save command to save your scripts. As you can see in the following screenshot, the /save command requires, at a minimum, a file name argument:

```
● ● ●                    ⌂ edljr — java ‹ jshell — 83×26
jshell> /help save                                                              ⊟
|
|                                      /save
|                                      =====
|
|  Save the specified snippets and/or commands to the specified file.
|
|  /save <file>
|        Save the source of current active snippets to the file.
|
|  /save -all <file>
|        Save the source of all snippets to the file.
|        Includes source of overwritten, failed, and startup code
|
|  /save -history <file>
|        Save the sequential history of all commands and snippets entered since the
|        jshell tool was launched.
|
|  /save -start <file>
|        Save the current startup definitions to the file
|
|  /save <id> <file>
|        Save the snippet with the specified snippet ID.
|        One or more IDs or ID ranges may used, see '/help id'
|
jshell> ▯
```

There are three options available to you with the /save command:

- The -all option can be used to save the source of all snippets to the specified file.
- The -history option saves a sequential history of all commands and snippets you have entered since JShell was launched. JShell's ability to perform this operation informs you that it maintains a history of everything you enter.
- The -start option saves the current startup definitions to the specified file.

Advanced scripting with JShell

What are the limits of JShell? There is so much you can do with this tool, and you are virtually only limited by your imagination and programming abilities.

Let's look at an advanced code base that can be used to compile and run Java programs from a JShell script:

```
import java.util.concurrent.*
import java.util.concurrent.*
import java.util.stream.*
import java.util.*

void print2Console(String thetext) {
  System.out.println(thetext);
  System.out.println("");
}

void runSomeProcess(String... args) throws Exception {
  String theProcess =
   Arrays.asList(args).stream().collect(Collectors.joining(" "));
  print2Console("You asked me to run: '"+theProcess+"'");
  print2Console("");
  ProcessBuilder compileBuilder = new ProcessBuilder(args).inheritIO();
  Process compileProc = compileBuilder.start();
  CompletableFuture<Process> compileTask = compileProc.onExit();
  compileTask.get();
}

print2Console("JShell session launched.")
print2Console("Preparing to compile Sample.java. . . ")

// run the Java Compiler to complete Sample.java
runSomeProcess("javac", "Sample.java")
print2Console("Compilation complete.")
print2Console("Preparing to run Sample.class...")

// run the Sample.class file
runSomeProcess("java", "Sample")
print2Console("Run Cycle compete.")

// exit JShell
print2Console("JShell Termination in progress...")
print2Console("Session ended.")

/exit
```

As you can see with this script, we created a `runSomeProcess()` method which you can use to explicitly compile and run external Java files. You are encouraged to experiment with this on your own so that you become familiar with the process.

Summary

In this chapter, we examined JShell, Java's REPL command-line tool. We started with introductory information regarding the tool and looked closely at the REPL concept. We spent considerable time reviewing JShell commands and command-line options. Our coverage included practical guides to feedback modes, asset listing, and editing in the shell. We also gained experience working with scripts.

In the next chapter, we will look at Java's default garbage collector. Specifically, we will look at the default garbage collection, depreciated garbage collection combinations, and examine garbage collection logging.

Questions

1. What is REPL?
2. What is JShell?
3. Can you name four recent features of JShell that make its use more time-efficient?
4. Where is JShell located in your computer's file system?
5. How do you quit JShell?
6. What JShell command would you use to list all declared variables and their corresponding values?
7. How can you obtain a full list of commands and syntax that can be used with JShell?
8. How can you obtain detailed help regarding a specific JShell command?
9. What is a feedback mode?
10. What are the default feedback modes?

Further reading

The following book is a good source for learning more about JShell:

- *Java 9 with JShell,* available at `https://www.packtpub.com/application-development/java-9-jshell`.

Leveraging the Default G1 Garbage Collector

7

In the previous chapter, we examined **Java Shell (JShell)**, Java's **Read-Eval-Print Loop (REPL)** command-line tool. We started with introductory information regarding the tool and looked closely at the REPL concept. We spent considerable time reviewing JShell commands and command-line options. Our coverage included practical guides to feedback modes, asset listing, and editing in the shell. We also gained experience working with scripts.

In this chapter, we will take an in-depth look at garbage collection and how it is handled in Java. We will start with an overview of garbage collection and then look at specifics in the pre-Java 9 realm. Armed with that foundational information, we will look at specific garbage collection changes in the Java 9 platform. Lastly, we will look at some garbage collection issues that persist, even after Java 11.

The following topics are covered in this chapter:

- Overview of garbage collection
- The pre-Java 9 garbage collection schema
- Collecting garbage with the new Java platform
- Persistent issues

Technical requirements

This chapter features Java 11. The Standard Edition (SE) of the Java platform can be downloaded from Oracle's official download site (`http://www.oracle.com/technetwork/java/javase/downloads/index.html`).

An IDE software package is sufficient. IntelliJ IDEA, from JetBrains, was used for all coding associated with this chapter and subsequent chapters. The Community version of IntelliJ IDEA can be downloaded from the website (`https://www.jetbrains.com/idea/features/`).

This chapter's source code is available on GitHub at: `https://github.com/PacktPublishing/Mastering-Java-11-Second-Edition`.

Overview of garbage collection

Garbage collection is the mechanism used in Java to deallocate unused memory. Essentially, when an object is created, memory space is allocated and dedicated to that object until it no longer has any references pointing to it. At that time, the system deallocates the memory.

Java performs this garbage collection automatically for us, which can lead to a lack of attention to memory usage and poor programming practices in the area of memory management and system performance. Java's garbage collection is considered an automatic memory management schema because programmers do not have to designate objects as ready to be deallocated. The garbage collection runs on a low-priority thread and, as you will read later in this chapter, has variable execution cycles.

In our overview of garbage collection, we will look at the following concepts:

- Object life cycle
- Garbage collection algorithms
- Garbage collection options
- Java methods relevant to garbage collection

We will look at each of these concepts in the sections that follow.

Object life cycle

In order to fully understand Java's garbage collection, we need to look at the entire life cycle of an object. Because the core of garbage collection is automatic in Java, it is not uncommon to see the terms **garbage collection** and **memory management** as assumed components of the object life cycle.

We will start our review of the object life cycle with object creation.

Object creation

Objects are declared and created. When we write an object declaration or declare an object, we are declaring a name or identifier so that we can refer to an object. For example, the following line of code declares `myObjectName` as the name of an object of type `CapuchinMonkey`. At this point, no object was created and no memory allocated for it:

```
CapuchinMonkey myObjectName;
```

We use the `new` keyword to create an object. The following example illustrates how to invoke the `new` operation to create an object. This operation results in:

```
myObjectName = new CapuchinMonkey();
```

Of course, we can combine the declaration and creation statements together by using `CapuchinMonkey myObjectName = new CapuchinMonkey();` instead of `CapuchinMonkey myObjectName;` and `myObjectName = new CapuchinMonkey();`. They were separated in the preceding example for illustrative purposes.

When an object is created, a specific amount of memory is allocated for storing that object. The amount of memory allocated can differ based on architecture and JVM.

Next, we will look at the mid-life of an object.

Object mid-life

Objects are created and Java allocates system memory for storing that object. If the object is not used, the memory allocated to it is considered wasted. This is something we want to avoid. Even with small applications, this type of wasted memory can lead to poor performance and even out-of-memory issues.

Our goal is to deallocate or release the memory, any previously allocated memory that we no longer need. Fortunately, with Java, there is a mechanism for handling this issue. It is called garbage collection.

When an object, such as our `myObjectName` example, no longer has any references pointing to it, the system will reallocate the associated memory.

Object destruction

The idea of Java having a garbage collector running in the dark shadows of your code (usually a low-priority thread) and deallocating memory currently allocated to unreferenced objects, is appealing. So, how does this work? The garbage collection system monitors objects and, as feasible, counts the number of references to each object.

When there are no references to an object, there is no way to get to it with the currently running code, so it makes perfect sense to deallocate the associated memory.

 The term **memory leak** refers to small memory chunks lost or improperly deallocated. These leaks are avoidable with Java's garbage collection.

Garbage collection algorithms

There are several garbage collection algorithms, or types, for use by the JVM. In this section, we will cover the following garbage collection algorithms:

- Mark and sweep
- **Concurrent Mark Sweep (CMS)** garbage collection
- Serial garbage collection
- Parallel garbage collection
- G1 garbage collection

Mark and sweep

Java's initial garbage collection algorithm, mark and sweep used a simple two-step process:

1. The first step, mark, is to step through all objects that have accessible references, marking those objects as alive

2. The second step, sweep, involves scanning the sea for any object that is not marked

As you can readily determine, the mark and sweep algorithm seems effective but is probably not very efficient due to the two-step nature of this approach. This eventually led to a Java garbage collection system with vastly improved efficiencies.

Concurrent Mark Sweep (CMS) garbage collection

The CMS algorithm for garbage collection scans heap memory using multiple threads. Similar to the mark and sweep method, it marks objects for removal and then makes a sweep to actually remove those objects. This method of garbage collection is essentially an upgraded mark and sweep method. It was modified to take advantage of faster systems and had performance enhancements.

To manually invoke the CMS garbage collection algorithm for your application, use the following command-line option:

```
-XX:+UseConcMarkSweepGC
```

If you want to use the CMS garbage collection algorithm and dictate the number of threads to use, you can use the following command-line option. In the following example, we are telling the Java platform to use the CMS garbage collection algorithm with eight threads:

```
-XX:ParallelCMSThreads=8
```

Serial garbage collection

Java's serial garbage collection works on a single thread. When executing, it freezes all other threads until garbage collection operations have concluded. Due to the thread-freezing nature of serial garbage collection, it is only feasible for very small programs.

To manually invoke the serial garbage collection algorithm for your application, use the following command-line option:

```
-XX:+UseSerialGC
```

Parallel garbage collection

In earlier versions of Java 8 and earlier, the parallel garbage collection algorithm was the default garbage collector. It uses multiple threads but freezes all non-garbage collection threads in the application until garbage collection functions have completed, just like the serial garbage collection algorithm.

G1 garbage collection

The G1 garbage collection algorithm was created for use with large memory heaps. This approach involves segmenting the memory heap into regions. Garbage collection, using the G1 algorithm, takes place in parallel with each heap region.

Another part of the G1 algorithm is that when memory is deallocated, the heap space is compacted. Unfortunately, the compacting operation takes place using the *Stop the World* approach.

The G1 garbage collection algorithm also prioritizes the regions based on those that have the most garbage to be collected.

 The **G1** name refers to **Garbage-First**.

To manually invoke the G1 garbage collection algorithm for your application, use the following command-line option:

```
-XX:+UseG1GC
```

Garbage collection options

Here is a list of JVM sizing options:

Sizing description	JVM option flag
This flag establishes the initial heap size (combined young and tenured space).	XX:InitialHeapSize=3g
This flag establishes the maximum heap size (combined young and tenured space).	-XX:MaxHeapSize=3g
This flag establishes the initial and maximum heap size (combined young and tenured space).	-Xms2048m -Xmx3g
This flag establishes the initial size of young space.	-XX:NewSize=128m

This flag establishes the maximum size of young space.	`-XX:MaxNewSize=128m`
This flag establishes young space size. It uses a ration of young versus tenured space. In the sample flag to the right, 3 means that young space will be three times smaller than tenured space.	`-XX:NewRation=3`
This flag establishes the size of single survivor space as a portion of Eden space size.	`-XX:SurvivorRatio=15`
This flag establishes the initial size of the permanent space.	`-XX:PermSize=512m`
This flag establishes the maximum size of the permanent space.	`-XX:MaxPermSize=512m`
This flag establishes the size of the stack area dedicated to each thread (in bytes).	`-Xss512k`
This flag establishes the size of the stack area dedicated to each thread (in kilobytes).	`-XX:ThreadStackSize=512`
This flag establishes the maximum size of off-heap memory available to the JVM.	`-XX:MaxDirectMemorySize=3g`

Here is a list of young generation garbage collection options:

Young generation garbage collection tuning option	Flag
Sets the tenuring threshold (threshold for collections before promotion occurs from young to tenured space).	`-XX:Initial\TenuringThreshold=16`
Sets the upper tenuring threshold.	`-XX:Max\TenuringThreshold=30`
Sets the maximum object size permitted in young space. If an object is larger than the maximum size, it will be allocated to tenured space and bypass young space.	`-XX:Pretenure\SizeThreshold=3m`
Used to promote all young objects surviving the young collection to tenured space.	`-XX:+AlwaysTenure`
With this tag, objects from young space never get promoted to tenured space as long as the survivor space has sufficient room for them.	`-XX:+NeverTenure`
We can indicate that we want to use thread local allocation blocks in the young space. This is enabled by default.	`-XX:+UseTLAB`
Toggle this to allow the JVM to adaptively resize the **TLAB** (short for **Thread Local Allocation Blocks**) for threads.	`-XX:+ResizeTLAB`
Sets the initial size of TLAB for a thread.	`-XX:TLABSize=2m`
Sets the minimum allowable size of TLAB.	`-XX:MinTLABSize=128k`

Here is a list of CMS tuning options:

CMS tuning option	Flag
Indicates that you want to solely use occupancy as a criterion for starting a CMS collection operation.	`-XX:+UseCMSInitiating\OccupancyOnly`
Sets the percentage CMS generation occupancy to start a CMS collection cycle. If you indicate a negative number, you are telling the JVM you want to use `CMSTriggerRatio`.	`-XX:CMSInitiating\OccupancyFraction=70`
Sets the percentage CMS generation occupancy that you want to initiate a CMS collection for bootstrapping collection statistics.	`-XX:CMSBootstrap\Occupancy=10`
This is the percentage of `MinHeapFreeRatio` in CMS generation that is allocated prior to a CMS cycle starting.	`-XX:CMSTriggerRatio=70`
Sets the percentage of `MinHeapFreeRatio` in the CMS permanent generation that is allocated before starting a CMS collection cycle.	`-XX:CMSTriggerPermRatio=90`
This is the wait duration after a CMS collection is triggered. Use the parameter to specify how long the CMS is allowed to wait for young collection.	`-XX:CMSWaitDuration=2000`
Enables parallel remark.	`-XX:+CMSParallel\RemarkEnabled`
Enables parallel remark of survivor space.	`-XX:+CMSParallel\SurvivorRemarkEnabled`
You can use this to force young collection before the remark phase.	`-XX:+CMSScavengeBeforeRemark`
Use this to prevent a scheduling remark if the Eden used is below the threshold value.	`-XX:+CMSScheduleRemark\EdenSizeThreshold`
Sets the Eden occupancy percentage that you want CMS to try and schedule a remark pause.	`-XX:CMSScheduleRemark\EdenPenetration=20`
This is where you want to start sampling Eden top at least before young generation occupancy reaches 1/4 (in our sample to the right) of the size at which you want to schedule a remark.	`-XX:CMSScheduleRemark\SamplingRatio=4`
You can select `variant=1` or `variant=2` of verification following a remark.	`-XX:CMSRemarkVerifyVariant=1`
Elects to use the parallel algorithm for young space collection.	`-XX:+UseParNewGC`
Enables the use of multiple threads for concurrent phases.	`-XX:+CMSConcurrentMTEnabled`
Sets the number of parallel threads used for concurrent phases.	`-XX:ConcGCThreads=2`
Sets the number of parallel threads you want used for stop-the-world phases.	`-XX:ParallelGCThreads=2`
You can enable **Incremental CMS (iCMS)** mode.	`-XX:+CMSIncrementalMode`
If this is not enabled, CMS will not clean permanent space.	`-XX:+CMSClassUnloadingEnabled`
This allows `System.gc()` to trigger concurrent collection instead of a full garbage collection cycle.	`-XX:+ExplicitGCInvokes\Concurrent`

This allows `System.gc()` to trigger concurrent collection of permanent space.	`-XX:+ExplicitGCInvokes\ConcurrentAndUnloadsClasses`

iCMS mode is intended for servers with a small number of CPUs. It should not be employed on modern hardware.

Here are some miscellaneous garbage collection options:

Miscellaneous garbage collection options	Flag
This will cause the JVM to ignore any `System.gc()` method invocations by an application.	`-XX:+DisableExplicitGC`
This is the (soft reference) time to live in milliseconds per MB of free space in the heap.	`-XX:SoftRefLRU\PolicyMSPerMB=2000`
This is the use policy used to limit the time spent in garbage collection before an `OutOfMemory` error is thrown.	`-XX:+UseGCOverheadLimit`
This limits the proportion of time spent in garbage collection before an `OutOfMemory` error is thrown. This is used with `GCHeapFreeLimit`.	`-XX:GCTimeLimit=95`
This sets the minimum percentage of free space after a full garbage collection before an `OutOfMemory` error is thrown. This is used with `GCTimeLimit`.	`-XX:GCHeapFreeLimit=5`

Finally, here are some G1 specific options. Note that these are all supported starting with JVM 6u26:

G1 garbage collection options	Flag
Size of the heap region. The default is 2,048 and the acceptable range is 1 MiB to 32 MiB.	`-XX:G1HeapRegionSize=16m`
This is the confidence coefficient pause prediction heuristics.	`-XX:G1ConfidencePercent=75`
This determines the minimum reserve in the heap.	`-XX:G1ReservePercent=5`
This is the garbage collection time per MMU--time slice in milliseconds.	`-XX:MaxGCPauseMillis=100`
This is the pause interval time slice per MMU in milliseconds.	`-XX:GCPauseIntervalMillis=200`

MiB stands for **Mebibyte**, which is a multiple of bytes for digital information.

Java methods relevant to garbage collection

Let's look at two specific methods associated with garbage collection.

The System.gc() method

Although garbage collection is automatic in Java, you can make explicit calls to the `java.lang.System.gc()` method to aid in the debugging process. This method does not take any parameters and does not return any value. It is an explicit call that runs Java's garbage collector. Here is a sample implementation:

```
System.gc();
System.out.println("Garbage collected and unused memory has been
deallocated.");
```

Let's look at a more in-depth example. In the following code, we start by creating an instance of `Runtime`, using `Runtime myRuntime = Runtime.getRuntime();`, which returns a singleton. This gives us access to the JVM. After printing some header information and initial memory stats, we create `ArrayList` with a size of `300000`. Then, we create a loop that generates `100000` array list objects. Lastly, we provide output in three passes, asking the JVM to invoke the garbage collector with `1` second pauses in between. Here is the source code:

```
package MyGarbageCollectionSuite;

import java.util.ArrayList;
import java.util.concurrent.TimeUnit;

public class GCVerificationTest {
  public static void main(String[] args) throws InterruptedException {
    // Obtain a Runtime instance (to communicate with the JVM)
    Runtime myRuntime = Runtime.getRuntime();

    // Set header information and output initial memory stats
    System.out.println("Garbage Collection Verification Test");
    System.out.println("-----------------------------------------------
-----------");
    System.out.println("Initial JVM Memory: " + myRuntime.totalMemory()
+
      "\tFree Memory: " + myRuntime.freeMemory());

    // Use a bunch of memory
    ArrayList<Integer> AccountNumbers = new ArrayList<>(300000);
    for (int i = 0; i < 100000; i++) {
      AccountNumbers = new ArrayList<>(3000);
```

```
      AccountNumbers = null;
   }

   // Provide update with with three passes
   for (int i = 0; i < 3; i++) {
      System.out.println("------------------------------------");
      System.out.println("Free Memory before collection number " +
         (i+1) + ": " + myRuntime.freeMemory());
      System.gc();
      System.out.println("Free Memory after collection number " +
         (i+1) + ": " + myRuntime.freeMemory());
      TimeUnit.SECONDS.sleep(1); // delay thread 5 second
   }
  }
 }
```

As you can see from the following output, the garbage collector did not reallocate all of the garbage during the first or even the second pass:

```
Garbage Collection Verification Test
------------------------------------------------------
Initial JVM Memory: 514850816    Free Memory: 509439928
------------------------------------
Free Memory before collection number 1: 768241776
Free Memory after collection number 1: 888052656
------------------------------------
Free Memory before collection number 2: 888052656
Free Memory after collection number 2: 887536992
------------------------------------
Free Memory before collection number 3: 887536992
Free Memory after collection number 3: 888061280
```

Garbage collection verification test

There is an alternative to using the System.gc() method to invoke the garbage collector. In our example, we could have used myRuntime.gc(), our earlier singleton example.

The finalize() method

You can think of Java's garbage collector as a death dealer. When it removes something from memory, it is gone. This so-called death dealer is not without compassion as it provides each method with their final last words. The objects give their last words through a finalize() method. If an object has a finalize() method, the garbage collector invokes it before the object is removed and the associated memory deallocated. The method takes no parameters and has a return type of void.

The finalize() method is only called once and there can be variability when it is run. Certainly, the method is invoked before it is removed, but when the garbage collector runs it is dependent on the system. If, as an example, you have a relatively small app that is running a memory-rich system, the garbage collector might not run at all. So, why include a finalize() method at all? It is considered poor programming practice to override the finalize() method. That being said, you can use the method if needed. In fact, you can add code there to add a reference to your object to ensure it is not removed by the garbage collector. Again, this is not advisable.

Because all objects in Java, even the ones you create yourself, are child classes of java.lang.Object, every object in Java has a finalize() method.

The garbage collector, as sophisticated as it is, might not close databases, files, or network connections the way you want it done. If your application requires specific considerations when its objects are collected, you can override the object's finalize() method.

Here is an example implementation that demonstrates a use case for when you might want to override an object's finalize() method:

```java
public class Animal {
   private static String animalName;
   private static String animalBreed;
   private static int objectTally = 0;

   // constructor
   public Animal(String name, String type) {
      animalName = name;
      animalBreed = type;

      // increment count of object
      ++objectTally;
   }

   protected void finalize() {
      // decrement object count each time this method
      // is called by the garbage collector
      --objectTally;

      //Provide output to user
      System.out.println(animalName + " has been removed from memory.");

      // condition for 1 animal (use singular form)
      if (objectTally == 1) {
         System.out.println("You have " + objectTally + " animal
         remaining.");
```

```
        }

        // condition for 0 or greater than 1 animals (use plural form)
        else {
          System.out.println("You have " + objectTally + " animals
          remaining.");
        }
      }
    }
```

As you can see in the preceding code, the `objectTally` count is incremented each time an object of type `Animal` is created and decremented when one is removed by the garbage collector.

 Overriding an object's `finalize()` method is usually discouraged. The `finalize()` method should normally be declared as `protected`.

The pre-Java 9 garbage collection schema

Java's garbage collection is not new to Java 9, it has existed since the initial release of Java. Java has long had a sophisticated garbage collection system that is automatic and runs in the background. By running in the background, we are referring to garbage collection processes running during idle times.

 Idle times refer to the time between input/output, such as between keyboard input, mouse clicks, and output generation.

This automatic garbage collection has been one of the key factors in developers selecting Java for their programming solutions. Other programming languages, such as C# and Objective-C, have implemented garbage collection following the success of the Java platform.

Let's next take a look at the following listed concepts before we look at the changes to garbage collection in the current Java platform:

- Visualizing garbage collection
- Garbage collection upgrades in Java 8
- Case study—games written with Java

Visualizing garbage collection

It can be helpful to visualize how garbage collection works and, perhaps more importantly, the need for it. Consider the following code snippet that progressively creates the string Garbage:

```
001 String var = new String("G");
002 var += "a";
003 var += "r";
004 var += "b";
005 var += "a";
006 var += "g";
007 var += "e";
008 System.out.println("Your completed String is: " + var + ".");
```

Clearly, the preceding code generates the output provided as follows:

Your completed String is Garbage.

What might not be clear is that the sample code results in five unreferenced string objects. This is due, in part, to strings being immutable. As you can see in the following table, with each successive line of code, the referenced object is updated and an additional object becomes unreferenced:

Line of Code	001	002	003	004	005	006	007
Code	String var = new String("G");	var+="a";	var+="r";	var+="b";	var+="a";	var+="g";	var+="e";
Referenced memory	var → "G"	var → "Ga"	var → "Gar"	var → "Garb"	var → "Garba"	var → "Garbag"	var → "Garbage"
Unreferenced memory		"G"	"G" "Ga"	"G" "Ga" "Gar"	"G" "Ga" "Gar" "Garb"	"G" "Ga" "Gar" "Garb" "Garba"	"G" "Ga" "Gar" "Garb" "Garbag"

Unreferenced object accumulation

The preceding unreferenced objects listed certainly will not break the memory bank, but it is indicative of how quickly a large number of unreferenced objects can accumulate.

Garbage collection upgrades in Java 8

As of Java 8, the default garbage collection algorithm was the parallel garbage collector. Java 8 was released with some improvements to the G1 garbage collection system. One of these improvements was the ability to use the following command-line option to optimize the heap memory by removing duplicative string values:

```
-XX:+UseStringDeduplication
```

The G1 garbage collector can view the character arrays when it sees a string. It then takes the value and stores it with a new, weak reference to the character array. If the G1 garbage collector finds a string with the same hash code, it will compare the two strings with a character-by-character review. If a match is found, both strings end up pointing to the same character array. Specifically, the first string will point to the character array of the second string.

This method can require substantial processing overhead and should only be used if deemed beneficial or absolutely necessary.

Case study – games written with Java

Multiplayer games require extensive management techniques, both for server and client systems. The JVM runs the garbage collection thread in a low-priority thread and is run periodically. Server administrators previously used an incremental garbage collection schema using the now depreciated -Xincgc command-line option to avoid server stalls that occur when the server is overloaded. The goal is to have garbage collection run more frequently and with much shorter execution cycles each time.

 When considering memory usage and garbage collection, it is important to use as little memory on the target system as possible and to limit pauses for garbage collection to the extent feasible. These tips are especially important for games, simulations, and other applications that require real-time performance.

The JVM manages the heap where Java memory is stored. The JVM starts with a small heap by default and grows as additional objects are created. The heap has two partitions—young and tenured. When objects are initially created, they are created in the young partition. Persistent objects are moved to the tenure partition. The creation of objects is usually very quick with not much more than pointer incrementation. Processing in the young partition is much faster than that of the tenured partition. This is important because it applies to the overall app, or in our case, a game's efficiency.

It becomes important for us to monitor our game's memory usage and when garbage collection occurs. To monitor garbage collection, we can add the `verbose` flag (`-verbose:gc`) when we launch our game, such as with the following example:

```
java -verbose:gc MyJavaGameClass
```

The JVM will then provide a line of formatted output for each garbage collection. Here is the format of the `verbose` GC output:

```
[<TYPE> <MEMORY USED BEFORE> -> MEMORY USED AFTER (TOTAL HEAP SIZE),
<TIME>]
```

Let's look at two examples. In this first example, we see `GC` for type, which refers to the young partition we previously discussed:

```
[GC 31924K -> 29732K(42234K), 0.0019319 secs]
```

In this second example, `Full GC` indicates that the garbage collection action was taken on the tenured partition of the memory heap:

```
[Full GC 29732K -> 10911K(42234K), 0.0319319 secs]
```

You can obtain more detailed information from the garbage collector using the `-XX:+PrintGCDetails` option, as shown here:

```
java -verbose:gc -XX:+PrintGCDetails MyJavaGameClass
```

Collecting garbage with the new Java platform

Java came out of the gate with automatic garbage collection, making it a development platform of choice for many programmers. It was commonplace to want to avoid manual memory management in other programming languages. We have looked in-depth at the garbage collection system to include the various approaches, or algorithms, used by the JVM. Java, starting with release 9 and through 11, which includes some relevant changes to the garbage collection system. Let's review the most significant changes:

- Default garbage collection
- Depreciated garbage collection combinations
- Unified garbage collection logging
- Garbage collection interface

- Parallel full garbage collection for G1
- Epsilon—an arbitrarily low-overhead **garbage collection (GC)**

We will review each one of these garbage collection concept issues in the following sections.

Default garbage collection

We previously detailed the following garbage collection approaches used by the JVM prior to Java 9. These are still plausible garbage collection algorithms:

- CMS garbage collection
- Serial garbage collection
- Parallel garbage collection
- G1 garbage collection

Let's briefly recap each of these approaches:

- **CMS garbage collection:** The CMS garbage collection algorithm scans heap memory using multiple threads. Using this approach, the JVM marks objects for removal and then makes a sweep to actually remove them.
- **Serial garbage collection:** This approach uses a thread-freezing schema on a single thread. When the garbage collection is in progress, it freezes all other threads until garbage collection operations have concluded. Due to the thread-freezing nature of serial garbage collection, it is only feasible for very small programs.
- **Parallel garbage collection:** This approach uses multiple threads but freezes all non-garbage collection threads in the application until garbage collection functions have completed, just like the serial garbage collection algorithm.
- **G1 garbage collection:** This is the garbage collection algorithm with the following characteristics:
  - Is used with large memory heaps
  - Involves segmenting the memory heap into regions
  - Takes place in parallel with each heap region
  - Compacts the heap space when memory is deallocated
  - Compacting operations take place using the *Stop the World* approach
  - Prioritizes the regions based on those that have the most garbage to be collected

Prior to Java 9, the parallel garbage collection algorithm was the default garbage collector. In Java 9, the G1 garbage collector is the new default implementation of Java's memory management system. This is true for both 32-bit and 64-bit server configurations.

Oracle assessed that the G1 garbage collector, mostly due to its low-pause nature, was a better performing garbage collection method than the parallel approach. This change was predicated on the following concepts:

- It is important to limit latency
- Maximizing throughput is less important than limiting latency
- The G1 garbage collection algorithm is stable

There are two assumptions involved with making the G1 garbage collection method the default method over the parallel approach:

- Making G1 the default garbage collection method will significantly increase its use. This increased usage might unveil performance or stability issues not realized before Java 9.
- The G1 approach is more processor-intensive than the parallel approach. In some use cases, this could be somewhat problematic.

On the surface, this change might seem like a great step for Java 9 and that very well might be the case. Caution, however, should be used when blindly accepting this new default collection method. It is recommended that systems be tested if switching to G1 to ensure your applications do not suffer from performance degradation or have unexpected issues that are caused by the use of G1. As previously suggested, G1 has not benefited from the widespread testing that the parallel method has.

This last point about the lack of widespread testing is significant. Making G1 the default automatic memory management (garbage collection) system with Java 9 is tantamount to turning developers into unsuspecting testers. While no major problems are expected, knowing that there is potential for performance and stability issues when using G1 with Java 9 will place greater emphasis on testing your Java 9 applications.

Depreciated garbage collection combinations

Oracle has been great about depreciating features, APIs, and libraries before removing them from a new release of the Java platform. With this schema in place, language components that were depreciated in Java 8 are subject for removal in Java 9. There are a few garbage collection combinations that were deemed to be rarely used and depreciated in Java 8.

Those combinations, listed here, have been removed in Java 9:

- DefNew + CMS
- ParNew + SerialOld
- Incremental CMS

These combinations, in addition to having been rarely used, introduced an unneeded level of complexity to the garbage collection system. This resulted in an extra drain on system resources without providing a commensurate benefit to the user or developer.

The following listed garbage collection configurations were affected by the aforementioned depreciation in the Java 8 platform:

Garbage collection configuration	Flag(s)
DefNew + CMS	`-XX:+UseParNewGC` `-XX:UseConcMarkSweepGC`
ParNew + SerialOld	`-XX:+UseParNewGC`
ParNew + iCMS	`-Xincgc`
ParNew + iCMS	`-XX:+CMSIncrementalMode` `-XX:+UseConcMarkSweepGC`

Defnew + iCMS	`-XX:+CMSIncrementalMode`
	`-XX:+UseConcMarkSweepGC`
	`-XX:-UseParNewGC`

With the release of Java 9, garbage collection combinations deprecated in JDK 8 were removed. Those combinations are listed along with the flags that control those combinations. In addition, the flags to enable CMS foreground collections were removed and are not present in JDK 9. Those flags are listed as follows:

Garbage collection combinations	Flag
CMS foreground	`-XX:+UseCMSCompactAtFullCollection`
CMS foreground	`-XX+CMSFullGCsBeforeCompaction`
CMS foreground	`-XX+UseCMSCollectionPassing`

The only assessed downside to the removal of the depreciated garbage collection combinations is that applications that use JVM startup files with any of the flags listed in this section, will need to have their JVM startup files modified to remove or replace the old flags.

Unified garbage collection logging

Unified GC logging, part of the JDK 9 enhancement, was intended to reimplement garbage collection logging using the unified JVM logging framework. So, let's first review the Unified JVM logging initiative.

Unified JVM logging

Creating a unified logging schema for the JVM included the following high-level list of goals:

- Create a JVM-wide set of command-line options for all logging operations.
- Use categorized tags for logging.
- Provide six levels of logging as follows:
  - Error
  - Warning
  - Information
  - Debug
  - Trace
  - Develop

This is not an exhaustive list of goals. We will discuss Java's unified logging schema in greater detail in `Chapter 14`, *Command-Line Flags*.

The changes to the JVM, in the context of logging, can be categorized into:

- Tags
- Levels
- Decorations
- Output
- Command-line options

Let's briefly look at these categories.

Tags

Logging tags are identified in the JVM and can be changed in the source code if needed. The tags should be self-identifying, such as `gc` for garbage collection.

Levels

Each log message has an associated level. As previously listed, the levels are error, warning, information, debug, trace, and develop. The following diagram shows how the levels have an increasing level of verbosity in respect to how much information is logged:

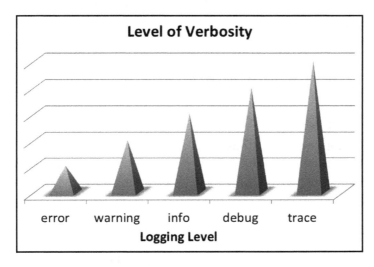

Level of verbosity

Decorations

In the context of Java's logging framework, decorations are metadata about the log message. Here is the alphabetic list of decorations that are available:

- level
- pid
- tags
- tid
- time
- timemillis
- timenanos
- uptime
- uptimemillis
- uptimenanos

For an explanation of these decorations, please refer to `Chapter 14`, *Command-Line Flags*.

Output

The Java 9 logging framework supports three types of output:

- `stderr`: Provides output to `stderr`
- `stdout`: Provides output to `stdout`
- text file: Writes the output to text files

Command-line options

Control of the JVM's logging operations is accomplished via the command-line. The `-Xlog` command-line option has an extensive array of parameters and possibilities. Here is one example:

-Xlog:gc+rt*=debug

In this example, we are telling the JVM to take the following actions:

- Log all messages tagged with, at a minimum, the `gc` and `rt` tags
- Use the `debug` level
- Provide output to `stdout`

Unified GC logging

Now that we have a general understanding of the changes to Java's logging framework, let's look at what changes were introduced. In this section, we will look at the following areas:

- Garbage collection logging options
- The `gc` tag
- Macros
- Additional considerations

Garbage collection logging options

Here is a list of garbage collection logging options and flags we had available to us before the introduction of Java's logging framework:

Garbage collection logging options	JVM option flag(s)
This prints the basic garbage collection information.	`-verbose:gc` or `-XX:+PrintGC`
This will print more detailed garbage collection information.	`-XX:+PrintGCDetails`
You can print timestamps for each garbage collection event. The seconds are sequential and begin from the JVM start time.	`-XX:+PrintGCTimeStamps`
You can print date stamps for each garbage collection event. Sample format: `2017-07-26T03:19:00.319+400:[GC . . . ]`	`-XX:+PrintGCDateStamps`
You can use this flag to print timestamps for individual garbage collection work thread tasks.	`-XX:+PrintGC\TaskTimeStamps`
Using this you can redirect garbage collection output to a file instead of the console.	`-Xloggc:`
You can print detailed information regarding young space following each collection cycle.	`-XX:+Print\TenuringDistribution`
You can use this flag to print TLAB allocation statistics.	`-XX:+PrintTLAB`
Using this flag, you can print the times for reference processing (that is, weak, soft, and so on) during *Stop the World* pauses.	`-XX:+PrintReferenceGC`
This reports if the garbage collection is waiting for native code to unpin objects in memory.	`-XX:+PrintJNIGCStalls`
This will print a pause summary after each *Stop the World* pause.	`-XX:+PrintGC\ApplicationStoppedTime`
This flag will print the time for each concurrent phase of garbage collection.	`-XX:+PrintGC\ApplicationConcurrentTime`
Using this flag will print a class histogram after a full garbage collection.	`-XX:+Print\ClassHistogramAfterFullGC`
Using this flag will print a class histogram before a full garbage collection.	`-XX:+Print\ClassHistogramBeforeFullGC`
This creates a heap dump file after full garbage collection.	`-XX:+HeapDump\AfterFullGC`
This creates a heap dump file before full garbage collection.	`-XX:+HeapDump\BeforeFullGC`
This creates a heap dump file in an out-of-memory condition.	`-XX:+HeapDump\OnOutOfMemoryError`
You use this flag to specify the path where you want your heap dumps saved on your system.	`-XX:HeapDumpPath=<path>`
You can use this to print CMS statistics, if n >= 1. Applies specifically to CMS only.	`-XX:PrintCMSStatistics=2`
This will print CMS initialization details. Applies specifically to CMS only.	`-XX:+Print\CMSInitiationStatistics`
You can use this flag to print additional information concerning free lists. Applies specifically to CMS only.	`-XX:PrintFLSStatistics=2`
You can use this flag to print additional information concerning free lists. Applies specifically to CMS only.	`-XX:PrintFLSCensus=2`
You can use this flag to print detailed diagnostic information following a promotion (young to tenure) failure. Applies specifically to CMS only.	`-XX:+PrintPromotionFailure`

This flag allows you to dump useful information regarding the state of the CMS old generation when a promotion (young to tenure) failure occurs. Applies specifically to CMS only.	-XX:+CMSDumpAt\PromotionFailure
When the -XX:+CMSDumpAt\PromotionFailure flag is used, you can use -XX:+CMSPrint\ChunksInDump to include additional details regarding free chunks. Applies specifically to CMS only.	-XX:+CMSPrint\ChunksInDump
When using the -XX:+CMSPrint\ChunksInDump flag, you can include additional information about the allocated objects using the -XX:+CMSPrint\ObjectsInDump flag. Applies specifically to CMS only.	-XX:+CMSPrint\ObjectsInDump

The gc tag

We can use the gc tag with the -Xlog option to inform the JVM to only log gc tagged items at the info level. As you will recall, this is similar to using -XX:+PrintGC. With both options, the JVM will log one line for each garbage collection operation.

It is important to note that the gc tag was not intended to be used on its own; rather, it is recommended that it be used in conjunction with other tags.

Macros

We can create macros to add logic to our garbage collection logging. Here is the general syntax for the log macro:

```
log_<level>(Tag1[,...])(fmtstr, ...)
```

Here is an example of a log macro:

```
log_debug(gc, classloading)("Number of objects loaded: %d.", object_count)
```

The following example skeleton log macro shows how you can use the new Java logging framework to create scripts for greater fidelity in logging:

```
LogHandle(gc, rt, classunloading) log;

if (log.is_error()) {
  // do something specific regarding the 'error' level
}

if (log.is_warning()) {
  // do something specific regarding the 'warning' level
}

if (log.is_info()) {
```

```
  // do something specific regarding the 'info' level
}

if (log.is_debug()) {
  // do something specific regarding the 'debug' level
}

if (log.is_trace()) {
  // do something specific regarding the 'trace' level
}
```

Additional considerations

Here are some additional items to be considered in regards to garbage collection logging:

- Using the new `-Xlog:gc` should produce similar results to the `-XX:+PrintGCDetails` command-line option and flag pairing
- The new `trace` level provides the level of detail previously provided with the `verbose` flag

Garbage collection interface

Improvements to Java's garbage collection did not stop with the major changes in Java 8 and Java 9. In Java 10, a clean garbage collector interface was introduced. The goal for the new interface was to increase the modularity for the internal garbage collection code specific to the HotSpot JVM. The increased modularity will make it easier for the new interface to be updated without negatively impacting core code bases. Another benefit is the relative ease with which garbage collection can be excluded from JDK builds.

Prior to Java 10, the garbage collection implementation was peppered in source code throughout the JVM's file structure. Cleaning this up so that the code is modular is a natural step toward optimizing Java's code base and modernizing garbage collection in a way that makes it easier to update and work with.

In Java, garbage collectors implement the `CollectedHeap` class, which manages the interaction between the JVM and garbage collection operations.

The new garbage collection interface is noteworthy, but is most applicable to garbage collection and JVM developers.

Parallel full garbage collection for G1

As mentioned earlier in this chapter, the G1 garbage collector has been the default garbage collector since Java 9. One of the efficiencies of the G1 garbage collector is that it uses concurrent garbage collection vice full collections. There are times when a full garbage collection is implemented, usually when concurrent garbage collection is not fast enough. Of note, prior to Java 9, the parallel collector was the default garbage collector and is a parallel full garbage collector.

For Java 10, the G1 full garbage collector was transitioned to parallel in order to mitigate any negative impact for developers that use full garbage collection. The mark-week-compact algorithm used for G1 full garbage collection was made parallel.

Epsilon – an arbitrarily low-overhead GC

The latest release of Java, version 11, comes with a passive GC that takes care of memory allocation. The passive nature of this GC, named the Epsilon GC, indicates that it does not perform garbage collection; rather, it continues to allocate memory until there is no room left on the heap. At that point, the JVM shuts down.

To enable the Epsilon GC, we use either of the following:

- `-XX:+UseEpsilonGC`
- `-XX:+UseNoGC`

The use of Epsilon GC is mostly seen in testing and it's low-overhead, due to the lack of garbage collection, improves testing efficiency.

Persistent issues

Even with the advent of the modern versions of Java 9, 10, and 11 there are downsides to Java's garbage collection system. Because it is an automatic process, we do not have complete control of when the collector runs. We, as developers, are not in control of garbage collection, the JVM is. The JVM makes the decision when to run garbage collection. As you have seen earlier in this chapter, we can ask the JVM to run garbage collection using the `System.gc()` method. Despite our use of this method, we are not guaranteed that our request will be honored or that it will be complied within a timely manner.

Earlier in this chapter, we reviewed several approaches and algorithms for garbage collection. We discussed how we, as developers, can take control of the process. That assumes that we have the ability to take control of garbage collection. Even when we specify a specific garbage collection technique (for example, using – XX:+UseConcMarkSweepGC for CMS garbage collection), we are not guaranteed that the JVM will use that implementation. So, we can do our best to control how the garbage collector works, but should remember that the JVM has the ultimate authority regarding how, when, and if garbage collection occurs.

Our lack of complete control over garbage collection underscores the importance of writing efficient code with memory management in mind. In the next sections, we will examine how to write code to explicitly make objects eligible for garbage collection by the JVM.

Making objects eligible for garbage collection

An easy method for making objects available for garbage collection is to assign null to the reference variable that refers to the object. Let's review this example:

```
package MyGarbageCollectionSuite;

public class GarbageCollectionExperimentOne {
   public static void main(String[] args) {
      // Declare and create new object.
      String junk = new String("Pile of Junk");

      // Output to demonstrate that the object has an active
      // reference and is not eligible for garbage collection.
      System.out.println(junk);

      // Set the reference variable to null.
      junk = null;

      // The String object junk is now eligible for garbage collection.
   }
}
```

As indicated in the in-code comments, once the string object reference variable is set to null, in this case using the junk = null; statement, the object becomes available for garbage collection.

In our next example, we will abandon an object by setting its reference variable to point to a different object. As you can see in the following code, that results in the first object being available for garbage collection:

```
package MyGarbageCollectionSuite;

public class GarbageCollectionExperimentTwo {
  public static void main(String[] args) {
    // Declare and create the first object.
    String junk1 = new String("The first pile of Junk");

    // Declare and create the second object.
    String junk2 = new String("The second pile of Junk");

    // Output to demonstrate that both objects have active references
    // and are not eligible for garbage collection.
    System.out.println(junk1);
    System.out.println(junk2);

    // Set the first object's reference to the second object.
    junk1 = junk2;

    // The String "The first pile of Junk" is now eligible for garbage
    //collection.
  }
}
```

Let's review one final method of making objects available for garbage collection. In this example, we have a single instance variable (objectNbr) that is a reference variable to an instance of the GarbageCollectionExperimentThree class. The class does not do anything interesting, other than create additional reference variables to instances of the GarbageCollectionExperimentThree class. In our example, we set the objectNbr2, objectNbr3, objectNbr4, and objectNbr5 references to null. Although these objects have instance variables and can refer to each other, their accessibility outside of the class has been terminated by setting their references to null. This makes them (objectNbr2, objectNbr3, objectNbr4, and objectNbr5) eligible for garbage collection:

```
package MyGarbageCollectionSuite;

public class GarbageCollectionExperimentThree
  {
  // instance variable
  GarbageCollectionExperimentThree objectNbr;

  public static void main(String[] args) {
```

```
GarbageCollectionExperimentThree objectNbr2 = new
GarbageCollectionExperimentThree();
GarbageCollectionExperimentThree objectNbr3 = new
GarbageCollectionExperimentThree();
GarbageCollectionExperimentThree objectNbr4 = new
GarbageCollectionExperimentThree();
GarbageCollectionExperimentThree objectNbr5 = new
GarbageCollectionExperimentThree();
GarbageCollectionExperimentThree objectNbr6 = new
GarbageCollectionExperimentThree();
GarbageCollectionExperimentThree objectNbr7 = new
GarbageCollectionExperimentThree();

// set objectNbr2 to refer to objectNbr3
objectNbr2.objectNbr = objectNbr3;

// set objectNbr3 to refer to objectNbr4
objectNbr3.objectNbr = objectNbr4;

// set objectNbr4 to refer to objectNbr5
objectNbr4.objectNbr = objectNbr5;

// set objectNbr5 to refer to objectNbr2
objectNbr5.objectNbr = objectNbr2;

// set selected references to null
objectNbr2 = null;
objectNbr3 = null;
objectNbr4 = null;
objectNbr5 = null;
    }
}
```

Summary

In this chapter, we took an in-depth review of garbage collection as a critical Java platform component. Our review included object life cycles, garbage collection algorithms, garbage collection options, and methods related to garbage collection. We looked at upgrades to garbage collection in Java 8, 9, 10, and 11 and looked at a case study to help our understanding of modern garbage collection.

We then turned our focus to the changes to garbage collection with the new Java 9 platform. Our exploration of garbage collection in Java included looks at default garbage collection, depreciated garbage collection combinations, and unified garbage collection logging. We concluded our exploration of garbage collection by looking at a few garbage collection issues that persist, even in the most recent version of Java.

In the next chapter, we will look at how to write performance tests using the **Java Microbenchmark Harness** (**JMH**), a Java harness library for writing benchmarks for the JVM.

Questions

1. Name five garbage collection algorithms.
2. What is G1?
3. What is iCMS used for?
4. What is MiB?
5. How do you make an explicit call to garbage collection?
6. How do you add a `finalize()` method to custom objects?
7. What do the following garbage collection combinations have in common?
    1. DefNew + CMS
    2. ParNew + Serial
    3. Old Incremental CMS
8. In Java, which class, implemented by garbage collectors, manages the interaction between the JVM and garbage collection operations?
9. What changes were made to the G1 full GC in Java 10?
10. What is the name of the passive GC introduced in Java 11?

Further reading

The following reference will help you dive deeper into the concepts presented in this chapter:

- *Java EE 8 High Performance [Video]*, available at `https://www.packtpub.com/ application-development/java-ee-8-high-performance-video`.

8
Microbenchmarking Applications with JMH

In the previous chapter, we took an in-depth review of garbage collection to include an object life cycle, garbage collection algorithms, garbage collection options, and methods related to garbage collection. We took a brief look at upgrades to garbage collection in Java 8 and focused on changes with the new Java platform. Our exploration of garbage collection in Java 11 included looks at default garbage collection, depreciated garbage collection combinations, unified garbage collection logging, and garbage collection issues that persist.

In this chapter, we will look at how to write performance tests using the **Java Microbenchmark Harness** (**JMH**), a Java harness library for writing benchmarks for the JVM. We will use Maven along with JMH to help illustrate the power of microbenchmarking with the new Java platform.

Specifically, we will cover the following topics:

- Microbenchmarking overview
- Microbenchmarking with Maven
- Benchmarking options
- Techniques for avoiding microbenchmarking pitfalls

Technical requirements

This chapter features Java 11. The **Standard Edition** (**SE**) of the Java platform can be downloaded from Oracle's official download site (`http://www.oracle.com/technetwork/java/javase/downloads/index.html`).

An IDE software package is sufficient. IntelliJ IDEA, from JetBrains, was used for all coding associated with this chapter and subsequent chapters. The Community version of IntelliJ IDEA can be downloaded from the site (`https://www.jetbrains.com/idea/features/`).

This chapter's source code is available on GitHub at the URL (`https://github.com/PacktPublishing/Mastering-Java-11-Second-Edition`).

Microbenchmarking overview

Microbenchmarking is used to test the performance of a system. This differs from macrobenchmarking, which runs tests on different platforms for efficiency comparison and subsequent analysis. With microbenchmarking, we typically target a specific slice of code on one system such as a method or loop. The primary purpose of microbenchmarking is to identify optimization opportunities in our code.

There are multiple approaches to benchmarking; we will focus on using the JMH tool. So, why benchmark at all? Developers do not always concern themselves with performance issues unless performance is a stated requirement. This can lead to post-deployment surprises that could have been avoided if microbenchmarking was conducted as part of the development process.

Microbenchmarking takes place across several phases of a process. As shown in the following diagram, the process involves design, implementation, execution, analysis, and enhancement:

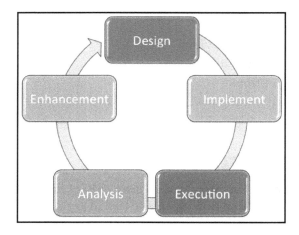

Microbenchmarking Process Phases

In the **Design** phase, we determine our goals and design our microbenchmark accordingly. In the **Implement** phase, we are writing the microbenchmark and then, in the **Execution** phase, we actually run the test. With microbenchmarking results in hand, we interpret and analyze the results in the **Analysis** phase. This leads to code improvements in the **Enhancement** phase. Once our code has been updated, we redesign the microbenchmarking test, adjust the implementation, or go straight to the **Execution** phase. This is a cyclical process that continues until we have achieved the performance optimization we identified in our goals.

Approach to using JMH

Oracle's documentation indicates that the most ideal JMH use case is to use a Maven project that is dependent on the application's JAR files. They further recommend that microbenchmarking takes place via the command line and not from within an IDE, as that could impact the results.

 Maven, also referred to as Apache Maven, is a project management and comprehension tool that we can use to manage our application project build, reporting, and documentation.

To use JMH, we will use bytecode processors (annotations) to generate the benchmark code. We use Maven archetypes to enable JMH.

In order to test the JMH, you must have an IDE with support for Maven and the version of Java you are using. If you do not yet have Java 11 or an IDE with Java 11 support, you can follow the steps in the next section.

Installing Java and Eclipse

You can download and install Java 11 from the JDK 11 Early-Access Builds page (http://jdk.java.net/11/).

Once you have Java 11 installed, download the latest version of Eclipse. At the time of writing this book, that was Oxygen. This is the relevant link https://www.eclipse.org/downloads/.

Hands-on experiment

Now that we have Eclipse Oxygen installed, you can run a quick test to determine if JMH is working on your development computer. Start by creating a new Maven project as illustrated in the following screenshot:

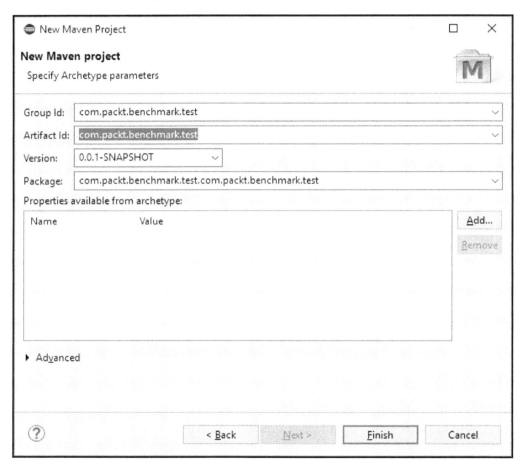

New Maven project

Next, we need to add a dependency. We can do this by editing the pom.xml file directly with the following code:

```
<dependency>
  <groupId>org.openjdk.jmh</groupId>
```

```
<artifactId>jmh-core</artifactId>
<version>0.1</version>
</dependency>
```

Alternatively, we can click the **Add...** button on the **New Maven project** dialog window (see the previous screenshot) to enter the data in a dialog window, as shown in the following screenshot. Using this form updates the pom.xml file with the preceding code:

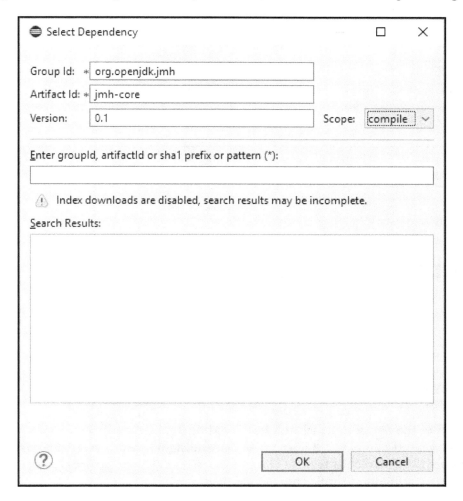

Dependency selection

Next, we need to write a class that contains a JMH method. This is just as an initial test to confirm our recently updated development environment. Here is sample code you can use for your test:

```
package com.packt.benchmark.test.com.packt.benchmark.test;
import org.openjdk.jmh.Main;

public class Test {
  public static void main(String[] args) {
    Main.main(args);
  }
}
```

We can now compile and run our very simple test program. The results are provided in the **Console** tab, or the actual console if you are using the command line. Here is what you will see:

```
<terminated> Test [Java Application] C:\Program Files\Java\jre1.8.0_131\bin\javaw.exe (Jul 30, 2017, 8:04:30 PM)
No matching benchmarks. Miss-spelled regexp? Use -v for verbose output.
```

JMH test results

Microbenchmarking with Maven

One approach to getting started with JMH is to use the JMH Maven archetype. The first step is to create a new JMH project. At our system's command prompt, we will enter the mvn command followed by a long set of parameters to create a new Java project and the necessary Maven pom.xml file:

```
mvn archetype:generate –DinteractiveMode=false –
DarchetypeGroupId=org.openjdk.jmh –DarchetypeArtifactId=jmh-java-benchmark-
archetype –DgroupId=com.packt –DartifactId=chapter8-benchmark –Dversion=1.0
```

Once you enter the mvn command and the preceding detailed parameters, you will see the results reported to you via the Terminal. Depending on your level of use, you might see a large number of downloads from https://repo.maven.apache.org/maven2/org/apache/maven/plugins/ and other similar repository sites.

You will also see an information section that informs you about the project build process, as shown in the following screenshot:

```
[INFO]
[INFO] ------------------------------------------------------------------------
[INFO] Building Maven Stub Project (No POM) 1
[INFO] ------------------------------------------------------------------------
[INFO]
[INFO] >>> maven-archetype-plugin:3.0.1:generate (default-cli) > generate-sources @ standalone-pom >>>
[INFO]
[INFO] <<< maven-archetype-plugin:3.0.1:generate (default-cli) < generate-sources @ standalone-pom <<<
[INFO]
[INFO]
[INFO] --- maven-archetype-plugin:3.0.1:generate (default-cli) @ standalone-pom ---
```

Maven build process

There will likely be additional plugin and other resources downloaded from the `https://repo.maven.apache.org` repositories. Then, you will see an informational feedback component that lets you know the project is being generated in batch mode, shown as follows:

```
[INFO] Generating project in Batch mode
[INFO] Archetype [org.openjdk.jmh:jmh-java-benchmark-archetype:1.19] found in catalog remote
```

Maven project generation

Finally, you will be presented with a set of parameters and a note that your project build was successful. As you can see with the following example, the process took less than 21 seconds to complete:

```
[INFO] ------------------------------------------------------------------------
[INFO] Using following parameters for creating project from Archetype: jmh-java-benchmark-archetype:1.19
[INFO] ------------------------------------------------------------------------
[INFO] Parameter: groupId, Value: com.packt
[INFO] Parameter: artifactId, Value: chapter8-benchmark
[INFO] Parameter: version, Value: 1.0
[INFO] Parameter: package, Value: com.packt
[INFO] Parameter: packageInPathFormat, Value: com/packt
[INFO] Parameter: package, Value: com.packt
[INFO] Parameter: groupId, Value: com.packt
[INFO] Parameter: artifactId, Value: chapter8-benchmark
[INFO] Parameter: version, Value: 1.0
[INFO] Project created from Archetype in dir: C:\chapter8-benchmark
[INFO] ------------------------------------------------------------------------
[INFO] BUILD SUCCESS
[INFO] ------------------------------------------------------------------------
[INFO] Total time: 20.753 s
[INFO] Finished at: 2017-07-31T18:03:27-05:00
[INFO] Final Memory: 18M/62M
[INFO] ------------------------------------------------------------------------
C:\>
```

New Maven project

A folder will be created based on the parameter we included in the `-DartifactId` option. In our example, we used `-DartifactId=chapter8-benchmark`, and Maven created a `chapter8-benchmark` project folder, shown as follows:

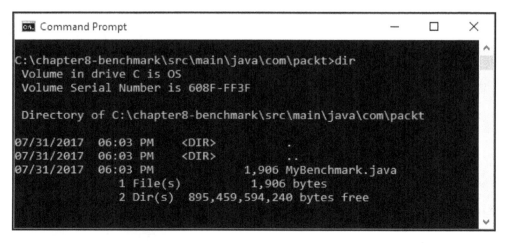

Benchmark project folder

You will see that Maven created the `pom.xml` file as well as a source (`src`) folder. In that folder, under the subdirectory structure of `C:\chapter8-benchmark\src\main\java\com\packt`, is the `MyBenchmark.java` file. Maven created a benchmark class for us, shown in the next screenshot:

```
C:\chapter8-benchmark\src\main\java\com\packt>dir
 Volume in drive C is OS
 Volume Serial Number is 608F-FF3F

 Directory of C:\chapter8-benchmark\src\main\java\com\packt

07/31/2017  06:03 PM    <DIR>          .
07/31/2017  06:03 PM    <DIR>          ..
07/31/2017  06:03 PM             1,906 MyBenchmark.java
               1 File(s)          1,906 bytes
               2 Dir(s)  895,459,594,240 bytes free
```

MyBenchmark.java file location

Here are the contents of the `MyBenchmark.java` class created by the JMH Maven
project creation process:

```
package com.packt;
import org.openjdk.jmh.annotations.Benchmark;
```

```
public class MyBenchmark {
  @Benchmark
  public void testMethod() {
    // This is a demo/sample template for building your JMH benchmarks.
    // Edit as needed.
    // Put your benchmark code here.
  }
}
```

Our next step is to modify `testMethod()` so that there is something to test. Here is the modified method we will use for the benchmark test:

```
@Benchmark
public void testMethod() {
  int total = 0;
  for (int i=0; i<100000; i++) {
    total = total + (i * 2 );
  }
System.out.println("Total: " + total);
}
```

With our code edited, we will navigate back to the project folder, `C:\chapter8-benchmark`, in our example, and execute `mvn clean install` at the command prompt.

You will see several repository downloads, source compilations, plugin installations and, finally the `Build Success` indicator, as shown here:

Build results

You will now see `.classpath` and `.project` files as well as a new `.settings` and `target` subfolders in the project directory, shown as follows:

```
Command Prompt                                    —    □    ×

C:\chapter8-benchmark>dir
 Volume in drive C is OS
 Volume Serial Number is 608F-FF3F

 Directory of C:\chapter8-benchmark

07/31/2017  07:09 PM    <DIR>          .
07/31/2017  07:09 PM    <DIR>          ..
07/31/2017  07:02 PM             1,024 .classpath
07/31/2017  07:02 PM               570 .project
07/31/2017  07:02 PM    <DIR>          .settings
07/31/2017  07:02 PM    <DIR>          bin
07/31/2017  06:03 PM             7,062 pom.xml
07/31/2017  06:03 PM    <DIR>          src
07/31/2017  07:09 PM    <DIR>          target
               3 File(s)          8,656 bytes
               6 Dir(s)  895,323,013,120 bytes free

C:\chapter8-benchmark>
```

Project directory

If you navigate to the `\target` subfolder, you will see that our `benchmarks.jar` file was created. This JAR contains what we need to run our benchmarks.

 External dependencies in `benchmarks.jar` are configured in the `pom.xml` file.

We can update our `MyBenchmark.java` file in an IDE, such as Eclipse. Then, we can execute `mvn clean install` again to overwrite our files. After the initial execution, our builds will be much faster, as nothing will need to be downloaded.

Here is a look at the output from the build process after the initial execution:

```
Command Prompt                                                    —    □    ✕

C:\chapter8-benchmark>mvn clean install
[INFO] Scanning for projects...
[INFO]
[INFO] ------------------------------------------------------------------------
[INFO] Building JMH benchmark sample: Java 1.0
[INFO] ------------------------------------------------------------------------
[INFO]
[INFO] --- maven-clean-plugin:2.5:clean (default-clean) @ chapter8-benchmark ---
[INFO] Deleting C:\chapter8-benchmark\target
[INFO]
[INFO] --- maven-resources-plugin:2.6:resources (default-resources) @ chapter8-benchmark ---
[INFO] Using 'UTF-8' encoding to copy filtered resources.
[INFO] skip non existing resourceDirectory C:\chapter8-benchmark\src\main\resources
[INFO]
[INFO] --- maven-compiler-plugin:3.1:compile (default-compile) @ chapter8-benchmark ---
[INFO] Changes detected - recompiling the module!
[INFO] Compiling 1 source file to C:\chapter8-benchmark\target\classes
[INFO]
[INFO] --- maven-resources-plugin:2.6:testResources (default-testResources) @ chapter8-bench
mark ---
[INFO] Using 'UTF-8' encoding to copy filtered resources.
[INFO] skip non existing resourceDirectory C:\chapter8-benchmark\src\test\resources
[INFO]
[INFO] --- maven-compiler-plugin:3.1:testCompile (default-testCompile) @ chapter8-benchmark
---
[INFO] No sources to compile
[INFO]
[INFO] --- maven-surefire-plugin:2.17:test (default-test) @ chapter8-benchmark ---
[INFO] No tests to run.
[INFO]
[INFO] --- maven-jar-plugin:2.4:jar (default-jar) @ chapter8-benchmark ---
[INFO] Building jar: C:\chapter8-benchmark\target\chapter8-benchmark-1.0.jar
[INFO]
[INFO] --- maven-shade-plugin:2.2:shade (default) @ chapter8-benchmark ---
[INFO] Including org.openjdk.jmh:jmh-core:jar:1.19 in the shaded jar.
[INFO] Including net.sf.jopt-simple:jopt-simple:jar:4.6 in the shaded jar.
[INFO] Including org.apache.commons:commons-math3:jar:3.2 in the shaded jar.
[INFO] Replacing C:\chapter8-benchmark\target\benchmarks.jar with C:\chapter8-benchmark\targ
et\chapter8-benchmark-1.0-shaded.jar
[INFO]
[INFO] --- maven-install-plugin:2.5.1:install (default-install) @ chapter8-benchmark ---
[INFO] Installing C:\chapter8-benchmark\target\chapter8-benchmark-1.0.jar to C:\Users\elavi\
.m2\repository\com\packt\chapter8-benchmark\1.0\chapter8-benchmark-1.0.jar
[INFO] Installing C:\chapter8-benchmark\pom.xml to C:\Users\elavi\.m2\repository\com\packt\c
hapter8-benchmark\1.0\chapter8-benchmark-1.0.pom
[INFO] ------------------------------------------------------------------------
[INFO] BUILD SUCCESS
[INFO] ------------------------------------------------------------------------
[INFO] Total time: 3.388 s
[INFO] Finished at: 2017-07-31T19:26:01-05:00
[INFO] Final Memory: 22M/73M
[INFO] ------------------------------------------------------------------------

C:\chapter8-benchmark>
```

Clean install process

Our last step is to run the benchmark tool from the `C:\chapter8-benchmark\target` folder. We can do that with the following command `-java -jar benchmarks.jar`. Even for small benchmarks on simplistic code, as with our example, the benchmarks could take some time to run. There will likely be several iterations including warm-ups to provide a more concise and valid set of benchmark results.

Our benchmark results are provided here. As you can see, the test ran for `00:08:08` hours:

```
Command Prompt                                              —    □    ×

Total: 319
24676.388 ops/s


Result "com.packt.MyBenchmark.testMethod":
  23847.961 ±(99.9%) 772.746 ops/s [Average]
  (min, avg, max) = (14864.509, 23847.961, 35528.242), stdev = 3271.857
  CI (99.9%): [23075.215, 24620.708] (assumes normal distribution)


# Run complete. Total time: 00:08:08

Benchmark                 Mode    Cnt      Score      Error   Units
MyBenchmark.testMethod    thrpt   200   23847.961 ±  772.746  ops/s

C:\chapter8-benchmark\target>
```

MyBenchmark.java file location

Benchmarking options

In the previous section, you learned how to run a benchmark test. In this section, we will look at the following configurable options for running our benchmarks:

- Modes
- Time units

Modes

The output of our benchmark results, from the previous section, included a `Mode` column that had the value of `thrpt`, which is short for throughput. This is the default mode and there are an additional four modes. All JMH benchmark modes are listed and described as follows:

Mode	Description
All	Measures all other modes sequentially.
Average Time	This mode measures the average time for a single benchmark to run.
Sample Time	This mode measures the benchmark execution time and includes min and max times.
Single Shot Time	With this mode, there is no JVM warm-up and the test is to determine how long a single benchmark method takes to run.
Throughput	This is the default mode and measures the number of operations per second.

To dictate which benchmark mode to use, you will modify your `@Benchmark` line of code to one of the following:

- `@Benchmark @BenchmarkMode(Mode.All)`
- `@Benchmark @BenchmarkMode(Mode.AverageTime)`
- `@Benchmark @BenchmarkMode(Mode.SampleTime)`
- `@Benchmark @BenchmarkMode(Mode.SingleShotTime)`
- `@Benchmark @BenchmarkMode(Mode.Throughput)`

Time units

In order to gain greater fidelity in benchmark outputs, we can designate a specific unit of time, listed here from shortest to longest:

- `NANOSECONDS`
- `MICROSECONDS`
- `MILLISECONDS`
- `SECONDS`
- `MINUTES`
- `HOURS`
- `DAYS`

In order to make this designation, we simply add the following code to our `@Benchmark` line:

```
@Benchmark @BenchmarkMode(Mode.AverageTime)
@OutputTimeUnit(TimeUnit.NANOSECONDS)
```

In the preceding example, we have designated the average mode and nanoseconds as the time unit.

Techniques for avoiding microbenchmarking pitfalls

Microbenchmarking is not something that every developer will have to worry about, but for those who do, there are several pitfalls that you should be aware of. In this section we will review the most common pitfalls and suggest strategies for avoiding them.

Power management

There are many subsystems that can be used to help you manage the balance between power and performance (that is, `cpufreq`). These systems can alter the state of time during benchmarks.

There are two suggested strategies for this pitfall:

- Disable any power management systems before running tests
- Run the benchmarks for longer periods

OS schedulers

Operating system schedulers, such as Solaris schedulers, help determine which software processes gain access to a system's resources. Use of these schedulers can have unreliable benchmarking results.

There are two suggested strategies for this pitfall:

- Refine your system scheduling policies
- Run the benchmarks for longer periods

Timesharing

Timesharing systems are used to help balance system resources. Use of these systems often results in irregular gaps between a thread's start and stop times. Also, the CPU load will not be uniform and our benchmarking data will not be as useful to us.

There are two suggested strategies to avoid this pitfall:

- Test all code before running benchmarks to ensure things work as they should
- Use JMH to measure only after all threads have started or all threads have stopped

Eliminating dead-code and constant folding

Dead-code and constant folding are often referred to as redundant code and our modern compilers are pretty good at eliminating them. An example of dead-code is code that will never be reached. Consider the following example:

```
. . .
int value = 10;
if (value != null) {
  System.out.println("The value is " + value + ".");
} else {
    System.out.println("The value is null."); // This is a line of Dead-
Code
}
. . .
```

In our preceding example, the line identified as dead-code is never reached since the variable value will never be equal to null. It is set to 10 immediately before the conditional if statement evaluates the variable.

The problem is that benchmarking code can sometimes be removed in the attempt to eliminate dead-code.

Constant folding is the compiler operation that occurs when compile-time constraints are replaced with actual results. The compiler performs constant folding to remove any redundant runtime computations. In the following example, we have a final int followed by a second int based on a mathematical calculation involving the first int:

```
. . .
static final int value = 10;
int newValue = 319 * value;
. . .
```

The constant folding operation would convert the two lines of the preceding code to the following:

```
int newValue = 3190;
```

There is one suggested strategy for this pitfall:

- Use the JMH API support to ensure your benchmarking code is not eliminated

Run-to-run variance

There is a plethora of issues that can drastically impact the run-to-run variance in benchmarking.

There are two suggested strategies for this pitfall:

- Run the JVM multiple times within every subsystem
- Use multiple JMH forks

Cache capacity

Dynamic Randomly Accessed Memory (**DRAM**) is very slow. This can result in very different performance results during benchmarking.

There are two suggested strategies to this pitfall:

- Run multiple benchmarks with varying problem sets. Keep track of your memory footprint during tests.
- Use the `@State` annotation to dictate the JMH state. This annotation is used to define the instance's scope. There are three states:
    - `Scope.Benchmark`: The instance is shared across all threads that are running the same test
    - `Scope.Group`: One instance is allocated per thread group
    - `Scope.Thread`: Each thread will have its own instance. This is the default state

Summary

In this chapter, we learned that the JMH is a Java harness library for writing benchmarks for the JVM. We experimented with writing performance tests using Maven along with JMH to help illustrate the procedures of microbenchmarking with the new Java platform. We started with a microbenchmarking overview, then dove deep into microbenchmarking with Maven, reviewed benchmarking options, and concluded with a few techniques for avoiding microbenchmarking pitfalls.

In the next chapter, we will learn to write an application that is managing other processes and utilizes the modern process management API of the Java platform.

Questions

1. What is microbenchmarking?
2. What are the major phases of microbenchmarking?
3. What is Maven?
4. What file is used to define dependencies?
5. What do modes and time units have in common with regards to benchmarking?
6. What are the JMH benchmark modes?
7. What are the time units used in benchmarking, in order of smallest to largest?
8. What are the suggested strategies for avoiding the power management pitfall?
9. What are the suggested strategies for avoiding the OS schedulers pitfall?
10. What are the suggested strategies for avoiding the timesharing pitfall?

Further reading

The following references listed will help you dive deeper into the concepts presented in this chapter:

- *Java EE Development with Eclipse*, available at https://www.packtpub.com/application-development/java-ee-development-eclipse.
- *Java EE Development with Eclipse - Second Edition*, available at https://www.packtpub.com/application-development/java-ee-development-eclipse-second-edition.

Making Use of the Process API

9

In the previous chapter, we learned that the **Java Microbenchmark Harness (JMH)** is a Java harness library for writing benchmarks for the JVM. We experimented with writing performance tests using Maven along with JMH to help illustrate the procedures of microbenchmarking with the new Java platform. We started with a microbenchmarking overview, then dove deep into microbenchmarking with Maven, reviewed benchmarking options, and concluded with a few techniques for avoiding microbenchmarking pitfalls.

In this chapter, we will focus on the updates to the `Process` class and the `java.lang.ProcessHandle` API. In earlier versions of Java, prior to Java 9, managing processes in Java was difficult. The API was insufficient with some features lacking and some tasks needed to be solved in a system-specific manner. For example, in Java 8, giving a process access to its own **process identifier (PID)** was an unnecessarily difficult task.

In this chapter, we will explore the requisite knowledge needed to write an application that manages other processes utilizing Java's process management API. Specifically, we will cover the following:

- Introducing processes
- Working with the `ProcessHandle` interface
- Reviewing a sample process controller app

Technical requirements

This chapter features Java 11. The **Standard Edition** (**SE**) of the Java platform can be downloaded from Oracle's official download site (`http://www.oracle.com/technetwork/java/javase/downloads/index.html`).

An IDE software package is sufficient. IntelliJ IDEA, from JetBrains, was used for all coding associated with this chapter and subsequent chapters. The Community version of IntelliJ IDEA can be downloaded from the site (`https://www.jetbrains.com/idea/features/`).

This chapter's source code is available on GitHub at the URL (`https://github.com/PacktPublishing/Mastering-Java-11-Second-Edition`)

Introducing processes

Processes, in the context of Java application programming, are execution units in the operating system. When you start a program, you start a process. When the machine boots the code, the first thing it does is execute the boot process. This process then starts other processes that become the children of the boot process. These child processes may start other processes. This way, when the machine runs, there are trees of processes running.

When the machine does something, it is done in some code executing inside some process. The operating system also runs as several processes that execute simultaneously. Applications are executed as one or more processes. Most of the applications run as a single process but, as an example, the Chrome browser starts several processes to do all the rendering and network communication operations that collectively function as a browser.

To get a better idea of what processes are, start the task manager on Windows or the **Activity Monitor** on OS X and click on the **Process** tab. You will see the different processes that currently exist on the machine. Using these tools, you can review the parameters of the processes, and you can kill processes individually.

 Individual processes have their memory allocated for their work and they are not allowed to freely access each other's memory.

The execution unit scheduled by the operating system is a thread. A process consists of one or more threads. These threads are scheduled by the operating system scheduler and are executed in time slots.

With every operating system, processes have a PID, which is a number that identifies the process. No two processes can be active at a time sharing the same PID. When we want to identify an active process in the operating system, we use the PID. On Linux and other Unix-like operating systems, the `kill` command terminates a process. The argument to be passed to this program is the PID of the process to terminate. Termination can be graceful. It is somewhat like asking the process to exit. If the process decides not to, it can keep running.

Programs can be prepared to stop upon such requests. For example, a Java application may add a `Thread` object calling the `Runtime.getRuntime().addShutdownHook(Thread t)` method. The thread passed should start when the process is asked to stop, so the thread can perform all tasks that the program has to do before it exits. Unfortunately, there is no guarantee that the thread will actually start. It depends on the actual implementation.

Working with the ProcessHandle interface

Two new interfaces were introduced in Java 9 that support handling operating system processes—`ProcessHandle` and `ProcessHandle.Info`.

A `ProcessHandle` object identifies an operating system process and provides methods to manage the process. In prior versions of Java, this was only possible with operating system-specific methods using the PID to identify the process. The major problem with this approach was that the PID is unique only while the process is active. When a process finishes, the operating system is free to reuse the PID for a new process. When we check to see if a process is still running, using the PID, we are really checking for an active process with that PID. Our process may be alive when we check it, but the next time our program queries the process state, it might be a different process.

The desktop and server operating systems try not to reuse the PID values for as long as possible. On some embedded systems the operating system may only use 16-bit values to store the PID. When only 16-bit values are used, there is a greater chance that the PIDs will be reused. We can now avoid this problem using the `ProcessHandle` API. We can receive `ProcessHandle` and can call the `handle.is.Alive()` method. This method will return `false` when the process finishes. This works even if the PID was reused.

Getting the PID of the current process

We can gain access to the PID of the processes via the `handle`. The `handle.getPid()` method returns `Long` representing the numerical value of the PID. Since it is safer to access the processes through the handle, the importance of this method is limited. It may come in handy when our code wants to give information about itself to some other management tool.

It is a common practice for programs to create a file that has the numeric PID as the name of the file. It may be a requirement that a certain program does not run in multiple processes. In that case, the code writes its own PID file to a specific directory. If a PID file with that name already exists, processing stops. If the previous process crashed or terminated without deleting the PID file, then the system manager can easily delete the file and start the new process. If the program hangs, then the system manager can easily kill the dead process if the PID is known.

To get the PID of the current process, the call chain `ProcessHandle.current().getPid()` can be used.

Getting information about processes

To get information about a process, we need access to the `Info` object of the process. This is available through `ProcessHandle`. We use a call to the `handle.info()` method to return it.

The `Info` interface defines query methods that deliver information about the process. These are:

- `command()` returns `Optional<String>` containing the command that was used to start the process
- `arguments()` returns `Optional<String[]>` that contains the arguments that were used on the command line after the command to start the process
- `commandLine()` returns `Optional<String>` that contains the whole command line
- `startInstant()` returns `Optional<Instant>`, which essentially represents the time the process was started
- `totalCpuDuration()` returns `Optional<Duration>`, which represents the CPU time used by the process since it was started

- `user()` returns `Optional<String>` that holds the name of the user the process belongs to

The values returned by these methods are all `Optional` because there is no guarantee that the operating system or the Java implementation can return the information. However, on most operating systems it should work and the returned values should be present.

The following sample code displays the information on a given process:

```
import java.io.IOException;
import java.time.Duration;
import java.time.Instant;

public class ProcessHandleDemonstration {
    public static void main(String[] args) throws InterruptedException,
    IOException {
        provideProcessInformation(ProcessHandle.current());
        Process theProcess = new
         ProcessBuilder("SnippingTool.exe").start();
        provideProcessInformation(theProcess.toHandle());
        theProcess.waitFor();
        provideProcessInformation(theProcess.toHandle());
    }
    static void provideProcessInformation(ProcessHandle theHandle) {
        // get id
        long pid = ProcessHandle.current().pid();
        // Get handle information (if available)
        ProcessHandle.Info handleInformation = theHandle.info();

        // Print header
        System.out.println("|==============================|");
        System.out.println("| INFORMATION ON YOUR PROCESS |");
        System.out.println("|==============================|\n");

        // Print the PID
        System.out.println("Process id (PID): " + pid);
        System.out.println("Process Owner: " +
        handleInformation.user().orElse(""));

        // Print additional information if available
        System.out.println("Command:" +
        handleInformation.command().orElse(""));
        String[] args = handleInformation.arguments().orElse (new String[]{});
        System.out.println("Argument(s): ");
        for (String arg: args) System.out.printf("\t" + arg);
          System.out.println("Command line: " +
          handleInformation.commandLine().orElse(""));
```

```
        System.out.println("Start time: " +
        handleInformation.startInstant().orElse(Instant.now()).
        toString());
        System.out.printf("Run time duration: %sms%n",
        handleInformation.totalCpuDuration().
        orElse(Duration.ofMillis(0)).toMillis());
    }
}
```

Here is the console output for the preceding code:

```
Problems  @ Javadoc  Declaration  Console  ⊠
<terminated> ProcessHandleDemonstration [Java Application] C:\Program Files\Java\jre-9\bin\javaw.exe (Sep 14, 2017, 1:24:00 PM)
|==============================|
|  INFORMATION ON YOUR PROCESS |
|==============================|

Process id (PID): 6176
Process Owner: DESKTOP-75PIVKB\elavi
Command:
Argument(s):
Command line:
Start time: 2017-09-14T18:24:00.490Z
Run time duration: 15ms
```

Listing processes

Prior to Java 9, we did not have the means to obtain a list of active processes. With Java 9, 10, and 11 it is possible to get the processes in Stream. There are three methods that return Stream<ProcessHandle> and are used to:

- List children processes
- List all the descendants
- List all processes

Each of these is reviewed in the next section.

Listing children

To get Stream of process handles for controlling children, the static method processHandle.children() should be used. This will create a snapshot of the children processes of the process represented by processHandle and create Stream. Since processes are dynamic, there is no guarantee that during the code execution, while our program attends to the handles, all children processes are still active. Some of them may terminate and our process may spawn new children, perhaps from a different thread. Thus, the code should not assume that each of the ProcessHandle elements of Stream represents an active and running process.

The following program starts 10 Command Prompts in Windows and then counts the number of children processes and prints them to a standard output:

```
import java.io.IOException;

public class ChildLister {
   public static void main(String[] args) throws IOException {
      for (int i = 0; i < 10; i++) {
         new ProcessBuilder().command("cmd.exe").start();
      }
      System.out.println("Number of children :" +
         ProcessHandle.current().children().count());
   }
}
```

Executing the program will result in the following:

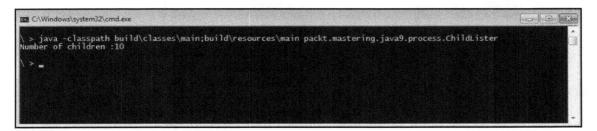

Listing descendants

Listing the descendants is very similar to listing children, but if we call the processHandle.descendants() method then Stream will contain all the children processes and the children processes of those processes, and so on.

The following program starts Command Prompts with command-line arguments so that they also spawn another cmd.exe that terminates:

```java
import java.io.IOException;
import java.util.stream.Collectors;

public class DescendantLister {
  public static void main(String[] args) throws IOException {
    for (int i = 0; i < 10; i++) {
      new ProcessBuilder().command("cmd.exe","/K","cmd").start();
    }
    System.out.println("Number of descendants: " +
      ProcessHandle.current().descendants().count();
  }
}
```

Running the command a few times will result in the following, nondeterministic output:

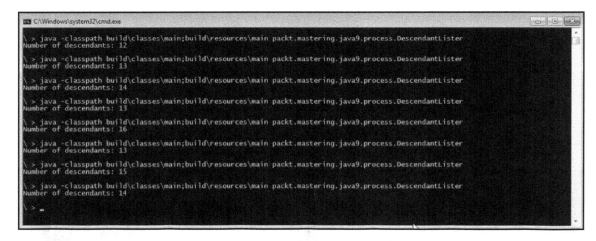

The output clearly demonstrates that when Stream of the descendants is created not all processes are alive. The sample code starts 10 processes and each of them starts another. Stream does not have 20 elements because some of these subprocesses were terminated during processing.

Listing all processes

Listing all the processes is slightly different from listing descendants and children.
The method `allProcess()` is static and returns `Stream` of handles of all processes that
are active in the operating system at the time of execution.

The following sample code prints the process commands to the console that seem to be
Java processes:

```java
import java.lang.ProcessHandle.Info;

public class ProcessLister {
  private static void out(String format, Object... params) {
    System.out.println(String.format(format, params));
  }
  private static boolean looksLikeJavaProcess(Info info) {
    return info.command().isPresent() && info.command().get().
      toLowerCase().indexOf("java") != -1;
  }

  public static void main(String[] args) {
    ProcessHandle.allProcesses().map(ProcessHandle::info).
      filter(info -> looksLikeJavaProcess(info)).
      forEach((info) -> System.out.println(info.command().
      orElse("---")));
  }
}
```

The output of the program lists all the process commands that have the string `java` inside,
shown as follows:

Your actual output may, of course, be different.

Waiting for processes

When a process starts another process, it may wait for the process many times because it needs the result of the other program. If the structure of the task can be organized in a way that the parent program can do something else while waiting for the child process to finish, then the parent process can invoke the isAlive() method on the process handle. Usually, the parent process has nothing to do until the spawned process finishes. Legacy applications implemented loops that called the Thread.sleep() method so the CPU was not excessively wasted and the process was checked periodically to see if it was still alive.

The current Java platform offers a much better approach to the waiting process. The ProcessHandle interface has a method called onExit() that returns CompletableFuture. This class makes it possible to wait for a task to be finished without looping. If we have the handle of a process we can simply call the handle.onExit().join() method to wait until the process finishes. The get() method of the returned CompletableFuture returns the ProcessHandle instance that was used to create it in the first place.

We can call the onExit() method on the handle many times and each time it will return a different CompletableFuture object, each related to the same process. We can call the cancel() method on the object, but it will only cancel the CompletableFuture object and not the process, and also does not have any effect on the other CompletableFuture objects that were created from the same ProcessHandle instance.

Terminating processes

To terminate a process we can call the destroy() method or the destroyForcibly() method on the ProcessHandle instance. Both of these methods will terminate the process. The destroy() method is expected to terminate the process, gracefully executing the process shutdown sequence. In this case, the shutdown hooks added to the runtime are executed if the actual implementation supports the graceful, normal termination of processes.

The destroyForcibly() method will enforce process termination, and in this case, the shutdown sequence will not be executed. If the process managed by the handle is not alive then nothing happens when the code calls any of these methods. If there are any CompletableFuture objects created calling the onExit() method on the handle, then they will be completed after the call to the destroy() or destroyForcefully() method when the process has terminated.

This means that the `CompletableFuture` object will return from a `join()` or some similar method after some time when the process termination is complete, and not immediately after `destroy()` or `destroyForcefully()` returns.

It is also important to note that process termination may depend on many things. If the actual process that is waiting to terminate another does not have the right to terminate the other process, then the request will fail. In this case, the return value of the method is `false`. A return value of `true` does not mean that the process has actually terminated. It only means that the termination request was accepted by the operating system and that the operating system will terminate the process at some point in the future. This will actually happen rather soon, but not instantaneously and therefore it should not be a surprise if the method `isAlive()` returns `true` for some time after the `destroy()` or `destroyForcefully()` method returns the value `true`.

The difference between `destroy()` and `destroyForcefully()` is implementation-specific. The Java standard does not state that `destroy()` terminate the process letting the shutdown sequence be executed. It only requests the process to be killed. Whether the process represented by this `ProcessHandle` object is normally terminated is implementation-dependent.

This is because some operating systems do not implement the graceful process termination feature. In such situations, the implementation of `destroy()` is the same as calling `destroyForcefully()`. The system-specific implementation of the interface `ProcessHandle` must implement the method `supportsNormalTermination()`, which should be `true` only if the implementation supports normal (not forceful) process termination. The method is expected to return the same value for all invocations in an actual implementation and should not change the return value during the execution of a JVM instance. There is no need to call the method multiple times.

The following examples demonstrate process starting, process termination, and waiting for the process to terminate. In our example, we use two classes. This first class demonstrates the `.sleep()` method:

```
public class WaitForChildToBeTerminated {
  public static void main(String[] args) throws InterruptedException {
    Thread.sleep(10_000);
  }
}
```

The second class in our example calls the `WaitForChildToBeTerminated` class:

```java
import java.io.IOException;
import java.util.Arrays;
import java.util.concurrent.CompletableFuture;
import java.util.stream.Collectors;

public class TerminateAProcessAfterWaiting {
  private static final int N = 10;
  public static void main(String[] args) throws IOException,
  InterruptedException {
    ProcessHandle ph[] = new ProcessHandle[N];
      for (int i = 0; i < N; i++) {
        final ProcessBuilder pb = ew ProcessBuilder().
          command("java", "-cp", "build/classes/main",
          "packt.mastering.java11.process.WaitForChildToBeTerminated");
        Process p = pb.start();
        ph[i] = p.toHandle();
      }

      long start = System.currentTimeMillis();
      Arrays.stream(ph).forEach(ProcessHandle::destroyForcibly);
      CompletableFuture.allOf(Arrays.stream(ph).
        map(ProcessHandle::onExit).collect(Collectors.toList()).
        toArray(new CompletableFuture[ph.length])).join();
      long duration = System.currentTimeMillis() - start;
      System.out.println("Duration " + duration + "ms");
  }
}
```

The preceding code starts 10 processes, each executing the program that sleeps for 10 seconds. It forcibly destroys the processes, or more specifically, the operating system is asked to destroy them. Our example joins the `CompletableFuture` that is composed from the array of `CompletableFuture` objects, which are created using the handles of the individual processes.

When all the processes are finished then it prints out the measured time in milliseconds. The time interval starts when the processes are created and the process creation loop is finished. The end of the measured time interval is when the processes are recognized by the JVM returning from the `join()` method.

The sample code sets the sleeping time to 10 seconds. This is a more noticeable time period. Running the code twice and deleting the line that destroys the processes can result in a much slower printout. Actually, the measured and printed elapsed times will also show that terminating the processes has an effect.

Reviewing a sample process controller app

This final section provides a sample process control application to demonstrate this chapter's content. The functionality of the application is very simple. It reads from a series of configuration file parameters how to start some processes and then, if any of them stops, it tries to restart the process.

This sample application can be used as a starting point for real-world applications. You can extend the set of parameters of the process with environment variable specifications. You can also add a default directory for the process, input, and output redirection, and even how much CPU consumption a process is allowed without the controlling application killing and restarting it.

The application consists of four classes:

- `Main`: This class contains the `public static void main` method and is used to start up the daemon.
- `Parameters`: This class contains the configuration parameters for a process. In this simple case, it will only contain one field, the command line. If the application gets extended, this class will contain the default directory, the redirections, and CPU use-limiting data.
- `ParamsAndHandle`: This class is nothing more than a data tuple holding a reference to a `Parameters` object and also a process handle. When a process dies and gets restarted the process handle is replaced by the new handle, but the reference to the `Parameters` object never changes its configuration.
- `ControlDaemon`: This class implements the `Runnable` interface and is started as a separate thread.

Main class

The `main()` method takes the name of the directory from the command-line argument. It treats this as relative to the current working directory. It uses a separate method from the same class to read the set of configurations from the files in the directory and then starts the control daemon. The following code is the `main()` method of the program:

```
public static void main(String[] args) throws IOException,
    InterruptedException {

    // DemoOutput.out() simulated - implementation not shown
    DemoOutput.out(new File(".").getAbsolutePath().toString());
    if (args.length == 0) {
```

```
      System.err.println("Usage: daemon directory");
      System.exit(-1);
    }

    Set<Parameters> params = parametersSetFrom(args[0]);
    Thread t = new Thread(new ControlDaemon(params));
    t.start();
  }
```

Although this is a daemon, we are starting it as a normal thread and not as a daemon thread. When a thread is set to be a daemon thread it will not keep the JVM alive. When all other non-daemon threads stop, the JVM will just exit and the daemon threads will be stopped. In our case, the daemon thread we execute is the only one that keeps the code running. After that has been started the main thread has nothing more to do, but the JVM should stay alive until it is killed by the operator issuing a Unix `kill` command or pressing *Ctrl* + *C* on the command line.

Getting the list of the files that are in the directory specified, and getting the parameters from the file, is simple using the new `Files` and `Paths` classes from the JDK:

```
    private static Set<Parameters>
      GetListOfFilesInDirectory(String directory) throws IOException {
        return Files.walk(Paths.get(directory)).map(Path::toFile)
          .filter(File::isFile).map(file -> Parameters.fromFile(file))
          .collect(Collectors.toSet());
    }
```

We get a stream of the files in the form of `Path` objects, map it to `File` objects, then filter out the directories if there are any in the `configuration` directory, and map the remaining plain files to `Parameters` objects using the static method from `File` of the `Parameters` class. Finally, we return `Set` of the objects.

Parameters class

Our `Parameters` class has a field and a constructor, listed as follows:

```
    final String[] commandLine;
    public Parameters(String[] commandLine) {
      this.commandLine = commandLine;
    }
```

The `Parameters` class has two methods. The first method, `getCommandLineStrings()`, retrieves the command-line strings from the properties. This array contains the command and the command-line parameters. If it was not defined in the file, then we return an empty array, shown as follows:

```
private static String[] getCommandLineStrings(Properties props) {
    return Optional.ofNullable(props.getProperty("commandLine"))
      .orElse("").split("\\s+");
}
```

The second method is the static `fromFile()` that reads the properties from a `properties` file, shown as follows:

```
public static Parameters fromFile(final File file) {
    final Properties props = new Properties();
    try (final InputStream is = new FileInputStream(file)) {
      props.load(is);
    } catch (IOException e) {
        throw new RuntimeException(e);
    }
    return new Parameters(getCommandLineStrings(props));
}
```

If the set of parameters handled by the program is extended, then this class should also be modified.

ParamsAndHandle

The `ParamsAndHandle` is a very simple class that holds two fields—one for the parameters and the other is the handle to the process handle that is used to access the process started using the parameters, as shown in the following:

```
public class ParamsAndHandle {
    final Parameters params;
    ProcessHandle handle;
    public ParamsAndHandle(Parameters params, ProcessHandle handle) {
      this.params = params;
      this.handle = handle;
    }

    public ProcessHandle toHandle() {
      return handle;
    }
}
```

Since the class is closely tied to the `ControlDaemon` class from where it is used, there is no mutator or accessor associated with the field. We see the two classes as something inside the same encapsulation boundaries. The `toHandle ()` method is there so that we can use it as a method handle, as we will see in `Chapter 10`, *Fine-Grained Stack Tracing*.

ControlDaemon

The `ControlDaemon` class implements the `Runnable` interface and is started as a separate thread. The constructor gets the set of the parameters that were read from the properties files and converts them to a set of `ParamsAndHandle` objects, shown as follows:

```
private final Set<ParamsAndHandle> handlers;
public ControlDaemon(Set<Parameters> params) {
  handlers = params.stream()
    .map( s -> new ParamsAndHandle(s,null))
    .collect(Collectors.toSet());
}
```

Because the processes are not started at this point, the handles are all `null`. The `run()` method is used to start the processes, as follows:

```
@Override
public void run() {
  try {
    for (ParamsAndHandle pah : handlers) {
      log.log(DEBUG, "Starting {0}", pah.params);
      ProcessHandle handle = start(pah.params);
      pah.handle = handle;
    }
    keepProcessesAlive();
    while (handlers.size() > 0) {
      allMyProcesses().join();
    }
  } catch (IOException e) {
    log.log(ERROR, e);
  }
}
```

Processing goes through the set of parameters and uses the method (implemented in this class later) to start the processes. The handles to each process get to the `ParamsAndHandle` object. After that, the `keepProcessesAlive()` method is called and waits for the processes to finish. When a process stops it gets restarted. If it cannot be restarted it will be removed from the set.

The `allMyProcesses()` method (also implemented in this class) returns a `CompletableFuture` that gets completed when all the started processes have stopped. Some of the processes may have been restarted by the time the `join()` method returns. As long as there is at least one process running, the thread should run.

Using the `CompletableFuture` to wait for the processes and the `while` loop, we use minimal CPU to keep the thread alive as long there is at least one process we manage to run, presumably even after a few restarts. We have to keep this thread alive even if it does not use CPU and executes no code most of the time to let the `keepProcessesAlive()` method do its work using `CompletableFutures`. The method is shown in the following code snippet:

```
private void keepProcessesAlive() {
  anyOfMyProcesses().thenAccept(ignore -> {
    restartProcesses();
    keepProcessesAlive();
  });
}
```

The `keepProcessesAlive()` method calls the `anyOfMyProcesses()` method that returns `CompletableFuture`, which is completed when any of the managed processes exits. The method schedules to execute the Lambda passed as an argument to the `thenAccept()` method for the time the `CompletableFuture` is completed. The Lambda does two things:

- Restarts the processes that are stopped (probably only one)
- Calls the `keepProcessesAlive()` method

It is important to understand that this call is not performed from within the `keepProcessesAlive()` method itself. This is not a recursive call. This is scheduled as a `CompletableFuture` action. We are not implementing a loop in a recursive call, because we would run out of stack space. We ask the JVM executors to execute this method again when the processes are restarted.

The JVM uses the default `ForkJoinPool` to schedule these tasks and this pool contains daemon threads. That is the reason we have to wait and keep the method running because that is the only non-daemon thread that prevents the JVM from exiting.

The next method, shown as follows, is `restartProcesses()`:

```
private void restartProcesses() {
  Set<ParamsAndHandle> failing = new HashSet<>();
  handlers.stream()
    .filter(pah -> !pah.toHandle().isAlive())
    .forEach(pah -> {
  try {
    pah.handle = start(pah.params);
  } catch (IOException e) {
      failing.add(pah);
    }
  });
  handlers.removeAll(failing);
}
```

This method starts the processes that are in our set of managed processes and which are not alive. If any of the restarts fail, it removes the failing processes from the set. (Be aware not to remove it in the loop to avoid `ConcurrentModificationException`). The `anyOfMyProcesses()` and `allMyProcesses()` methods are using the auxiliary `completableFuturesOfTheProcessesand()` method and are straightforward, shown as follows:

```
private CompletableFuture anyOfMyProcesses() {
  return CompletableFuture.anyOf(
    completableFuturesOfTheProcesses());
}

private CompletableFuture allMyProcesses() {
  return CompletableFuture.allOf(
    completableFuturesOfTheProcesses());
}
```

The `completableFuturesOfTheProcesses()` method returns an array of `CompletableFutures` created from the currently running managed processes calling their `onExit()` method. This is done in a compact and easy-to-read functional programming style, as shown here:

```
private CompletableFuture[] completableFuturesOfTheProcesses() {
  return handlers.stream()
    .map(ParamsAndHandle::toHandle)
    .map(ProcessHandle::onExit)
    .collect(Collectors.toList())
    .toArray(new CompletableFuture[handlers.size()]);
}
```

The set is converted to a `Stream`, mapped to a `Stream` of `ProcessHandle` objects (this is why we needed the `toHandle()` method in the `ParamsAndHandle` class). Then the handles are mapped to the `CompletableFuture` stream using the `onExit()` method and finally, we collect it to a list and convert it to an array.

Our last method to complete our sample application is as follows:

```
private ProcessHandle start(Parameters params)
  throws IOException {
     return new ProcessBuilder(params.commandLine)
       .start().toHandle();
}
```

This method starts the process using `ProcessBuilder` and returns `ProcessHandle` so that we can replace the old one in our set and manage the new process.

Summary

In this chapter, we discussed how the current Java platform enables us to manage processes. This represents a vast improvement from earlier versions of Java, which required operating system-specific implementations and was less than optimal in terms of CPU use and coding practice. The modern API, with new classes like `ProcessHandle`, makes it possible to handle almost all aspects of processes. We examined the new API and reviewed sample code snippets for the use of each of them. We also constructed a full application, managing processes where the learned API was put into practice.

In the next chapter, we will take a detailed look at the Java Stack Walking API. We will use code samples to illustrate how to use the API.

Questions

1. What are processes?
2. What two interfaces support handling operating system processes?
3. What method returns `false` when a process finishes?
4. How can you gain access to the PID of a process?
5. How do you retrieve the PID of the current process?
6. Name six query methods used by the `Info` interface to deliver information about a process.

7. What method is used to get the `Stream` of process handles for controlling children?
8. What method is used to get the `Stream` of process handles for descendants?
9. What method can be used to retrieve a list of all children and descendants?
10. What does the `onExit()` method return?

Further reading

For more information, you can visit the following link:

- *Java 9 High Performance*, available at `https://www.packtpub.com/application-development/java-9-high-performance`.

10
Fine-Grained Stack Tracing

In the last chapter, we explored the `Process` class and the `java.lang.ProcessHandle` API. In earlier versions of Java, process management from within Java required OS-specific implementations and was less than optimal in terms of CPU use and coding practice. The modern API, with new classes such as `ProcessHandle`, makes it possible to handle almost all aspects of process management. Specifically, we covered an introduction to processes, working with the `ProcessHandle` interface, and reviewed a sample process controller application.

In this chapter, we will focus on Java's `StackWalker` API. The API supports special functionality that is rarely needed by ordinary programs. The API can be useful for some very special cases, such as with functionality that is delivered by a framework. So, if you want an efficient means of stack walking that gives you filterable access to stack trace information, you will enjoy using the `StackWalker` API. The API provides fast and optimized access to the call stack, implementing lazy access to the individual frames.

Specifically, we will cover the following topics:

- Overview of the Java Stack
- The importance of stack information
- Working with `StackWalker`
- `StackFrame`
- Performance

Technical requirements

This chapter, and subsequent chapters, feature Java 18.9, also referred to as Java 11. The Standard Edition (SE) of the Java platform can be downloaded from Oracle's official download site (`http://www.oracle.com/technetwork/java/javase/downloads/index.html`).

An Integrated Development Environment (IDE) software package is sufficient. IntelliJ IDEA, from JetBrains, was used for all coding associated with this chapter and subsequent chapters. The Community version of IntelliJ IDEA can be downloaded from the following site (`https://www.jetbrains.com/idea/features/`).

Overview of the Java Stack

Before we dive into `StackWalker`, let's start by covering the Java Stack. We will review basic stack information, not specific to `StackWalker`.

The Java runtime has a class named `Stack`, which can be used to store objects using the **last-in-first-out** (**LIFO**) policy. Arithmetic expressions are calculated using a stack. If we add *A* and *B* in our code, first *A* is pushed on the **operand stack**, then *B* is pushed on the operand stack and, finally, the addition operation is executed, which fetches the two topmost elements of the operand stack and pushes the result, *A* + *B* there.

The JVM is written in C and executes calling C functions and returning from there. This call-return sequence is maintained using the **Native Method Stack,** just like any other C program.

Finally, when the JVM creates a new thread, it also allocates a call stack containing frames that in turn contain the local variables, a reference to the previous frame, and reference to the class that contains the executing method. When a method is invoked, a new frame is created. The frame is destroyed when a method finishes its execution; in other words, it returns or throws an exception. This stack, the **Java Virtual Machine Stack**, is the one that the `StackWalker` API manages.

The importance of stack information

Generally speaking, we need the stack information when we want to develop caller dependent code. Having information about the caller allows our code to make decisions based on that information. In general practice, it is not a good idea to make functionality dependent on the caller. Information that affects the behavior of a method should be available via parameters. Caller dependent code development should be fairly limited.

The JDK accesses stack information with native methods that are not available to Java applications. The `SecurityManager` class is a class that defines an application's security policy. This class checks that the caller of a reflection API is allowed to access the non-public members of another class. To do that, it has to have access to the caller class and it does that through a protected native method.

This is an example of implementing some security measures without having to walk through a stack. We open our code for external developers to use it as a library. We also call methods of classes provided by the library user and they may call back to our code. There is some code that we want to allow library users to call, but only if they were not called from our code. If we did not want to allow some of the code to be accessed directly by the library using the code, we could use Java's modular structure and not export the package containing the classes not to be invoked. This is the reason we set the extra condition that the code is available for the callers from outside, except if they were called by our code:

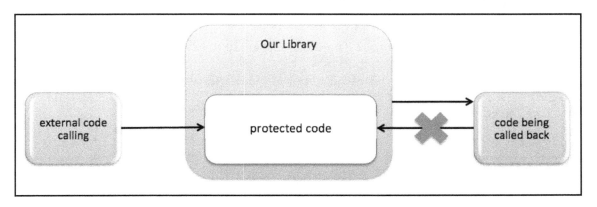

Isolating protected code

Another example is when we want to get access to a logger. Java applications use many different loggers and the logging system is usually very flexible so that the output of the different loggers can be switched on and off based on the actual need to introspect into the code. The most common practice is to use a different logger for each class and the name of the logger is usually the name of the class. The practice is so common that the logging framework even provides logger access methods that accept the reference to the class itself instead of the name. It essentially means that the call to get the handle of a logger looks something like the following:

```
private static final Logger LOG = Logger.getLogger(MyClass.class);
```

A problem can arise when we create new classes from existing classes if we forget to alter the name of the class name in the call for getting a new logger. This is not a serious problem, but it is common. In that case, our code will use the logger of the other class and it will actually work, but may create confusion when we analyze the log files. It would be much nicer if we had a method that returned the logger that is named as the class of the caller.

Let's continue our exploration of stack information in the next two sections with example code snippets.

Example – restricting callers

In this section, we will develop a sample library with two methods. The `hello()` method prints `hello` to the standard output. The `callMe()` method accepts `Runnable` as an argument and runs it. The first method, however, is restricted. It executes only if the caller is purely outside of the library. It throws `IllegalCallerException` if the caller obtained the control in a way that the library was called out, presumably via the second method invoking the passed `Runnable`. The implementation of the API is simple:

```
package packt.java9.deep.stackwalker.myrestrictivelibrary;
public class RestrictedAPI {
  public void hello() {
    CheckEligibility.itIsNotCallBack();
    System.out.println("hello");
  }
  public void callMe(Runnable cb) {
    cb.run();
  }
}
```

The code that performs the eligibility checking is implemented in a separate class to keep things simple; we will examine that code later in this section. First, let's review the main code used to start our demonstration:

```
package packt.java9.deep.stackwalker.externalcode;
import packt.java9.deep.stackwalker.myrestrictivelibrary.RestrictedAPI;

public class DirectCall {
    public static void main(String[] args) {
        RestrictedAPI api = new RestrictedAPI();
        api.hello();
        api.callMe(() -> { api.hello();
        });
    }
}
```

This code creates an instance of our API class and then directly invokes the `hello()` method. It should work and should print the characters `hello` onscreen. The next code line asks the `callMe()` method to call back `Runnable` provided in the form of a Lambda expression. In this case, the call will fail, because the caller is outside but was called from inside the library.

Let's now look at how the eligibility check is implemented:

```
package packt.java9.deep.stackwalker.myrestrictivelibrary;
import static java.lang.StackWalker.Option.RETAIN_CLASS_REFERENCE;

public class CheckEligibility {
    private static final String packageName
        = CheckEligibility.class.getPackageName();
    private static boolean notInLibrary(StackWalker.StackFrame f) {
        return !inLibrary(f);
    }

    private static boolean inLibrary(StackWalker.StackFrame f) {
        return f.getDeclaringClass().getPackageName()
            .equals(packageName);
    }

    public static void itIsNotCallBack() {
        boolean eligible = StackWalker
            .getInstance(RETAIN_CLASS_REFERENCE)
            .walk(s -> s.dropWhile(CheckEligibility::inLibrary)
            .dropWhile(CheckEligibility::notInLibrary)
            .count() == 0
        );
```

```
        if (!eligible) {
          throw new IllegalCallerException();
        }
      }
    }
```

The `itIsNotCallBack()` method is the one called from the `hello()` method. This method creates `StackWalker` and invokes the `walk()` method. The argument of the `walk()` method is a function that converts `Stream` of `StackFrame` objects to some other value that the `walk()` method will return.

At first, this argument setting might seem complex and difficult to understand. It would be more logical to return `Stream` that provides the `StackFrame` objects instead of forcing the caller to define a function that will get this as an argument.

The sample code uses a Lambda expression to define the function as an argument to the `walk()` method. The argument to the Lambda expression is the stream. Since the first element of this stream is the actual call, we drop it. Because these calls should also be refused if the caller is not eligible even though the call to the `hello()` method was through some other class and method that is already inside the library, we drop all elements from the frame that belong to classes inside the package of the `CheckEligibility` class. This package is `packt.java9.deep.stackwalker.myrestrictivelibrary` and in the code, this string is stored in the `packageName` field. The resulting stream contains only the `StackFrame` objects that are from outside of the library. We drop these also until the stream exhausts or until we find `StackFrame` that again belongs to the library. If all the elements were dropped, we are good. In this case, the result of `count()` is zero. If we find a class in `StackFrame` that belongs to the library, it means that the outside code was called from the library and, in this case, we have to refuse to work. In this case, the variable `eligible` will be `false` and we throw an exception, as depicted in the following screenshot:

```
c DirectCall.java      c CheckEligibility.java

       DirectCall  main()   -> Runnable
  1    package packt.java9.deep.stackwalker.externalcode;
  2
  3    import packt.java9.deep.stackwalker.myrestrictivelibrary.RestrictedAPI;
  4
  5 ▶  public class DirectCall {
  6
  7 ▶      public static void main(String[] args) {
  8            RestrictedAPI api = new RestrictedAPI();
  9            api.hello();
 10 ●↑        api.callMe(() -> {
 11                api.hello();|
 12            });
 13        }
 14    }

Run  DirectCall
  ▶  ↑   /Library/Java/JavaVirtualMachines/jdk-9.jdk/Contents/Home/bin/java "-javaagent:/Applications/IntelliJ IDEA CE
     ↓   Exception in thread "main" java.lang.IllegalCallerException
         hello
             at stackwalker/packt.java9.deep.stackwalker.myrestrictivelibrary.CheckEligibility.itIsNotCallBack(CheckEligibility.java:31)
             at stackwalker/packt.java9.deep.stackwalker.myrestrictivelibrary.RestrictedAPI.hello(RestrictedAPI.java:6)
             at stackwalker/packt.java9.deep.stackwalker.externalcode.DirectCall.lambda$main$0(DirectCall.java:11)
             at stackwalker/packt.java9.deep.stackwalker.myrestrictivelibrary.RestrictedAPI.callMe(RestrictedAPI.java:11)
             at stackwalker/packt.java9.deep.stackwalker.externalcode.DirectCall.main(DirectCall.java:10)

         Process finished with exit code 1
```

Class in library found by StackFrame

Example – getting loggers for callers

In Java, we use an API to get `Logger`. Using the API, a module can provide an implementation for the service `LoggerFinder`, which in turn can return `Logger` implementing the `getLogger()` method. This eliminates the dependency of libraries on specific loggers or logger facades, which is a huge advantage. The smaller but still annoying issue requiring us to write the name of the class again as the parameter to the `getLogger()` method remains.

To avoid this cumbersome task, we create a helper class that looks up the caller class and retrieves the logger that is suitable for the caller class and module. Because in this case there is no need for all the classes referenced in the stack trace, we will call the `getCallerClass()` method of the `StackWalker` class. We create a class named `Labrador` in the `packt.java9.deep.stackwalker.logretrieve` package:

```
package packt.java9.deep.stackwalker.logretriever;
import java.lang.System.Logger;
import java.lang.System.LoggerFinder;
import static java.lang.StackWalker.Option.RETAIN_CLASS_REFERENCE;
```

```
public class Labrador {
  public static Logger retrieve() {
    final Class clazz = StackWalker
      .getInstance(RETAIN_CLASS_REFERENCE)
      .getCallerClass();
    return LoggerFinder.getLoggerFinder().getLogger(
      clazz.getCanonicalName(), clazz.getModule());
  }
}
```

Prior to Java 9, the solution for this issue was getting the StackTrace array from the Thread class and looking up the name of the caller class from there. Another approach was extending SecurityManager, which has a protected method, getClassContext(), which returns an array of all the classes on the stack. Both solutions walk through the stack and compose an array although we only need one element from the array. In the case of Logger retrieval, it may not be a significant performance penalty since loggers are usually stored in private static final fields and thus are initialized once per class during class initialization. In other use cases, the performance penalty may be significant.

Next, we will look at the details of StackWalker.

Working with StackWalker

In this section, you will become familiar with how to work with StackWalker. We will explore the following topics in this section:

- Getting an instance of StackWalker
- Enum options
- Accessing classes
- Walking methods

Getting an instance of StackWalker

To perform walking over the stack elements we need an instance of StackWalker. To do that, we invoke the getInstance() method. As shown here, there are four overloaded versions of this method:

- static StackWalker getInstance()
- static StackWalker getInstance(StackWalker.Option option)

- `static StackWalker getInstance(Set<StackWalker.Option> options)`
- `static StackWalker getInstance(Set<StackWalker.Option> options, int estimateDepth)`

The first version does not take any arguments and returns a `StackWalker` instance that will let us walk through normal stack frames. This is usually what we would be interested in. The other versions of the method accept a `StackWalker.Option` value or values. The enum `StackWalker.Option`, as the name suggests, is inside the `StackWalker` class and has three values:

- `RETAIN_CLASS_REFERENCE`
- `SHOW_REFLECT_FRAMES`
- `SHOW_HIDDEN_FRAMES`

Enum options

The `RETAIN_CLASS_REFERENCE`, `SHOW_REFLECT_FRAMES`, and `SHOW_HIDDEN_FRAMES` enum options have self-descriptive names and are explained in the following sections.

RETAIN_CLASS_REFERNCE

If we specify the first option enum constant, `RETAIN_CLASS_REFERENCE`, as an argument to the `getInstance()` method, the returned instance grants us access to the classes that the individual stack frames reference during the walking.

SHOW_REFLECT_FRAMES

The `SHOW_REFLECT_FRAMES` enum constant will generate a walker that includes the frames that source from some reflective calling.

SHOW_HIDDEN_FRAMES

Finally, the enum constant option, `SHOW_HIDDEN_FRAMES` will include all the hidden frames, which contain reflective calls as well as call frames that are generated for Lambda function calls.

Here is a simple demonstration of reflective and hidden frames:

```
package packt;
import static java.lang.StackWalker.Option.SHOW_HIDDEN_FRAMES;
import static java.lang.StackWalker.Option.SHOW_REFLECT_FRAMES;
public class Main {
```

The `main` method allowing us to execute this code directly calls the `simpleCall()` method:

```
public static void main(String[] args) {
  simpleCall();
}
```

The `simpleCall()` method simply calls on, as the name suggests:

```
static void simpleCall() {
  reflectCall();
}
```

The next method in the chain is a bit more complex. Although this also only calls the next one, it does so using reflection:

```
static void reflectCall() {
  try {
    Main.class.getDeclaredMethod("lambdaCall",
      new Class[0]).invoke(null, new Object[0]);
  } catch (Exception e) {
      throw new RuntimeException();
  }
}
```

In this next example, we have a method that calls using a Lambda:

```
static void lambdaCall() {
  Runnable r = () -> {
    walk();
  };
  r.run();
}
```

The last method before the actual walking is called `walk()`:

```
static void walk() {
  noOptions();
  System.out.println();
  reflect();
  System.out.println();
```

```
    hidden();
  }
```

The preceding `walk()` method calls three methods, one after the other. These methods are very similar to each other and are shown here:

```
static void noOptions() {
  StackWalker
    .getInstance()
    .forEach(System.out::println);
}

static void reflect() {
  StackWalker
    .getInstance(SHOW_REFLECT_FRAMES)
    .forEach(System.out::println);
}

static void hidden() {
  StackWalker
    .getInstance(SHOW_HIDDEN_FRAMES)
    .forEach(System.out::println);
}
```

The preceding three methods print out the frames to the standard output. They use the `forEach()` method of `StackWalker`. Here is the output of the stack walking program:

```
stackwalker/packt.Main.noOptions(Main.java:45)
stackwalker/packt.Main.walk(Main.java:34)
stackwalker/packt.Main.lambda$lambdaCall$0(Main.java:28)
stackwalker/packt.Main.lambdaCall(Main.java:30)
stackwalker/packt.Main.reflectCall(Main.java:19)
stackwalker/packt.Main.simpleCall(Main.java:12)
stackwalker/packt.Main.main(Main.java:8)
```

This output only contains the frames that belong to calls that are in our code. The `main()` method calls `simpleCall()`, which calls `reflectCall()`, that in turn calls `lambdaCall()`, which calls a Lambda expression, which calls `walk()`, and so on. The fact that we did not specify any option does not delete the Lambda call from the stack. We performed that call, thus it must be there. What it deletes are the extra stack frames that are needed by the JVM to implement the Lambda. We can see in the next output, when the option was `SHOW_REFLECT_FRAMES`, that the reflective frames are already there:

```
stackwalker/packt.Main.reflect(Main.java:58)
stackwalker/packt.Main.walk(Main.java:36)
stackwalker/packt.Main.lambda$lambdaCall$0(Main.java:28)
stackwalker/packt.Main.lambdaCall(Main.java:30)
```

```
java.base/jdk.internal.reflect.NativeMethodAccessorImpl.invoke0(NativeMetho
d)
java.base/jdk.internal.reflect.NativeMethodAccessorImpl.invoke(NativeMethod
AccessorImpl.java:62)
java.base/jdk.internal.reflect.DelegatingMethodAccessorImpl.invoke(Delegati
ngMethodAccessorImpl.java:43)
java.base/java.lang.reflect.Method.invoke(Method.java:547)
stackwalker/packt.Main.reflectCall(Main.java:19)
stackwalker/packt.Main.simpleCall(Main.java:12)
stackwalker/packt.Main.main(Main.java:8)
```

In this case, the difference is that we can see that the call from the `reflectCall()` method to the `lambdaCall()` method is not direct. The `reflectCall()` method calls the `invoke()` method that calls another method of the same name defined in a different class that in turn calls the `invoke()` method, which is a native method provided by the JVM. After that, we finally get to the `lambdaCall()` method.

In the output, we can also see that these reflective calls belong to the `java.base` module and not our `StackWalker` module.

If we include the hidden frames in addition to the reflective frames, specifying the option `SHOW_HIDDEN_FRAMES`, then we will see the following output:

```
stackwalker/packt.Main.hidden(Main.java:52)
 stackwalker/packt.Main.walk(Main.java:38)
stackwalker/packt.Main.lambda$lambdaCall$0(Main.java:28)
stackwalker/packt.Main$$Lambda$46/269468037.run(Unknown Source)
stackwalker/packt.Main.lambdaCall(Main.java:30)
java.base/jdk.internal.reflect.NativeMethodAccessorImpl.invoke0(NativeMetho
d)
java.base/jdk.internal.reflect.NativeMethodAccessorImpl.invoke(NativeMethod
AccessorImpl.java:62)
java.base/jdk.internal.reflect.DelegatingMethodAccessorImpl.invoke(Delegati
ngMethodAccessorImpl.java:43)
java.base/java.lang.reflect.Method.invoke(Method.java:547)
stackwalker/packt.Main.reflectCall(Main.java:19)
stackwalker/packt.Main.simpleCall(Main.java:12)
stackwalker/packt.Main.main(Main.java:8)
```

This includes an extra hidden frame that the JVM is using to execute the Lambda call. In addition, the reflective frames are also included.

Final thoughts on enum constants

We can also specify more than one option giving a set of the options. The simplest way of doing that is to use the static `of()` method of the `java.util.Set` interface. This way, the `RETAIN_CLASS_REFERENCE` option can be combined with either the `SHOW_REFLECT_FRAMES` option or the `SHOW_HIDDEN_FRAMES` option.

Although it is technically possible to combine `SHOW_REFLECT_FRAMES` and `SHOW_HIDDEN_FRAMES` as an option set, there is really no advantage in doing that. The latter includes the first, so the combination of the two is exactly the same as the second.

Accessing classes

When we want to access the class objects during a stack walk, we have to specify the `RETAIN_CLASS_REFERENCE` option. Although the `StackFrame` interface defines the `getClassName()` method, that could be used to access a class of the name using the `Class.forName()` method, doing so would not guarantee that the class the `StackFrame` object refers to was loaded by the same class loader as the code calling `Class.forName()`. In some special cases, we could end up with two different classes of the same name loaded by two different class loaders.

When the option is not used during the creation of the `StackWalker` instance, the methods that otherwise return a class object will throw an `UnsupportedOperationException` exception. That way, `getDeclaringClass()` cannot be used on `StackFrame` and `getCallerClass()` on `StackWalker`.

Walking methods

The `StackWalker` class defines the `forEach()` method that expects `Consumer` (preferably in the form of a Lambda expression) that is invoked for each element of the stack trace walking up the stack. The argument to the `Consumer` method is a `StackFrame` object.

Although a method named `forEach` is also defined by the `Stream` interface and the `walk()` method passes a `Stream` object to the function it gets as an argument, we should not confuse the two. The `forEach()` method of `StackWalker` is a simpler, and most of the time, a less effective way to get through all the elements of the stack trace.

It is less effective, in most cases, because it forces the StackWalker instance to get all the elements of the stack trace so that the forEach() method can traverse through each element to the end. If we know that we will not traverse through the stack trace to the end, we should use the walk() method that is accessing the stack the lazy way and thus leave more room for performance optimization.

The StackWalker class has the walk() method, which is the defining method that makes it a walker. The method accepts a function that is called by StackWalker. The return value of the walk() method will be the object returned by the function. The argument to the function is Stream<StackFrame> that delivers the stack frames. The first frame is the one that contains the walk() method call, the next is the one that was calling the method that contains the call to walk(), and so on.

The function can be used to calculate some value based on the StackFrame objects that come from the stream and decide if a caller is eligible to call our code or not.

You might wonder, after reviewing the walk() method, which needs a function, which in turn gets a Stream<StackFrame> as an argument, why it is so complicated. Ideally, we would be able to get Stream<StackFrame> directly from the StackWalter instance. The simplest approach would be to pass the stream back from the function. Consider the following example:

```
// EXAMPLE OF WHAT NOT TO DO!!!!
public static void itIsNotCallBack() {
  Stream<StackWalker.StackFrame> stream = StackWalker
    .getInstance(RETAIN_CLASS_REFERENCE)
    .walk(s -> s);
  // The following results in an EXCEPTION
  boolean eligible = stream
    .dropWhile(CheckEligibility::inLibrary)
    .dropWhile(CheckEligibility::notInLibrary)
    .count() == 0;
  if (!eligible) {
    throw new IllegalCallerException();
  }
}
```

What we were doing is simply returning the stream directly from the walker call and walking through it afterward doing the same calculation. Our results are an IllegalStateException exception instead of the eligibility check.

The reason for this is that the implementation of StackWalker is highly optimized. It does not copy the whole stack to provide source information for the stream. It works from the actual, living stack. To do that, it has to be sure that the stack is not modified while the stream is in use. This is something very similar to the ConcurrentModificationException exception that we might get if we alter a collection while we iterate over it. If we passed the stream up in the call stack and then wanted to get StackFrame out of it, the stream would try to get the information from the stack frame that is long gone, since we returned from the method that it belonged to. That way, StackWalker does not make a snapshot of the whole stack but rather it works from the actual one, and it must ensure that the part of the stack it needs does not change. We may call methods from the function and that way we can dig deeper in the call chain, but we cannot get higher while the stream is in use.

The StackWalker class is a final class and cannot be extended.

StackFrame

In previous sections, we iterated through the StackFrame elements and provided sample code snippets. Next, we will examine it more closely. StackFrame is an interface defined inside the StackWalker class. It defines accessors and is a converter that can be used to convert the information to StackTraceElement.

The accessors the interface defines are the following:

- getClassName() will return the binary name of the class of the method represented by StackFrame.
- getMethodName() will return the name of the method represented by StackFrame.
- getDeclaringClass() will return the class of the method represented by StackFrame. If Option.RETAIN_CLASS_REFERENCE was not used during the creation of the StackWalker instance, the method will throw UnsupportedOperationException.

- `getByteCodeIndex()` gets the index to the code array containing the execution point of the method represented by `StackFrame`. The use of this value can be helpful during bug hunting when looking at the disassembled Java code that the command line tool `javap` can give us. The programmatic use of this value can only be valuable for applications that have direct access to the bytecode of the code, Java agents, or libraries that generate bytecode during runtime. The method will return a negative number if the method is native.
- `getFileName()` returns the name of the source file the method represented by `StackFrame` was defined.
- `getLineNumber()` returns the line number of the source code.
- `isNativeMethod()` returns `true` if the method represented by `StackFrame` is native and `false` otherwise.

`StackFrame` does not provide any means to access the object that the method belongs to. You cannot access the arguments and the local variables of the method represented by `StackFrame` and there is no other way you can accomplish that. This is important. Such access would be too invasive and is not possible.

Performance

Our coverage of `StackWalker` would not be complete without a look at performance considerations.

`StackWalker` is highly optimized and does not create huge memory structures that go unused. This is the reason why we have to use that function passed to the `walker()` method as an argument. This is also the reason why `StackTrace` is not automatically converted to `StackTraceElement` when created. This only happens if we query the method name, the line number of the specific `StackTraceElement`. It is important to understand that this conversion takes a significant amount of time, and if it was used for some debugging purpose in the code, it should not be left there.

To make `StackWalker` even faster, we can provide an estimate of the number of `StackFrame` elements that we will work within the stream. If we do not provide such an estimate, the current implementation in the JDK will use eight `StackFrame` objects preallocated and when that is exhausted, the JDK will allocate more. The JDK will allocate the number of elements based on our estimate unless we estimate a value larger than 256. In that case, the JDK will use 256.

Summary

In this chapter, we learned how to use the `StackWalker` API and examined sample code snippets to strengthen our understanding. Our detailed review of the API included different usage scenarios, options, and information. We explored the API's complexity and shared how and how not to use the class. We closed with some related performance issues that developers should be aware of.

In our next chapter, we will cover over a dozen tools and tool enhancements relevant to the modern Java platform. The featured changes will cover a wide range of tools and updates to APIs that are aimed at making developing with Java easier and the ability to create optimized Java applications. We will look at the new HTTP client, changes to the Javadoc and Doclet API, the new JavaScript parser, JAR and JRE changes, the new Java-level JVM compiler interface, support for TIFF images, platform logging, XML catalog support, collections, new platform-specific desktop features, enhancements to method handling, and the depreciation annotation.

Questions

1. How does Java store objects using a stack?
2. What stack does Java use for call return sequences?
3. What stack does the `StackWalker` API manage?
4. How can you retrieve a logger?
5. What class does the `getCallerClass()` method belong to?
6. What are the possible values of the `StackWalker.Option` enum?
7. What is the `RETAIN_CLASS_REFERNCE` enum used for?
8. What is the `SHOW_REFLECT_FRAMES` enum used for?
9. What is the `SHOW_HIDDEN_FRAMES` enum used for?
10. How can the `StackWalker` class be extended?

11
New Tools and Tool Enhancements

In the previous chapter, we learned how to use the `StackWalker` API and examined sample code snippets to strengthen our understanding. Our detailed review of the API included different usage scenarios, options, and information. We explored the API's complexity and shared specifics on class usage. We ended the chapter with a look at performance issues related to the `StackWalker` API.

In this chapter, we will cover over a dozen tools and tool enhancements relevant to the modern Java platform. The featured changes will cover a wide range of tools and updates to APIs that are aimed at making developing with Java easier and enhance the ability to create optimized Java applications.

More specifically, we will review the following topics:

- HTTP client
- Javadoc and the Doclet API
- mJRE changes
- JavaScript parser
- Multiple-release JAR files
- The Java-level JVM compiler interface
- TIFF support
- Platform logging
- XML catalogs
- Collections
- Platform-specific desktop features
- Enhanced method handling
- Enhanced depreciation
- The native header generation tool (`javah`)

Technical requirements

This chapter features Java 11. The **Standard Edition** (**SE**) of the Java platform can be downloaded from Oracle's official download site: `http://www.oracle.com/technetwork/java/javase/downloads/index.html`.

An IDE software package is sufficient. IntelliJ IDEA, from JetBrains, was used for all coding associated with this chapter and subsequent chapters. The Community version of IntelliJ IDEA can be downloaded from the website (`https://www.jetbrains.com/idea/features/`).

This chapter's source code is available at GitHub at the URL (`https://github.com/PacktPublishing/Mastering-Java-11-Second-Edition`).

Working with the HTTP client

In this section, we will review Java's **Hypertext Transfer Protocol** (**HTTP**) client, starting with a look at the old, pre-Java 9 client and then diving into the new HTTP client that is part of the current Java platform. Finally, we will take a look at the limitations of the current HTTP client. This approach is needed to support an understanding of the changes.

The pre-Java 9 HTTP client

JDK version 1.1 introduced the `HttpURLConnection` API that supported HTTP-specific features. This was a robust class that included the following fields:

• chunkLength	• HTTP_LENGTH_REQUIRED	• HTTP_PROXY_AUTH
• fixedContentLength	• HTTP_MOVED_PERM	• HTTP_REQ_TOO_LONG
• fixedContentLengthLong	• HTTP_MOVED_TEMP	• HTTP_RESET
	• HTTP_MULT_CHOICE	• HTTP_SEE_OTHER
• HTTP_ACCEPTED	• HTTP_NO_CONTENT	• HTTP_SERVER_ERROR
• HTTP_BAD_GATEWAY	• HTTP_NOT_ACCEPTABLE	• HTTP_UNAUTHORIZED
• HTTP_BAD_METHOD	• HTTP_NOT_AUTHORITATIVE	• HTTP_UNAVAIABLE
• HTTP_BAD_REQUEST		• HTTP_UNSUPPORTED_TYPE
• HTTP_CLIENT_TIMEOUT	• HTTP_NOT_FOUND	• HTTP_USE_PROXY
• HTTP_CONFLICT	• HTTP_NOT_IMPLEMENTED	• HTTP_VERSION
• HTTP_CREATED	• HTTP_NOT_MODIFIED	• instanceFollowRedirects
• HTTP_ENTITY_TOO_LARGE	• HTTP_OK	• method
• HTTP_FORBIDDEN	• HTTP_PARTIAL	• responseCode
• HTTP_GONE	• HTTP_PAYMENT_REQUIRED	• responseMessage
• HTTP_INTERNAL_ERROR	• HTTP_PRECON_FAILED	

As you can see from the preceding list of fields, there was already great support for HTTP. In addition to a constructor, there are a plethora of available methods, including the following:

- disconnect()
- getErrorStream()
- getFollowRedirects()
- getHeaderField(int n)
- getHeaderFieldDate(String name, long Default)
- getHeaderFieldKey(int n)
- getInstanceFollowRedirects()
- getPermission()
- getRequestMethod()
- getResponseCode()
- getResponseMessage()
- setChunkedStreamingMode(int chunklen)
- setFixedLengthStreamingMode(int contentLength)
- setFixedlengthStreamingMode(long contentLength)
- setFollowRedirects(boolean set)
- setInstanceFollowRedircts(boolean followRedirects)
- setRequestMethod(String method)
- usingProxy()

The class methods listed earlier are in addition to the methods inherited from the `java.net.URLConnection` class and the `java.lang.Object` class.

There were problems with the original HTTP client that made it ripe for updating with the new Java platform. Those problems were as follows:

- The base `URLConnection` API had defunct protocols such as Gopher and FTP becoming an increasing issue over the years
- The `HttpURLConnection` API predated HTTP 1.1 and was overly abstract, making it less usable
- The HTTP client was woefully under documented, making the API frustrating and difficult to use
- The client only functioned on one thread at a time
- The API was extremely difficult to maintain due to it predating HTTP 1.1 and lacking sufficient documentation

Now that we know what was wrong with the previous HTTP client, let's look at the current HTTP client.

The Java 11 HTTP client

There were several goals associated with creating the new HTTP client for the modern Java platform, available with Java 9, 10, and 11. The primary goals are listed in the following table. These goals are presented in the broad categories of ease of use, core capabilities, additional capabilities, and performance:

Ease of use	• The API was designed to provide up to 90 percent of HTTP-related application requirements. • The new API is usable, without unnecessary complexity, for the most common use cases. • A simplistic blocking mode is included. • The API supports modern Java language features. Lambda expressions, a major new introduction released with Java 8, is an example.
Core capabilities	• Support HTTPS/TLS • Supports HTTP/2 • Provides visibility on all details related to HTTP protocol requests and responses • Supports standard/common authentication mechanisms • Provides header received event notifications • Provides response body received event notifications • Provides error event notifications
Additional capabilities	• The new API can be used for WebSocket handshakes • It performs security checks in concert with the current networking API

Performance	• For HTTP/1.1:
	   ○ The new API must perform at least as effectively as the previous API.
	   ○ Memory consumption must not exceed that of Apache HttpClient, Netty, and Jetty, when being used as a client API.
	• For HTTP/2:
	   ○ Performance must exceed that of HTTP/1.1.
	   ○ The new performance must match or exceed that of Netty and Jetty when being used as a client API. Performance degradation should not be a result of the new client.
	   ○ Memory consumption must not exceed that of Apache HttpClient, Netty, and Jetty, when being used as a client API.
	• Avoids running timer threads.

Limitations of the HTTP client API

There are some intentional shortcomings of the HTTP client API. While this might sound counter-intuitive, the new API was not intended to completely replace the current `HttpURLConnection` API. Instead, the new API is intended to eventually replace the current one.

The following code snippet provides an example of how to implement the `HttpURLConnect` class to open and read a URL in a Java application:

```
/*
import statements
*/

public class HttpUrlConnectionExample {
  public static void main(String[] args) {
    new HttpUrlConnectionExample();
  }

  public HttpUrlConnectionExample() {
    URL theUrl = null;
    BufferedReader theReader = null;
    StringBuilder theStringBuilder;

    // put the URL into a String
    String theUrl = "https://www.packtpub.com/";

    // here we are creating the connection
    theUrl = new URL(theUrl);
    HttpURLConnection theConnection = (HttpURLConnection)
      theUrl.openConnection();

    theConnection.setRequestedMethod("GET");
```

```
    // add a delay
    theConnection.setReadTimeout(30000); // 30 seconds
    theConnection.connect();

    // next, we can read the output
    theReader = new BufferedReader(
      new InputStreamReader(theConnection.getInputStream()));
    theStringBuilder = new StringBuilder();

    // read the output one line at a time
    String theLine = null;
    while ((theLine = theReader.readLine() != null) {
      theStringBUilder.append(line + "\n");
    }

    // echo the output to the screen console
    System.out.println(theStringBuilder.toString());

    // close the reader
    theReader.close();
  }
}
. . .
```

 The preceding code does not include exception handling for brevity.

Here are some specific limitations of the new API:

- Not all HTTP-related functionality is supported. It is estimated that about 10 percent of the HTTP's protocol is not exposed by the API.
- Standard/common authentication mechanisms have been limited to basic authentication.
- The overarching goal of the new API was the simplicity of use, which means that performance improvements might not be realized. Certainly, there will be no performance degradation, but it's unlikely that there will be an overwhelming level of improvement, either.
- There is no support for filtering on requests.
- There is no support for filtering on responses.
- The new API does not include a pluggable connection cache.
- There is a lack of a general upgrade mechanism.

Understanding Javadoc and the Doclet API

Javadoc and the Doclet API are closely related. Javadoc is a documentation tool, and the Doclet API provides functionality so that we can inspect the Javadoc comments embedded at the source levels of libraries and programs. In this section, we will review the earlier status of the Doclet API (pre-Java 9) and then explore the changes introduced to the Doclet API in the current Java platform. Finally, we will review Javadoc.

The pre-Java 9 Doclet API

The pre-Java 9 Doclet API, or the `com.sun.javadoc` package, gives us access to look at Javadoc comments located in the source code. Invoking a Doclet is accomplished by using the `start` method. This method's signature is `public static boolean start(RootDoc root)`. We will use the `RootDoc` instance as a container for the program's structure information.

In order to call Javadoc, we need to pass the following:

- Package names
- Source file names (for classes and interfaces)
- An access control option—one of the following:
  - package
  - private
  - protected
  - public

When the preceding listed items are used to call `javadoc`, a documented set is provided as a filtered list. If our aim is to obtain a comprehensive, unfiltered list, we can use `allClasses(false)`.

Let's review an example Doclet:

```
// Mandatory import statement
import com.sun.javadoc.*;

// We will be looking for all the @throws documentation tags
public class AllThrowsTags extends Doclet {

    // This is used to invoke the Doclet.
    public static boolean start(Rootdoc myRoot) {
        // "ClassDoc[]" here refers to classes and interfaces.
```

```
    ClassDoc[] classesAndInterfaces = myRoot.classesAndInterfaces();
    for (int i = 0; i < classesAndInterfaces.length; ++i) {
      ClassDoc tempCD = classesAndInterfaces[i];
      printThrows(tempCD.contructors());
      printThrows(tempCD.methods());
    }
    return true;
  }

  static void printThrows(ExecutableMemberDoc[] theThrows) {
    for (int i = 0; i < theThrows.length; ++i) {
      ThrowsTag[] throws = theThrows[i].throwsTags();
      // Print the "qualified name" which will be
      // the class or interface name
      System.out.println(theThrows[i].qualifiedName());
      // A loop to print all comments with the
      // Throws Tag that belongs to the previously
      // printed class or interface name
      for (int j = 0; j < throws.length; ++j) {
        // A println statement that calls three
        // methods from the ThrowsTag Interface:
        // exceptionType(), exceptionName(),
        // and exceptionComment().
        System.out.println("--> TYPE: " +
          throws[j].exceptionType() +
          " | NAME: " + throws[j].exceptionName() +
          " | COMMENT: " + throws[j].exceptionComment());
      }
    }
  }
}
```

As you can see by the thoroughly commented code, gaining access to the `javadoc` content is relatively easy. In our preceding example, we would invoke the `AllThrows` class by using the following code in the command line:

```
javadoc -doclet AllThrowsTags -sourcepath <source-location> java.util
```

The output of our result will consist of the following structure:

```
<class or interface name>
TYPE: <exception type> | NAME: <exception name> | COMMENT: <exception
comment>
TYPE: <exception type> | NAME: <exception name> | COMMENT: <exception
comment>
TYPE: <exception type> | NAME: <exception name> | COMMENT: <exception
comment>
<class or interface name>
```

```
TYPE: <exception type> | NAME: <exception name> | COMMENT: <exception
comment>
TYPE: <exception type> | NAME: <exception name> | COMMENT: <exception
comment>
```

API enums

The API consists of one enum, `LanguageVersion`, which provides the Java programming language version. The constants for this enum are `Java_1_1` and `Java_1_5`.

API classes

The `Doclet` class provides an example of how to create a class to start a Doclet. It contains an empty `Doclet()` constructor and the following methods:

- `languageVersion()`
- `optionLength(String option)`
- `start(RootDoc root)`
- `validOptions(String[][] options, DocErrorReporter reporter)`

API interfaces

The Doclet API contains the following listed interfaces. The interface names are self-explanatory. You can consult the documentation for additional details:

• AnnotatedType • AnnotationDesc • AnnotationDesc.ElementValuePair • AnnotationTypeDoc • AnnotationTypeElementDoc • AnnotationValue • ClassDoc • ConstructorDoc • Doc	• DoCErrorReporter • ExecutableMemberDoc • FieldDoc • MemberDoc • MethodDoc • PackageDoc • Parameter • ParameterizedType • ParamTag	• ProgramElementDoc • RootDoc • SeeTag • SerialFieldTag • SourcePosition • Tag • ThrowsTag • Type • TypeVariable • WildcardType

Problems with the pre-existing Doclet API

Fueling the need for a new Doclet API were several issues with the pre-existing Doclet API:

- It was not ideal for testing or concurrent usage. This stemmed from its implementation of static methods.
- The language model used in the API had several limitations and became more problematic with each successive Java upgrade.
- The API was inefficient, largely due to its heavy use of substring matching.
- There was no reference provided regarding the specific location of any given comment. This made diagnostics and troubleshooting difficult.

Java 9's Doclet API

Now that you have a good handle on the Doclet API as it existed prior to Java 9, let's look at what changes have been made and delivered with the Java 9 platform. The new Doclet API is in the `jdk.javadoc.doclet` package.

At a high level, the changes to the Doclet API are as follows:

- Updates the `com.sun.javadoc` Doclet API to take advantage of several Java SE and JDK APIs
- Updates the `com.sun.tools.doclets.standard.Standard` Doclet to use the new API
- Supports the updated Taglet API that is used to create custom `javadoc` tags

In addition to the aforementioned changes, the new API uses the following two APIs:

- The compiler tree API
- The language model API

Let's explore each of these in the following sections.

Compiler tree API

The compiler tree API is in the `com.sun.source.doctree` package. It provides several interfaces to document source-level comments. These APIs are represented as **abstract syntax trees (ASTs)**.

There are two enums as follows:

- `AttributeTree.ValueKind`, with the following constants:
  - `DOUBLE`
  - `EMPTY`
  - `SINGLE`
  - `UNQUOTED`

- `DocTree.Kind`, with the following constants:
  - `ATTRIBUTE`
  - `AUTHOR`
  - `CODE`
  - `COMMENT`
  - `DEPRECATED`
  - `DOC_COMMENT`
  - `DOC_ROOT`
  - `END_ELEMENT`
  - `ENTITY`
  - `ERRONEOUS`
  - `EXCEPTION`
  - `IDENTIFIER`
  - `INHERIT_DOC`
  - `LINK`
  - `LINK_PLAIN`
  - `LITERAL`
  - `OTHER`
  - `PARAM`
  - `REFERENCE`
  - `RETURN`
  - `SEE`
  - `SERIAL`
  - `SERIAL_DATA`
  - `SERIAL_FIELD`

- SINCE
- START_ELEMENT
- TEXT
- THROWS
- UNKNOWN_BLOCK_TAG
- UNKNOWN_INLINE_TAG
- VALUE
- VERSION

The `com.sun.source.doctree` package contains several interfaces. They are detailed in the following table:

Interface name	Extends	A tree node for	Non-inherited methods
AttributeTree	DocTree	A HTML element	getName(), getValue(), getValueKind()
AuthorTree	BlockTagTree, DocTree	@author block tag	getName()
BlockTagTree	DocTree	The base class for different types of block tags	getTagName()
CommentTree	DocTree	An embedded HTML comment with the following HTML tags—`<!--text-->`	getBody()
DeprecatedTree	BlockTagTree	@deprecated block tag	getBody()
DocCommentTree	DocTree	Body block tags	getBlockTags(), getBody(), getFirstSentence()
DocRootTree	InlineTagTree	@docroot inline tag	N/A
DocTree	N/A	A common interface for all	accept(DocTreeVisitor<R,D>visitor,Ddata), getKind()
DocTreeVisitor<R,P>	N/A	R = return type of visitor's methods; P = type of the additional parameter	visitAttribute(AttributeTree node, P p), visitAuthor(AuthorTree node, P p), visitComment(CommentTree node, P p), visitDeprecated(DeprecatedTree node, P p), visitDocComment(DocCommentTree node, P p), visitDocRoot(DocRootTree node, P p), visitEndElement(EndElementTree node, P p), visitEntity(EntityTree node, P p), visitErroneous(ErroneousTree node, P p), visitIdentifier(IdentifierTree node, P p), visitInheritDoc(InheritDocTree node, P p), visitLink(LinkTree node, P p), visitLiteral(LiteralTree node, P p), visitOther(DocTree node, P p), visitParam(ParamTree node, P p), visitReference(ReferenceTree node, P p), visitReturn(ReturnTree node, P p), visitSee(SeeTree node, P p), visitSerial(SerialTree node, P p), visitSerialData(SerialDataTree node, P p), visitSerialField(SerialFieldTree node, P p), visitSince(SinceTree node, P p), visitStartElement(StartElementTree node, P p), visitText(TextTree node, P p), visitThrows(ThrowsTree node, P p), visitUnknownBlockTag(UnknownBlockTagTree node, P p), visitUnknownInlineTag(UnknownInlineTagTree node, P p), visitValue(ValueTree node, P p), visitVersion(VersionTree node, P p)
EndElementTree	DocTree	End of an HTML element `</name>`	getName()
EntityTree	DocTree	An HTML entity	getName()

ErroneousTree	TextTree	This is for malformed text	getDiagnostic()
IdentifierTree	DocTree	An identifier in a comment	getName()
InheritDocTree	InlineTagTree	@inheritDoc inline tag	N/A
InlineTagTree	DocTree	A common interface for inline tags	getTagName()
LinkTree	InlineTagTree	@link or @linkplan inline tags	getLabel(), getReference()
LiteralTree	InlineTagTree	@literal or @code inline tags	getBody()
ParamTree	BlockTagTree	@param block tags	getDescription(),getName(),isTypeParameter()
ReferenceTree	DocTree	Used to reference a Java lang element	getSignature()
ReturnTree	BlockTagTree	@return block tags	getDescription()
SeeTree	BlockTagTree	@see block tags	getReference()
SerialDataTree	BlockTagTree	@serialData block tags	getDescription()
SerialFieldTree	BlockTagTree	@serialData block tags and @serialField field names and descriptions	getDescription(),getName(),getType()
SerialTree	BlockTagTree	@serial block tags	getDescription()
SinceTree	BlockTagTree	@since block tags	getBody()
StartElementTree	DocTree	Start of an HTML element < name [attributes] [/] >	getAttributes(),getName(),isSelfClosing()
TextTree	DocTree	Plain text	getBody()
ThrowsTree	BlockTagTree	@exception or @throws block tags	getDescription(), getExceptionname()
UnknownBlockTagTree	BlockTagTree	Unrecognized inline tags	getContent()
UnknownInlineTagTree	InlineTagTree	Unrecognized inline tags	getContent()
ValueTree	InlineTagTree	@value inline tags	getReference()
VersionTree	BlockTagTree	@version block tags	getBody()

Language model API

The language model API is in the `java.lang.model` package. It includes packages and classes that are used for language processing and language modeling. It consists of the following components:

- The `AnnotatedConstruct` interface
- The `SourceVersion` enum
- The `UnknownEntityException` exception

Each of these language model API components is further explored in the following three sections.

The AnnotatedConstruct interface

The `AnnotatedConstruction` interface provides an annotatable construct to the language model API that has been part of the Java platform since version 1.8. It is applicable to constructs that are either an element (Interface `Element`) or a type (Interface `TypeMirror`). The annotations for each of these constructs differ, as shown in the following table:

Construct type	Interface	Annotation
element	Element	Declaration
type	TypeMirror	Based on the use of a type name

The `AnnotatedConstruction` interface has three methods:

- `getAnnotation(Class<A> annotationType)`: This method returns the type of the construct's annotation
- `getAnnotationMirrors()`: This method returns a list of annotations that are on the construct
- `getAnnotationsByType(Class<A> annotationType)`: This method returns the construct's associated annotations

The SourceVersion enum

The `SourceVersion` enum consists of the following constants:

- `RELEASE_0`
- `RELEASE_1`
- `RELEASE_2`
- `RELEASE_3`
- `RELEASE_4`
- `RELEASE_5`
- `RELEASE_6`
- `RELEASE_7`
- `RELEASE_8`
- `RELEASE_9`

 It is anticipated that the `SourceVersion` enum will be updated to include `RELEASE_10` and `RELEASE_11`, as these versions of the Java platform are officially released.

This enum also contains several methods, which are as follows:

Method name: isIdentifier:

```
public static boolean isIdentifier(CharSequence name)
```

This method returns true if the parameter string is a Java identifier or keyword.

Method name: isKeyword:

```
public static boolean isKeyword(CharSequence s)
```

This method returns true if the given CharSequence is a literal or keyword.

Method name: isName:

```
public static boolean isName(CharSequence name)
```

This method returns true if the CharSequence is a valid name.

Method name: latest:

```
public static SourceVersion latest()
```

This method returns the latest source version for modeling purposes.

Method name: latestSupported:

```
public static SourceVersion latestSupported()
```

This method returns the latest source version that can be fully supported for modeling.

Method name: valueOf:

```
public static SourceVersion valueOf(String name)
```

This method returns the enum constant based on the parameter string provided.

 You should be aware that the value(String name) method throws two exceptions: IllegalArgumentException and NullPointerException.

Method name: values:

```
public static SourceVersion[] values()
```

This method returns an array of the enum constants.

The UnknownEntityException exception

The `UnknownEntityException` class extends `RuntimeException` and is a superclass of unknown exceptions. The class constructor is as follows:

```
protected UnknownEntityException(String message)
```

The constructor creates a new instance of `UnknownEntityException` with the message provided as a string argument. The method does not take additional arguments.

This class does not have its own methods, but inherits methods from both the `java.lang.Throwable` and `class.java.lang.Object` classes, as shown here:

The `java.lang.Throwable` class methods are as follows:

- `addSuppressed()`
- `fillInStackTrace()`
- `getCause()`
- `getLocalizedMessage()`
- `getMessage()`
- `getStackTrace()`
- `getSuppressed()`
- `initCause()`
- `printStackTrace()`
- `setStackTrace()`
- `toString()`

The `java.lang.Object` class methods are as follows:

- `clone()`
- `equals()`
- `finalize()`
- `getClass()`
- `hashCode()`
- `notify()`
- `notifyAll()`
- `wait()`

Using the HTML5 Javadoc

The Javadoc tool has been updated for the modern Java platform, defined as Java 9 and later. It can generate HTML 5 markup output in addition to HTML 4. The Javadoc tool provides support for both HTML 4 and HTML 5. HTML 5, as of Java 10, is the default output markup format.

The following short Java application simply generates a 319-wide by 319-high frame. It is shown here without any Javadoc tags, which we will discuss later in this section:

```java
import javax.swing.JFrame;
import javax.swing.WindowConstants;

public class JavadocExample {

  public static void main(String[] args) {
    drawJFrame();
  }

  public static void drawJFrame() {
    JFrame myFrame = new JFrame("Javadoc Example");
    myFrame.setSize(319,319);
    myFrame.setDefaultCloseOperation(
      WindowConstants.EXIT_ON_CLOSE);
    myFrame.setVisible(true);
  }
}
```

Once your package or class is completed, you can generate a Javadoc using the Javadoc tool. You can run the Javadoc tool, located in your JDK /bin directory, from the command line or from within your IDE. Each IDE handles Javadoc generation differently. For example, in Eclipse, you would select **Project** from the drop-down menu and then choose **Generate Javadoc**. In the IntelliJ IDEA IDE, you select the **Tools** drop-down menu and then choose **Generate Javadoc**.

The following screenshot shows the IntelliJ IDEA interface for the **Generate Javadoc** functionality. As you can see, the `-html5` command-line argument has been included:

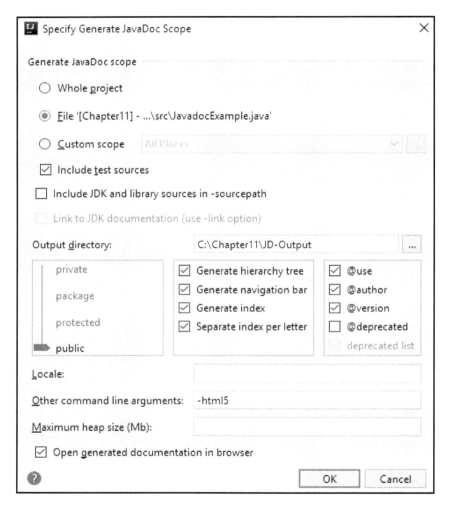

Generate Javadoc

When the **OK** button is clicked, you will see a series of status messages, as shown in the following example:

```
"C:\Program Files\Java\jdk-9\bin\javadoc.exe" -public -splitindex -use -
author -version -nodeprecated -html5
@C:\Users\elavi\AppData\Local\Temp\javadoc1304args.txt -d
C:\Chapter11\JDOutput
Loading source file C:\Chapter11\src\JavadocExample.java...
Constructing Javadoc information...
Standard Doclet version 9
Building tree for all the packages and classes...
Generating C:\Chapter11\JD-Output\JavadocExample.html...
Generating C:\Chapter11\JD-Output\package-frame.html...
Generating C:\Chapter11\JD-Output\package-summary.html...
Generating C:\Chapter11\JD-Output\package-tree.html...
Generating C:\Chapter11\JD-Output\constant-values.html...
Generating C:\Chapter11\JD-Output\class-use\JavadocExample.html...
Generating C:\Chapter11\JD-Output\package-use.html...
Building index for all the packages and classes...
Generating C:\Chapter11\JD-Output\overview-tree.html...
Generating C:\Chapter11\JD-Output\index-files\index-1.html...
Generating C:\Chapter11\JD-Output\index-files\index-2.html...
Generating C:\Chapter11\JD-Output\index-files\index-3.html...
Building index for all classes...
Generating C:\Chapter11\JD-Output\allclasses-frame.html...
Generating C:\Chapter11\JD-Output\allclasses-frame.html...
Generating C:\Chapter11\JD-Output\allclasses-noframe.html...
Generating C:\Chapter11\JD-Output\allclasses-noframe.html...
Generating C:\Chapter11\JD-Output\index.html...
Generating C:\Chapter11\JD-Output\help-doc.html...
javadoc exited with exit code 0
```

Once the Javadoc tool exits, you are ready to view the Javadoc. Here is a screenshot of what was generated based on the previously provided code. As you can see, it is formatted in the same manner in which the formal Java documentation from Oracle is documented:

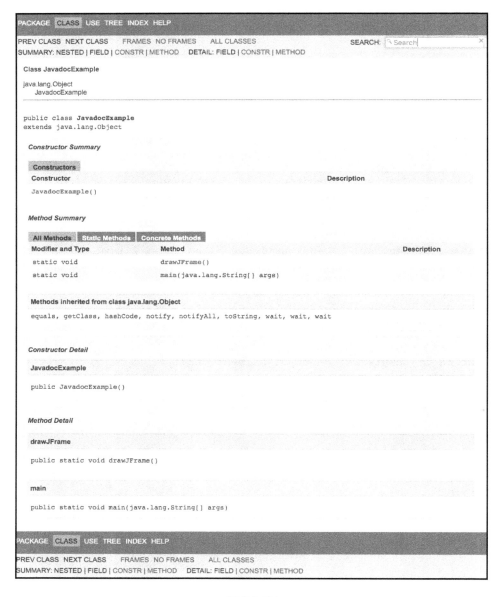

Sample Javadoc

When we generated the Javadoc, multiple documents were created, as illustrated by the directory tree provided in the following screenshot:

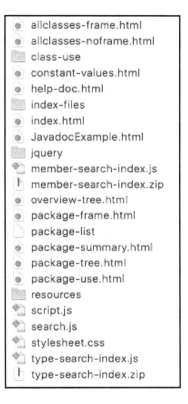

Javadoc directory tree

You can also add optional tags that are recognized by the Javadoc tool. These tags are provided here:

- @author
- @code
- @deprecated
- @docRoot
- @exception
- @inheritDoc
- @link
- @linkplain

- @param
- @return
- @see
- @serial
- @serialData
- @serialField
- @since
- @throws
- @value
- @version

> For more information on how to write document comments for the Javadoc tool, you can visit Oracle's official instructions at http://www.oracle.com/technetwork/articles/java/index-137868.html.

Javadoc search

Prior to Java 9, the standard Doclet generated API documentation pages were difficult to navigate. Unless you were very familiar with the layout of these documentation pages, you would have likely used the browser-based find functionality to search text. This was considered clunky and suboptimal.

The current platform includes a search box as part of the API documentation. This search box is granted by the standard Doclet and can be used to search for text within the documentation. This represents a great convenience for developers and is likely to change our usage of Doclet-generated documentation.

With the new Javadoc search functionality, we have the ability to search for the following indexed components:

- Module names
- Package names
- Types
- Members
- Terms/phrases that are indexed by using the new @index inline tag

Introducing Camel Case search

The Javadoc search functionality includes a great shortcut by using Camel Case search. As an example, we can search for `openED` to find the `openExternalDatabase()` method.

Changes to the Multiple JRE feature

The **mJRE** (short for **Multiple JRE**) feature was previously used to specify a specific JRE version, or range of versions, for launching our applications. We would accomplish this via the command-line option `-version` or with an entry in the JAR file's manifest. The following flowchart illustrates what happens based on our selection:

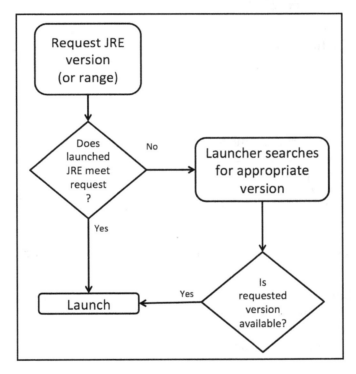

Multiple JRE flow

This functionality was introduced with JDK 5 and was not fully documented in that release or any subsequent release prior to JDK 9.

The following specific changes were introduced with the modern platform:

- The mJRE feature has been removed.
- The launcher will now produce an error whenever the `-version` command-line option is used. This is a Terminal error in that processing will not continue.
- In Java 9, a warning will be produced if there is a `-version` entry in a JAR's manifest. The warning will not stop the execution.
- In Java 10 and 11, the presence of a `-version` entry in a manifest file will result in a Terminal error.

JavaScript Parser

A recent change to the Java platform was the creation of an API for Nashorn's ECMAScript AST. In this section, we will individually look at Nashorn, ECMAScript, and then at the Parser API.

Nashorn

Oracle Nashorn is a JavaScript engine for the JVM that was developed in Java by Oracle. It was released with Java 8 and was created to provide developers with a highly efficient and lightweight JavaScript runtime engine. Using this engine, developers were able to embed JavaScript code in their Java applications. Prior to Java 8, developers had access to the JavaScript engine that was created by Netscape. That engine, introduced in 1997, was maintained by Mozilla.

Nashorn can be used both as a command-line tool and as an embedded interpreter in Java applications. Let's look at examples of both.

 Nashorn is the German word for rhinoceros. The name spawned from the Rhino-named JavaScript engine from the Mozilla Foundation. Rhino is said to have originated from the picture of the animal on a JavaScript book cover. File this one under interesting facts.

Using Nashorn as a command-line tool

The Nashorn executable file, `jjs.exe`, resides in the `\bin` folder. To access it, you can navigate to that folder or, if your system path is set up appropriately, you can launch into the shell by entering the `jjs` command in a Terminal/Command Prompt window on your system:

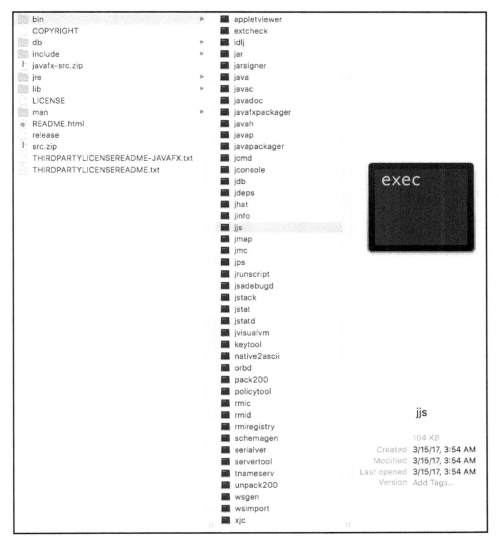

Location of the Nashorn executable file

Here, you can see an open Terminal window that first checks the version of Java and then uses the `jjs -version` command to launch the Nashorn shell. In this example, both Java and Nashorn are of version 1.8.0.121. Alternatively, we can simply launch Nashorn with the `jjs` command, and the shell will open without the version identification:

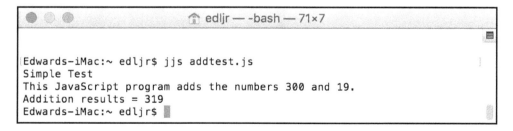

```
Edwards-iMac:~ edljr$ java -version
java version "1.8.0_121"
Java(TM) SE Runtime Environment (build 1.8.0_121-b13)
Java HotSpot(TM) 64-Bit Server VM (build 25.121-b13, mixed mode)
Edwards-iMac:~ edljr$ jjs -version
nashorn 1.8.0_121
jjs>
```

Launching Nashorn with the jjs command

Next, let's create a short JavaScript and run it using Nashorn. Consider the following simple JavaScript code that has three simple lines of output:

```
var addtest = function() {
  print("Simple Test");
  print("This JavaScript program adds the
    numbers 300 and 19.");
  print("Addition results = " + (300 + 19));
}
addtest();
```

To have Java run this JavaScript application, we will use the `jjs addtest.js` command. Here is the output:

```
Edwards-iMac:~ edljr$ jjs addtest.js
Simple Test
This JavaScript program adds the numbers 300 and 19.
Addition results = 319
Edwards-iMac:~ edljr$
```

Running a JavaScript with Java

There is a lot you can do with Nashorn. From the Terminal/Command Prompt window, we can execute `jjs` with the `-help` option to view a full list of command-line commands:

```
● ● ●                        🏠 edljr — -bash — 105×47

[Edwards-iMac:~ edljr$ jjs -help
jjs [<options>] <files> [-- <arguments>]
        -D (-Dname=value. Set a system property. This option can be repeated.)

        -cp, -classpath (-cp path. Specify where to find user class files.)

        -doe, -dump-on-error (Dump a stack trace on errors.)
                param: [true|false]    default: false

        -fv, -fullversion (Print full version info of Nashorn.)
                param: [true|false]    default: false

        -fx (Launch script as an fx application.)
                param: [true|false]    default: false

        -h, -help (Print help for command line flags.)
                param: [true|false]    default: false

        --language (Specify ECMAScript language version.)
                param: [es5|es6]    default: es5

        -ot, --optimistic-types (Use optimistic type assumptions with deoptimizing recompilation.
                                This makes the compiler try, for any program symbol whose type cannot
                                be proven at compile time, to type it as narrow and primitive as
                                possible. If the runtime encounters an error because symbol type
                                is too narrow, a wider method will be generated until steady stage
                                is reached. While this produces as optimal Java Bytecode as possible,
                                erroneous type guesses will lead to longer warmup. Optimistic typing
                                is currently disabled by default, but can be enabled for significantly
                                better peak performance.)
                param: [true|false]    default: false

        -scripting (Enable scripting features.)
                param: [true|false]    default: false

        -strict (Run scripts in strict mode.)
                param: [true|false]    default: false

        -t, -timezone (Set timezone for script execution.)
                param: <timezone>    default: America/Chicago

        -v, -version (Print version info of Nashorn.)
                param: [true|false]    default: false

Edwards-iMac:~ edljr$ █
```

The -help component

As you can see, using the -scripting option gives us the ability to create scripts by using Nashorn as a text editor. There are several built-in functions that are useful when using Nashorn:

- echo(): This is similar to a System.out.print() Java method
- exit(): This exits Nashorn
- load(): This loads a script from a given path or URL

- `print()`: This is similar to a `System.out.print()` Java method
- `readFull()`: This reads a file's contents
- `readLine()`: This reads a single line from `stdin`
- `quit()`: This exits Nashorn

Using Nashorn as an embedded interpreter

A more common use of Nashorn, compared to using it as a command-line tool, is using it as an embedded interpreter. The `javax.script` API is public and can be accessed via the `nashorn` identifier. The following code demonstrates how we can gain access to Nashorn, define a JavaScript function, and obtain the results, all from within a Java application:

```
// required imports
import javax.script.ScriptEngine;
import javax.script.ScriptEngineManager;

public class EmbeddedAddTest {
  public static void main(String[] args)
    throws Throwable {
    // instantiate a new ScriptEngineManager
    ScriptEngineManager myEngineManager =
      new ScriptEngineManager();

    // instantiate a new Nashorn ScriptEngine
    ScriptEngine myEngine = myEngineManager.
      getEngineByName("nashorn");

    // create the JavaScript function
    myEngine.eval("function addTest(x, y)
      { return x + y; }");

    // generate output including a call to the
    // addTest function via the engine
    System.out.println("The addition results are:
      " + myEngine.eval("addTest(300, 19);"));
  }
}
```

Here is the output that's provided in the console window:

```
Problems   Javadoc   Declaration   Console ⊠
<terminated> EmbeddedAddTest [Java Application] /Library/Java/JavaVirtualMachines/jdk1.8.0_131.jdk/Contents/Home/bin/java (Aug 8, 2017, 1:44:24 PM)
The addition results are: 319.0
```

Console output

This is a simplistic example to give you an idea of what is possible with the embedded use of Nashorn. There are ample examples in Oracle's official documentation.

ECMAScript

The **ECMA** (short for **European Computer Manufacturers Association**) was formed in 1961 as a standards organization for both information systems and communications systems. Today, the ECMA continues to develop standards and issue technical reports to help standardize how consumer electronics, information systems, and communications technologies are used. There are over 400 ECMA standards, most of which have been adopted.

 You will notice that ECMA is not spelled with all capital letters as it is no longer considered an acronym. In 1994, the **European Computer Manufacturers Association** formally changed its name to **ECMA**.

ECMAScript, also referred to as ES, was created in 1997 as a scripted language specification. JavaScript implements this specification, which includes the following:

- Complementary technologies
- Libraries
- Scripting language syntax
- Semantics

Parser API

One of the most recent changes to the Java platform was to provide specific support for Nashorn's ECMAScript abstract syntax tree. The goals of the new API are to provide the following:

- Interfaces to represent Nashorn syntax tree nodes
- The ability to create parser instances that can be configured with command-line options
- A visitor pattern API for interfacing with AST nodes
- Test programs to use the API

The new API, `jdk.nashorn.api.tree`, was created to permit future changes to the Nashorn classes. Prior to the new Parser API, IDEs used Nashorn's internal AST representations for code analysis. According to Oracle, use of the `jdk.nashorn.internal.ir` package prevented the modernization of Nashorn's internal classes.

Here is a look at the class hierarchy of the new `jdk.nashorn.api.tree` package:

Class Hierarchy

- java.lang.**Object**
  - jdk.nashorn.api.tree.**SimpleTreeVisitorES5_1**<R,P> (implements jdk.nashorn.api.tree.TreeVisitor<R,P>)
    - jdk.nashorn.api.tree.**SimpleTreeVisitorES6**<R,P>
  - java.lang.**Throwable** (implements java.io.Serializable)
    - java.lang.**Exception**
      - java.lang.**RuntimeException**
        - jdk.nashorn.api.tree.**UnknownTreeException**

The jdk.nashorn.api.tree class hierarchy

The following graphic illustrates the complexity of the new API, featuring a full interface hierarchy:

Interface Hierarchy

- jdk.nashorn.api.tree.**Diagnostic**
- jdk.nashorn.api.tree.**DiagnosticListener**
- jdk.nashorn.api.tree.**LineMap**
- jdk.nashorn.api.tree.**Parser**
- jdk.nashorn.api.tree.**Tree**
  - jdk.nashorn.api.tree.**CaseTree**
  - jdk.nashorn.api.tree.**CatchTree**
  - jdk.nashorn.api.tree.**CompilationUnitTree**
  - jdk.nashorn.api.tree.**ExportEntryTree**
  - jdk.nashorn.api.tree.**ExpressionTree**
    - jdk.nashorn.api.tree.**ArrayAccessTree**
    - jdk.nashorn.api.tree.**ArrayLiteralTree**
    - jdk.nashorn.api.tree.**AssignmentTree**
    - jdk.nashorn.api.tree.**BinaryTree**
    - jdk.nashorn.api.tree.**ClassExpressionTree**
    - jdk.nashorn.api.tree.**CompoundAssignmentTree**
    - jdk.nashorn.api.tree.**ConditionalExpressionTree**
    - jdk.nashorn.api.tree.**ErroneousTree**
    - jdk.nashorn.api.tree.**FunctionCallTree**
    - jdk.nashorn.api.tree.**FunctionExpressionTree**
    - jdk.nashorn.api.tree.**IdentifierTree**
    - jdk.nashorn.api.tree.**InstanceOfTree**
    - jdk.nashorn.api.tree.**LiteralTree**
    - jdk.nashorn.api.tree.**MemberSelectTree**
    - jdk.nashorn.api.tree.**NewTree**
    - jdk.nashorn.api.tree.**ObjectLiteralTree**
    - jdk.nashorn.api.tree.**ParenthesizedTree**
    - jdk.nashorn.api.tree.**RegExpLiteralTree**
    - jdk.nashorn.api.tree.**SpreadTree**
    - jdk.nashorn.api.tree.**TemplateLiteralTree**
    - jdk.nashorn.api.tree.**UnaryTree**
    - jdk.nashorn.api.tree.**YieldTree**
  - jdk.nashorn.api.tree.**ImportEntryTree**
  - jdk.nashorn.api.tree.**ModuleTree**
  - jdk.nashorn.api.tree.**PropertyTree**
  - jdk.nashorn.api.tree.**StatementTree**
    - jdk.nashorn.api.tree.**BlockTree**
    - jdk.nashorn.api.tree.**ClassDeclarationTree**
    - jdk.nashorn.api.tree.**DebuggerTree**
    - jdk.nashorn.api.tree.**EmptyStatementTree**
    - jdk.nashorn.api.tree.**ExpressionStatementTree**
    - jdk.nashorn.api.tree.**FunctionDeclarationTree**
    - jdk.nashorn.api.tree.**GotoTree**
      - jdk.nashorn.api.tree.**BreakTree**
      - jdk.nashorn.api.tree.**ContinueTree**
    - jdk.nashorn.api.tree.**IfTree**
    - jdk.nashorn.api.tree.**LabeledStatementTree**
    - jdk.nashorn.api.tree.**LoopTree**
      - jdk.nashorn.api.tree.**ConditionalLoopTree**
        - jdk.nashorn.api.tree.**DoWhileLoopTree**
        - jdk.nashorn.api.tree.**ForLoopTree**
        - jdk.nashorn.api.tree.**WhileLoopTree**
      - jdk.nashorn.api.tree.**ForInLoopTree**
      - jdk.nashorn.api.tree.**ForOfLoopTree**
    - jdk.nashorn.api.tree.**ReturnTree**
    - jdk.nashorn.api.tree.**SwitchTree**
    - jdk.nashorn.api.tree.**ThrowTree**
    - jdk.nashorn.api.tree.**TryTree**
    - jdk.nashorn.api.tree.**VariableTree**
    - jdk.nashorn.api.tree.**WithTree**
- jdk.nashorn.api.tree.**TreeVisitor<R,P>**

Nashorn interface hierarchy

The last component of the `jdk.nashorn.api.tree` package is the enum hierarchy, which is shown here:

```
Enum Hierarchy

  ○ java.lang.Object
      ○ java.lang.Enum<E> (implements java.lang.Comparable<T>, java.io.Serializable)
          ○ jdk.nashorn.api.tree.Diagnostic.Kind
          ○ jdk.nashorn.api.tree.Tree.Kind
```

Enum hierarchy

Multiple-release JAR files

The JAR file format has been extended in the Java platform and now permits multiple versions of class files to exist in a single JAR file. The class versions can be specific to a Java release version. This enhancement allows developers to use a single JAR file to house multiple releases of their software.

The JAR file enhancement includes the following:

- Support for the `JarFile` API
- Support for standard class loaders

The changes to the JAR file format resulted in necessary changes to core Java tools so that they are able to interpret the new multiple-release JAR files. These core tools include the following:

- `javac`
- `javap`
- `jdeps`

Finally, the new JAR file format supports modularity as the key characteristic of the modern Java platform. The changes to the JAR file format have not resulted in a reduced performance of the related tools or processes.

Identifying multi-release JAR files

Multi-release JAR files will have a new attribute, `Multi-Release: true`. This attribute will be located in the JAR `MANIFEST.MF` main section.

The directory structure will differ between standard JAR files and multi-release JAR files. Here is a look at a typical JAR file structure:

```
jar root
      Apple.class
      Banana.class
      Coconut.class
      Dragonfruit.class
      Elderberry.class
```

Javadoc directory tree

The following illustration shows the new multi-release JAR file structure with Java version-specific class files for both Java 8 and Java 9:

```
jar root
      Apple.class
      Banana.class
      Coconut.class
      Dragonfruit.class
      Elderberry.class
      META-INF
            versions
                  8
                        Apple.class
                        Banana.class
                        Coconut.class
                        Dragonfruit.class
                        Elderberry.class
                  9
                        Apple.class
                        Banana.class
                        Coconut.class
                        Dragonfruit.class
                        Elderberry.class
```

JAR file structure

Related JDK changes

Several changes had to be made to the JDK to support the new multi-release JAR file format. These changes include the following:

- The `URLClassLoader` is JAR-based and was modified so that it can read class files from the specified version.
- The new module-based class loader, new to Java 9, was written so that it can read class files from the specified version.
- The `java.util.jar.JarFile` class was modified so that it selects the appropriate class version from the multi-release JAR files.
- The JAR URL scheme's protocol handler was modified so that it selects the appropriate class version from the multi-release JAR files.
- The Java compiler, `javac`, was made to read identified versions of the class files. These version identifications are made by using the `-target` and `-release` command-line options with the `JavacFileManager` API and the `ZipFileSystem` API.
- The following tools were modified to take advantage of the changes to the `JavacFileManager` API and the `ZipFileSystem` API:
    - `javah`: This generates C header and source files
    - `schemagen`: This is the schema generator for namespaces in Java classes
    - `wsgen`: This is the parser for web service deployment

- The `javap` tool was updated to support the new versioning schema.
- The `jdeps` tool was modified to support the new versioning schema.
- The JAR packing tool set was updated accordingly. This toolset consists of `pack200` and `unpack200`.
- Of course, the JAR tool was enhanced so that it can create the multi-release JAR files.

All related documentation has been updated to support all the changes involved in establishing and supporting the new multi-release JAR file format.

Java-level JVM Compiler Interface

The Java-based **JVM Compiler Interface (JVMCI)** enables a Java compiler (which must have been written in Java) to be used as a dynamic compiler by the JVM.

The reasoning behind the desire for the JVMCI is that it would be a highly optimized compiler that does not require low-level language features. Some JVM subsystems require low-level functionality, such as with garbage collection and bytecode interpretation. So, the JVMCI was written in Java instead of C or C++. This provides the collateral benefit of some of Java's greatest features, such as the following:

- Exception handling
- IDEs that are both free and robust
- Memory management
- Runtime extensibility
- Synchronization
- Unit testing support

As JVMCI was written in Java, it is arguably easier to maintain.

There are three primary components of the JVMCI API:

- Virtual machine data structure access
- Installing compiled code with its metadata
- Using the JVM's compilation system

The JVMCI actually existed, to some extent, in Java 8. The JVMCI API was only accessible via a class loader that worked for code on the boot classpath. In Java 9, this changed. It is still experimental in the current Java platform, but more accessible. In order to enable the JVMCI, the following series of command-line options must be used:

```
-XX:+UnlockExperimentalVMOptions -XX:+EnableJVMCI -XX:+UseJVMCICompiler -
Djvmci.Compiler=<name of compiler>
```

Oracle is keeping the JVMCI experimental in Java 9 to permit further testing and to afford the greatest level of protection for developers.

BeanInfo annotations

The @beaninfo Javadoc tags have been replaced with more appropriate annotations. Furthermore, these new annotations are now processed at runtime so that BeanInfo classes can be generated dynamically. The modularity of Java resulted in this change. The creation of custom BeanInfo classes has been simplified and the client library has been modularized.

In order to fully grasp this change, we will review JavaBean, BeanProperty, and SwingContainer before going any further into this JEP.

JavaBean

A JavaBean is a Java class. Like other Java classes, JavaBeans are reusable code. They are unique in their design because they encapsulate several objects into one. There are three conventions that a JavaBean class must follow:

- The constructor should not take any arguments
- It must be serializable
- It must contain mutator and accessor methods for its properties

Here is an example JavaBean class:

```
public class MyBean implements java.io.Serializable {

  // instance variables
  private int studentId;
  private String studentName;

  // no-argument constructor
  public MyBean() {
  }

  // mutator/setter
  public void setStudentId(int theID) {
    this.studentId = theID;
  }

  // accessor/getter
  public int getStudentId() {
    return studentId;
  }

  // mutator/setter
```

```
    public void setStudentName(String theName) {
      this.studentName = theName;
    }

    // accessor/getter
    public String getStudentName(){
      return studentName;
    }
  }
```

Accessing JavaBean classes is as simple as using the mutator and accessor methods. This is likely not new to you, but there is a good chance you did not know that those carefully coded classes you created were called JavaBean classes.

BeanProperty

BeanProperty is an annotation type. We use this annotation to specify a property so that we can automatically generate BeanInfo classes. This is a relatively new annotation for Java, starting with Java 9.

The BeanProperty annotation has the following optional elements:

- boolean bound
- String description
- String[] enumerationValues
- boolean expert
- boolean hidden
- boolean preferred
- boolean required
- boolean visualUpdate

SwingContainer

SwingContainer is an annotation type. We use this annotation to specify a swing-related property so that we can automatically generate BeanInfo classes.

The SwingContainer annotation has the following optional elements:

- String delegate
- boolean value

Now that we have reviewed `JavaBean`, `BeanProperty`, and `SwingContainer`, let's take a look at the `BeanInfo` classes.

BeanInfo classes

For the most part, `BeanInfo` classes are automatically generated at runtime. The exception is with `Swing` classes. These classes generate `BeanInfo` classes based on the `@beaninfo` Javadoc tags. This is done at compile time, not runtime. Starting with Java 9, the `@beaninfo` tags have been replaced with the `@interface JavaBean`, `@interface BeanProperty`, and `@interface SwingContainer` annotations.

These new annotations are used to set the corresponding attributes based on the optional elements noted in the previous sections. As an example, the following code snippet sets the attributes for `SwingContainer`:

```
package javax.swing;

public @interface SwingContainer {
  boolean value() default false;
  String delegate() default "";
}
```

This provides us with three benefits:

- It will be much easier to specify attributes in `Bean` classes instead of having to create individual `BeanInfo` classes
- We will be able to remove autogenerated classes
- The client library is much more easily modularized with this approach

TIFF support

The image input/output plugins have been extended for the modern Java platform to include support for the TIFF image format. The `ImageIO` class extends the `Object` class and is part of Java SE. The class contains several methods for encoding and decoding images. Here is a list of static methods:

Method	Return Value
`createImageInputStream(Object input)`	`ImageInputStream`
`createImageOutputStream(Object output)`	`ImageOutputStream`

`getCacheDirectory()`	Current value of the `CacheDirectory`
`getImageReader(ImageWriter writer)`	`ImageReader`
`getImageReaders(Object input)`	Iterator of the current `ImageReaders`
`getImageReadersByFormatName(String formatName)`	Iterator of the current `ImageReaders` with the specified format name
`getImageReadersByMIMEType(String MIMEType)`	Iterator of the current `ImageReaders` of the specified MIME type
`getImageReadersBySuffix(String fileSuffix)`	Iterator of the current `ImageReaders` with the specified suffix
`getImageTranscoders(ImageReader reader)`	Iterator of the current `ImageTranscoders`
`getImageWriter(ImageReader reader)`	`ImageWriter`
`getImageWriters(ImageTypeSpecifier type, String formatName)`	Iterator of the current `ImageWriters` that can encode to the specified type
`getImageWritersByFormatName(String formatName)`	Iterator of the current `ImageWriters` with the specified format name
`getImageWritersByMIMEType(String MIMEType)`	Iterator of the current `ImageWriters` of the specified MIME type
`getImageWritersBySuffix(String fileSuffix)`	Iterator of the current `ImageWriters` with the specified suffix
`getReaderFileSuffixes()`	String array with file suffixes that are understood by current readers
`getReaderFormatNames()`	String array with format names that are understood by current readers
`getReaderMIMETypes()`	String array with MIME types that are understood by current readers
`getUseCache()`	`UseCache` value
`getWriterFileSuffixes()`	String array of file suffixes that are understood by current writers

`getWriterFormatNames()`	String array with format names that are understood by current writers
`getWriterMIMETypes()`	String array with MIME types that are understood by current writers
`read(File input)`	`BufferedImage` with `ImageReader`
`read(ImageInputStream stream)`	`BufferedImage` with `ImageInputStream` and `ImageReader`
`read(InputStream input)`	`BufferedImage` with `InputStream` and `ImageReader`
`read(URL input)`	`BufferedImage` with `ImageReader`

There are also a few static methods that do not return a value or return a Boolean:

Method	Description
`scanForPlugins()`	Performs the following actions: • Scans the application classpath for plugins • Loads plugin service provider classes • Registers service provider instances in the IIORegistry
`setCacheDirectory(File cacheDirectory)`	This is where the cache files will be stored.
`setUseCache(boolean useCache)`	This method toggles if the cache will be disk-based or not. This applies to `ImageInputStream` and `ImageOutputStream` instances.
`write(RenderedImage im, String formatName, File output)`	Writes an image to the specified file.
`write(RenderedImage im, String formatName, ImageOutputStream output)`	Writes an image to `ImageOutputStream`.
`write(RenderedImage im, String formatName, OutputStream output)`	Writes an image to `OutputStream`.

As you can glean from the provided methods, the image input/output framework provides us with a convenient way of using image codecs. As of Java 7, the following image format plugins were implemented by `javax.imageio`:

- BMP
- GIF
- JPEG
- PNG
- WBMP

TIFF is, as you can see, not on the list of image file formats. TIFFs are a common file format and, in 2001, macOS, with the release of macOS X, used the format extensively.

The current Java platform includes `ImageReader` and `ImageWriter` plugins for the TIFFs. These plugins have been written in Java and have been bundled in the new `javax.imageio.plugins.tiff` package.

Platform logging

The modern Java platform includes a logging API that enables platform classes to log messages. It has a commensurate service for manipulating the logs. Before we go too far into what is new regarding the logging API and service, let's review `java.util.logging.api`, which was introduced in Java 7.

The java.util.logging package

The `java.util.logging` package includes classes and interfaces that collectively comprise Java's core logging features. This functionality was created with the following goals:

- Problem diagnosis by end users and system administrators
- Problem diagnosis by field service engineers
- Problem diagnosis by the development organization

As you can see, the primary purpose was to enable maintenance of remote software.

The `java.util.logging` package has two interfaces:

- `public interface Filter`:
    - Purpose: This provides fine-grain control over logged data
    - Method: `isLoggable(LogRecord record)`

- `public interface LoggingMXBean`:
    - Purpose: This is the logging facility's management interface
    - Methods:
        - `getLoggerLevel(String loggerName)`
        - `getLoggerNames()`
        - `getparentLoggerName(String loggerName)`
        - `setLoggerLevel(String loggerName, String levelName)`

The following table provides the `java.util.logging` package classes, along with a brief description regarding what each class provides in respect to logging functionality and management:

Class	Definition	Description
ConsoleHandler	`public class ConsoleHandler extends StreamHandler`	Publishes log records to `System.err`
ErrorManager	`public class ErrorManager extends Object`	Used to process errors during logging
FileHandler	`public class FileHandler extends StreamHandler`	File logging
Formatter	`public abstract class Formatter extends Object`	For formatting `LogRecords`
Handler	`public abstract class Handler extends Object`	Exports `Logger` messages
Level	`public class Level extends Object implements Serializable`	Controls level of logging. The levels, in descending order, are—severe, warning, info, config, fine, finer, and finest
Logger	`public class Logger extends Object`	Logs messages

LoggingPermission	public final class LoggingPermission extends BasicPermission	SecurityManager checks
LogManager	public class LogManager	For maintaining a shared state between loggers and logging services
LogRecord	public class LogRecord extends Object implements Serializable	Passed between handlers
MemoryHandler	public class MemoryHandler extends Handler	Buffer requests in memory
SimpleFormatter	public class SimpleFormatter extends Formatter	Provides human-readable LogRecord metadata
SocketHandler	public class SocketHandler extends StreamHandler	Network logging handler
StreamHandler	public class StreamHandler extends Handler	Stream-based logging handler
XMLFormatter	public class XMLFormatter extends Formatter	Formats logs into XML

Next, let's review what changes were made in the modern Java platform.

Logging in the modern Java platform

Prior to Java 9, there were multiple logging schemas available, including java.util.logging, SLF4J, and Log4J. The latter two are third-party frameworks that have a separate facade and implementation components. These patterns have been replicated in the current Java platform.

The java.base module has been updated to handle logging functions and does not rely on the java.util.logging API. It has a separate facade and implementation components. This means that, when using third-party frameworks, the JDK only needs to provide the implementation component and return platform loggers that work with the requesting logging framework.

As you can see in the following illustration, we use the `java.util.ServiceLoader` API to load our `LoggerFinder` implementation. The JDK uses a default implementation if a concrete implementation is not found when using the system class loader:

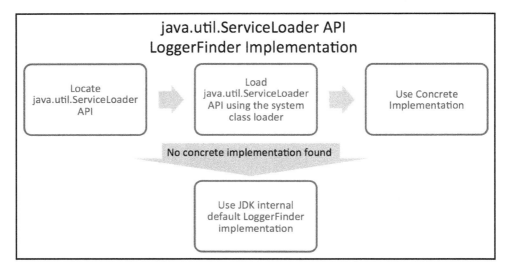

ServiceLoader API's LoggerFinder implementation

XML Catalogs

The modern Java platform includes a standard XML Catalog API to support the OASIS XML Catalogs Standard v1.1. The new API defines catalog and catalog-resolve abstractions so that JAXP processors can use them. In this section, we will look at the following:

- The OASIS XML Catalog standard
- JAXP processors
- Earlier XML Catalogs
- Current XML Catalogs

The OASIS XML Catalog standard

XML (eXtensible Markup Language) Catalogs are XML documents consisting of catalog entries. Each entry pairs an identifier to another location. OASIS is a not-for-profit consortium, with the mission of advancing open standards. They published the XML catalog standard, version 1.1, in 2005. This standard has two basic use cases:

- To map an external identifier to a URI reference
- To map a URI reference to another URI reference

Here is a sample XML catalog entry:

```
<public publicId="-//Packt Publishing Limited//Mastering Java 9//EN"
uri="https://www.packtpub.com/application-development/mastering-java-9"/>
```

The complete OASIS XML Catalog standard can be found at the official site:
`https://www.oasis-open.org/committees/download.php/14809/xml-catalogs.html`.

JAXP processors

The Java API for XML processing is referred to as JAXP. As its name suggests, this API is used for parsing XML documents. There are four related interfaces:

- **DOM**: Document Object Model parsing
- **SAX**: Simple API for XML parsing
- **StAX**: Streaming API for XML parsing
- **XSLT**: Interface to transform XML documents

Earlier XML Catalogs

The Java platform has had an internal catalog resolver since JDK 6. There was no public API, so external tools and libraries were used to access its functionality. Moving into modern Java platforms, that is, versions 9, 10, and 11, the goal was to make the internal catalog resolver a standard API for common use and ease of support.

Current XML Catalogs

The new XML Catalog API, delivered with Java 9, follows the OASIS XML Catalogs standard, v1.1. Here are the feature and capability highlights:

- Implements `EntityResolver`.
- Implements `URIResolver`.
- Creation of XML Catalogs is possible via the `CatalogManager`.
- `CatalogManager` will be used to create `CatalogResolvers`.
- OASIS open catalog file semantics will be followed:
  - Maps an external identifier to a URI reference
  - Maps a URI reference to another URI reference
- `CatalogResolvers` will implement the JAXP `EntityResolver` interface.
- `CatalogResolvers` will implement the JAXP `URIResolver` interface.
- The SAX `XMLFilter` will be supported by the resolver.

Since the new XML Catalog API is public, the pre-Java 9 internal catalog resolver has been removed, as it is no longer necessary.

Collections

The Java programming language does not support collection literals. Adding this feature to the Java platform was proposed in 2013 and revisited in 2016, but it only gained exposure as a research proposal, and not for future implementation.

 Oracle's definition of a collection literal is *a syntactic expression form that evaluates to an aggregate type, such as an array, list, or map* (http://openjdk.java.net/jeps/186).

Of course, that is until Java 9 was released. Implementing collection literals in the Java programming language is reported to have the following benefits:

- Performance improvement
- Increased safety
- Reduction of boilerplate code

Even without being part of the research group, our knowledge of the Java programming language clues us into additional benefits:

- The ability to write shorter code
- The ability to write space-efficient code
- The ability to make collection literals immutable

Let's look at two cases—using collections prior to the modern Java platform, and then with the new support for collection literals in the new Java platform.

Using collections prior to the modern Java platform

Here is an example of how we would create our own collections prior to the modern Java platform. This first class defines the structure for PlanetCollection. It has the following components:

- A single instance variable
- A one-argument constructor
- A mutator/setter method
- An accessor/getter method
- A method to print the object

Here is the code that implements the previously listed constructor and methods:

```
public class PlanetCollection {

  // Instance Variable
  private String planetName;

  // constructor
  public PlanetCollection(String name) {
    setPlanetName(name);
  }

  // mutator
  public void setPlanetName(String name) {
    this.planetName = name;
  }

  // accessor
  public String getPlanetName() {
```

```
      return this.planetName;
   }

   public void print() {
      System.out.println(getPlanetName());
   }
}
```

Now, let's look at the driver class that populates the collection:

```
import java.util.ArrayList;

public class OldSchool {

   private static ArrayList<PlanetCollection>
      myPlanets = new ArrayList<>();

   public static void main(String[] args) {
      add("Earth");
      add("Jupiter");
      add("Mars");
      add("Venus");
      add("Saturn");
      add("Mercury");
      add("Neptune");
      add("Uranus");
      add("Dagobah");
      add("Kobol");

      for (PlanetCollection orb : myPlanets) {
         orb.print();
      }
   }

   public static void add(String name) {
      PlanetCollection newPlanet =
         new PlanetCollection(name);
      myPlanets.add(newPlanet);
   }
}
```

Here is the output from this application:

```
  Problems    Javadoc    Declaration   Console  
<terminated> OldSchool [Java Application] /Library/Java/JavaVirtualMachines/jdk1.8.0_131.jdk/Contents/Home/bin/java (Aug 9, 2017, 7:02:41 PM)
Earth
Jupiter
Mars
Venus
Saturn
Mercury
Neptune
Uranus
Dagobah
Kobol
```

OldSchool class output

This code is, unfortunately, very verbose. We populated our collection in static initializer blocks instead of using a field initializer. There are other methods for populating our list, but they are all more verbose than they should have to be. These other methods have additional problems, such as the need to create extra classes, the use of the obscure code, and hidden references.

Now, let's take a look at the solution to this problem, which is provided by the modern Java platform. We will look at what is new in the next section.

Using new collection literals

In order to rectify the currently required code's verbosity in creating collections, we need library APIs for creating collection instances. Look at our earlier code snippet from the previous section and then consider this possible refactoring:

```
PlanetCollection<String> myPlanets = Set.of(
    "Earth",
    "Jupiter",
    "Mars",
    "Venus",
    "Saturn",
    "Mercury",
    "Neptune",
    "Uranus",
    "Dagobah",
    "Kobol");
```

This code is highly human-readable and not verbose.

The new implementation will include static factory methods on the following interfaces:

- `List`
- `Map`
- `Set`

So, we are now able to create unmodifiable instances of `List` collections, `Map` collections, and `Set` collections. They can be instantiated with the following syntax:

- `List.of(a, b, c, d, e);`
- `Set.of(a, b, c, d, e);`
- `Map.of();`

The `Map` collections will have a set of fixed arguments.

Platform-specific desktop features

The modern Java platform includes a public API that enables us to write applications with access to platform-specific desktop features. These features include interacting with taskbars/docks and listening for application and system events.

The macOS X `com.apple.eawt` package was an internal API and, starting with Java 9, is no longer accessible. In support of Java's embedded platform-specific desktop features, `apple.applescript` classes have been removed without replacement. They are not available in Java 9, 10, or 11.

The new API has been added to the `java.awt.Desktop` class and provides the following:

- It creates a public API to replace the functionality in `com.apple.{east,eio}`.
- It ensures that OS X developers do not lose functionality. To this end, the current Java platform has replacements for the following packages:
  - `com.apple.eawt`
  - `com.apple.eio`

- It provides developers with a near-common set of features for platforms (that is, Windows and Linux) in addition to OS X. These common features include the following:
    - A login/logout handler with event listeners
    - A screen lock handler with event listeners
- Taskbar/dock actions to include the following:
    - Requesting user attention
    - Indicating task progress
    - Action shortcuts

Enhanced method handling

The modern Java platform includes enhanced method handles as a way to improve the following listed classes in order to make common usage easier with improved optimizations:

- The `MethodHandle` class
- The `MethodHandles` class
- The `MethodHandles.Lookup` class

The preceding classes are all part of the `java.lang.invoke` package, which has been updated for the modern Java platform. These improvements were made possible through the use of lookup refinement with `MethodHandle` combinations, `for` loops, and `try...finally` blocks.

In this section, we will look at the following regarding:

- The reason for the enhancement
- Lookup functions
- Argument handling
- Additional combinations

The reason for the enhancement

This enhancement stemmed from developer feedback and the desire to make the `MethodHandle`, `MethodHandles`, and `MethodHandles.Lookup` classes much easier to use. There was also the call to add additional use cases.

These changes resulted in the following benefits:

- Enabled precision in the usage of the `MethodHandle` API
- Instantiation reduction
- Increased JVM compiler optimizations

Lookup functions

Changes regarding lookup functions include the following:

- `MethodHandles` can now be bound to non-abstract methods in interfaces
- The lookup API allows class lookups from different contexts

The `MethodHandles.Lookup.findSpecial(Class<?> refs, String name, MethodType type, Class<?> specialCaller)` class has been modified to permit locating super-callable methods on interfaces.

In addition, the following methods have been added to the `MethodHandles.Lookup` class:

- `Class<?> findClass(String targetName)`
- `Class<?> accessClass(Class<?> targetClass)`

Argument handling

Three recent updates were made to improve `MethodHandle` argument handling. These changes are highlighted as follows:

- Argument folding using `foldArguments(MethodHandle target, MethodHandle combinator)` did not previously have a position argument:
  - Argument collection using the `MethodHandle.asCollector(Class<?> arrayType, int arrayLength)` method did not previously support collecting the arguments into an array except for the trailing element. This has been changed, and there is now an additional `asCollector` method to support that functionality.

- Argument spreading using the
  `MethodHandle.asSpreader(Class<?> arrayType, int arrayLength)`
  method spreads the contents of the trailing array to a number of arguments, in a reverse method of argument collection. Argument spreading has been modified to support the expansion of an array anywhere in the method signature.

 The new method definitions for the updated `asCollector` and `asSpreader` methods are provided in the next section.

Additional combinations

The following additional combinations have been added to support the ease of use and optimizations for the `MethodHandle`, `MethodHandles`, and `MethodHandles.Lookup` classes of the `java.lang.invoke` package:

- Generic loop abstraction:
  - `MethodHandle loop(MethodHandle[] . . . clauses)`
- `While` loops:
  - `MethodHandle whileLoop(MethodHandle init, MethodHandle pred, MethodHandle body)`
- `Do...while` loops:
  - `MethodHandle doWhileLoop(MethodHandle init, MethodHandle body, MethodHandle pred)`
- Counting loops:
  - `MethodHandle countedLoop(MethodHandle iterations, MethodHandle init, MethodHandle body)`
- Data structure iteration:
  - `MethodHandle iteratedLoop(MethodHandle iterator, MethodHandle init, MethodHandle body)`
- `Try...finally` blocks:
  - `MethodHandle tryFinally(MethodHandle target, MethodHandle cleanup)`

- Argument handling:
  - Argument spreading:
    - `MethodHandle asSpreader(int pos,`
      `Class<?> arrayType, int arrayLength)`
  - Argument collection:
    - `MethodHandle asCollector(int pos, Class<?>`
      `arrayType, int arrayLength)`
  - Argument folding:
    - `MethodHandle foldArguments(MethodHandle target,`
      `int pos, MethodHandle combiner)`

Enhanced depreciation

There are two facilities for expressing deprecation:

- `@Deprecated` annotation
- `@deprecated` Javadoc tag

These facilities were introduced in Java SE 5 and JDK 1.1, respectively. The `@Deprecated` annotation was intended to annotate program components that should not be used because they were deemed dangerous and/or there was a better option. That was the intended use. Actual use varied, and because warnings were only provided at compile time, there was little reason to ignore the annotated code.

The Enhanced deprecation effort was taken on to provide developers with clearer information regarding the intended disposition of the APIs in the specification documentation. Work on this also resulted in a tool for analyzing a program's use of deprecated APIs.

To support this fidelity in information, the following components have been added to the `java.lang.Deprecated` annotation type:

- `forRemoval()`:
  - Returns Boolean `true` if the API element has been slated for future removal
  - Returns Boolean `false` if the API element has not been slated for future removal but is deprecated
  - The default is `false`

- since():
    - Returns a string containing the release or version number, at which point the specified API was marked as deprecated

What the @Deprecated annotation really means

When an API, or methods within an API, has/have been marked with the @Deprecated annotation, one or more of the following conditions typically exists:

- There are errors in the API and there is no plan to fix them
- Using the API is likely to result in errors
- The API has been replaced by another API
- The API is experimental

The native header generation tool (javah)

The Java header tool (javah) was introduced to the Java platform with Java 8. It provided developers with the ability to write native headers. Starting with Java 10, the javah tool has been replaced by functionality that's included in the Java compiler (javac).

Instead of using javah, developers will simply use javac -h.

Summary

In this chapter, we covered several upgrades regarding the modern platform. These updates cover a wide range of tools and updates to APIs to make developing with Java easier, with greater optimization possibilities for our resulting programs. Our review included a look at the new HTTP client, changes to Javadoc and the Doclet API, the new JavaScript parser, JAR and JRE changes, the new Java-level JVM compiler interface, new support for TIFF images, platform logging, XML Catalog support, collections, and the new platform-specific desktop features. We also looked at enhancements for method handling and the deprecation annotation.

In the next chapter, we will cover concurrency enhancements. Our primary focus will be the support for reactive programming that is provided by the Flow class API. We will also explore additional concurrency enhancements.

Questions

1. What was the primary reason for upgrading the HTTP client?
2. List the limitations of the new HTTP client API.
3. What three components must be passed to use `javadoc`?
4. Name one or more methods, other than the constructor, that are part of the Doclet class.
5. What are the enums in the compiler tree API?
6. What is the default output for the Javadoc tool?
7. What is Nashorn?
8. What is ECMAScript (ES)?
9. Name two primary JAR file enhancements.
10. What are the three conventions of `JavaBean`?

Further reading

Here is a list of information you can refer to:

- *Docker Fundamentals [Integrated Course]*, available at `https://www.packtpub.com/virtualization-and-cloud/docker-fundamentals-integrated-course`.
- *Java 9: Building Robust Modular Applications*, available at `https://www.packtpub.com/application-development/java-9-building-robust-modular-applications`.

12
Concurrency Enhancements

In the previous chapter, we covered several enhancements for the modern Java platform. These enhancements represented a wide range of tools and updates to APIs to make developing with Java easier, with greater optimization possibilities for our Java applications. We looked at the new HTTP client, changes to Javadoc and the Doclet API, the new JavaScript parser, JAR and JRE changes, the new Java-level JVM compiler interface, new support for TIFF images, platform logging, XML catalog support, collections, and the new platform-specific desktop features. We also looked at enhancements to method handling and the deprecation annotation.

In this chapter, we will cover concurrency enhancements for the Java platform. Our primary focus will be on the support for reactive programming, a concurrency enhancement that is provided by the `Flow` class API. Reactive programming was first released in Java 9 and remains an important feature of Java 10 and 11. We will also explore additional concurrency enhancements.

More specifically, we will cover the following topics:

- Reactive programming
- The `Flow` API
- Additional concurrency updates
- Spin-wait hints

Technical requirements

This chapter, and subsequent chapters, feature Java 11. The SE of the Java platform can be downloaded from Oracle's official site (`http://www.oracle.com/technetwork/java/javase/downloads/index.html`).

An Integrated Development Environment (IDE) software package is sufficient. IntelliJ IDEA, from JetBrains, was used for all coding associated with this chapter and subsequent chapters. The Community version of IntelliJ IDEA can be downloaded from the site (`https://www.jetbrains.com/idea/features/`).

Reactive programming

Reactive programming is when applications react to an asynchronous data stream as it occurs. The following diagram illustrates this flow:

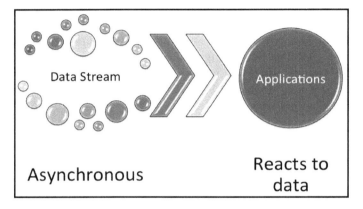

Reactive programming flow

Reactive programming is not a fancy software engineering term that's only used by academics. It is, in fact, a programming model that can result in much greater efficiencies as opposed to the more common method of having applications iterate over data that is in memory.

There is more to reactive programming. First, let's consider that the data stream is provided by a publisher in an asynchronous manner to the subscriber.

 A data streams is a binary input/output of strings and primitive data types. The `DataInput` interface is used for an input stream and the `DataOutput` interface is used for output streams.

Processors, or a chain of processors, can be used to transform the data stream without the publisher or subscriber being involved. In the following example, the **Processors** work on the stream of data without **Publisher** or **Subscriber** involvement, or even awareness:

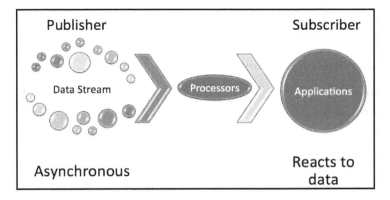

Processor-subscriber relationship

In addition to greater efficiency, reactive programming represents several additional benefits, which are highlighted as follows:

- The code base can be less verbose, making it:
  - Easier to code
  - Easier to maintain
  - Easier to read

- Stream processing results in memory efficiencies
- This is a solution for a variety of programming applications
- Less boilerplate code needs to be written, so development time can be focused on programming core functionalities
- The following types of programming require less time and code:
  - Concurrency
  - Low-level threading
  - Synchronization

Reactive programming standardization

There are standards in many aspects of software development, and reactive programming has not escaped this. There is a **Reactive Streams** initiative to standardize asynchronous stream processing. The specific focus, in the context of Java, is with the JVM and JavaScript.

The Reactive Streams initiative aims at tackling the issue of governing how the data stream is exchanged between threads. As you will recall from the previous section, the idea of processors is predicated on there being no impact on the publisher or receiver. This no-impact mandate stipulates that the following are not required:

- Data buffering
- Data translation
- Conversion

The basic semantics of the standard defines the regulation of data stream element transmission. This standard was specifically established for delivery with the Java 9 platform. Reactive Streams includes a library that will help developers convert between `org.reactivestreams` and `java.util.concurrent.Flow` namespaces.

The key to being successful with reactive programming and the Reactive Streams standardization is understanding the relevant terminology:

Term	Description
Demand	Demand refers to the subscriber's request for more elements as well as referring to the total number of elements requested that have not been fulfilled by the publisher yet.
Demand	Demand also refers to the total number of elements requested that have not been fulfilled by the publisher yet.
External synchronization	External access coordination for thread safety.
Non-obstructing	Methods are said to be non-obstructing if they rapidly execute without the requirement of heavy computations. Non-obstructing methods do not delay a subscriber's thread execution.
NOP	NOP execution is execution that can be called repeatedly without impacting on the calling thread.
Responsivity	This term refers to a component's ability to respond.
Return normally	Return normally refers to when there are no errors—the normal condition. The `onError` method is the only way permitted by the standard to inform the subscriber of a failure.
Signal	One of the following methods: • `cancel()` • `onComplete()` • `onError()` • `onNext()` • `onSubscribe()` • `request()`

In the following section, we will look at `Flow` APIs in the Java platform, since they correspond to the Reactive Streams specification.

The Flow API

The `Flow` class is part of the `java.util.concurrent` package. It helps developers incorporate reactive programming in their applications. The class has one method, `defaultBufferSize()`, and four interfaces.

The `defaultBufferSize()` method is a static method that returns the default buffer size for publishing and subscribing buffering. Its default value is `256` and it is returned as an `int`.

Let's look at the four interfaces.

The Flow.Publisher interface

The `Flow.Publisher` interface is a functional interface. A `Publisher` is a producer of data sent to subscribers:

```
@FunctionalInterface
public static interface Flow.Publisher<T>
```

This functional interface can serve as a Lambda expression assignment target. It only takes one argument—the subscribed item type `<T>`. It has one method, that is, `void subscribe(Flow.Subscriber subscriber)`.

The Flow.Subscriber interface

The `Flow.Subscriber` interface is used to receive messages, and its implementation is shown here:

```
public static interface Flow.Subscriber<T>
```

This interface is set up to receive messages. It only takes one argument—the subscribed item type, `<T>`. It has the following methods:

- `void onComplete()`
- `void onError(Throwable throwable)`

- `void onNext(T item)`
- `void onSubscribe(Flow.Subscription subscription)`

The Flow.Subscription interface

The `Flow.Subscription` interface ensures that only subscribers receive what is requested. Also, as you will see here, a subscription can be canceled at any time:

```
public static interface Flow.Subscription
```

This interface does not take any arguments and is the link that controls the messages between instances of `Flow.Publisher` and `Flow.Subscriber`. It has the following methods:

- `void cancel()`
- `void request(long n)`

The Flow.Processor interface

The `Flow.Processor` interface can serve as both `Subscriber` and `Publisher`. The implementation is provided here:

```
static interface Flow.Processor<T,R> extends Flow.Subscriber<T>,
Flow.Publisher<R>
```

This interface takes two arguments—the subscribed item type `<T>` and the published item type `<R>`. It does not have its own methods, but does inherit the following method from `java.util.concurrent.Flow.Publisher`:

```
void subscribe(Flow.Subscriber<? super T> subscriber)
```

`Flow.Processor` also inherits the following methods from `java.util.concurrent.Flow.Subscriber` interface:

- `void onComplete()`
- `void onError(Throwable throwable)`
- `void onNext(T item)`
- `void onSubscribe(Flow.Subscription subscription)`

Sample implementation

In any given implementation of reactive programming, we will have `Subscriber`, which requests data, and `Publisher`, which provides the data. First, let's look at a sample `Subscriber` implementation:

```
import java.util.concurrent.Flow.*;

public class packtSubscriber<T> implements Subscriber<T> {

  private Subscription theSubscription;

  // We will override the four Subscriber interface methods
  @Override
  public void onComplete() {
    System.out.println("Data stream ended");
  }

  @Override
  public void onError(Throwable theError) {
    theError.printStackTrace();
  }

  @Override
  public void onNext(T theItem) {
    System.out.println("Next item received: " + theItem);
    theSubscription.request(19); // arbitrary number
  }

  @Override
  public void onSubscribe(Subscription theSubscription) {
    this.theSubscription = theSubscription;
    theSubscription.request(19);
  }
}
```

As you can see, implementing `Subscriber` is not difficult. The heavy work is done by the processors in-between the `Subscriber` and `Publisher`. Let's look at a sample implementation where the `Publisher` publishes a data stream to subscribers:

```
import java.util.concurrent.SubmissionPublisher;
. . .
// First, let's create a Publisher instance
SubmissionPublisher<String> packtPublisher =
  newSubmissionPublisher<>();

// Next, we will register a Subscriber
```

```
PacktSubscriber<String> currentSubscriber =
  new PacktSubscriber<>();
packtPublisher.subscribe(currentSubscriber);

// Finally, we will publish data to the Subscriber
// and close the publishing effort
System.out.println("||---- Publishing Data Stream ----||");
. . .
packtPublisher.close();
System.out.println("||---- End of Data Stream Reached ----||");
```

Additional concurrency updates

The Java platform was recently enhanced to improve the use of concurrency. In this section, we will briefly explore the concept of Java concurrency and look at related enhancements to the Java platform, including:

- Java concurrency
- Supporting Reactive Streams
- CompletableFuture API enhancements

Java concurrency

In this section, we will start with a brief explanation of concurrency, then look at system configurations, cover Java threads, and finally look at concurrency improvements.

Concurrency explained

Concurrent processing has been around since the 1960s. In those formative years, we already had systems that permitted multiple processes to share a single processor. These systems are more clearly defined as pseudo-parallel systems because it only appeared as though multiple processes were being simultaneously executed. To this day, our computers still operate in this manner. The difference between the 1960s and the current day is that our computers can have multiple CPUs, each with multiple cores, which better supports concurrency.

Concurrency and parallelism are often used as interchangeable terms. Concurrency is when multiple processes overlap, although the start and stop times could be different. Parallelism occurs when tasks start, run, and stop at the same time.

System configurations

There are several different processor configurations that need to be considered. This section features two common configurations. The first configuration is that of shared memory, and is illustrated here:

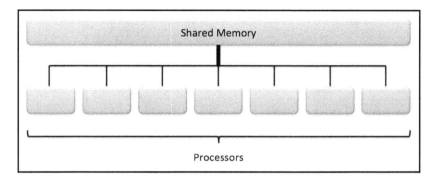

Shared memory configuration

As you can see, the shared memory system configuration has multiple processors that all share a common system memory. The second featured system configuration is a distributed memory system:

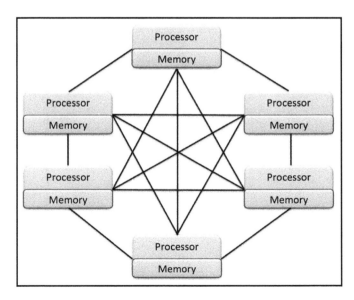

Distributed memory system

With the distributed memory system, each processor has its own memory, and each individual processor is fully linked with the other processors, making for a distributed system that is fully linked.

Java threads

A thread in Java is a program execution and is built into the JVM. The Thread class is part of the java.lang package (java.lang.Thread). Threads have priorities that control in what order the JVM executes them. While the concept is simple, implementation is not. Let's start by taking a close look at the Thread class.

The Thread class has one nested class:

- public static enum Thread.State

Also relevant to the Thread class is the following interface:

- public static interface Thread.UncaughtExceptionHandler

There are three class variables for managing thread priorities:

- public static final int MAX_PRIORITY
- public static final int MIN_PRIORITY
- public static final int NORM_PRIORITY

The Thread class has eight constructors, all of which allocate a new Thread object. Here are the constructor signatures:

- public Thread()
- public Thread(Runnable target)
- public Thread(Runnable target, String name)
- public Thread(String name)
- public Thread(ThreadGroup group, Runnable target)
- public Thread(ThreadGroup group, Runnable target, String name)
- public Thread(ThreadGroup group, Runnable target, String name, long stackSize)
- public Thread(ThreadGroup group, String name)

The `Thread` class also has 43 methods, six of which have been deprecated. The remaining methods are listed here, save for the accessors and mutators, which are listed separately. You can consult the documentation for details about each of these methods:

- `public static int activeCount()`
- `public final void checkAccess()`
- `protected Object clone() throws CloneNotSupportedException`
- `public static Thread currentThread()`
- `public static void dumpStack()`
- `public static int enumerate(Thread[] array)`
- `public static boolean holdsLock(Object obj)`
- `public void interrupt()`
- `public static boolean interrupted()`
- `public final boolean isAlive()`
- `public final boolean isDaemon()`
- `public boolean isInterrupted()`
- Join methods:
    - `public final void join() throws InterruptedException`
    - `public final void join(long millis) throws InterruptedException`
    - `public final void join(long millis, int nano) throws InterruptedException`
- `public void run()`
- Sleep methods:
    - `public static void sleep(long mills) throws InterruptedException`
    - `public static void sleep(long mills, int nano) throws InterruptedException`
- `public void start()`
- `public String toString()`
- `public static void yield()`

Here is the list of accessors/getters and mutators/setters for the `Thread` class:

- Accessors/getters:
  - `public static Map<Thread, StackTraceElement[]> getAllStacktraces()`
  - `public ClassLoader getContextClassLoader()`
  - `public static Thread.UncaughtExceptionHandler getDefaultUncaughtExceptionHandler()`
  - `public long getId()`
  - `public final String getName()`
  - `public final int getPriority()`
  - `public StackTraceElement[] getStackTrace()`
  - `public Thread.State getState()`
  - `public final ThreadGroup getThreadGroup()`
  - `public Thread.UncaughtExceptionHandler getUncaughtExceptionHandler()`

- Mutators/setters:
  - `public void setContextClassLoader(ClassLoader cl)`
  - `public final void setDaemon(boolean on)`
  - `public static void setDefaultUncaughtExceptionHandler(Thread.UncaughtException Handler eh)`
  - `public final void setName(String name)`
  - `public final void setPriority(int newPriority)`
  - `public void setUncaughtExceptionHandler(Thread.UncaughtException Handler eh)`

In Java, concurrency is commonly referred to as multithreading. As indicated earlier, managing threads, and especially multithreads, requires great fidelity in control. Java a couple of techniques, including the use of locks. Code segments can be locked to ensure that only a single thread can execute that code at any given time. We can lock classes and methods with the use of the synchronized keyword. Here is an example of how to lock an entire method:

```
public synchronized void protectedMethod() {
  . . .
}
```

The following code snippet demonstrates how to use the synchronized keyword to lock blocks of code within a method:

```
. . .
public class unprotectedMethod() {
  . . .
  public int doSomething(int tValue) {
    synchronized (this) {
      if (tValue != 0) {
        // do something to change tValue
        return tValue;
      }
    }
  }
}
```

Concurrency improvements

The ability to employ multiple threads in our Java applications stands to greatly improve efficiency and leverages the increasing processing capabilities of modern computers. The use of threads in Java gives us great granularity in our concurrency controls.

Threads are at the core of Java's concurrency functionality. We can create a thread in Java by defining a run method and instantiating a Thread object. There are two methods of accomplishing this set of tasks. Our first option is to extend the Thread class and override the Thread.run() method. Here is an example of that approach:

```
. . .
class PacktThread extends Thread {
  . . .
  public void run() {
    . . .
  }
```

```
}
. . .
Thread varT = new PacktThread();
. . .
// This next line is start the Thread by
// executing the run() method.
varT.start();
. . .
```

A second approach is to create a class that implements the Runnable interface and pass an instance of the class to the constructor of Thread. Here is an example:

```
. . .
class PacktRunner implements Runnable {
  . . .
  public void run() {
    . . .
  }
}
. . .
PacktRunner varR = new PacktRunner();
Thread varT = new Thread(varR);
. . .
// This next line is start the Thread by
// executing the run() method.
varT.start();
. . .
```

Both of these methods work equally well, and which one you use is considered to be the developer's choice. Of course, if you are looking for additional flexibility, the second approach is probably a better one to use. You can experiment with both methods to help you make a decision.

CompletableFuture API enhancements

The CompletableFuture<T> class is part of the java.util.concurrent package. This class extends the Object class and implements Future<T> and CompletionStage<T> interfaces. This class is used to annotate threads that can be completed. We can use the CompletableFuture class to represent a future result. When the complete method is used, that future result can be completed.

It is important to realize that if multiple threads attempt to simultaneously complete (finish or cancel), all but one will fail. Let's look at the class and then look at the enhancements.

Class details

The `CompletableFuture<T>` class has one nested class that marks asynchronous tasks:

```
public static interface CompletableFuture.AsynchronousCompletionTask
```

The constructor for the `CompletableFuture<T>` class has to be in sync with the provided constructor signature. It also must not take any arguments. The class has the following methods, which are organized by what they return:

Returns `CompletionStage`:

- `public CompletableFuture<Void> acceptEither(CompletionStage<? extends T> other, Consumer<? super T> action)`
- `public CompletableFuture<Void> acceptEitherAsync(CompletionStage<? extends T> other, Consumer<? super T> action)`
- `public CompletableFuture<Void> acceptEitherAsync(CompletionStage<? extends T> other, Consumer<? super T> action, Executor executor)`
- `public <U> CompletableFuture<U> applyToEither(CompletionStage<? extends T> other, Function<? super T, U> fn)`
- `public <U> CompletableFuture<U> applyToEitherAsync(CompletionStage<? extends T> other, Function<? super T, U> fn)`
- `public <U> CompletableFuture<U> applyToEitherAsync(CompletionStage<? extends T> other, Function<? super T, U> fn, Executor executor)`
- `public static <U> CompletedStage<U> completedStage(U value)`
- `public static <U> CompletionStage<U> failedStage(Throwable ex)`
- `public <U> CompletableFuture<U> handle(BiFunction<? super T, Throwable, ? extends U> fn)`

- `public <U> CompletableFuture<U> handleAsync(BiFunction<? super T, Throwable, ? extends U> fn)`
- `public <U> CompletableFuture<U> handleAsync(BiFunction<? super T, Throwable, ? extends U> fn, Executor executor)`
- `public CompletionStage<T> minimalCompletionStage()`
- `public CompletableFuture<Void> runAfterBoth(CompletionStage<?> other, Runnable action)`
- `public CompletableFuture<Void> runAfterBothAsync(CompletionStage<?> other, Runnable action)`
- `public CompletableFuture<Void> runAfterBothAsync(CompletionStage<?> other, Runnable action, Executor executor)`
- `public CompletableFuture<Void> runAfterEither(CompletionStage<?> other, Runnable action)`
- `public CompletableFuture<Void> runAfterEitherAsync(CompletionStage<?> other, Runnable action)`
- `public CompletableFuture<Void> runAfterEitherAsync(CompletionStage<?> other, Runnable action, Executor executor)`
- `public CompletableFuture<T> whenComplete(BiConsumer<? super T, ? super Throwable> action)`
- `public CompletableFuture<T> whenCompleteAsync(BiConsumer<? super T, ? super Throwable> action)`
- `public CompletableFuture<T> whenCompleteAsync(BiConsumer<? super T, ? super Throwable> action, Executor executor)`

These methods return `CompletionStage`:

- `public CompletableFuture<Void> thenAccept(Consumer<? super T> action)`
- `public CompletableFuture<Void> thenAcceptAsync(Consumer<? super T> action)`
- `public CompletableFuture<Void> thenAcceptAsync(Consumer<? super T> action, Executor executor)`

- public <U> CompletableFuture<Void>
  thenAcceptBoth(CompletionStage<? extends U> other, BiConsumer<?
  super T, ? super U> action)

- public <U> CompletableFuture<Void>
  thenAcceptBothAsync(CompletionStage<? extends U> other,
  BiConsumer<? super T, ? super U> action)

- public <U> CompletableFuture<Void>
  thenAcceptBothAsync(CompletionStage<? extends U> other,
  BiConsumer<? super T, ? super U> action, Executor executor)

- public <U> CompletableFuture<U> thenApply(Function<? super T, ?
  extends U> fn)

- public <U> CompletableFuture<U> thenApplyAsync(Function<? super
  T, ? extends U> fn)

- public <U> CompletableFuture<U> thenApplyAsync(Function<? super
  T, ? extends U> fn, Executor executor)

- public <U, V> CompletableFuture<V>
  thenCombine(CompletionStage<? extends U> other, BiFunction<?
  super T, ? super U, ? extends V> fn)

- public <U, V> CompletableFuture<V>
  thenCombineAsync(CompletionStage<? extends U> other,
  BiFunction<? super T, ? super U, ? extends V> fn)

- public <U, V> CompletableFuture<V>
  thenCombineAsync(CompletionStage<? extends U> other,
  BiFunction<? super T, ? super U, ? extends V> fn, Executor
  executor)

- public <U> CompletableFuture<U> thenCompose(Function<? super T,
  ? extends CompletionStage<U>> fn)

- public <U> CompletableFuture<U> thenComposeAsync(Function<?
  super T, ? extends CompletionStage<U>> fn)

- public <U> CompletableFuture<U> thenComposeAsync(Function<?
  super T, ? extends CompletionStage<U>> fn, Executor executor)

- public CompletableFuture<Void> thenRun(Runnable action)

- public CompletableFuture<Void>thenRunAsync(Runnable action)

- public CompletableFuture<Void>thenRunAsync(Runnable action,
  Executor executor)

These methods return `CompletableFuture`:

- `public static CompletableFuture<Void> allOf(CompletableFuture<?>...cfs)`
- `public static CompletableFuture<Object> anyOf(CompletableFuture<?>... cfs)`
- `public CompletableFuture<T> completeAsync(Supplier<? extends T> supplier, Executor executor)`
- `public CompletableFuture<T> completeAsync(Supplier<? extends T> supplier)`
- `public static <U> CompletableFuture<U> completedFuture(U value)`
- `public CompletableFuture<T> completeOnTimeout(T value, long timeout, TimeUnit unit)`
- `public CompletableFuture<T> copy()`
- `public CompletableFuture<T> exceptionally(Function<Throwable, ? extends T> fn)`
- `public static <U> CompletableFuture<U> failedFuture(Throwable ex)`
- `public <U> CompletableFuture<U> newIncompeteFuture()`
- `public CompletableFuture<T> orTimeout(long timeout, TimeUnit unit)`
- `public static ComletableFuture<Void> runAsync(Runnable runnable)`
- `public static CompletableFuture<Void> runAsync(Runnable runnable, Executor executor)`
- `public static <U> CompletableFuture<U> supplyAsync(Supplier<U> supplier)`
- `public static <U> CompletableFuture<U> supplyAsync(Supplier<U. supplier, Executor executor)`
- `public CompletableFuture<T> toCompletableFuture()`

These methods return `Executor`:

- `public Executor defaultExecutor()`
- `public static Executor delayedExecutor(long delay, Timeunit unit, Executor executor)`
- `public static Executor delayedExecutor(long delay, Timeunit unit)`

These methods return `boolean`:

- `public boolean cancel(boolean mayInterruptIfRunning)`
- `public boolean complete(T value)`
- `public boolean completeExceptionally(Throwable ex)`
- `public boolean isCancelled()`
- `public boolean isCompletedExceptionally()`
- `public boolean isDone()`

No return type:

- `public void obtrudeException(Throwable ex)`
- `public void obtrudeValue(T value)`

Additional methods:

- `public T get(long timeout, TimeUnit unit) throws InterruptedException, ExecutionException, TimeoutException`
- `public T get() throws InterruptedException, ExecutionException`
- `public T getNow(T valueIfAbsent)`
- `public int getNumberOfDependents()`
- `public T join()`
- `public String toString()`

Enhancements

The `CompletableFuture<T>` class received the following enhancements as part of the current Java platform:

- Added time-based enhancements:
  - This enables completion based on lapsed time
  - Delayed executions are now also supported

- Significant enhancement to subclasses:
  - Extending `CompletableFuture` is easier
  - Subclasses support alternative default executors

Specifically, the following methods were added in Java 9:

- `newIncompleteFuture()`
- `defaultExecutor()`
- `copy()`
- `minimalCompletionStage()`
- `completeAsync()`
- `orTimeout()`
- `completeOnTimeout()`
- `delayedExecutor()`
- `completedStage()`
- `failedFuture()`
- `failedStage()`

Spin-wait hints

With concurrency, we need to ensure that threads waiting to be executed actually get executed. The concept of spin-wait is a process that continually checks for a true condition. The Java platform has an API that permits Java code to issue hints that a spin loop is currently being executed.

While this is not a feature that every Java developer will use, it can be useful for low-level programming. The hint system simply issues hints—indications and performs no other actions. Justifications for adding these hints include the following assumptions:

- A spin loop's action time can be improved when using a spin hint
- Use of spin hints will reduce thread-to-thread latency
- CPU power consumption will be reduced
- Hardware threads will execute faster

This hint functionality will be contained in a new `onSpinWait()` method as part of the `java.lang.Thread` class. Here is an example of implementing the `onSpinWait()` method:

```
. . .
volatile boolean notInReceiptOfEventNotification
. . .
while ( notInReceiptOfEventNotification ); {
  java.lang.Thread.onSpinWait();
```

```
}
// Add functionality here to read and process the event
. . .
```

Summary

In this chapter, we covered concurrency enhancements of the Java platform. We took a deep look at concurrency both as a core Java concept and with an eye as to what Java provides. We also explored the `Flow` class API, which supports reactive programming. In addition, we explored concurrency enhancements and the new spin-wait hints.

In the next chapter, we will highlight the security enhancements of the Java platform, along with practical examples.

Questions

1. What is reactive programming?
2. What is a data stream?
3. What is the primary benefit of using reactive programming?
4. What are the stipulations of the no-impact mandate of reactive programming?
5. What package is the `Flow` class a part of?
6. List the four interfaces of the `Flow` class.
7. What is concurrency?
8. What is the distinction between concurrency and parallelism?
9. Explain the shared memory system configuration.
10. Explain the distributed memory system configuration.

Further reading

Here is a list of information you may refer to:

- *Reactive Programming With Java 9*, available at `https://www.packtpub.com/application-development/reactive-programming-java-9`.
- *Java 9 Concurrency-Advanced Elements [Video]*, available at `https://www.packtpub.com/application-development/java-9-concurrency-advanced-elements-video`.

13
Security Enhancements

In the last chapter, we covered concurrency enhancements of the modern Java platform. We took an in-depth look at concurrency, both as a core concept and as a series of enhancements for Java. We also explored the `Flow` class API, which supports Reactive Programming. In addition, we explored concurrency enhancements and the spin-wait hints for Java.

In this chapter, we will look at several recent changes that have been made to the JDK, which involve security. The size of these changes does not reflect their significance. The security enhancements for the modern Java platform provide developers with a greater ability to write and maintain applications that are more secure than previously possible.

More specifically, we will review the following topics in this chapter:

- Datagram Transport Layer Security
- Creating PKCS12 keystores
- Improving security application performance
- TLS application-layer protocol negotiation extension
- Leveraging CPU instructions for GHASH and RSA
- OCSP stapling for TLS
- DRBG-based `SecureRandom` implementations

Technical requirements

This chapter and subsequent chapters feature Java 11. The **Standard Edition (SE)** of the Java platform can be downloaded from Oracle's official site (http://www.oracle.com/technetwork/java/javase/downloads/index.html).

An IDE software package is sufficient. IntelliJ IDEA, from JetBrains, was used for all coding associated with this chapter and subsequent chapters. The Community version of IntelliJ IDEA can be downloaded from the website (`https://www.jetbrains.com/idea/features/`).

Datagram Transport Layer Security

Datagram Transport Layer Security (**DTLS**) is a communications protocol. This protocol provides a layer of security for datagram-based applications. DTLS permits secure communications and is based on the **Transport Layer Security** (**TLS**) protocol. Embedded security helps ensure that messages are not forged, tampered with, or eavesdropped.

Let's review the relevant terminology:

- **Communication protocol**: A set of rules that govern how information is transmitted.
- **Datagram**: A structured transfer unit.
- **Eavesdropping**: Undetected when listening to in-transit data packets.
- **Forgery**: Transmission of a packet with a falsified sender.
- **Network packet**: A formatted unit of data for transmission.
- **Tampering**: The altering of data packets after the sender transmits them and before the intended receiver receives them.
- **TLS protocol**: The most common network security protocol. As an example, it uses IMPA and POP for email.

The recent DTLS Java enhancements were aimed at creating an API for versions 1.0 and 1.2 of the DTLS.

In the sections that follow, we will look at each of the DTLS versions, 1.0 and 1.2, and then review the changes made to the Java platform.

DTLS protocol version 1.0

DTLS protocol version 1.0 was established in 2006 and provides communications security for datagram protocols. Here are its basic characteristics:

- Permits client/server applications to communicate without permitting:
    - Eavesdropping
    - Tampering
    - Message forgery

- Based on the TLS protocol
- Provides security guarantees
- The DLS protocol's datagram semantics are preserved

The following diagram illustrates where the **Transport Layer** fits into the overall schema of **SSL/TLS** protocol layers and the protocols for each layer:

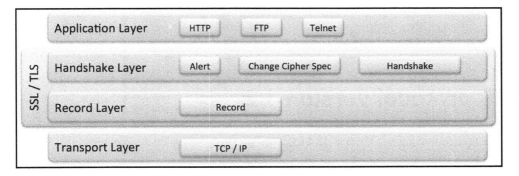

SSL/TLS protocol layers

DTLS protocol version 1.0 provides detailed specifications of the major areas of coverage, and are as follows:

- Ciphers:
    - Anti-replay block cipher
    - New cipher suites
    - Standard (or null) stream ciphers

- Denial of service countermeasures

- Handshake:
  - Message format
  - Protocol
  - Reliability

- Messages:
  - Fragmentation and reassembly
  - Loss-insensitive messaging
  - Size
  - Timeout and retransmission
  - Packet loss

- **Path Maximum Transition Unit (PMTU)** discovery
- Record layer
- Record payload protection
- Reordering
- Replay detection
- Transport layer mapping

DTLS protocol version 1.2

DTLS protocol version 1.2 was published in January 2012 and is copyrighted by the **Internet Engineering Task Force (IETF)**. This section shares code samples that illustrate the changes made in version 1.2.

The following code illustrates the TLS 1.2 handshake message header. This format supports:

- Message fragmentation
- Message loss
- Reordering:

```
// Copyright (c) 2012 IETF Trust and the persons identified
// as authors of the code. All rights reserved.

struct
{
  HandshakeType msg_type;
  uint24 length;
  uint16 message_seq; // New field
```

```
  uint24 fragment_offset; // New field
  uint24 fragment_length; // New field
  select (HandshakeType)
  {
    case hello_request: HelloRequest;
    case client_hello: ClientHello;
    case hello_verify_request: HelloVerifyRequest; // New type
    case server_hello: ServerHello;
    case certificate:Certificate;
    case server_key_exchange: ServerKeyExchange;
    case certificate_request: CertificateRequest;
    case server_hello_done:ServerHelloDone;
    case certificate_verify: CertificateVerify;
    case client_key_exchange: ClientKeyExchange;
    case finished: Finished;
  } body;
} Handshake;
```

 The code presented in this section is from the DTLS protocol documentation and is republished here in accordance with IETF's *Legal Provisions Relating to IETF Documents*.

The record layer contains the information that we intend to send into records. The information starts off inside a DTLSPlaintext structure and then after the handshake takes place, the records are encrypted and are eligible to be sent by the communication stream. The record layer format follows with new fields in version 1.2, and is annotated with the // New field in-code comments, as follows:

```
// Copyright (c) 2012 IETF Trust and the persons identified
// as authors of the code. All rights reserved.

struct
{
  ContentType type;
  ProtocolVersion version;
  uint16 epoch; // New field
  uint48 sequence_number; // New field
  uint16 length;
  opaque fragment[DTLSPlaintext.length];
} DTLSPlaintext;

struct
{
  ContentType type;
  ProtocolVersion version;
  uint16 epoch; // New field
```

```
    uint48 sequence_number; // New field
    uint16 length;
    opaque fragment[DTLSCompressed.length];
  } DTLSCompressed;

  struct
  {
    ContentType type;
    ProtocolVersion version;
    uint16 epoch; // New field
    uint48 sequence_number; // New field
    uint16 length;
    select (CipherSpec.cipher_type)
    {
      case block: GenericBlockCipher;
      case aead: GenericAEADCipher; // New field
    } fragment;
  } DTLSCiphertext;
```

Finally, here is the updated handshake protocol:

```
// Copyright (c) 2012 IETF Trust and the persons identified
// as authors of the code. All rights reserved.

enum {
  hello_request(0), client_hello(1),
  server_hello(2),
  hello_verify_request(3), // New field
  certificate(11), server_key_exchange (12),
  certificate_request(13), server_hello_done(14),
  certificate_verify(15), client_key_exchange(16),
  finished(20), (255) } HandshakeType;

  struct {
    HandshakeType msg_type;
    uint24 length;
    uint16 message_seq; // New field
    uint24 fragment_offset; // New field
    uint24 fragment_length; // New field
    select (HandshakeType) {
      case hello_request: HelloRequest;
      case client_hello: ClientHello;
      case server_hello: ServerHello;
      case hello_verify_request: HelloVerifyRequest; // New field
      case certificate:Certificate;
      case server_key_exchange: ServerKeyExchange;
      case certificate_request: CertificateRequest;
      case server_hello_done:ServerHelloDone;
```

```
      case certificate_verify: CertificateVerify;
      case client_key_exchange: ClientKeyExchange;
      case finished: Finished;
   } body; } Handshake;

struct {
   ProtocolVersion client_version;
   Random random;
   SessionID session_id;
   opaque cookie<0..2^8-1>; // New field
   CipherSuite cipher_suites<2..2^16-1>;
   CompressionMethod compression_methods<1..2^8-1>; } ClientHello;

struct {
   ProtocolVersion server_version;
   opaque cookie<0..2^8-1>; } HelloVerifyRequest;
```

DTLS support in Java

Java's implementation of the DTLS API is transport-independent and lightweight. The design considerations for the API were as follows:

- Read timeouts will not be managed
- The implementation will use a single TLS record for each wrap/unwrap operation
- The application, not the API, will be required to:
  - Determine timeout values
  - Assemble out-of-order application data

The DTLS is a protocol that is used to secure data from the application-layer before that data is passed to a transport layer protocol. DTLS is a good solution for encrypting and transmitting real-time data. Caution should be exercised so that we do not introduce vulnerabilities in our application's implementation. Here are some security considerations that are specific to implementing DTLS in your Java applications:

- Implement DTLS v1.2, since that is the latest version supported by Java.
- Avoid **Rivest-Shamir-Adleman** (**RSA**) encryption. If RSA must be used, add additional security to your private keys since this is a weak point for RSA.
- Use 192 bits or more when using the **Elliptic Curve Diffie-Hellman** (**ECDH**) anonymous key agreement protocol. The 192-bit value is based on a **National Institute of Standards and Technology** (**NIST**) recommendation.

- The use of **Authenticated Encryption with Associated Data** (**AEAD**), a form of encryption, is highly recommended. AEAD provides authenticity, confidentiality, and integrity assurances on the data being encrypted and decrypted.
- Always implement the `renegotiation_info` extension when implementing a handshake renegotiation.
- Establish a **Forward Secrecy** (**FS**) capability in all Java applications using a communication protocol. Implementing FS ensures past session encryption keys are not compromised when long-term encryption keys are compromised. Ideally, a **Perfect Forward Secrecy** (**PFS**), where each key is only valid for a single session, would be used in the Java applications that call for the greatest security of transmitted data.

Creating PKCS12 keystores

The Java platform provides increased security for keystores. Before creating PKCS12 keystores by default, we will first review the concept of keystores, look at the `KeyStore` class, and then look at recent updates to the Java platform.

Keystore primer

The concept of `KeyStore` is relatively simple. It is essentially a database file, or data repository file, that stores public key certificates and private keys. The `KeyStore` will be stored in the `/jre/lib/security/cacerts` folder. As you will see in the next section, this database is managed by Java's `java.security.KeyStore` class methods.

The features of `KeyStore` include the following:

- Contains one of the following entry types:
    - Private keys
    - Public key certificates

- Unique alias string names for every entry
- Password protection for each key

Java Keystore (JKS)

The `java.security.KeyStore` class is the storage facility for cryptographic keys and certificates. This class extends `java.lang.Object`, as follows:

```
public class KeyStore extends Object
```

There are three types of entries that are managed by `KeyStore`, and each implements the `KeyStore.Entry` interface, one of the three interfaces provided by the `KeyStore` class. The entry implementations are defined in the following table:

Implementation	Description
`KeyStore.PrivateKeyEntry`	Contains the `PrivateKey`, which it can store in a protected format. Contains the certificate chain for the public key.
`KeyStore.SecretKeyEntry`	Contains the `SecretKey`, which it can store in a protected format.
`KeyStore.TrustedCertifcateEntry`	Contains a single public key `Certificate` from an external source.

This class has been part of the Java platform since version 1.2. It has one constructor, three interfaces, six subclasses, and several methods. The constructor definition is as follows:

```
protected KeyStore(KeyStoreSpi keyStoresSpi, Provider provider, String type)
```

The `KeyStore` class contains the following interfaces:

- `public static interface KeyStore.Entry`: This interface serves as a marker for `KeyStore` entry types and contains no methods.
- `public static interface KeyStore.LoadStoreParameter`: This interface serves as a marker for load and store parameters and has the following method that returns null, or the parameter used to protect the `KeyStore` data:
    - `getProtectionParameter()`
- `public static interface KeyStore.ProtectionParameter`: This interface serves as a marker for `KeyStore` protection parameters and contains no methods.

The `java.security.KeyStore` class also contains the six nested classes, each of these are examined in the subsequent sections.

The `KeyStoreSpi` class defines the Key Store's **Service Provider Interface (SPI)**.

Understanding the KeyStore.Builder

The `KeyStore.Builder` class is used when you want to defer the instantiation of `KeyStore`:

```
public abstract static class KeyStore.Builder extends Object
```

This class provides the necessary information for instantiating a `KeyStore` object. The class has the following methods:

- `public abstract KeyStore getKeyStore() throws KeyStoreException`.
- `public abstractKeyStore.ProtectionParameter getProjectionParameter(String alias) throws KeyStoreException`.
- Three options for `newInstance`:
  - `public static KeyStore.Builder newInstance(KeyStore keyStore, KeyStore.ProtectionParameter protectionParameter)`
  - `public static KeyStore.Builder newInstance(String type, Provider provider, File file, KeyStore.ProtectionParameter protection)`
  - `public static KeyStore.Builder newInstance(String type, Provider provider, KeyStore.ProtectionParameter protection)`

The CallbackHandlerProtection class

The `KeyStore.CallbackHandlerProtection` class definition is as follows:

```
public static class KeyStore.CallbackHandlerProtection extends Object
implements KeyStore.ProtectionParameter
```

This class provides `ProtectionParameter` to encapsulate `CallbackHandler` and has the following method:

```
public CallbackHandler getCallbackHandler()
```

The PasswordProtection class

The `KeyStore.PasswordProtection` class definition is as follows:

```
public static class KeyStore.PasswordProtection extends Object implements
KeyStore.ProtectionParameter, Destroyable
```

This call provides an implementation of `ProtectionParameter` that is password-based. This class has the following methods:

- `public void destroy() throws DestroyFailedException`: This method clears the password
- `public char[] getPassword()`: Returns a reference to the password
- `public boolean isDestroyed()`: Returns true if the password was cleared

The PrivateKeyEntry class

The `KeyStore.PrivateKeyEntry` class definition is as follows:

```
public static final class KeyStore.PrivateKeyEntry extends Object
implements KeyStore.Entry
```

This creates an entry to hold `PrivateKey` and the corresponding `Certificate` chain. This class has the following methods:

- `public Certificate getCertificate()`: Returns the end entity `Certificate` from the `Certificate` chain
- `public Certificate[] getCertificateChain()`: Returns the `Certificate` chain as an array of `Certificates`
- `public PrivateKey getPrivateKey()`: Returns the `PrivateKey` from the current entry
- `public String toString()`: Returns the `PrivateKeyEntry` as `String`

The SecretKeyEntry class

The `KeyStore.SecretKeyEntry` class definition is as follows:

```
public static final class KeyStore.SecretKeyEntry extends Object implements
KeyStore.Entry
```

This class holds `SecretKey` and has the following methods:

- `public SecretKey getSecretKey()`: Returns the entry's `SecretKey`
- `public String toString()`: Returns the `SecretKeyEntry` as `String`

The TrustedCertificateEntry class

The `KeyStore.TrustedCertificateEntry` class definition is as follows:

```
public static final class KeyStore.TrustedCertificateEntry extends Object
implements KeyStore.Entry
```

This class holds a trusted `Certificate` and has the following methods:

- `public Certificate getTrustedCertificate()`: Returns the entry's trusted `Certificate`
- `public String toString()`: Returns the entry's trusted `Certificate` as `String`

The key to using this class is understanding its flow. First, we must load `KeyStore` by using the `getInstance` method. Next, we must request access to the `KeyStore` instance. Then, we must gain access so that we can read and write to `Object`:

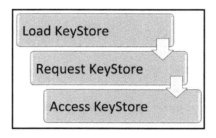

Keystore load-request-access pattern

The following code snippet shows the load-request-access implementation:

```
. . .
try {
  // KeyStore implementation will be returned for the default type
  KeyStore myKS = KeyStore.getInstance(KeyStore.getDefaultType());

  // Load
  myKS.load(null, null);
```

```
// Instantiate a KeyStore that holds a trusted certificate
TrustedCertificateEntry myCertEntry =
  new TrustedCertificateEntry(generateCertificate());

// Assigns the trusted certificate to the "packt.pub" alias
myKS.setCertificateEntry("packt.pub",
  myCertEntry.getTrustedCertificate());

return myKS;
}
catch (Exception e) {
  throw new AssertionError(e);
}
}
. . .
```

PKCS12 default in Java 9, 10, and 11

Prior to Java 9, the default `KeyStore` type was **Java KeyStore (JKS)**. The current Java platform uses PKCS as the default `KeyStore` type, more specifically, PKCS12.

 PKCS is an acronym for **Public Key Cryptography Standards**.

This change to PKCS provides stronger cryptographic algorithms as compared to JKS. As you would expect, JDK 9, 10, and 11 are still compatible with JKS to support previously developed systems.

Improving security application performance

The modern Java platform includes performance improvements when running applications with a security manager installed. Security managers can result in processing overhead and less than ideal application performance.

This is an impressive undertaking, as current CPU overhead when running security managers is estimated to result in 10-15 percent performance degradation. It is not feasible to completely remove the CPU overhead, as some CPU processing is required to run the security manager. That being said, the goal was to decrease the overhead percentage as much as possible.

This effort resulted in the following optimizations, with each detailed in the subsequent sections:

- Security policy enforcement
- Permission evaluation
- Hash code
- Package checking algorithm

Security policy enforcement

The JDK uses `ConcurrentHashMap` for mapping `ProtectionDomain` to `PermissionCollection`. `ConcurrentHashMap` is typically used for high concurrency in applications. It has the following characteristics:

- Thread safe
- The enter map does not need to be synchronized
- Fast reads
- Writes use locks
- No object-level locking
- Locking at a very granular level

The `ConcurrentHashMap` class definition is as follows:

```
public class ConcurrentHashMap<K, V> extends AbstractMap<K, V> implements
ConcurrentMap<K, V>, Serializable
```

In the preceding class definition, `K` refers to the type of keys maintained by the hash map, and `V` indicates the type of mapped values. There is a `KeySetView` subclass and several methods.

There are three additional classes related to enforcing security policy—`ProtectionDomain`, `PermissionCollection`, and `SecureClassLoader`:

- The `ProtectionDomain` class is used to encapsulate a group of classes so that permissions can be granted to the domain.
- The `PermissionCollection` class represents a collection of permission objects.
- The `SecureClassLoader` class, which extends the `ClassLoader` class, provides additional functionality for defining classes with permissions for retrieval by the system policy. In Java, this class uses `ConcurrentHashMap` for increased security.

Permission evaluation

Under the category of permission evaluation, three optimizations were made:

- The `identifyPolicyEntries` list previously had policy provider code for synchronization. This code has been removed and is not available in Java 9, 10, or 11.
- `PermissionCollection` entries are now stored in `ConcurrentHashMap`. They were previously stored as `HashMap` in a `Permission` class.
- Permissions are now stored in concurrent collections in subclasses of `PermissionCollection`.

The java.Security.CodeSource package

A hash code is an object-generated number that is stored in a hash table for rapid storage and retrieval. Every object in Java has a hash code. Here are some characteristics and rules for hash codes:

- Hash codes are the same for equal objects within a running process
- Hash codes can change between execution cycles
- Hash codes should not be used as keys

The Java platform includes a modified `hashCode` method of `java.security.CodeSource` to optimize DNS lookups. These can be processor intensive, so a string version of the code source URL is used to compute hash codes.

The `CodeSource` class definition is as follows:

```
public class CodeSource extends Object implements Serializable
```

This class has the following methods:

- `public boolean equals(Object obj)`: Returns true if the objects are equal. This overrides the equals method in the `Object` class.
- `public final Certificate[] getCertificates()`: Returns an array of certificates.
- `public final CodeSigner[] getCodeSigners()`: Returns an array of the code signers associated with the `CodeSource`.
- `public final URL getLocation()`: Returns the URL.
- `public int hashCode()`: Returns the hash code value for the current object.

- `public boolean implies(CodeSource codesource)`: Returns true if the given code source meets the following criteria:
    - Is not null
    - The object's certificates are not null
    - The object's location is not null
- `public String toString()`: Returns a string with information about the `CodeSource` to include the location and certificates.

Package checking algorithm

Java's most recent performance improvement, when running applications with a security manager installed, came in the form of the `java.lang.SecurityManager` package enhancements. More specifically, the `checkPackageAccess` method's package checking algorithm was modified.

The `java.lang.SecurityManager` class allows applications to implement security policies on specific operations. The `public void checkPackageAccess(String pkg)` method of this class receives a comma-delimited list of restricted packages from the `getProperty()` method. As illustrated here, depending on the evaluation, the `checkPackageAccess` method can throw one of two exceptions:

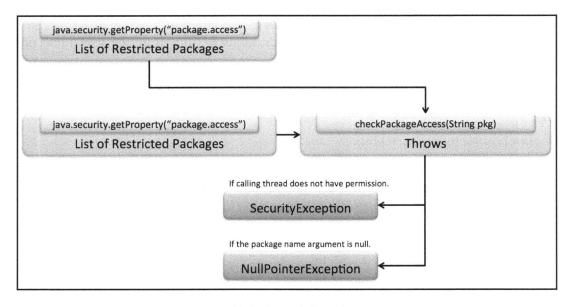

checkPackageAccess method's exceptions

The TLS application-layer protocol negotiation extension

The `javax.net.ssl` package has recently been enhanced so that it supports the **Transport Layer Security (TLS) ALPN** (short for **Application-Layer Protocol Negotiation**) extension. This extension permits application protocol negotiation for TLS connections.

TLS ALPN extension

ALPN is a TLS extension and can be used to negotiate regarding which protocol to implement when using a secure connection. ALPN represents an efficient means of negotiating protocols. As indicated in the following diagram, there are five basic steps to TLS handshakes:

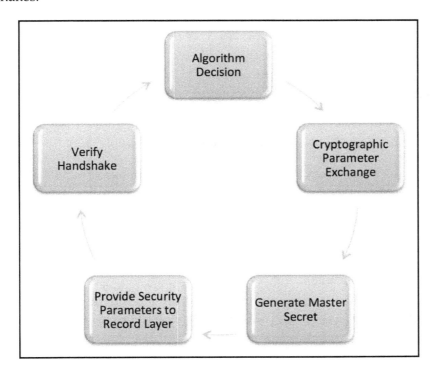

The five steps of TLS handshakes

The javax.net.ssl package

The `java.net.ssl` package contains classes relating to secure socket packages. This permits us to use SSL, as an example, for the reliable detection of errors that are introduced to the network byte stream. It also provides the ability to encrypt the data as well as provide authentication of the client and server.

This package includes the following interfaces:

- `public interface HandshakeCompletedListener extends EventListener`
- `public interface HostnameVerifier`
- `public interface KeyManager`
- `public interface ManagerFactoryParameters`
- `public interface SSLSession`
- `public interface SSLSessionBindingListener extends EventListener`
- `public interface SSLSessionContext`
- `public interace TrustManager`
- `public interface X509KeyManager extends KeyManager`
- `public interface X509TrustManager extends TrustManager`

The `java.net.ssl` package also has the following subclasses:

- `public class CertPathTrustManagerParameters extends Object implements ManagerFactoryParameters`
- `public abstract class ExtendedSSLSession extends Object implements SSLSession`
- `public class HandshakeCompleteEvent extends EventObject`
- `public abstract class HttpsURLConnection extends HttpURLConnection`
- `public class KeyManagerFactory extends Object`
- `public abstract class KeyManagerFactorySpi`
- `public class KeyStoreBuilderParameters extends Object implements ManagerFactoryParameters`
- `public class SSLContext extends Object`

- `public abstract class SSLContextSpi extends Object`
- `public abstract class SSLEngine extends Object`
- `public class SSLEngineResult extends Object`
- `public class SSLParameters extends Object`
- `public final class SSLPermission extends BasicPermission`
- `public abstract class SSLServerSocket extends ServerSocket`
- `public abstract class SSLServerSocketFactory extends ServerSocketFactory`
- `public class SSLSessionBindingEvent extends EventObject`
- `public abstract class SSLSocket extends Socket`
- `public abstract class SSLSocketFactory extends SocketFactory`
- `public class TrustManagerFactory extends Object`
- `public abstract class TrustManagerFactorySpi extends Object`
- `public abstract class X509ExtendedKeyManager extends Object implements X509KeyManager`
- `public abstract class X509ExtendedTrustManager extends Object implements x509TrustManager`

The java.net.ssl package extension

This change to the `java.net.ssl` package in the Java platform makes it so that it now supports the TLS ALPN extension. Key benefits of this change are as follows:

- TLS clients and servers can now use multiple application-layer protocols, which may or may not use the same transport-layer port
- The ALPN extension permits clients to prioritize application-layer protocols it supports
- Servers can select a client protocol for the TLS connection
- Supports HTTP/2

The following illustration was previously presented as the five basic steps to TLS handshakes. Updated for Java 9 and presented here, the following illustration indicates where the protocol names are shared between the client and server:

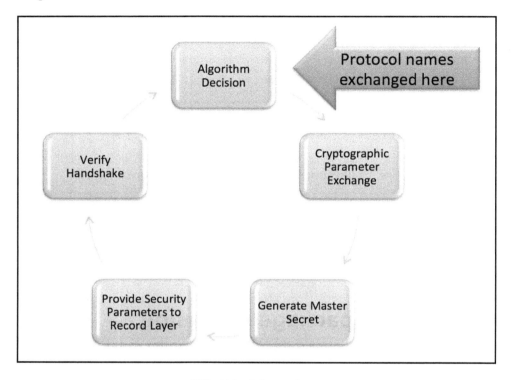

TLS handshakes: sharing protocol names

Once the client's list of application-layer protocols is received, the server can select the server's preferred intersection value and externally scan initial plaintext ClientHellos and select an ALPN protocol. An application server will do one of the following:

- Select any of the supported protocols
- Decide that the ALPN values (remotely offered and locally supported) are mutually exclusive
- Ignore the ALPN extension

Other key behaviors with regards to the ALPN extension are as follows:

- The server can alter connection parameters
- After the SSL/TLS handshake starts, the application can query to see if an ALPN value has been selected yet
- After the SSL/TLS handshake ends, the application can review which protocol was used

`ClientHello` is the first message in the TLS handshake. It has the following structure:

```
struct {
    ProtocolVersion client_version;
    Random random;
    SessionID session_id;
    CipherSuite cipher_suites<2..2^16-1>;
    CompressionMethod compression_methods<1..2^8-1>;
    Extension extensions<0..2^16-1>;
} ClientHello;
```

Leveraging CPU instructions for GHASH and RSA

The modern Java platform includes an improved performance of cryptographic operations, specifically GHASH and RSA. This performance improvement has been achieved in Java by leveraging the newest SPARC and Intel x64 CPU instructions.

This enhancement did not require new or modified APIs as part of the Java platform.

Hashing

Galois HASH (GHASH) and **RSA** are cryptosystem hashing algorithms. Hashes are a fixed length string or number that is generated from a string of text. Algorithms, more specifically hashing algorithms, are devised so that the resultant hashes cannot be reverse engineered. We use hashing to store passwords that are generated with a salt.

 Salts, in cryptology, are random data that are used as input for a hashing function to generate a password. Salts help protect against rainbow table attacks and dictionary attacks.

The following graphic illustrates the basics of how hashing works:

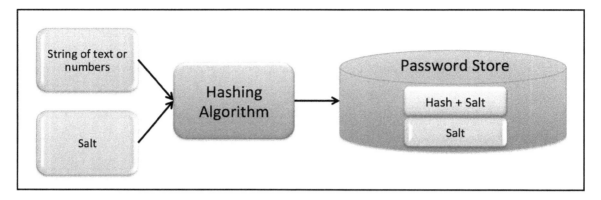

Hashing overview

As you can see, the **Hashing Algorithm** is fed with plaintext and a **Salt**, resulting in a new hashed password and the **Salt** being stored. Here is the same graphic with a sample input/output to demonstrate the functionality:

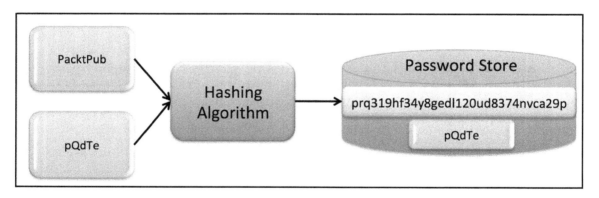

Hash and salt functionality

The validation process, as shown in the following diagram, starts with the user entering their plain text password. The hashing algorithm takes that plain text and rehashes it with the stored salt. Then, the resulting hashed password is compared to the stored one:

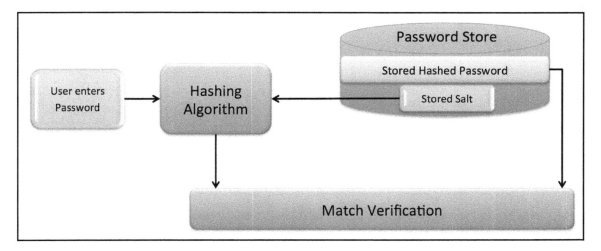

Hashing match verification

OCSP stapling for TLS

Online Certificate Status Protocol (**OCSP**) stapling is the method of checking the revocation status of digital certificates. The OCSP stapling approach for determining an SSL certificate's validity is assessed as being both safe and quick. The determination speed is achieved by permitting web servers to provide the validity information on its organic certificates instead of the lengthier process of requesting validating information from the certificate's issuing vendor.

OCSP stapling was previously referred to as the TLS certificate status request extension.

OCSP stapling primer

THE OCSP stapling process involves several components and validity checks. The following graphic illustrates the OCSP stapling process:

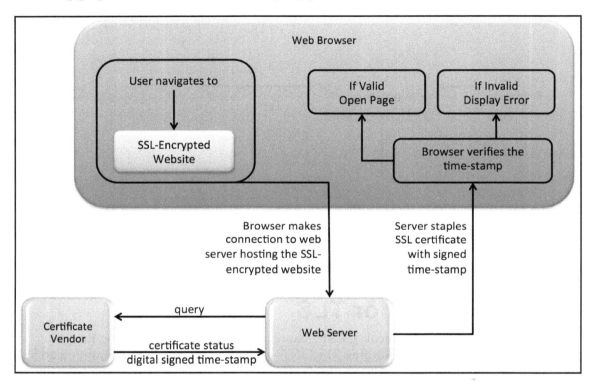

Hashing match verification

As you can see, the process starts when the user attempts to open an SSL-encrypted website via their browser. The browser queries the web server to ensure that the SSL-encrypted website has a valid certificate. The web server queries the certificate's vendor and is provided with both the certificate status and the digitally signed timestamp. The web server takes those two components, staples them together, and returns the stapled set to the requesting browser. The browser can then check the validity of the timestamp and decide whether to display the SSL-encrypted website or to display an error.

Recent changes to the Java platform

OCSP stapling for TLS implements OCSP stapling via the TLS certificate status request extension. OSCP stapling checks the validity of X.509 certificates.

 X.509 certificates are digital certificates that use the X509 **Public Key Infrastructure (PKI)**.

Prior to Java 9, the certificate validity check (really, the check to see if the certificate has been revoked) could be enabled on the client side and had the following inefficiencies:

- OCSP responder performance bottlenecks
- Performance degradation based on multiple passes
- Additional performance degradation if OCSP checking is performed on the client side
- False **fails** when browsers do not connect to an OCSP responder
- Susceptibility to denial of service attacks on OCSP responders

The new OCSP stapling for TLS includes the following system property changes for Java 9, 10, and 11:

- `jdk.tls.client.enableStatusRequestExtension`:
    - Default setting: true
    - Enables the `status_request` extension
    - Enables the `status_request_v2` extension
    - Enables processing `CertificateStatus` messages from the server
- `jdk.tls.server.enableStatusRequestExtension`:
    - Default setting: false
    - Enables OCSP stapling support server-side
- `jdk.tls.stapling.responseTimeout`:
    - Default setting: 5,000 milliseconds
    - Controls maximum time allocated by the server to obtain OCSP responses

- `jdk.tls.stapling.cacheSize`:
  - Default setting: 256
  - Controls maximum number of cache entries
  - Can set maximum to zero eliminates ceiling
- `jdk.tls.stapling.cacheLifetime`:
  - Default setting: 3,600 seconds (1 hour)
  - Controls the maximum lifetime of a cached response
  - Can set the value to zero in order to disable the cache's lifetime
- `jdk.tls.stapling.responderURI`:
  - Default setting: none
  - Can set a default URI for certificates without the **Authority Info Access** (**AIA**) extension
  - Does not override the AIA extension unless the `jdk.tls.stapling.Override` property is set
- `jdk.tls.stapling.respoderOverride`:
  - Default setting: false
  - Allows `jdk.tls.stapling.responderURI` provided property to override AIA extension values
- `jdk.tls.stapling.ignoreExtensions`:
  - Default setting: false
  - Disables OCSP extension forwarding, as specified in `status_request` or `status_request_v2` TLS extensions

The `status_request` and `status_request_v2` TLS hello extensions are now supported by both client and server-side Java implementations.

DRBG-based SecureRandom implementations

In earlier versions of Java, that is, version 8 and earlier, the JDK had two approaches to generating secure random numbers. One method, written in Java, used SHA1-based random number generation and was not terribly strong. The other method was platform-dependent and used preconfigured libraries.

Deterministic Random Bit Generator (**DRBG**) is a method for generating random numbers. It has been approved by the NIST, a branch of the U.S. Department of Commerce. DRBG methodologies include modern and stronger algorithms for generating secure random numbers.

Recently, three specific DRBG mechanisms were implemented. These mechanisms are listed as follows:

- `Hash_DRBG`
- `HMAC_DRBG`
- `CTR_DRBG`

 You can learn the specifics of each of the DRBG mechanisms at `http://nvlpubs.nist.gov/nistpubs/SpecialPublications/NIST.SP.800` `-90Ar1.pdf`.

Here are the three new APIs:

- `SecureRandom`: New methods, allowing for the configuration of `SecureRandom` objects with the following configurable properties:
    - Seeding
    - Reseeding
    - Random-bit-generation
- `SecureRandomSpi`: New methods to implement the `SecureRandom` methods.
- `SecureRandomParameter`: New interfaces so that input can be passed to the new `SecureRandom` methods.

Summary

In this chapter, we looked at several small, but significant changes to the JDK that involve security. The featured security enhancements provide developers with the distinct ability to write and maintain applications that implement security. More specifically, we covered DTLS, keystores, improving security application performance, the TLS ALPN, leveraging CPU instructions for GHASH and RSA, OCSP stapling for TLS, and DRBG-based `SecureRandom` implementations.

In the next chapter, we will explore the new command-line flags used in Java as well as changes to various command-line tools. Our coverage will include managing Java's JVM runtime and compiler using the new command-line options and flags.

Questions

1. What is DTLS?
2. What is TLS?
3. What is a security consideration regarding handshake renegotiation?
4. Why should you establish an FS capability in Java applications?
5. What is `KeyStore`?
6. Where is `KeyStore` stored?
7. What is the purpose of the `Builder` class?
8. What are the characteristics of `ConcurrentHashMap`?
9. What is a hash code?
10. What is GHASH?

Further reading

Here is a list of information you can refer to:

- *Instant Java Password and Authentication Security*, available at `https://www.packtpub.com/application-development/instant-java-password-and-authentication-security-instant`.

14
Command-Line Flags

In the previous chapter, we looked at several security changes to the JDK. Java's security enhancements provide developers with the ability to write and maintain applications that implement security. More specifically, we covered datagram transport layer security, keystores, improving security application performance, the TLS ALPN, leveraging CPU instructions for GHASH and RSA, OCSP stapling for TLS, and DRBG-based `SecureRandom` implementations.

In this chapter, we will explore several changes to the modern Java platform with the common theme of command-line flags. More specifically, we will cover the following concepts:

- Unified JVM logging
- Compiler control
- Diagnostic commands
- The heap profiling agent
- Removing your JHAT
- Command-line flag argument validation
- Compiling for older platform versions
- The experimental Java-based JIT compiler

Technical requirements

This chapter and subsequent chapters feature Java 11. The **Standard Edition** (**SE**) of the Java platform can be downloaded from Oracle's official site (http://www.oracle.com/technetwork/java/javase/downloads/index.html).

An IDE software package is sufficient. IntelliJ IDEA, from JetBrains, was used for all coding associated with this chapter and subsequent chapters. The Community version of IntelliJ IDEA can be downloaded from the site (https://www.jetbrains.com/idea/features/).

Unified JVM logging

Creating a unified logging schema for the JVM was introduced in Java 9. Here is a comprehensive list of the goals of that effort:

- To create a JVM-wide set of command line options for all logging operations
- To use categorized tags for logging
- To permit messages to have multiple tags, also referred to as tag sets
- To provide six levels of logging:
  - Error
  - Warning
  - Information
  - Debug
  - Trace
  - Develop

- To select which messages are logged based on levels
- To optionally direct logging to the console or a file:
  - Print one line at a time and do not support interleaving within the same line
- To permit the output of multiple line logs (non-interleaved)
- To format all logging messages so that they are easily human-read
- To add decorations such as uptime, level, and tags
- Like levels, to select which messages are logged based on decorations
- To convert pre-Java 9 `tty>print` logging to use unified logging as the output
- To permit dynamic message configuration using `jcmd` and `MBeans`
- To permit the ability to enable and disable individual log messages
- To add the ability to determine the order in which decorations are printed

The unified logging changes to the JVM can be grouped into the following five categories:

- Command-line options
- Decorations
- Levels
- Output
- Tags

Let's briefly look at each of these categories.

Command-line options

The new command-line option, -Xlog, is a crucial component of Java's logging framework. This command-line option has an extensive array of parameters and possibilities. The basic syntax is simply -Xlog, followed by an option.

Here is the formal basic syntax:

```
-Xlog[:option]
```

Here is a basic example with all option:

```
-Xlog:all
```

Here is the extensive command-line syntax used to configure the new, unified logging:

```
-Xlog[:option]
option := [<what>][:[<output>][:[<decorators>][:<outputoptions>]]]
'help'
'disable'

what := <selector>[,...]
selector := <tag-set>[*][=<level>]
tag-set := <tag>[+..]
'all'
tag := name of tag
level := trace
debug
info
warning
error

output := 'stderr'
'stdout'
[file=]<filename>
decorators := <decorator>[,...]
'none'

decorator := time
uptime
timemillis
uptimemillis
timenanos
uptimenanos
pid
tid
level
tags
```

```
output-options := <output_option>[,...]
output-option := filecount=<file count>
filesize=<file size in kb>
parameter=value
```

The following `-Xlog` examples are followed by a description:

-Xlog:all

In the preceding example, we are telling the JVM to take the following actions:

- Log all messages
- Use the `info` level
- Provide output to `stdout`

 With this example, all `warning` messages will still be output to `stderr`.

The following example, logs messages at the `debug` level:

-Xlog:gc+rt*=debug

In the preceding example, we are telling the JVM to take the following actions:

- Log all messages tagged with, at a minimum, the `gc` and `rt` tags
- Use the `debug` level
- Provide output to `stdout`

The following example pushes the output to an external file:

-Xlog:disable – Xlog:rt=debug:rtdebug.txt

In the preceding example, we are telling the JVM to take the following actions:

- Disable all messages except those tagged with `rt` tags
- Use the `debug` level
- Provide output to a file named `rtdebug.txt`

Decorations

In the context of Java's logging framework, decorations are metadata about the log message. Here is an alphabetic list of decorations that are available:

- `level`: The level associated with the logged message
- `pid`: PID = Processor Identifier
- `tags`: The tag set associated with the logged message
- `tid`: TID = Thread Identifier
- `time`: Refers to the current date and time, using the ISO-8601 format
- `timemillis`: Current time in milliseconds
- `timenanos`: Current time in nanoseconds
- `uptime`: Time, in seconds and milliseconds, since the JVM started
- `uptimemillis`: Time, in milliseconds, since the JVM started
- `uptimenanos`: Time, in nanoseconds, since the JVM started

Decorations can be surpassed or included in unified logging output. Regardless of which decorations are used, they will appear in the output in the following order:

1. `time`
2. `uptime`
3. `timemillis`
4. `uptimemillis`
5. `timenanos`
6. `uptimenanos`
7. `pid`
8. `tid`
9. `level`
10. `tags`

Levels

Logged messages are individually associated with a verbosity level. As previously listed, the levels are **error**, **warning**, **info**, **debug**, **trace**, and **develop**. The following chart shows how the levels have an increasing level of verbosity with respect to how much information is logged. The develop level is for development purposes only and is not available in on-product application builds:

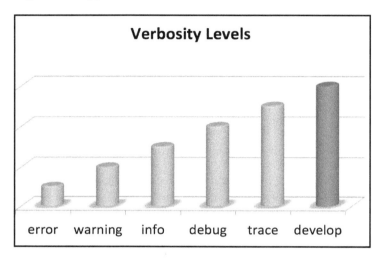

The verbosity levels of the log messages

Working with Xlog output

The Java logging framework supports three types of output with examples of direct use with the -Xlog command-line syntax:

In the following example, we provide output to stderr:

```
-Xlog:all=warning:stderr:none
```

The following example provides output to stdout:

```
-Xlog:all=warning:stdout:none
```

The following example writes the output to a text file:

```
-Xlog:all=warning:file=logmessages.txt:none
```

Tags

The new logging framework consists of a set of tags that are identified in the JVM. These tags can be changed in the source code if needed. The tags should be self-identifying, such as `gc` for garbage collection.

When more than one tag is grouped together, they form a tag set. When we add our own tags via source code, each tag should be associated with a tag set. This will help ensure that the tags stay organized and are easily human-readable.

Compiler control

Controlling **Java Virtual Machine** (**JVM**) compilers might seem like an unnecessary task, but for many developers, this is an important aspect of testing. This is accomplished with method-dependent compiler flags.

In this section, we will start with a look at JVM compilation modes and then look at the compiler that can be controlled using the Java platform.

Compilation modes

The changes in the modern Java platform include granular control of both the **C1** and **C2** JVM compilers. As you can see in the following illustration, the Java HotSpot JVM has two JIT compilation modes **C1** and **C2**:

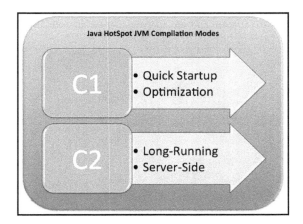

Java hotSpot JVM compilation modes

The **C1** and **C2** compilation modes use different compilation techniques and, if used on the same code base, can produce different sets of machine code.

The C1 compilation mode

The C1 compilation mode inside the Java HotSpot VM is typically used for applications that have the following characteristics:

- Quick startup
- Increased optimization
- Client-side

The C2 compilation mode

The second compilation mode, C2, is used by applications with the following listed characteristics:

- Long runtimes
- Server-side

Tiered compilation

Tiered compilation allows us to use both **C1** and **C2** compilation modes. Starting with Java 8, tiered compilation is the default process. As illustrated here, **C1** mode is used at startup to help provide greater optimization. Then, once the app has sufficiently warmed up, **C2** mode is employed:

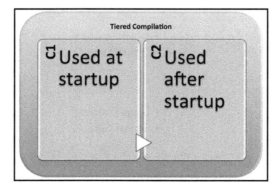

Tiered compilation

Compiler control in Java 11

Java comes with the promise of the ability to have finite control over JVM compilers and to make changes at runtime. These additional abilities do not degrade performance. This permits greater fidelity of testing and testing optimization as we can run small compiler tests without having to relaunch the entire JVM.

To control compiler operations, we need to create a directives file. These files contain compiler directives that consist of a set of options with values. Directive files essentially use a subset of JSON:

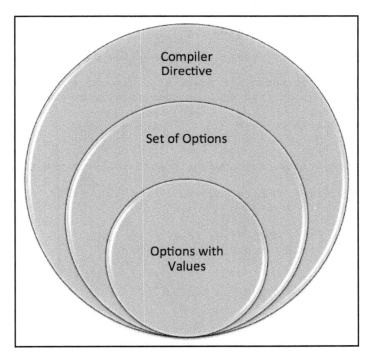

Compiler directive structure

The **JavaScript Object Notation (JSON)** format is used for data-interchange. The directive files have the following formatting differences from JSON:

- `int` and `doubles` are the only supported number formats
- The double forward slash (//) can be used for comment lines
- Trailing commas (,) can be used in arrays and objects

- Escape characters are not supported
- Option names are formatted as strings and do not have to be quoted

You can learn more about JSON at `http://www.json.org`.

We can add our directive file using the following syntax at the command line:

-XX:CompilerDirectivesFile=<file>

Here is a shell example of a directives file:

```
[ // Open square bracket marks the start of the directives file

{ // Open curly brace marks the start of a directive block
  // A directives block that applies specifically to the C1 mode
  c1: {
      // directives go here
    },

  // A directives block that applies specifically to the C2 mode
  c2: {
      // directives go here
    },

  // Here we can put a directives that do not apply to
  // a specific compiler mode
},

{ // can have multiple directive blocks

  c1: {
      // directives go here
    }

  c2: {
      // directives go here
    }
}
] // Close square bracket marks the start of the directives file
```

Diagnostic commands

Seven new diagnostic commands where added to the modern Java platform to enhance the ability to diagnose the JDK and the JVM. The new diagnostic commands are detailed here.

The `print_codegenlist` command prints methods that are currently queued for compilation. Since C1 and C2 compilation modes are on separate queues, this command would need to be issued to a specific queue.

The `dump_codelist` diagnostic command will print the following listed information for the compiled methods:

- Full signature
- Address range
- State:
    - Alive
    - Non-entrant
    - Zombie

In addition, the `dump_codelist` diagnostic command allows the output to be directed to `stdout` or to a specified file. The output can be in XML form or standard text.

The `print_codeblocks` command allows us to print the following:

- The code cache size
- The code cache list
- A list of blocks in the code cache
- Addresses for code blocks

The `datadump_request` diagnostic command sends a dump request to the **Java Virtual Machine Tool Interface (JVMTI)**. This replaces the **Java Virtual Machine Debug Interface (JVMDI)** and the **Java Virtual Machine Profiling Interface (JVMPI)**.

With the `set_vmflag` command, we can set a command-line flag or option in the JVM or the libraries.

The `print_class_summary` diagnostic command prints a list of all loaded classes as well as the structure of their inheritance.

The `print_utf8pool` command prints all UTF-8 string constants.

The heap profiling agent

The JVM TI `hprof` agent was recently removed from the Java platform. Here are the key terms associated with this change:

- **Tool Interface** (**TI**): This is a native programming interface that allows tools to control the execution of applications that are being run inside the Java Virtual Machine. The interface also permits state inquiries. The full nomenclature for this tool is the Java Virtual Machine Tool Interface, or JVM TI.
- **Heap Profiling** (**HPROF**): This is an internal JDK tool that's used for profiling a JVM's use of CPUs and the heap. The most common exposure developers have to `hprof` is the file that is generated when following a crash. The generated file contains a heap dump.

The Java 11 JDK does not contain the `hprof` agent. It was removed largely because there are superior alternatives available. Here is a table of their related functionality:

HPROF Functionality	Alternative
Allocation Profiler (heap=sites)	Java VisualVM
CPU Profiler (cpu=samples) (cpu=times)	Java VisualVM Java Flight Recorder
Heap Dumps (heap=dump)	Internal JVM functionality: • `GC.heap_dump`(`icmd <pid> GC.heap_dump`) • `jmap -dump`

Interestingly, when HPROF was originally created, it was not intended to be used in production. In fact, it was only meant to test code for the **JVM Tool Interface**. So, with the advent of the modern Java platform, the HPROF library (`libhprof.so`) will no longer be part of the JDK.

Removing your JHAT

The **Java Heap Analysis Tool** (**JHAT**) is used to parse Java heap dump files. The syntax for this heap dump file parsing tool is as follows:

```
jhat
    [-stack <bool>]
    [-refs <bool>]
    [-port <port>]
```

```
        [-baseline <file>]
        [-debug <int>]
        [-version]
        [-h|-help]
     <file>
```

Here is a quick look at the options associated with the JHAT command:

Option	Description	Default
-J<flag>	This passes <flag> to the runtime system	N/A
-stack<bool>	This toggles tracking of the object allocation call stack	true
-refs<bool>	This toggles tracking of references to objects	true
-port<port>	This indicates the port for the JHAT HTTP server	7000
-exclude<exclude-filename>	This excludes the indicated file from reachable objects	N/A
-baseline<filename>	This specifies the baseline heap dump for use in comparisons	N/A
-debug<int>	This sets the verbosity of the output	N/A
-version	This simply outputs the JHAT release number	N/A
-h -help	This provides help text	N/A

JHAT has been part of the Java platform since JDK-6 in an experimental form. It was not supported and has been deemed to be outdated. Starting with Java 9, this tool is no longer be part of the JDK.

Command-line flag argument validation

In this chapter, you have gained exposure to much of the command-line flag's usage with the Java platform. A concerted effort was taken to ensure all JVM command-line flags with arguments were validated. The primary goals of this effort were to:

- Avoid JVM crashes
- Provide error messages to inform you of invalid flag arguments

As you can see from the following diagram, there was no attempt to autocorrect the flag argument errors; rather, just to identify the errors and prevent the JVM from crashing:

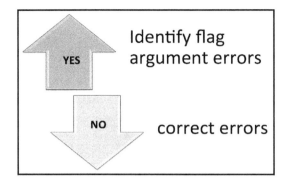

Flag argument errors

A sample error message is provided here and indicates that the flag argument was out of range. This error would be displayed during the flag argument range check that's performed during the JVM's initialization:

```
exampleFlag UnguardOnExecutionViolation = 4 is outside the allowed range [0
   . . . 3]
```

Here are some specifics regarding this change to the Java platform:

- Expand on the current `globals.hpp` source file to ensure that complete flag default values and permissible ranges are documented
- Define a framework to support adding new JVM command-line flags in the future:
  - This will include value ranges and value sets
  - This will ensure that validity checking will apply to all newly added command-line flags

- Modify macro tables:
  - Add min/max for the optional range
  - Add constraint entries for the following:
    - Ensure constraint checks are performed each time a flag changes
    - All manageable flags will continue to be checked while the JVM is running

Compiling for older platform versions

The Java compiler, `javac`, was updated in Java 9 to ensure that it can be used to compile Java programs to run on user-selected older versions of the Java platform. As you can see in the following screenshot, `javac` has several options, including `-source` and `-target`. The `javac` presented in the following screenshot is from Java 8:

```
● ● ●                          ⬆ edljr — -bash — 125×37
Edwards-iMac:~ edljr$ javac -help
Usage: javac <options> <source files>
where possible options include:
  -g                         Generate all debugging info
  -g:none                    Generate no debugging info
  -g:{lines,vars,source}     Generate only some debugging info
  -nowarn                    Generate no warnings
  -verbose                   Output messages about what the compiler is doing
  -deprecation               Output source locations where deprecated APIs are used
  -classpath <path>          Specify where to find user class files and annotation processors
  -cp <path>                 Specify where to find user class files and annotation processors
  -sourcepath <path>         Specify where to find input source files
  -bootclasspath <path>      Override location of bootstrap class files
  -extdirs <dirs>            Override location of installed extensions
  -endorseddirs <dirs>       Override location of endorsed standards path
  -proc:{none,only}          Control whether annotation processing and/or compilation is done.
  -processor <class1>[,<class2>,<class3>...] Names of the annotation processors to run; bypasses default discovery process
  -processorpath <path>      Specify where to find annotation processors
  -parameters                Generate metadata for reflection on method parameters
  -d <directory>             Specify where to place generated class files
  -s <directory>             Specify where to place generated source files
  -h <directory>             Specify where to place generated native header files
  -implicit:{none,class}     Specify whether or not to generate class files for implicitly referenced files
  -encoding <encoding>       Specify character encoding used by source files
  -source <release>          Provide source compatibility with specified release
  -target <release>          Generate class files for specific VM version
  -profile <profile>         Check that API used is available in the specified profile
  -version                   Version information
  -help                      Print a synopsis of standard options
  -Akey[=value]              Options to pass to annotation processors
  -X                         Print a synopsis of nonstandard options
  -J<flag>                   Pass <flag> directly to the runtime system
  -Werror                    Terminate compilation if warnings occur
  @<filename>                Read options and filenames from file

Edwards-iMac:~ edljr$ ▊
```

javac options in Java 8

The `-source` option is used to dictate the Java version that's accepted by the compiler. The `-target` option informs you of which version of class files `javac` will produce. By default, `javac` generates class files in the most recent Java version and that of the platform APIs. This can cause a problem when the compiled application uses APIs that are only available in the most recent platform version. This would render the application ineligible to run on older platform versions, despite what is dictated with `-source` and `-target` options.

To address the aforementioned problem, a new command-line option is available in Java. This option is the `--release` option and, when used, will automatically configure `javac` to generate class files that link against a specific platform version. The following screenshot shows the `javac` options with the current Java platform. As you can see, the new `--release` option is included:

```
Command Prompt                                                    —    □    ✕
C:\Users\elavi>javac -help
Usage: javac <options> <source files>
where possible options include:
  @<filename>                     Read options and filenames from file
  -Akey[=value]                   Options to pass to annotation processors
  --add-modules <module>(,<module>)*
                    Root modules to resolve in addition to the initial modules, or all modules
                    on the module path if <module> is ALL-MODULE-PATH.
  --boot-class-path <path>, -bootclasspath <path>
                    Override location of bootstrap class files
  --class-path <path>, -classpath <path>, -cp <path>
                    Specify where to find user class files and annotation processors
  -d <directory>                  Specify where to place generated class files
  -deprecation
                    Output source locations where deprecated APIs are used
  -encoding <encoding>            Specify character encoding used by source files
  -endorseddirs <dirs>            Override location of endorsed standards path
  -extdirs <dirs>                 Override location of installed extensions
  -g                              Generate all debugging info
  -g:{lines,vars,source}          Generate only some debugging info
  -g:none                         Generate no debugging info
  -h <directory>
                    Specify where to place generated native header files
  --help, -help                   Print this help message
  --help-extra, -X                Print help on extra options
  -implicit:{none,class}
                    Specify whether or not to generate class files for implicitly referenced files
  -J<flag>                        Pass <flag> directly to the runtime system
  --limit-modules <module>(,<module>)*
                    Limit the universe of observable modules
  --module <module-name>, -m <module-name>
                    Compile only the specified module, check timestamps
  --module-path <path>, -p <path>
                    Specify where to find application modules
  --module-source-path <module-source-path>
                    Specify where to find input source files for multiple modules
  --module-version <version>
                    Specify version of modules that are being compiled
  -nowarn                         Generate no warnings
  -parameters
                    Generate metadata for reflection on method parameters
  -proc:{none,only}
                    Control whether annotation processing and/or compilation is done.
  -processor <class1>[,<class2>,<class3>...]
                    Names of the annotation processors to run; bypasses default discovery process
  --processor-module-path <path>
                    Specify a module path where to find annotation processors
  --processor-path <path>, -processorpath <path>
                    Specify where to find annotation processors
  -profile <profile>
                    Check that API used is available in the specified profile
  --release <release>
                    Compile for a specific VM version. Supported targets: 6, 7, 8, 9
  -s <directory>                  Specify where to place generated source files
  -source <release>
                    Provide source compatibility with specified release
  --source-path <path>, -sourcepath <path>
                    Specify where to find input source files
  --system <jdk>|none             Override location of system modules
  -target <release>               Generate class files for specific VM version
  --upgrade-module-path <path>
                    Override location of upgradeable modules
  -verbose                        Output messages about what the compiler is doing
  --version, -version             Version information
  -Werror                         Terminate compilation if warnings occur

C:\Users\elavi>
```

javac options in Java 18.9

Here is the syntax for the new option:

```
javac --release <release> <source files>
```

The experimental Java-based JIT compiler

The Java-based **Just in Time** (**JIT**) compiler was enabled in Java 10 so that it could be used as an experimental JIT compiler for Linux/x64 platforms. The Java-based JIT compiler is referred to as Graal.

This change was made in the hope that experimentation would serve as a proof of concept for adding the JIT compiler to the JDK.

Summary

In this chapter, we explored several changes to the modern Java platform, with the common theme of command-line flags. Specifically, we covered unified JVM logging, compiler control, new diagnostic commands, removal of the HPROF heap profiling agent, the removal of JHAT, command-line flag argument validation, and the ability to compile for older platform versions.

In the next chapter, we will focus on best practices with additional utilities provided in Java. These will include UTF-8, Unicode 7.0, Linux, and more.

Questions

1. What is the schema introduced in Java 9 in regards to JVM logging?
2. What are the five categories of logging?
3. What are decorations?
4. What are the levels of verbosity in logs?
5. Which verbosity level is the highest?
6. Which verbosity level is the lowest?
7. How can logging tags be changed?

8. What is used for controlling the JVM?
9. What are the JIT compilation modes for the Java HotSpot JVM?
10. Which compilation mode features a quick startup?

Further reading

Here is a list of information you may refer to:

- *Getting Started with Clean Code Java SE 9 [Video]*, available at `https://www.`
  `packtpub.com/application-development/getting-started-clean-code-java-`
  `se-9-video`.

15
Additional Enhancements to the Java Platform

In the last chapter, we explored several changes regarding command-line flags in Java. Specifically, we covered unified JVM logging, compiler control, new diagnostic commands, removal of the HPROF heap profiling agent, the removal of the **Java Heap Analysis Tool** (**JHAT**), command-line flag argument validation, and the ability to compile for older platform versions.

In this chapter, we will focus on best practices with additional utilities provided with the Java platform. Specifically, we will cover the following topics:

- Support for UTF-8
- Unicode support
- Linux/AArch64 port
- Multiresolution images
- **Common Locale Data Repository** (**CDLR**)

Technical requirements

This chapter and subsequent chapters feature Java 11. The **Standard Edition** (**SE**) of the Java platform can be downloaded from Oracle's official download site (`http://www.oracle.com/technetwork/java/javase/downloads/index.html`).

An IDE software package is sufficient. IntelliJ IDEA, from JetBrains, was used for all coding associated with this chapter and subsequent chapters. The Community version of IntelliJ IDEA can be downloaded from the website (`https://www.jetbrains.com/idea/features/`).

Support for UTF-8

Unicode Transformation Format-8 (**UTF-8**) is a character set that encapsulates all Unicode characters, using one to four eight-bit bytes. It is the byte-oriented encoded form of Unicode. UTF-8 is and has been the predominant character set for encoding web pages since 2009.

Here are some characteristics of UTF-8:

- It can encode all 1,112,064 Unicode code points
- It uses one to four eight-bit bytes
- It accounts for nearly 90% of all web pages
- It is backward compatible with ASCII
- It is reversible

The pervasive use of UTF-8 underscores the importance of ensuring the Java platform fully supports UTF-8. With Java applications, we have the ability to specify property files that have UTF-8 encoding. The Java platform includes changes to the `ResourceBundle` API to support UTF-8.

Let's take a look at the premodern Java (Java 8 and earlier) `ResourceBundle` class, followed by what changes were made to this class in the modern Java platform.

The ResourceBundle class

The following class provides developers with the ability to isolate locale-specific resources from a resource bundle. This class significantly simplifies localization and translation:

```
public abstract class ResourceBundle extends Object
```

Creating resource bundles needs a purposeful approach. For example, let's imagine that we are creating a resource bundle that will support multiple languages for a business application. Our button labels, among other things, will be displayed differently depending on the current locale. So, for our example, we can create a resource bundle for our buttons. We can call it `buttonResources`. Then, for each locale, we can create `buttonResource_<identifier>`. Here are some examples:

- `buttonResource_ja`: for Japanese
- `buttonResource_uk`: for UK English

- `buttonResource_it`: for Italian
- `buttonResource_lh`: for Lithuanian

We can use a resource bundle with the same name as the base name for our default bundle. So, `buttonResource` would contain our default bundle.

To obtain a locale-specific object, we make a call to the `getBundle` method. An example follows:

```
. . .
ResourceBundle = buttonResource =
  ResourceBundle.getBundle("buttonResource", currentLocale);
. . .
```

In the next sections, we will examine the `ResourceBundle` class by looking at its nested class, field, and constructor, and included methods.

The nested class

There is one nested class associated with the `ResourceBundle` class, that is the `ResourceBundle.Control` class. It provides callback methods that are used when the `ResourceBundle.getBundle` method is used, shown as follows:

```
public static class ResourceBundle.Control extends Object
```

The `ResourceBundle.Control` class has the following fields:

- `public static final List<String> FORMAT_CLASS`
- `public static final List<String> FORMAT_DEFAULT`
- `public static final List<String> FORMAT_PROPERTIES`
- `public static final long TTL_DONT_CACHE`
- `public static final long TTL_NO_EXPIRATION_CONTROL`

The class has a single, empty constructor and the following methods:

- `getCandidateLocales()`:

    ```
    public List<Locale> getCandidateLocales(String baseName, Locale locale)
    ```

Let's look at the details for the `getCandidateLocales()` method:

Component	Details
Throws	`NullPointerException` (if `baseName` or `locale` is null)
Parameters	`baseName`: A fully qualified class name `locale`: The desired `locale`
Returns	List of candidate locales

- `getControl()`:

```
public static final ResourceBundle.Control getControl(List<String>
formats)
```

Let's look at the details for the `getControl()` method:

Component	Details
Throws	• `IllegalArgumentException` (if `formats` is unknown) • `NullPointerException` (if `formats` is null)
Parameters	`formats`: These are the formats that will be returned by the `ResourceBundle.Control.getFormats` method
Returns	`ResourceBundle.Control` that supports the formats specified

- `getFallbackLocale()`:

```
public Locale getFallbackLocale(String baseName, Locale locale)
```

Let's look at the details for the `getFallbackLocale()` method:

Component	Details
Throws	`NullPointerException` (if `baseName` or `locale` is null)
Parameters	• `baseName`: A fully qualified class name • `locale`: The desired `locale` that could not be found with the `ResourceBundle.getBundle` method
Returns	The fallback `locale`

- `getFormats()`:

```
public List<String> getFormats(String baseName)
```

Let's look at the details for the `getFormats()` method:

Component	Details
Throws	`NullPointerException` (if `baseName` is null)
Parameters	`baseName`: A fully qualified class name
Returns	A list of strings with their formats so the resource bundles can be loaded

- `getNoFallbackControl()`:

```
public static final ResourceBundle.Control
getNoFallbackControl(List<String> formats)
```

Let's look at the details for the `getNoFallbackControl()` method:

Component	Details
Throws	• `IllegalArgumentException` (if `formats` is unknown) • `NullPointerException` (if `formats` is null)
Parameters	`formats`: These are the formats that will be returned by the `ResourceBundle.Control.getFormats` method
Returns	`ResourceBundle.Control` that supports the formats specified without a fallback `locale`.

- `getTimeToLive()`:

```
public long getTimeToLive(String baseName, Locale locale)
```

Let's look at the details for the `getTimeToLive()` method:

Component	Details
Throws	`NullPointerException` (if `baseName` is null)
Parameters	• `baseName`: A fully qualified class name • `locale`: The desired `locale`
Returns	Zero or a positive millisecond that is offset from the cached time

- `needsReload()`:

```
public boolean needsReload(String baseName, Locale locale, String
format, ClassLoader loader, ResourceBundle bundle, long loadTime)
```

Let's look at the details for the `needsReload()` method:

Component	Details
Throws	`NullPointerException` (if any of the following listed parameters are null): • `baseName` • `locale` • `format` • `loader` • `bundle`
Parameters	• `baseName`: A fully qualified class name • `locale`: The desired `locale` • `format`: The resource bundle format • `loader`: The `ClassLoader` that should be used to load the bundle • `bundle`: The expired bundle • `loadTime`: A time bundle was added to the cache
Returns	`true/false` to indicate whether the expired bundle needs to be reloaded

- `newBundle()`:

```
public ResourceBundle newBundle(String baseName, Locale locale,
String format, ClassLoader loader, boolean reload)
```

Let's look at the details for the `newBundle()` method:

Component	Details

Throws	• `ClassCastException` (if the loaded class cannot be cast to `ResourceBundle`)
	• `ExceptionInInitializerError` (if initialization fails)
	• `IllegalAccessException` (if the class or constructor is not accessible)
	• `IllegalArgumentException` (if the format is unknown)
	• `InstantiationException` (if the class instantiation fails)
	• `IOException` (resource reading error)
	• `NullPointerException` (if any of the following listed parameters are null):
	  ○ `baseName`
	  ○ `locale`
	  ○ `format`
	  ○ `loader`
	• `SecurityException` (if access to new instances is denied)

Parameters	• `baseName`: A fully qualified class name • `locale`: The desired locale • `format`: The resource bundle format • `loader`: The `ClassLoader` that should be used to load the bundle • `reload`: `true/false` flag indicating if the resource bundle has expired
Returns	Instance of the resource bundle

- `toBundleName()`:

      public String toBundleName(String baseName, Locale locale)

Let's look at the details for the `toBundleName()` method:

Component	Details
Throws	`NullPointerException` (if `baseName` or `locale` is null)
Parameters	• `baseName`: A fully qualified class name • `locale`: The desired `locale`
Returns	The bundle name

- `toResourceName()`:

      public final String toResourceName(String bundleName, String
      suffix)

Let's look at the details for the `toResourceName()` method:

Component	Details
Throws	`NullPointerException` (if `bundleName` or `suffix` is null)
Parameters	• `bundleName`: The name of the bundle • `suffix`: The suffix for the file name
Returns	The converted resource name

Fields and constructors

The `ResourceBundle` class has one field, as described here:

    protected Resourcebundle parent

The parent bundle is searched by the `getObject` method when a specified resource is not found.

The constructor for the `ResourceBundle` class is as follows:

    public ResourceBundle() {
    }

Methods

The `ResourceBundle` class has 18 methods, each described here:

- `clearCache()`:

      public static final void clearCache()

  As you can see from the following table, the `clearCache()` method does not throw any exceptions, does not take any parameters, and has no return value:

Component	Details
Throws	None
Parameters	None
Returns	None

  Here is a version of the `clearCache()` method that takes `ClassLoader` as a parameter:

      public static final void clearCache(ClassLoader loader)

  Here are the details of the version of the `clearCache()` method that takes a `ClassLoader` as a parameter:

Component	Details
Throws	`NullPointerException` (if `loader` is null)
Parameters	`loader`: The class `loader`
Returns	None

- `containsKey()`:

      public boolean containsKey(String key)

  Let's look at the details for the `containsKey()` method:

Component	Details
Throws	`NullPointerException` (if key is null)
Parameters	key: Resource `key`
Returns	`true`/`false` depending on if `key` is in `ResourceBundle` or parent bundles

- `getBundle()`:

      public static final ResourceBundle getBundle(String baseName)

Let's look at the details for the first version `getBundle()` method:

Component	Details
Throws	• `MissingResourceException` (if the resource bundle for the provided `baseName` is not found) • `NullPointerException` (if `baseName` is null)
Parameters	`baseName`: Fully qualified class name
Returns	Resource bundle based on the given `baseName` and the default `locale`

The following is the syntax for the second version of the `getBundle()` method:

```
public static final ResourceBundle getBundle(String baseName,
Resourcebundle.Control control)
```

Let's look at the details for the second version of the `getBundle()` method:

Component	Details
Throws	• `IllegalArgumentException` (if the passed control performs improperly) • `MissingResourceException` (if the resource bundle for the provided `baseName` is not found) • `NullPointerException` (if `baseName` is null)
Parameters	• `baseName`: Fully qualified class name • `control`: The `control` provides information so the `resource` bundle can be loaded
Returns	Resource bundle based on the given `baseName` and the default `locale`

The following is the syntax for the third version of the `getBundle()` method:

```
public static final ResourceBundle getBundle(String baseName,
Locale locale)
```

Let's look at the details for the third version of the `getBundle()` method:

Component	Details
Throws	• `MissingResourceException` (if the resource bundle for the provided `baseName` is not found) • `NullPointerException` (if `baseName` or `locale` is null)
Parameters	• `baseName`: Fully qualified class name • `locale`: Desired `locale`
Returns	Resource bundle based on the given `baseName` and `locale`

The following is the syntax for the fourth version of the `getBundle()` method:

```
public static final ResourceBundle getBundle(String baseName,
Locale targetLocale, Resourcebundle.Control control)
```

Let's look at the details for the fourth version of the `getBundle()` method:

Component	Details
Throws	• `IllegalArgumentException` (if the passed `control` performs improperly) • `MissingResourceException` (if the resource bundle for the provided `baseName` is not found in any of the `locales`) • `NullPointerException` (if `baseName`, `control`, or `locale` is null)
Parameters	• `baseName`: Fully qualified class name • `control`: The `control` provides information so the resource bundle can be loaded • `targetLocale`: Desired `locale`
Returns	Resource bundle based on the given `baseName` and `locale`

The following is the syntax for the fifth version of the `getBundle()` method:

```
public static final ResourceBundle getBundle(String baseName,
Locale locale, ClassLoader loader)
```

Let's look at the details for the fifth version of the `getBundle()` method:

Component	Details
Throws	• `MissingResourceException` (if the resource bundle for the provided `baseName` is not found in any of the `locales`) • `NullPointerException` (if `baseName`, `loader`, or `locale` is null)
Parameters	• `baseName`: Fully qualified class name • `locale`: Desired `locale` • `loader`: Class `loader`
Returns	Resource bundle based on the given `baseName` and `locale`

The following is the syntax for the sixth version of the `getBundle()` method:

```
public static final ResourceBundle getBundle(String baseName,
Locale targetLocale, ClassLoader loader, ResourceBundle.Control
control)
```

Let's look at the details for the sixth version of the `getBundle()` method:

Component	Details
Throws	• `IllegalArgumentException` (if the passed `control` performs improperly) • `MissingResourceException` (if the resource bundle for the provided `baseName` is not found in any of the `locales`) • `NullPointerException` (if `baseName`, `control`, `loader`, or `targetLocale` is null)
Parameters	• `baseName`: Fully qualified class name • `control`: The control providing information so the resource bundle can be loaded • `loader`: Class `loader` • `targetLocale`: Desired `locale`
Returns	Resource bundle based on the given `baseName` and `locale`

- `getKeys()`:

```
public abstract Enumeration<String> getKeys()
```

Let's look at the details for the `Enumeration()` method:

Component	Details
Throws	None
Parameters	None
Returns	Enumeration of keys in `ResourceBundle` and parent bundles

- `getLocale()`:

```
public Locale getLocale()
```

Let's look at the details for the `getLocale()` method:

Component	Details
Throws	None
Parameters	None
Returns	The `locale` of the current resource bundle

- getObject():

```
public final Object getObject(String key)
```

Let's look at the details for the getObject() method:

Component	Details
Throws	• MissingResourceException (if the resource for the provided key is not found) • NullPointerException (if key is null)
Parameters	key: This is key for the desired object
Returns	The object for key provided

- getString():

```
public final String getString(String key)
```

Let's look at the details for the getString() method:

Component	Details
Throws	• ClassCastException (if the found object is not key) • MissingResourceException (if the resource for the provided key is not found) • NullPointerException (if key is null)
Parameters	key: This is the key for the desired String
Returns	String for the key provided

- getStringArray():

```
public final String[] getStringArray(String key)
```

Let's look at the details for the getStringArray() method:

Component	Details
Throws	• ClassCastException (if the found object is not a String array) • MissingResourceException (if the resource for the provided key is not found) • NullPointerException (if key is null)
Parameters	key: This is the key for the desired String array
Returns	The String array for the key provided

- handleGetObject():

  ```
  protected abstract Object handleGetObject(String key)
  ```

Let's look at the details for the handleGetObject() method:

Component	Details
Throws	NullPointerException (if key is null)
Parameters	key: key for the desired Object
Returns	The object for the given key

- handleKeySet():

  ```
  protected Set<String> handleKeySet()
  ```

Let's look at the details for the handleKeySet() method:

Component	Details
Throws	None
Parameters	None
Returns	Set of keys in ResourceBundle

- keySet():

  ```
  public Set<String> keySet()
  ```

Let's look at the details for the keySet() method:

Component	Details
Throws	None
Parameters	None
Returns	Set of keys in ResourceBundle and its parent bundles

- setParent():

  ```
  protected void setParent(ResourceBundle parent)
  ```

Let's look at the details for the setParent() method:

Component	Details
Throws	None
Parameters	parent: The parent bundle for the current bundle
Returns	None

Changes in the modern Java platform

The properties file format, based on ISO-8859-1, was previously supported by the Java platform. That format does not easily support escape characters, although it does provide an appropriate escape mechanism. The use of ISO-8859-1 requires conversion between the text characters and their escaped form.

The current Java platform includes a modified `ResourceBundle` class with the default file encoding set to UTF-8 vice ISO-8859-1. This saves applications the time it takes to make the aforementioned escape mechanism conversions.

Unicode support

As Unicode specifications are updated, so is the Java platform. Java 8 supported Unicode 6.2, Java 9 supported Unicode 7.0, and Java 11 supports Unicode 10.0.0, released on June 20, 2017.

 You can learn more about Unicode Version 10.0.0 at the official specification page at `http://unicode.org/versions/Unicode10.0.0/`.

The following Unicode Standards have not been implemented by the Java platform:

- **Unicode Technical Standard #10 (UTS #10)**: Unicode collation algorithm—details how to compare Unicode strings
- **Unicode Technical Standard #39 (UTS #39)**: Unicode Security Mechanisms
- **Unicode Technical Standard #46 (UTS #46)**: Unicode **Internationalizing Domain Names in Applications (IDNA)**—permits the use of ASCII string labels by applications to represent non-ASCII labels
- **Unicode Technical Standard #51 (UTS #51)**: Unicode emoji

The core Java platform changes, specific to Unicode support, include the following Java classes:

- `java.lang` package includes the following:
  - `Character`
  - `String`

- `java.text` package includes the following:
  - `Bidi`
  - `BreakIterator`
  - `Normalizer`

Let's take a quick look at each of those classes to help solidify our comprehension of the broad impact that support for Unicode 10.0.0 has on the Java platform.

The java.lang package

The `java.lang.package` provides fundamental classes used in nearly every Java application. In this section, we will look at the `Character` and `String` classes.

This is the `Character` class:

```
public final class Character extends Object implements
   Serializable, Comparable<Character>
```

This is one of the many core classes that has been around since the first version of Java. An object of the `Character` class consists of a single field of type, `char`.

This is the `String` class:

```
public final class String extends Object implements
   Serializable, Comparable<String>, CharSequence
```

Strings (a string is another core-originating class) are immutable character strings.

Modifying the `Character` and `String` classes to support a newer version of Unicode, Version 7.0 for Java 9 and later, is an important step to help keep Java relevant as the premier programming language.

The java.text package

The `Bidi`, `BreakIterator`, and `Normalizer` classes are not as widely used as the `Character` and `String` classes. Here is a brief overview of those classes:

This is the `Bidi` class:

```
public final class Bidi extends Object
```

This class is used to implement Unicode's bidirectional algorithm. This is used to support Arabic or Hebrew.

 For specific information on the *UNICODE BIDIRECTIONAL ALGORITHM*, visit `http://unicode.org/reports/tr9/`.

The `BreakIterator` class is used for finding text boundaries:

```
public abstract class BreakIterator extends Object implements Cloneable
```

This is the `Normalizer` class:

```
public final class Normalizer extends Object
```

This class contains two methods:

- `isNormalized`: Used to determine whether `char` values of a given sequence are normalized
- `normalize`: Normalizes a sequence of `char` values

Additional significance

As previously stated, JDK 8 supports Unicode 6.2. Version 6.3 was released on September 30, 2013 with the following listed highlights:

- Bidirectional behavior improvements
- Improved Unihan data
- Better support for Hebrew

Version 7.0.0, released on June 16, 2014, introduced the following changes:

- Added 2,834 characters
    - Increased support for Azerbaijan, Russian, and high-German dialects
    - Pictographic symbols
    - Historic scripts for several countries and regions
- Updates to the Unicode bidirectional algorithm.
- Nearly 3,000 new Cantonese pronunciation entries.
- Major enhancements to the Indic script properties.

The vast changes to Unicode with versions 6.3 and 7.0.0 underscore the importance of the current Java platform supporting 7.0.0, as opposed to 6.3, as with Java 8.

Linux/AArch64 port

Starting with JDK 9, the JDK has been ported to Linux/AArch64. To understand what this means to us as Java developers, let's talk a bit about hardware.

ARM is a British company that has been creating computing cores and architectures for over three decades. Their original name was Acorn RISC Machine, with **RISC** standing for **Reduced Instruction Set Computer**. Somewhere along the way, the company changed its name to **Advanced RISC Machine** (**ARM**), and, finally, to **ARM Holdings**, or just **ARM**. It licenses its architectures to other companies. ARM reports that there have been over 100 billion ARM processors manufactured.

In late 2011, ARM came out with a new ARM architecture called **ARMv8**. This architecture included a 64-bit optional architecture called **AArch64**, which, as you would expect, came with a new instruction set. Here is an abbreviated list of AArch64 features:

- A64 instruction set:
  - 31 general-purpose 64-bit registers
  - Dedicated zero or stack pointer registers
  - The ability to take 32-bit or 64-bit arguments
- Advanced SIMD (NEON)-enhanced:
  - 32 x 128-bit registers
  - Supports double-precision floating points
  - AES encrypt/decrypt and SHA-1/SHA-2 hashing
- New exception system

Oracle did a great job of identifying this architecture as something that needs to be supported in the modern Java platform. The new AArch64 architecture is said to be, essentially, an entirely new design. JDK 9, 10, and 11 have been successfully ported to Linux/AArch64 with the following implementations:

- Template interpreter
- C1 JIT compiler
- C2 JIT compiler

For information about the C1 and C2 JIT compilers, refer to `Chapter 14`, *Command-Line Flags*.

Multiresolution images

Java 11 includes an API that supports multiresolution images. Specifically, it allows a multiresolution image to encapsulate several resolution variants of the same image. This API is located in the `java.awt.image` package. The following diagram shows how multiresolution can encapsulate a set of images, with different resolutions, into a single image:

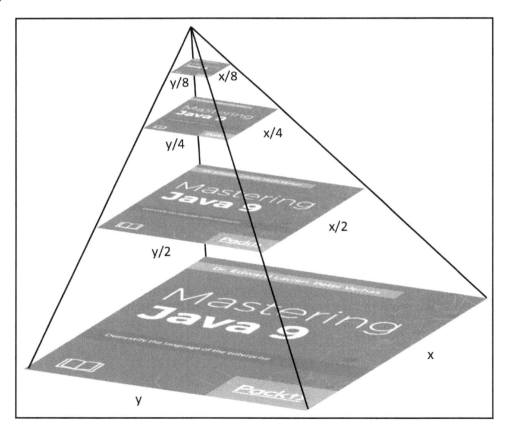

Multiimage resolution encapsulation

This new API will give developers the ability to retrieve all image variants or to retrieve a resolution-specific image. This is a powerful set of capabilities. The `java.awt.Graphics` class is used to retrieve the desired variant from the multiresolution image.

Here is a quick look at the API:

```
package java.awt.image;

public interface MultiResolutionImage {
   Image getResolutionVariant(float destinationImageWidth,
     float destinationImageHeight);

   public List <Image> getResolutionVariants();
}
```

As you can see from the preceding code example, the API contains the `getResolutionVariant` and `getResolutionVariants` that return an image and a list of images respectively. Since `MultiResolutionImage` is an interface, we will need an abstract class to implement it.

Common Locale Data Repository

Java 11 implements the decision to use locale data from the Unicode Common Locale Data Repository by default. CLDR is a key component of many software applications that support multiple languages. It is touted as the largest locale data repository and is used by a plethora of large software providers, including Apple, Google, IBM, and Microsoft. The widespread use of CLDR has made it the unofficial industry standard repository for locale data. Making this the default repository in the current Java platform further solidifies it as the software industry standard.

Interestingly, CLDR was already part of JDK 8, but was not the default library. In Java 8, we had to enable CLDR by setting a system property, as shown here:

```
java.locale.providers=JRE,CLDR
```

Now, in Java, we no longer have to enable CLDR, as it will be the default repository.

There are additional locale data repositories in the current Java platform. They are listed here in their default lookup order:

- CLDR
- COMPAT (previously JRE)
- **Service Provider Interface** (**SPI**)

To change the lookup order, we can change the `java.locale.providers` setting as illustrated:

```
java.locale.providers=SPI,COMPAT,CLDR
```

In the preceding example, `SPI` would be first, followed by `COMPAT`, and then `CLDR`.

Summary

In this chapter, we focused on best practices with additional utilities provided by the current Java platform. Specifically, we covered UTF-8 property files, Unicode 7.0.0, Linux/AArch64 port, multiresolution images, and the Common Locale Data Repository.

In the next chapter, we will look at the future direction of the Java platform by looking ahead to what we can expect from Java 19.3 (Java 12) and Java 19.9 (Java 13).

Questions

1. What is UTF-8?
2. List five characteristics of UTF-8.
3. What class provides developers with the ability to isolate locale-specific resources from a resource bundle?
4. What does the `clearCache()` method return?
5. What does the `getBundle()` method return?
6. What version of Unicode does Java 11 support?
7. JDK 9, 10, and 11 have been successfully ported to Linux/AArch64. List three implementations.
8. What is a multi-resolution image?
9. What class is used to retrieve the desired variant from a multi-resolution image?
10. What is CLDR?

16
Future Directions

In the last chapter, we focused on best practices with some exciting utilities provided by the Java platform. Specifically, we covered UTF-8 property files, Unicode, Linux/AArch64 port, multiresolution images, and the common locale data repository.

This chapter provides an overview of the future development of the Java platform, beyond Java 11. We will look at what is planned for Java 19.3(12) and 19.9(13) and what further changes we are likely to see in the future. We will start with a brief overview of the JEP.

Specifically, this chapter covers the following:

- JEP overview
- JEP Candidates
- JEP Submitted
- JEP Drafted
- Ongoing special projects

Technical requirements

This and subsequent chapters feature Java 11. The **Standard Edition** (**SE**) of the Java platform can be downloaded from Oracle's official download site (http://www.oracle.com/technetwork/java/javase/downloads/index.html).

An IDE software package is sufficient. IntelliJ IDEA, from JetBrains, was used for all coding associated with this chapter and subsequent chapters. The Community version of IntelliJ IDEA can be downloaded from the website (https://www.jetbrains.com/idea/features/).

An overview of the JDK Enhancement Proposal

The **JDK Enhancement Proposal** (**JEP**) consists of a list of proposed changes to the JDK. This publicly available list serves to inform developers and provide a long-term plan for the Java platform.

At the core of the JEP are the enhancements themselves. The criteria for an enhancement include:

- Must indicate a significant change to the JDK.
- Must have broad informational appeal.
- Further, it must meet one of the following additional criteria:
  - Requires significant engineering work to implement (at least two weeks)
  - Involves a significant change to the JDK or its infrastructure
  - Is a high demand item from Java developers or users

JEPs have the following sequential states:

1. **Draft**: This is the earliest state and is used when the JEP has been written and the author is circulating it for consensus
2. **Posted**: Once the author obtains consensus, the JEP can be logged into the JEP archive
3. **Submitted**: The author sets this status once the JEP is deemed ready for formal evaluation
4. **Candidate**: Once the OpenJDK lead accepts the JEP, it is changed to this state
5. **Funded**: Funded indicates a functional area lead or a group lead has judged the JEP to be fully funded
6. **Completed**: This state indicates work on the enhancement has been completed and delivered in a version release

Not every JEP makes it through the entire six-stage workflow. Additional states include **Active**, **Rejected**, and **Withdrawn**.

Each potential change to the Java platform will be characterized as targeted, submitted, or drafted. Targeted refers to changes that have been earmarked for a future Java release, submitted refers to a change that has been submitted but does not target a specific version of the Java platform, and changes that are drafted are still on the drawing board and are not ready to be submitted or designated as targeted.

The next sections cover **JDK Enhancement Proposals** with the status of Candidate, Submitted, and Draft.

JEP Candidates

This section features five JEPs that, at the time of writing this book, had the status of Candidate. Those JEPs are as follow:

- JEP 326: Raw String Literals
- JEP 334: JVM Constants API
- JEP 337: RDMA Network Sockets
- JEP 338: Vector API
- JEP 339: Edwards-Curve Digital Signature Algorithm

JEP 326: Raw String Literals

In a future release, we are likely to see raw string literals added to the Java platform. There are two important features of raw string literals:

- They can span more than one line of source code
- Escape sequences are not interpreted

The goal of this enhancement is essentially to make it easier for developers. This change will permit developers to provide strings that take more than one line of code, without having to provide characters to indicate a new line.

JEP 334: JVM Constants API

The JVM relies on a constant pool to determine the class layout, instances, interfaces, and arrays. Every class has a constant pool. Current Java data types for modeling these loadable constants are inefficient and inadequate. The aim of this JEP is to provide the ability for Java to manipulate classes and methods.

JEP 337: RDMA Network Sockets

The **remote direct memory access** (**RDMA**) allows one computer to access another computer's memory without having to go through the operating system. This JEP hopes to add RDMA to the JDK Networking API. This will, at least initially, be available for Linux systems.

JEP 338: Vector API

A new Vector API will be created so that vector computations can reliably be compiled into vector hardware instructions that are optimized for specific CPUs. This should give developers the ability to provide efficient scalar computations.

JEP 339: Edwards-Curve Digital Signature Algorithm

The **Edwards-Curve Digital Signature Algorithm** (**EdDSA**) is a cryptographic signature. This JEP plans to implement that algorithm.

JEP Submitted

The following JEPs had a status of Submitted at the time of writing this book:

- Experimental features will be disabled by default
- The default CDS archive will be included in the JDK binary
- Javadoc tags will be created in order to discern the difference between APIs, implementations, notes, and specifications
- New JMX annotations will be used to register managed resources
- The GTK3 will undergo modernization in regards to its layout
- New REST APIs will be created for JMX

Detailed information on each of these proposals can be obtained from `http://openjdk.java.net/jeps/0`.

JEP Drafted

The following JEPs had a status of Drafted at the time of writing this book:

- Abortable mixed collections for G1
- Allocation of old generation of Java heap on alternate memory devices
- Better hash codes
- Concurrent monitor deflation
- Dynamic max memory limit
- Efficient array comparison intrinsic
- Enable execution of Java methods on GPU
- Enhanced `ManderblotSet` demo using value types
- Enhanced pseudo-random number generators
- Improved IPv6 support
- Isolated methods
- Java thread sanitizer
- `JWarmup` precompiled Java hot methods at application startup
- Key Derivation API
- Packaging tool
- Provide stable USDT probe points on JVM compiled methods
- Support `ByteBuffer` mapped over non-volatile memory
- Timely reducing unused committed memory
- Type operator expressions in the JVM
- Unboxed argument lists for method handles
- Use UTF-8 as default charset

Detailed information on each of these proposals can be obtained from `http://openjdk.java.net/jeps/0`.

Ongoing special projects

Java enhancement proposals present design and implementation changes to the Java platform. As previously stated, the criteria for a JEP being drafted is that the work must meet at least one of the following:

- Requires significant engineering work to implement (at least two weeks)
- Involves a significant change to the JDK or its infrastructure
- Is a high demand item from Java developers or users

Projects, on the other hand, represent collaborative efforts that are sponsored by one of the following groups:

- 2D Graphics
- Adoption
- **Abstract Window Toolkit (AWT)**
- Build
- Compatibility and specification review
- Compiler
- Conformance
- Core libraries
- Governing board
- HotSpot
- Internationalization
- JMX
- Members
- Networking
- NetBeans projects
- Porters
- Quality
- Security
- Serviceability
- Sound
- Swing
- Vulnerability
- Web

Groups are formal and new ones can be proposed.

The following listed active projects represent possible future enhancement areas to the Java platform. Brief information about each project is provided later in this section and provides insight into general areas of future changes:

- Annotations Pipeline 2.0
- Audio Synthesis Engine
- Caciocavallo
- Common VM Interface
- Compiler Grammar
- Device I/O
- Graal
- HarfBuzz Integration
- Kona
- OpenJFX
- Panama
- Shenandoah

Annotations Pipeline 2.0

This project explores improvements to how annotations are handled within the Java compiler pipeline. There is no intention to propose changing specifications; rather, the focus is on performance enhancements.

Audio Synthesis Engine

This project is looking at the creation of a new midi-synthesizer for the JDK. The current midi-synthesizer belongs to a licensed library. The working group would like to see the new midi-synthesizer as an open source JDK asset.

Caciocavallo

The Caciocavallo project aims to improve the OpenJDK AWT internal interfaces. This extends to 2D subsystems. The proposed improvement stands to ease the way AWT is ported to new platforms.

Common VM Interface

The Common VM Interface project has the goal of documenting the VM interface for OpenJDK. This should make it easier for classpath VMs and other VMs to use OpenJDK.

Compiler Grammar

The Compiler Grammar project is working on an experimental Java compiler that is based on ANTLR grammar. **ANTLR** (short for **Another Tool for Language Recognition**), is a parser that reads, processes, and executes structured text or binary files. The project team hopes this Java compiler will replace the current one as it uses a hand-written parser, **LALR** (short for **Look-Ahead Left to Right**). The LALR parser has been identified by the project group as fragile and difficult to extend.

Device I/O

This project intends to provide access to generic peripheral devices via a Java-level API. The initial list of peripheral devices the project team wants to support include:

- **GPIO** (short for **General Purpose Input/Output**)
- **I2C** (short for **Inter-Integrated Circuit Bus**)
- **SPI** (short for **Serial Peripheral Interface**)
- **UART** (short for **Universal Asynchronous Receiver/Transmitter**)

Graal

The Graal project has the goal of exposing VM functionality via Java APIs. This exposure will permit developers to write, in Java, dynamic compilers for a given language runtime. This effort includes the development of a multilanguage interpreter framework.

HarfBuzz integration

The HarfBuzz Integration project hopes to integrate the HarfBuzz layout engine into the Java Development Kit. This is intended to replace the ICU layout engine with the HarfBuzz layout engine. The ICU layout engine has been deprecated, solidifying the importance of this project's future success.

Kona

The Kona project is working to define and implement Java APIs to support the **Internet of Things** (**IoT**) domain. This includes networking technologies and protocols. Although not stated, safety and security will be paramount to this effort's implementation success.

OpenJFX

There are not many details available regarding the OpenJFX project. The stated goal of this project is to create the next-generation Java client toolkit. Based on the project title, it can be assumed that the group wants to create an OpenJFX version of JavaFX, which is a set of packages used to create rich internet applications.

Panama

Project Panama is focused on enhancing the connections between the JVM and non-Java APIs.

The project includes the following selected components:

- Native function calls
- Native data access from the JVM
- Native data access inside the JVM heap
- New data layouts in the JVM heap
- API extraction tools for header files

The project team has generated a repository tree that matches JDK 9's structure. This significantly increases the likelihood of the project's success.

Shenandoah

Project Shenandoah has the goal of significantly reducing the pause times with garbage collection operations. The approach is to have more garbage collection operations run concurrently with the Java application. In `Chapter 7`, *Leveraging the Default G1 Garbage Collector*, you read about CMS and G1. The Shenandoah project intends to add concurrent compaction to the possible garbage collection approaches.

Summary

In this chapter, we provided an overview of the future developments of the Java platform, beyond Java 11. Each potential change to the Java platform was characterized as Candidate, Submitted, or Drafted.

In the next chapter, you will learn how you can contribute to the Java community and the benefits of doing so.

Questions

1. What is the JEP?
2. What type of appeal must a proposal have for it to be considered for the JEP?
3. What are the three criteria that proposals must meet one of?
4. Where can the list of active JEPs be found?
5. What does the Draft JEP state signify?
6. What does the Posted JEP state signify?
7. What does the Submitted JEP state signify?
8. What does the Candidate JEP state signify?
9. What does the Funded JEP state signify?
10. What does the Completed JEP state signify?

17
Contributing to the Java Platform

In the last chapter, we looked at the future development of the Java platform, beyond Java 11. We looked at what is planned for Java 19.3 and 19.9, and what further changes we are likely to see in the future. We started with a brief overview of the JEP and covered existing JEPs and ongoing special projects.

Key to the future of the Java platform is the Java community. That is the focus of this chapter. We will discuss the Java community and ways developers can contribute to the Java platform. Specifically, we will cover the following Java community-related topics:

- The Java community
- Participating in a Java User Group
- **Java Community Process** (**JCP**)
- Oracle Technology Network
- Writing technical articles

Technical requirements

This chapter features Java 11. The **Standard Edition** (**SE**) of the Java platform can be downloaded from Oracle's official site (`http://www.oracle.com/technetwork/java/javase/downloads/index.html`).

An IDE software package is sufficient. IntelliJ IDEA, from JetBrains, was used for all coding associated with this chapter. The Community version of IntelliJ IDEA can be downloaded from the following site (`https://www.jetbrains.com/idea/features/`).

The Java Community

The Java community consists of millions of developers that are involved in one or more ways to support one another and contribute to the Java platform. This is one of the reasons that Java is such a strong development platform. Community involvement can include following and participating on Twitter with `@java` or liking `<3 Java` on Facebook.

There are also a plethora of list serves, blogs, and forums that you can participate in to help developers with questions. This is a good way to support the community and stay current on changes to the Java platform. Oracle has approximately 200 official blogs that are worth reviewing and following. Not all of Oracle's blogs are specific to Java but are at least ancillary to Java.

 You can browse Oracle's blog directory at `http://blogs.oracle.com`.

There are several Java forums available on the internet. Oracle hosts an official Java Community space at `http://community.oracle.com`. The Java Community space is organized into the following spaces:

JavaOne	Java Champions
#Java20	Java Community Process
Java Essentials	Java APIs
Database Connectivity	Java SE
Java Security	Java HotSpot Virtual Machine
Java EE	Embedded Technologies
Java development tools	Article Archive
Java.net Forge Sunset	JavaScript Nashorn

Ideas for the New Java Space	Java User Groups
NightHacking	

Some Java developers have created how-to video playlists on YouTube and many of those are used by academic institutions. These can be fun to create and are a good way of giving back to the community.

Participating in a Java User Group

Java User Groups also referred to as **JUGs**, are comprised of community-minded Java professionals with an aim to share their Java knowledge. There are over 200 JUGs and participation is voluntary. Like other professional user groups, JUGs offer the following opportunities:

- Networking with fellow Java professionals
- Sharing tips, techniques, and resources
- Learning from others
- Increasing your knowledge of Java

JUGs have global reach. Some of them are organized by country and others by cities. As you explore the JUGs in your geographic region, you might find that they have periodic in-person meet-ups.

Java Community Process

The **Java Community Process**^{SM} (**JCP**^{SM}) is the structured approach for developing technical specification standards in regards to the Java platform. All developers can register at `http://jcp.org`. Once registered, users can review **Java Specification Requests (JSR)** and submit feedback.

Furthermore, you can even submit your own JSR proposals and join a JSRs experts group.

At the JCP site, you can search and browse current JSRs.

Oracle Technology Network

Oracle has an **Oracle Technology Network (OTN)** for which membership is free. For further details, visit `https://www.oracle.com/technetwork/community/join/overview/index.html`.

OTN membership has the following benefits:

- The opportunity to participate in discussion forums
- Free software
- Free online workshops
- Access to Java API documentation
- Community engagement
- Access to technical articles
- Blogs featured by Oracle employees
- Access to sample code
- Newsletter subscription
- Discounts on events, books, products, and other resources
- Social engagement via:
  - Twitter
  - YouTube
  - Facebook
  - Blogs

Writing technical articles

If you are an academic, professional, or just want to have an article published, you can submit them to Oracle. If accepted, Oracle will publish them under the umbrella of the OTN.

The following site provides details on writing technical articles for Oracle `https://www.oracle.com/technetwork/articles/otn-submit-100481.html`.

This site provides the following categorized information:

- Editorial needs
- Article specifications
- Submission and editorial processes

- Authorization to publish an article
- Response to your article submission
- Editorial process
- Commissioned articles

Summary

In this chapter, we discussed the Java community and ways that you can contribute to the Java platform. Specifically, we covered the Java community, participating in a Java user group, the JCP, the OTN, and writing technical articles for Oracle.

You made it to the end of the book. Thank you for reading. Happy coding!

Questions

1. What is a JUG?
2. How many JUGs are there?
3. How are JUGs organized?
4. What type of discounts comes with OTN membership?
5. What is the **Java Community Process**^{SM}?
6. How big is the Java community?
7. List four benefits of JUG membership.
8. Where can you learn more about writing technical articles for Oracle?
9. What is the prerequisite for submitting feedback to JSRs?
10. Who can submit JSRs?

Assessment

Chapter 1

1. 19.3.
2. Developers no longer need to wait very long for releases to the Java platform. More significant is the fact that no release will represent a major change to the platform.
3. Modularization of the Java platform.
4. CORBA.
5. Faster startup.
6. A low-overhead garbage collector.
7. Identifier.
8. Java 18.3(10).
9. Java 9, 10 (18.3), and 11 (18.9).
10. G1.

Chapter 2

1. When a thread is in a queue for a currently locked object, it is said to be in contention for that lock.
2. A code cache is the area of memory where the **Java Virtual Machine (JVM)** stores generated native code.
3. `-XX:NonProfiledCodeHeapSize`.
4. Lint and doclint are sources that report warnings to `javac`.
5. `hotspot/test/testlibrary/jit-tester`.
6. `-Xshare:off`.
7. FXML.
8. Prior to Java 9, string data was stored as an array of `chars`.
9. Starting with Java 9, strings are now internally represented using a byte array along with a flag field for encoding references.
10. OpenType is an HTML formatted font format specification.

Chapter 3

1. In Java, a fence operation is what `javac` does to force a constraint on memory in the form of a barrier instruction. These operations occur before and after the barrier instruction, essentially fencing them in.
2. Project Coin was a feature set of minor changes introduced in Java 7.
3. Starting with Java 9, we can use the `@SafeVarargs` annotation with private instance methods.
4. Starting with Java 9, the order we list import statements in our classes and files will no longer impact the compilation process.
5. The Java platform includes a set of root certificates in the `cacerts` keystore.
6. The `var` identifier is technically a reserved type name.
7. Declarations can be inferred through use of the new `var` identifier.
8. The underscore character (_) can no longer be used as a legal identifier name.
9. The `java.util.concurrent.atomic` package is a collection of 12 subclasses that support operations on single variables that are threadsafe and lock-free.
10. Variable handlers are typed references to variables and are governed by the `java.lang.invoke.VarHandle` abstract class.

Chapter 4

1. The JDK, JRE, and JAR were all too large.
2. Modular systems have the following requirements:
   - There must be a common interface to permit interoperability among all connected modules
   - Isolated and connected testing must be supported
   - Compile time operations must be able to identify which modules are in use
   - Runtime support for modules

3. Java modules are a collection of the following:
   - Packages
   - Classes
   - Interfaces
   - Code
   - Data
   - Resources
4. `java.`
5. The major components of the JDK are as follows:
   - Development tools
   - JavaFX tools
   - **Java Runtime Environment (JRE)**
   - Source code
   - Library
   - C Header Files
   - Database
6. Maintainability, Performance, and Security.
7. `bin`, `conf`, and `lib`.
8. `bin`, `conf`, `lib`, `demo`, `sample`, `man`, `include`.
9. Link time.
10. The Java Linker.

Chapter 5

1. Insufficient specificity in library information when more than one version of a library was located on the development computer, problems with the classloader, lengthy classpaths.
2. Java 9.
3. Modules solve the pre-Java 9 JDK monolithic issue by providing strong encapsulation.
4. `java.base`.

5. Encapsulation in Java is driven by the information in the `module-info.java` file.
6. The `jdk.unsupported` JDK module.
7. `module-info.java`.
8. Java Network Launch Protocol (**JNLP**).
9. It is an illegal identifier, starting with Java 10.
10. `--add-opens`, `--add-exports`, and `--permit-illegal-access`.

Chapter 6

1. The Read-Eval-Print Loop is often referred to as REPL, taking the first letter from each word in the phrase. It is also known as language shell or interactive top-level.
2. It is an interactive Read-Eval-Print Loop tool that is used to evaluate the following Java programming language components—declarations, statements, and expressions. It has its own API so that it can be used by external applications.
3. As listed here:

   - Tabcompletion
   - Autocompletion for end-of-statement semicolons
   - Autocompletion for imports
   - Autocompletion for definitions

4. JShell is a command-line tool that is located in the /bin folder.
5. Exiting the shell is as easy as entering `/exit`.
6. `/vars`.
7. Entering the `/help` or `/?` command in the JShell provides a complete list of commands and syntax that can be used in the shell.
8. Additional help can be obtained from within the JShell by using the `/help` command followed by the command you want additional help with.
9. Command-line tools usually provide relatively sparse feedback in an effort to not overcrowd the screen or otherwise become a nuisance to developers. JShell has several feedback modes, in addition to giving developers the ability to create their own custom modes.
10. There are four feedback modes: `concise`, `normal`, `silent`, and `verbose`.

Chapter 7

1. The following are Garbage collection algorithms:

   - Mark and sweep
   - CMS garbage collection
   - Serial garbage collection
   - Parallel garbage collection
   - G1 garbage collection

2. The G1 name refers to Garbage First.
3. **iCMS** (short for **Incremental Concurrent Mark Sweep**) mode is intended for servers with a small number of CPUs. It should not be employed on modern hardware.

4. MiB stands for Mebibyte, which is a multiple of bytes for digital information.

5. Although garbage collection is automatic in Java, you can make explicit calls to the `java.lang.System.gc()` method to aid in the debugging process. This method does not take any parameters and does not return any value.

6. Because all objects in Java, even the ones you create yourself, are child classes of `java.lang.Object`, every object in Java has a `finalize()` method.

7. These combinations have been removed in Java 9.
8. The `CollectedHeap` class.
9. For Java 10, the G1 full garbage collector was transitioned to parallel in order to mitigate any negative impact for developers that use full garbage collection.

10. Epsilon GC.

Chapter 8

1. Microbenchmarking is used to test the performance of a system. This differs from macrobenchmarking, which runs tests on different platforms for efficiency comparison and subsequent analysis. With microbenchmarking, we typically target a specific slice of code on one system such as a method or loop. The primary purpose of microbenchmarking is to identify optimization opportunities in our code.

2. Microbenchmarking takes place across several phases of a process design, implementation, execution, analysis, and enhancement.

3. Maven, also referred to as Apache Maven, is a project management and comprehension tool that we can use to manage our application project build, reporting, and documentation.

4. `pom.xml`.

5. They are both configurable options.

6. All, AverageTime, SampleTime, SingleShotTime, and Throughput.

7. Nanoseconds, Microseconds, Milliseconds, Seconds, Minutes, Hours, Days.

8. There are two suggested strategies to the Power Management pitfall:

   - Disable any power management systems before running tests
   - Run the benchmarks for longer periods

9. There are two suggested strategies to the OS Schedulers pitfall:

   - Refine your system scheduling policies
   - Run the benchmarks for longer periods

10. There are two suggested strategies to the Time Sharing pitfall:

    - Test all code before running benchmarks to ensure things work as they should
    - Use JMH to measure only once all threads have started or all threads have stopped

Chapter 9

1. Processes, in the context of Java application programming, are executional units in the operating system. When you start a program, you start a process.

2. Two new interfaces were introduced in Java 9 that support handling operating system processes: `ProcessHandle` and `ProcessHandle.Info`.

3. The `handle.is.Alive()` method returns false when the process finishes.

4. We can gain access to the PID of the processes via the handle. The `handle.getPid()` method returns `Long`, representing the numerical value of the PID.

5. To get the PID of the current process, the call chain `ProcessHandle.current().getPid()` can be used.

6. `command(), arguments(), commandLine(), startInstant(), totalCpuDuration(), user()`.

7. To get the `Stream` of process handles for controlling children, the static method `processHandle.children()` should be used.

8. `processHandle.descendants()`.

9. `allProcess()`.

10. `CompletableFuture`.

Chapter 10

1. The Java runtime has a class named `Stack`, which can be used to store objects using the **last-in-first-out** (**LIFO**) policy.

2. The JVM is written in C and executes calling C functions and returning from there.
   This call-return sequence is maintained using the Native Method Stack, just like any other C program.

3. The Java Virtual Machine `Stack`.

4. In Java, we use an API to get `Logger`. Using the API, a module can provide an implementation for the service `LoggerFinder`, which in turn can return a `Logger` implementing the `getLogger()` method.

5. The `StackWalker` class.

6. `RETAIN_CLASS_REFERENCE`, `SHOW_REFLECT_FRAMES`, and `SHOW_HIDDEN_FRAMES`.

7. If we specify the first option enum constant, `RETAIN_CLASS_REFERENCE`, as an argument to the `getInstance()` method, the returned instance grants us access to the classes that the individual stack frames reference during the walking.

8. The `SHOW_REFLECT_FRAMES` enum constant will generate a walker that includes the frames that source from some reflective calling.

9. The enum constant option, `SHOW_HIDDEN_FRAMES`, will include all the hidden frames, which contain reflective calls as well as call frames that are generated for Lambda function calls.

10. The `StackWalker` class is a final class and cannot be extended.

Chapter 11

1. Ease of use.
2. Approximately 10 percent of the HTTP's protocol is not exposed by the API:
   - Standard/common authentication mechanisms have been limited to basic authentication
   - Performance improvements might not be realized
   - There is no support for filtering on requests
   - There is no support for filtering on responses
   - The new API does not include a pluggable connection cache
   - There is a lack of a general upgrade mechanism

3. Package names, source file names, access control option.
4. `languageVersion()`, `optionLength(String option)`, `start(RootDoc root)`, `validOptions(String[][] options, DocErrorReporter reporter)`.
5. `AttributeTree.ValueKind` and `DocTree.Kind`.
6. HTML5.
7. A JavaScript engine for the JVM.
8. European Computer Manufacturers Association scripting language specification for JavaScript.
9. Support for the JarFile API and support for standard class loaders.
10. The constructor should not take any arguments.
    - It must be serializable
    - It must contain mutator and accessor methods for its properties

Chapter 12

1. Reactive programming is when applications react to an asynchronous data stream as it occurs.
2. Data streams are a binary input/output of strings and primitive data types.
3. Efficiency.
4. The following are not required—data buffering, data translation, and conversion.
5. `java.util.concurrent`.
6. `Flow.Publisher`, `Flow.Subscriber`, `Flow.Subscription`, `Flow.Processor`.
7. Multiple processes sharing a single processor.
8. Concurrency and parallelism are often used as interchangeable terms. Concurrency is when multiple processes overlap, although the start and stop times could be different. Parallelism occurs when tasks start, run, and stop at the same time.
9. The shared memory system configuration has multiple processors that all share a common system memory.
10. With the distributed memory system, each processor has its own memory and each individual processor is fully linked with the other processors, making for a distributed system that is fully linked.

Chapter 13

1. **Datagram Transport Layer Security (DTLS)** is a communications protocol.

2. **Transport Layer Security (TLS)** is the most common network security protocol.

3. Always implement the `renegotiation_info` extension when implementing a handshake renegotiation.

4. Implementing FS ensures past session encryption keys are not compromised when long-term encryption keys are compromised.

5. It is essentially a database file or a data repository file that stores public key certificates and private keys.

6. The `KeyStore` will be stored in the `/jre/lib/security/cacerts` folder.

7. The `KeyStore.Builder` class is used when you want to defer the instantiation of `KeyStore`.

8. It has the following characteristics:
   - Thread safe
   - Enter map does not need to be synchronized
   - Fast reads
   - Writes use locks
   - No object-level locking
   - Locking at a very granular level

9. A hash code is an object-generated number that is stored in a hash table for rapid storage and retrieval.

10. **Galois HASH (GHASH)** is a crypto system-hashing algorithm.

Chapter 14

1. Unified logging schema.
2. Command-line options, decorations, levels, output, and tags.
3. In the context of Java's logging framework, decorations are metadata about the log message.

4. Error, warning, information, debug, trace, and develop.
5. Develop.
6. Error.
7. In source code.
8. Method-dependent compiler flags.
9. C1 and C2.
10. C1.

Chapter 15

1. **Unicode Transformation Format-8** (**UTF-8**) is a character set that encapsulates all Unicode characters using one to four eight-bit bytes. It is the byte-oriented encoded form of Unicode.
2. Here are some characteristics of UTF-8:

   - Can encode all 1,112,064 Unicode code points
   - Uses one to four 8-bit bytes
   - Accounts for nearly 90 percent of all web pages
   - Is backward compatible with ASCII
   - Is reversible

3. The `ResourceBundle` class.
4. Nothing.
5. Resource bundle based on the given `baseName` and the default `locale`
6. Java 18.9 (Java 11) supports Unicode 10.0.0, released June 20, 2017.
7. JDK 9, 10, and 11 have been successfully ported to Linux/AArch64 with the following implementations:
   - Template interpreter
   - C1 JIT compiler
   - C2 JIT compiler

8. A multiresolution image encapsulates several resolution variants of the same image.

9. The `java.awt.Graphics` class is used to retrieve the desired variant from the multiresolution image.

10. **CLDR** (short for **Common Locale Data Repository**) is a key component of many software applications that support multiple languages. It is touted as the largest locale data repository and is used by a plethora of large software providers to include Apple, Google, IBM, and Microsoft.

Chapter 16

1. A list of proposed changes to the JDK.

2. Broad informational appeal.

3. Proposals must meet one of the following criteria:
     - Requires significant engineering work to implement (at least two weeks)
     - Involves a significant change to the JDK or its infrastructure
     - Is a high demand item from Java developers or users

4. Draft—this is the earliest state and is used when the JEP has been written and the author is circulating it for consensus.

5. Posted—once the author obtains consensus, the JEP can be logged into the JEP Archive.

6. Submitted—the author sets this status once the JEP is deemed ready for formal evaluation.

7. Candidate—once the OpenJDK Lead accepts the JEP, and it is changed to this state.

8. Funded—funded indicates a functional area lead or a group lead has judged the JEP to be fully funded.

9. Completed—this state indicates that work on the enhancement has been completed and delivered in a version release.

10. `http://openjdk.java.net/jeps/0`.

Chapter 17

1. Java User Group.
2. There are over 200 JUGs.
3. Geographically.
4. Discounts on events, books, products, and other resources.
5. The **Java Community Process**[SM] is the structured approach for developing technical specification standards in regards to the Java platform.
6. The Java Community consists of millions of developers.
7. The four benefits are as follows:

   - Networking with fellow Java professionals
   - Sharing tips, techniques, and resources
   - Learning from others
   - Increasing your knowledge of Java

8. `https://www.oracle.com/technetwork/articles/otn-submit-100481.html`.
9. Register at `http://jcp.org`.
10. Any registered member.

Other Books You May Enjoy

If you enjoyed this book, you may be interested in these other books by Packt:

Java Projects - Second Edition
Peter Verhas

ISBN: 978-1-78913-189-5

- Compile, package, and run a program using a build management tool
- Get to know the principles of test-driven development
- Separate the wiring of multiple modules from application logic
- Use Java annotations for configuration
- Master the scripting API built into the Java language
- Understand static versus dynamic implementation of code

Design Patterns and Best Practices in Java

Kamalmeet Singh, Adrian Ianculescu, Lucian-Paul Torje

ISBN: 978-1-78646-359-3

- Understand the OOP and FP paradigms
- Explore the traditional Java design patterns
- Get to know the new functional features of Java
- See how design patterns are changed and affected by the new features
- Discover what reactive programming is and why is it the natural augmentation of FP
- Work with reactive design patterns and find the best ways to solve common problems using them
- See the latest trends in architecture and the shift from MVC to serverless applications
- Use best practices when working with the new features

Leave a review - let other readers know what you think

Please share your thoughts on this book with others by leaving a review on the site that you bought it from. If you purchased the book from Amazon, please leave us an honest review on this book's Amazon page. This is vital so that other potential readers can see and use your unbiased opinion to make purchasing decisions, we can understand what our customers think about our products, and our authors can see your feedback on the title that they have worked with Packt to create. It will only take a few minutes of your time, but is valuable to other potential customers, our authors, and Packt. Thank you!

Index

@

@Deprecated annotation 309

A

abstract syntax trees (ASTs) 264
Abstract Window Toolkit (AWT) 404
Advanced RISC Machine (ARM) 395
Annotations Pipeline 2.0 project 405
ANTLR (Another Tool for Language Recognition) 406
application deployment
  about 133
  JNLP update 134
  JRE version, selecting 133
  serialized applets 133
ARMv8 395
Audio Synthesis Engine project 405

B

benchmarking options
  about 211
  modes 212
  time units 212, 213

C

Caciocavallo project 405
Certification Authority (CA) 66
class-data sharing (CDS) 7, 15, 19
CMS garbage collection 185
collection literals
  reference 300
  using 303
collections
  about 300
  prior to modern Java platform, creating 301, 303
command-line flag argument validation 373

Common Locale Data Repository (CLDR) 397
Common Object Request Broker Architecture
    (CORBA) modules
  removing 68
Common VM Interface project 406
compact profiles 10
Compiler Grammar project 406
CompletableFuture API enhancements
  about 324, 329
  class details 325
concurrency
  about 318
  CompletableFuture API enhancements 324
  improvements 323
  Java concurrency 318
Concurrent Mark Sweep (CMS) 172
contended locking
  about 21
  improvement goals 22
CPU instructions
  leveraging, for GHASH 353
  leveraging, for RSA 353

D

Datagram Transport Layer Security (DTLS)
  about 334
  protocol version 1.0 335
  protocol version 1.2 336
  support, in Java 339
  terminologies 334
depreciation
  expressing 308
Deterministic Random Bit Generator (DRBG)
  based SecureRandom implementations 358
  reference 359
diagnostic commands 371
Doclet API, Java 9

about 264
Compiler tree API 264
language model API 267
Doclet API
about 261
of Java 9 264
pre-existing Doclet API, issues 264
pre-Java 9 Doclet API 261
dynamic class-file constant 67
Dynamic Randomly Accessed Memory (DRAM)
215

E

Eclipse
reference 119
encapsulation
breaking, --add-opens option used 126
breaking, with --permit-illegal-access option 127
breaking, with--add-exports option 126
enum options, StackWalker
enum constants 249
RETAIN_CLASS_REFERNCE 245
SHOW_HIDDEN_FRAMES 245
SHOW_REFLECT_FRAMES 245
Epsilon 194
European Computer Manufacturers Association
(ECMA) 283
experimental Java-based Just in Time (JIT)
compiler 377

F

Flow API
about 315
Flow.Processor interface 316
Flow.Publisher interface 315
Flow.Subscriber interface 315
Flow.Subscription interface 316
sample implementation 317

G

G1 garbage collection 185
Galois HASH (GHASH) 353
garbage collection algorithms
Concurrent Mark Sweep (CMS) garbage
collection 173

G1 garbage collection 174
mark and sweep 172
parallel garbage collection 174
serial garbage collection 173
garbage collection
algorithms 172
approaches 185
depreciated combinations 186
interface 193
object life cycle 171
options 174
overview 170
parallel full garbage collection 194
relevant Java methods 178
unified JVM logging 188
unified logging 188
with Java platform 184
Garbage-First (G1) 132
Graal project 406

H

HarfBuzz integration project 406
hashing algorithm 353
heap allocation
alternative memory devices 66
heap profiling agent
Heap Profiling (HPROF) 372
Tool Interface (TI) 372
Hypertext Transfer Protocol (HTTP) client
about 256
Java 11 HTTP client 258
limitations 259
pre-Java 9 HTTP client 256

I

import statement depreciation warnings 56
import statement
member resolution 63
processing 63
type resolution 63
integrated development environment (IDE) 7
IntelliJ
reference 119
internal APIs
encapsulating 98

Internet of Things (IoT) 407

J

Java 10 features
    about 13
    application class-data sharing 15
    experimental Java-based JIT compiler 16
    garbage collection interface 14
    heap allocation, on alternative memory devices
        15
    JDK forest consolidation, into sigle repository 14
    local variable type inference 14
    native-header generation tool (javah), removing
        15
    parallel full garbage collector, for G1 15
    root certificates 16
    thread-local handshakes 15
    Unicode language-tag extensions 15
Java 11 features
    about 16
    CORBA modules, removing 17
    dynamic class, file constants 16
    Java EE, removing 17
    local variable syntax, for Lambda parameters 17
    low-overhead garbage collector 17
Java 11
    compiler control 369
Java 9
    external process, controlling 11
    HTTP 2.0 13
    importance 9
    Java Shell, using 11
    performance, boosting with G1 12
    performance, measuring with JMH 12
    platform, enhancing 10
    reactive programming, encompassing 13
Java application
    migration, planning 109
    potential migration issues 112
    testing 109
Java ARchive (JAR) 73
Java Community Process
    reference 411
Java Community
    about 410

reference 410
Java concurrency
    about 318
    Java threads 320
    system configurations 319
Java Connected Device Configuration (CDC) 10
Java Development Kit (JDK) 7, 73
Java Enterprise Edition (Java EE)
    about 17
    removing 68
Java Environment (jEnv) 137
Java Heap Analysis Tool (JHAT)
    removing 372
Java Keystore (JKS)
    about 341
    CallbackHandlerProtection class 342
    KeyStore.Builder 342
    PasswordProtection class 343
    PrivateKeyEntry class 343
    SecretKeyEntry class 343
    TrustedCertificateEntry class 344
Java landscape
    base module 105
    modules, fitting in 104
    reliable configuration 107
    strong encapsulation 108
Java Linker
    about 91, 96
    features 92
Java methods, garbage collection
    finalize() method 179
    System.gc() method 178
Java Microbenchmark Harness (JMH)
    about 7
    Eclipse, installing 201
    hands-on experiment 202, 203, 204
    Java, installing 201
    using 201
Java Native Interface (JNI) 83
Java Network Launch Protocol (JNLP)
    about 117, 133
    file syntax 136
    FX XML extension 134
    nested resources 134
    numeric version comparison 137

updating 134
Java Packager
  about 91
  options 92, 96
Java Platform Module System (JPMS) 74
Java Runtime Environment (JRE) 73
Java Specification Requests (JSR) 411
Java Stack
  about 238
  callers, restricting 240, 242
  information 239
  loggers, obtaining for callers 243
Java User Group
  participating 411
Java Virtual Machine (JVM) 367
Java Virtual Machine Debug Interface (JVMDI) 371
Java Virtual Machine Profiling Interface (JVMPI) 371
Java Virtual Machine Tool Interface (JVMTI) 371
Java-level JVM Compiler Interface (JVMCI)
  about 289
  BeanInfo annotations 290
  BeanInfo classes 292
  SwingContainer 291
Javadoc
  about 261
  Camel Case search 277
  HTML5 Javadoc, using 271
  search option 276
javah tool 309
JavaScript Object Notation (JSON) 369
JavaScript Parser
  about 278
  ECMAScript 283
  Nashorn 278
  Parser API 284
JDK Enhancement Proposal (JEP)
  about 19, 63
  candidates 401
  overview 400
  sequential states 400
JDK source code organization
  about 78
  C header files 83

database 84
development tools 79
internationalization 79
Java application, deployment 79
Java runtime environment 81
JavaFX tools 81
libraries 82
Remote Method Invocation (RMI) 80
security tools 80
source code 81
tools, monitoring 80
troubleshooting 80
web services 81
JEP Candidates
  about 401
  Edwards-Curve Digital Signature Algorithm (EdDSA) 402
  JVM Constants API 401
  Raw String Literals 401
  remote direct memory access (RDMA) network sockets 402
  vector API 402
JEP Drafted status 403
JEP Submitted status 402
just-in-time (JIT) compiler 16
JVM compiler
  C1 compilation mode 368
  C2 compilation mode 368
  controlling 367
  modes 367
  tiered compilation mode 368
JVM tool interface (JVM TI) 83

K

Kona project 407

L

Lambda parameters
  local variable syntax 65
language model API
  about 267
  AnnotatedConstruct interface 268
  SourceVersion enum 268
  UnknownEntityException exception 270
last-in-first-out (LIFO) 238

link time 101
Linux/AArch64 port 395
local variables
inferring 64
Look-Ahead Left to Right (LAIR) 406

M

M2Eclipse IDE
obtaining 140, 142
Maven
about 139
download link 139
method handling
additional combinations 307
argument handling 306
enhanced feature 305
enhancement feature 305
lookup functions 306
microbenchmarking
approach, to Java Microbenchmark Harness
(JMH) 201
cache capacity 215
constant folding, eliminating 214, 215
dead-code, eliminating 214, 215
OS schedulers 213
overview 200, 201
power management 213
run-to-run variance 215
techniques 213
timesharing 214
with Maven 204, 205, 206, 208, 209, 210, 211
Milling Project Coin
@SafeVarargs annotation, using 57
about 57
diamond operator, using 59
private interface methods, using 61
try-with-resource statement 58
underscore use, discontinuing 60
modular JDK
about 74, 77
JDK source code reorganization 84
source code 77
source code organization 78
modular primer 72, 73
module system

about 87
access-control boundary violations 89
module paths 88
runtime 89
Multiple JRE (mJRE) feature
modifying 277
multiple-release JAR files
about 286
identifying 287
related JDK changes 288
multiresolution images 396

N

Nashorn
about 278
using, as command-line tool 279, 281
using, as embedded interpreter 282
Native Method Stack 238
NetBeans
reference 119

O

object life cycle
object destruction 172
object mid-life 171
with object creation 171
oDevice I/O project 406
older platform versions
compiling for 375
ongoing projects 404, 406
Online Certificate Status Protocol (OCSP)
for TLS 355
Java platform, changes 357
stapling primer 356
Open Services Gateway Initiative (OSGi Alliance)
10
OpenJFX project 407
operand stack 238
Oracle Technology Network (OTN)
benefits 412
reference 412
Oracle
-source and -target options 121
application, compiling 119
encapsulation, breaking 126

features 117
jdeps, executing 122
JDK early access build, obtaining 118
preparatory steps 118
program, executing before recompiling 118
third-party libraries and tools, updating 119

P

Panama project 407
parallel garbage collection 185
persistent issues, garbage collection
    about 194
    object eligibility 195, 196
PKCS12 keystores
    creating 340
    default in Java versions 345
    Java Keystore (JKS) 341
    primer 340
platform logging
    about 295
    in modern Java platform 297
    java.util.logging package 295
platform-specific desktop features 304
potential migration issues, Java application
    extension mechanism 115
    internal APIs, accessing 113
    internal JARs, accessing 114
    JAR URL depreciation 114
    JDK's modularization 116
    JRE 112
pre-Java 9 Doclet API
    about 261
    classes 263
    enums 263
    interfaces 263
pre-Java 9 garbage collection schema
    about 181
    games, writing with Java 183
    upgrades, in Java 8 183
    visualizing 182
process identifier (PID) 217
processes
    about 218, 219
    children, listing 223
    descendants, listing 223, 224

listing 222, 225
terminating 226, 227, 228
waiting 226
ProcessHandle interface
    PID, current process 220
    processes, information 220, 221
    processes, listing 222
    working with 219
Project Jigsaw
    classpath 103
    JDK, monolithic nature 103
    review 102
Public Key Cryptography Standards (PKCS) 345

R

reactive programming
    about 312, 313
    standardization 313
Reduced Instruction Set Computer (RISC) 395
ResourceBundle class
    fields and constructors 385
    methods 386, 391
    nested class 381, 384
Rich Internet Applications (RIAs) 134
root certificates 66
RSA 353
runtime image
    changes 127
    Java version schema 127
    JDK's layout 128
    JRE's layout 128
    removed content, checking 131
    updated garbage collection 132
runtime images, Java modular
    about 84
    common operations, supporting 87
    existing behaviors, preserving 87
    JDK classes, deprivileging 87
    restructure 85
    runtime format, adopting 85

S

sample process controller app
    ControlDaemon 232, 233, 234, 235
    main class 229

parameters class 230, 231
ParamsAndHandle 231, 232
reviewing 229
Scalable Processor Architecture (SPARC) 66
security application performance
    java.Security.CodeSource package, using 347
    improving 345
    package checking algorithm 348
    permission evaluation 347
    policy enforcement 346
segmented code cache
    about 22
    memory allocation 23
serial garbage collection 185
Service Provider Interface (SPI) 398
Shenandoah project 407
spin-wait hints 330
StackFrame 251
StackWalker
    classes, accessing 249
    enum options 245
    instance, obtaining 244
    methods 249
    performance 252
    working with 244
Standard Edition (SE)
    about 199, 218
    download link 7
sun.misc.Unsafe class
    using 55

T

technical articles
    reference 412
    writing 412
thread-local handshakes 66
TIFF support 292
time-based releases
    feature releases 9
    long-term support release 9
    update releases 9
TLS application-layer protocol negotiation (ALPN)
    about 349
    extension 349
    java.net.ssl package extension 351

javax.net.ssl package 350
tools
    for application migration to Java platform 137

U

Unicode Transformation Format-8 (UTF-8)
    about 380
    characteristics 380
    ResourceBundle class, changes 392
    ResourceBundle class, using 380
Unicode
    java.lang package 393
    java.text package 393
    significance 394
    standards 392
unified GC logging
    about 190
    considerations 193
    gc tag 192
    macros 192
    options 191
unified JVM logging
    about 188, 362
    command-line options 190, 363
    decorations 189, 365
    levels 189, 366
    output 190
    tags 188, 367
    Xlog output, working with 366
Uniform Resource Identifier (URI) 84
URL (Uniform Resource Locator) 85

V

var identifier
    used, for inferring declarations 65
variable handlers
    AtoMiC ToolKit, working with 54
    sun.misc.Unsafe class, using 55
    working with 52, 53
versioning model, Java platform
    about 8
    feature-driven releases 8
    time-based releases 9

X

XML (eXtensible Markup Language) 299
XML Catalogs
  about 298

current version 300
earlier version 299
JAXP processors 299
OASIS XML Catalog standard 299

www.ingramcontent.com/pod-product-compliance
Lightning Source LLC
Chambersburg PA
CBHW060645060326
40690CB00020B/4518